# Computers and Microprocessors

# TUTORIAL GUIDES IN ELECTRONIC ENGINEERING

*Series editors*
Professor G.G. Bloodworth, *University of York*
Professor A.P. Dorey, *University of Lancaster*
Professor J.K. Fidler, *University of York*

This series is aimed at first- and second-year undergraduate courses. Each text is complete in itself, although linked with others in the series. Where possible, the trend towards a 'systems' approach is acknowledged, but classical fundamental areas of study have not been excluded. Worked examples feature prominently and indicate, where appropriate, a number of approaches to the same problem.

A format providing marginal notes has been adopted to allow the authors to include ideas and material to support the main text. These notes include references to standard mainstream texts and commentary on the applicability of solution methods, aimed particularly at covering points normally found difficult. Graded problems are provided at the end of each chapter, with answers at the end of the book.

1. Transistor Circuit Techniques: discrete and integrated (2nd edition) — G.J. Ritchie
2. Feedback Circuits and Op. Amps — D.H. Horrocks
3. Pascal for Electronic Engineers — J. Attikiouzel
4. Computers and Microprocessors: Components and Systems (3rd edition) — A.C. Downton
5. Telecommunications Principles (2nd edition) — J.J. O'Reilly
6. Digital Logic Techniques: principles and practice (2nd edition) — T.J. Stonham
7. Transducers and Interfacing: principles and techniques — B.R. Bannister and D.G. Whitehead
8. Signals and Systems: Models and behaviour (2nd edition) — M.L. Meade and C.R. Dillon
9. Basic Electromagnetism and its Applications — A.J. Compton
10. Electromagnetism for Electronic Engineers (2nd edition) — R.G. Carter
11. Power Electronics — D.A. Bradley
12. Semiconductor Devices: how they work — J.J. Sparkes
13. Electronic Components and Technology: engineering applications — S.J. Sangwine
14. Optoelectronics — J. Watson
15. Control Engineering — C.C. Bissell
16. Basic Mathematics for Electronic Engineers: models and applications — J.E. Szymanski
17. Software Engineering — D. Ince
18. Integrated Circuit Design and Technology — M.J. Morant

# Computers and Microprocessors

## Components and systems

## Third edition

**A.C. Downton**
*Senior Lecturer*
*Department of Electronic Systems Engineering*
*University of Essex*

**CHAPMAN & HALL**
University and Professional Division
London · New York · Tokyo · Melbourne · Madras

**Published by Chapman & Hall, 2–6 Boundary Row, London SE1 8HN**

Chapman & Hall, 2–6 Boundary Row, London SE1 8HN, UK

Van Nostrand Reinhold Inc., 115 5th Avenue, New York NY10003, USA

Chapman & Hall Japan, Thomson Publishing Japan, Hirakawacho
Nemoto Building, 6F, 1-7-11 Hirakawa-cho, Chiyoda-ku, Tokyo 102,
Japan

Chapman & Hall Australia, Thomas Nelson Australia, 102 Dodds Street,
South Melbourne, Victoria 3205, Australia

Chapman & Hall India, R. Seshadri, 32 Second Main Road, CIT East,
Madras 600 035, India

First edition 1984
Second edition 1988
Reprinted 1990
Third edition 1992
© 1984, 1988, 1992 A.C. Downton

Typeset in 10/12pt Times by Colset Pte Ltd, Singapore
Printed in Hong Kong

ISBN 0 412 40300 5    0 442 31536 8 (USA)

A catalogue record for this book is available from the British Library

Library of Congress Cataloging-in-Publication data available

To Pippa, Polly, Matthew and Christopher

# Contents

# Preface

In spite of the large number of texts on computers and microprocessors which are available, very few have achieved an integrated approach to computers and microprocessors which places equal emphasis on components and systems, application and design. On the one hand, the traditional introductions to computer technology cover the components of the computer and its peripherals very well, but contain very little information to guide students in either software or hardware design processes. On the other hand, many recent microprocessor textbooks fail even to discuss the components beyond the microcomputer and leave students singularly ill-equipped to deal with an engineering world where computers represent the main tool for design, simulation and analysis. It is in an attempt to reconcile the dual role of the computer as a general-purpose computing machine and as an electronic component that this book has been written.

Computers are also a notoriously circular subject where almost any explanatory statement presupposes knowledge of some other aspect of the problem. Partly this can be attributed to the jargon of the subject (in this book cross-references and marginal notes have been used extensively to explain technical terms), but even so, learning about computers appears to be a very non-linear process; the student can struggle in complete ignorance for quite some time before suddenly making a mysterious transition to clear understanding. One explanation for this may be that most textbooks seem to concentrate almost entirely on *how* computers work rather than considering *why* they are designed in the way they are.

For these reasons particular attention has been paid in this book to the sequence in which topics are introduced. The book presupposes some knowledge of digital electronics, and familiarity with a high-level programming language is also useful though not essential; both of these topics are covered by companion volumes in this series. The subject of computers and microprocessors is introduced in broad terms by means of a brief review of their history, high-lighting developments and concepts which subsequently proved to be crucial, and developing an outline computer structure which is capable of implementing the functions required of a general-purpose computing machine. Subsequent chapters then examine each component of this machine (memory, central processing unit, input and output interfaces) in detail, and consideration also is given to the ways in which instructions and data may be represented within the computer. Once the components of the computer are understood, the elements of programming are examined, with particular attention being focused on assembly languages and addressing modes. Comparisons are made with high-level languages to illustrate the advantages and limitations of each. At this stage the student is beginning to become aware of the hardware infrastructure required to support computer programming, so the next two chapters introduce the peripheral components associated with general-purpose computers (tape, disks, terminal, etc.) and the software tools required to undertake useful applications programming. The final chapter takes the student step by step through a typical (though simplified) design example, emphasising the importance of a structured approach.

The rate of change of microprocessor technology dictates that this book be revised to reflect current trends at regular intervals. In the three years since the second edition was published, the MC68000 family of processors has continued to be widely adopted for academic teaching, but the Z80 is clearly reaching the end of its life cycle. In fact, there is a strong trend away from 8-bit general purpose microprocessor applications in one of two directions: where the processing power demands it, a 16- or 32-bit general-purpose microprocessor is now the preferred solution; but for simple low-cost applications, a single-chip 8-bit microprocessor (or microcomputer) is used. Thus the traditional 8-bit microprocessor market is being replaced by a variety of single-chip microcomputers, mirroring the changes in the 4-bit microprocessor market in the late 1970s. For this reason, it seems that any coverage of 8-bit devices in this book should now reflect this trend, and accordingly, coverage of the MC6809 has been replaced by the MC68HC11, a single-chip 8-bit CMOS microcomputer whose architecture derives directly from the MC6809.

Perhaps the most significant trend over the last three years has been the emergence into widespread use of reduced instruction set computer (RISC) architectures. It now seems clear that RISC is set to dominate the PC and workstation market over the next decade, and therefore it is appropriate that an example of RISC architecture be included in this book. In fact, the inclusion of a RISC processor reinforces one of my primary objectives, of writing a book which critically compares alternative processor architectures, since the development of the RISC philosophy is based upon a fundamental reconsideration of such issues.

Although the market is currently dominated by computers based upon the SPARC and MIPS chips, the example I have chosen is the Acorn RISC Machine (ARM). This is because the ARM is currently the only RISC device available in a low-cost personal computer, for which simple parallel, serial and analogue input/output ports are available (via the Acorn Archimedes microcomputer), thus allowing the processor to be readily connected to 'real-world' I/O devices. These characteristics make it suitable for use as part of a first year Electronics undergraduate laboratory, as we have been doing at Essex since the 1989/90 academic year. For those who wish to support a course based on this book with laboratory work based around the ARM/Archimedes, copies of our laboratory script and support software can be obtained by writing to me.

This book is based upon my experience over several years of teaching first, second and third year undergraduate courses and MSc courses on computers and microprocessors, and of a number of short courses prepared for industry. Naturally, many of my colleagues have contributed to the ideas embodied in this book over this period of time, and in particular I would like to mention the contributions made by Professor A.F. Newell, Professor K.G. Nichols and Mr E.J. Zaluska in helping to crystallise my thoughts. I would also like to thank my consultant editor, Professor A.P. Dorey, for his help and encouragement in preparing my manuscript.

# Computers and microprocessors

☐ To introduce the terminology used to describe computers and their major components.

☐ To describe the history of computers, and the major landmarks in their development.

☐ To describe the basic structure of a computer, and its important computing features.

## Introduction

Over the last few decades, computers, and microprocessors in particular, have begun to have an enormous impact upon our lives. In the early stages of their development, computers were large, centralised machines which were seldom seen, though their presence was sometimes felt in the form of computerised bills or salary slips. All this has changed fundamentally as microelectronics has reduced the cost of computing power and increased the data processing capabilities of a single silicon chip. The scale of the change — about a tenfold increase in capacity (for a given chip size) every three years — now affects all aspects of society, by making available cheap and virtually unlimited computing power and generating applications for computers which previously would have seemed beyond the bounds of possibility. Twenty years ago, the possibility that a washing machine, a car which talks to us, an oven, a watch, even a doorbell could contain a computer would have been dismissed as nonsense. Yet all these products now exist, and just around the corner looms the prospect of shopping by computer terminal connected to our telephone, possibly even the demise of money in its conventional form, to be replaced ultimately by electronic funds transfer using a super credit card.

> This exponential increase in chip packing density was first proposed in the 1960s and has since become known as *Moore's Law*. It is expected that it will continue to hold for at least the next decade.

These changes in the consumer environment are paralleled by similar, and if anything even faster changes in the industrial world, where computer-controlled robots, computerised parts distribution and assembly lines are changing many traditional crafts. Large-scale automation has also reached the office environment as computers have become cheap enough to be used even by the smallest business, and specific office applications such as word processors have been developed.

> The impact of the computer revolution is explored more fully in Forester, T. (ed.) *The Microelectronics Revolution* (Blackwell, 1980), a series of definitive papers on the subject published during the 1970s.

The examples above serve to illustrate the versatility of the modern computer and its range of applications. These go far beyond the conventional concept of a computer as a sophisticated number-crunching calculator, and every increase in chip complexity or decrease in cost spurs further applications development. In spite of this versatility the fundamental principles of computers remain the same whether one is discussing the smallest single-chip microcomputer or the largest mainframe computer. It is the objective of this book to impart a clear understanding both of the principles of operation of a computer, and of the techniques which are used to design computer-based products.

To illustrate many of the points, reference will be made to three specific types of microprocessor. The Motorola MC68000 has been chosen to illustrate the capabilities of current 16- and 32-bit devices. The MC68000 is widely used in many popular PCs such as the Atari ST, Commodore Amiga and Apple Macintosh. More powerful upwardly compatible microprocessors based upon the MC68000 architecture (the MC68020, MC68030 and MC68040) form the basis of many current workstations (for example, the Sun 3 family and Apollo Domain series) and high-performance PCs (for example, Apple's Macintosh II family). The MC68000 represents the continuing tradition of complex instruction set computers (CISCs), as also embodied in the Intel 80X86 family.

A key architectural development in the 1980s has been the successful introduction of reduced instruction set computers (RISCs), which seem set to dominate computing in the 1990s, and have already taken over a substantial proportion of the workstation market. Therefore it is appropriate that the second example processor should reflect this new design philosophy. The Acorn RISC machine (ARM) embodies most of the key concepts of RISC design, and is available in a low-cost personal computer, the Acorn Archimedes.

Although there is a strong trend away from 8-bit general purpose micro-processors towards 16- and 32-bit devices, single-chip 8-bit microcomputers, typically derived from the architecture of their general-purpose predecessors, still find extensive use in simple, low-cost applications: domestic equipment, simple controllers and peripheral processors. The Motorola MC68HC11 (which is derived from the MC6800 and MC6809 architectures) is used to illustrate the characteristics of these devices.

**Early history of computers**

The history of computers and calculators goes back a very long way. At its lowest level, the principle of any calculator is to represent a number by some physical means (which may be simply a collection of stones or marks on paper) and to manipulate the representation to perform the required calculation. By using a physical medium to represent the abstract numbers, the ease of performing the calculation is increased and the chance of error reduced.

It is important to realise that not all numeric representations are equally useful. As an example, roman numerals, though perfectly adequate for representing numbers, become almost unusable if required to perform arithmetic. For this reason, the Romans were forced to resort to a *mechanical device* (the abacus) for even the simplest calculations, which we could perform in our heads. The advantage which we have is *arabic numerals*, which are fundamentally easier to manipulate than roman numerals not only because they have a consistent and limited set of symbols to represent numeric values, but also because they use a *positional notation* to supply additional information about the value of a numeral. It is easy to underestimate the importance of this concept, without which computing, as we know it, could never have been invented.

In comparing notations it should be borne in mind that a notation which is convenient for humans is not necessarily the ideal notation for the computer to

The abacus, invented in about 3000 BC, was probably the earliest recorded example of a mechanical calculator.

As a comparison, compare the difficulty of performing the calculation LV × IV with the calculation 55 × 4.

use. This need not matter, as long as some straightforward method exists for converting from one notation to the other. Thus, an appropriate human number system is the decimal system (presumably because we have ten fingers and ten toes), whereas an appropriate number system for modern computers is the binary system, because each binary digit can be represented by one switch or transistor, which has two physical conditions, *on* and *off*, corresponding to the binary numbers 0 and 1.

For many centuries after the adoption of arabic numerals, people were content to use their own brain-power to perform arithmetic. As commerce and trade grew and money rather than bartering became more common, so the need for arithmetic increased, and with it, the desire to reduce the drudgery associated with arithmetic. The first significant contribution to this area was the discovery by John Napier in the seventeenth century of *logarithms*, which are based upon the idea that if numbers are represented as a power of an appropriate base, they can be multiplied or divided by adding or subtracting the powers respectively. His discovery led to the significant mathematics activity of generating log and anti-log tables, but more importantly to the development of the slide rule as a mechanical implementation of the logarithm process. Surprisingly, this was not invented by Napier, who instead produced a machine called *Napier's bones*, which was, in effect, a set of cylindrical multiplication tables.

Later in the same century, and independently of Napier, Blaise Pascal developed the first truly mechanical calculator, which he called the *Pascaline* (see Fig. 1.1). In concept the device very closely resembled the mechanical adders which were widely used until quite recently, in which ten-teethed cogs were rotated to add or subtract numbers. Pascal's real contribution to the machine, however, was the concept of the *carry*, used to convert an overflow on one cog to an increment on the next higher digit. The major weakness of the machine was that multiplication or division could only be accomplished by repeated addition or subtraction. This was rectified later by Gottfried Leibnitz who, in 1671, introduced a multiplier wheel with teeth of different lengths.

The computer programming language PASCAL is named after Blaise Pascal.

All the devices developed up to now were essentially calculators; they could perform only limited addition, subtraction, multiplication and division. The next

Fig. 1.1   Replica of Pascal's calculating machine (reproduced by courtesy of the Science Museum, London).

conceptual leap, the idea of a *programmable* calculator or computer which was not restricted only to performing one fixed task, but could perform a number of different tasks according to the pattern of instructions which it was given, did not come until 1833.

The designer of the first true computer was Charles Babbage, an English inventor and mathematician. Babbage had spent several years attempting to build a special-purpose calculator (called the *Difference Engine*) for calculating the long lists of numbers required in log tables. Based upon this work he developed in 1833 the design of a much more ambitious machine called the *Analytical Engine* which was essentially the first programmable computer. The most remarkable aspect of the Analytical Engine is its similarity in concept to the modern computer. The machine contained a store for data, a *mill* for performing arithmetic operations, a control unit which determined the operation to be performed and performed operations in the required sequence, and input and output mechanisms. The *program* for the machine was specified using punched cards, an idea borrowed from the Jacquard loom developed at around the same time, and input data was also specified using punched cards. Sadly, though Babbage's ideas were perfectly sound, he was far ahead of his time. The mechanical machining accuracy possible at that time was simply inadequate to enable the complex hardware which Babbage had designed to be fabricated successfully. Even Babbage's earlier and much simpler Difference Engine was not successfully built until 1855, by a Swedish engineer named George Scheutz.

In the 1840s, Lady Ada Lovelace, a mathematician and the daughter of Lord Byron, became involved in Babbage's work and worked closely with him for some time. She published a number of notes about the machine entitled *Observations on Mr. Babbage's Analytical Engine*, setting down the principles of the computer program or software. For this reason Lady Lovelace is often thought of as the first software engineer.

As the nineteenth century continued, more advanced mechanical calculators began to appear. Notable at this time was Herman Hollerith who in 1887 won a competition to produce a machine for counting the 1890 US Census. He went on to set up the Tabulating Machine Company to manufacture and market his machine in 1890; this subsequently became the Computing Tabulating and Recording Company in 1911, and is now the company known as IBM.

Mechanical calculators continued to become further refined; nevertheless, the development of true computers was still inhibited by the lack of a suitable implementation medium. In spite of this, considerable advances were being made in the theory of computing; a definitive paper on this subject, *On Computable Numbers*, was published by the British mathematician Alan Turing in 1937.

At about the same time, a German scientist, Konrad Zuse, designed and built the first relay-based computer. Fortunately for the Allies, Adolf Hitler was not convinced of the value of this type of research, and though Zuse considered the possibility of replacing his relays with electronic valves which could have operated thousands of times faster, he never found the financial support to make this idea practicable.

The Americans, also, were experimenting with relay-based computers: Howard Aiken at Harvard built the Harvard Mark I computer between 1937 and 1943, sponsored by IBM. It was an enormous machine containing nearly a million electromechanical devices, and to this day is the only noisy computer ever built, becoming obsolete almost before it was completed.

An anthology of original papers describing the early history of computers has been published by Brian Randell. (Randell, B. *The Origins of Digital Computers* (Springer-Verlag, 1973)).

Babbage's mill is what we would call the arithmetic and logic unit on a modern computer. Refer to the section *A Simple Computer*, later in this chapter.

This historical interpretation has recently been challenged: a current project at the Science Museum is attempting to build an Analytical Engine using Babbage's original designs.

The computer programming language ADA is named after Lady Lovelace.

Turing, A. *On Computable Numbers, with an Application to the Entscheidungsproblem*, Proceedings of the London Mathematical Society, v. 42, pp. 230–265, 1937.

The Second World War provided the final spur needed to produce a genuine electronic computer. The British government's pressing need to decode German intelligence produced using the Enigma machine led to the setting up of a team led by Turing, I J Good and D Michie. This team produced *Colossus*, the first valve-based computer, though it was in fact a special-purpose machine. It is commonly held that Britain would not have won the Second World War without it. At about the same time, work on a general-purpose electronic computer was also beginning at the Moore School of Engineering in Pennsylvania, USA, led by J W Mauchly and J P Eckert. This machine, called *ENIAC*, was started in 1943 and finally completed in 1946. Again, it was an astounding piece of engineering perseverance, containing nearly 19 000 valves and consuming 150 kW of power. In order to operate the machine as reliably as possible, it had to remain switched on at all times, to reduce the chance of valve heaters burning out during the switch-on power surge. It is chastening to realise that the same sort of calculating power is now available in an electronic calculator costing a few pounds.

ENIAC differed only in one significant way from the computers of today: its program was stored externally. This meant that the program had to be executed sequentially at the speed at which instructions could be read by the primitive card and paper tape readers used at the time. But in 1944 John von Neumann became involved in the project, and he suggested that the computer program should actually be stored electronically inside the computer. This was the final breakthrough in computer design, because it meant not only that the computer program could be executed at a speed limited only by the electronic logic of the computer (rather than the mechanical limitation imposed by the card or paper tape reader) but also that computer programs could be designed to take decisions based upon the result of their processing, and modify their action accordingly. This was possible because the instruction execution sequence could be instantaneously modified since all instructions were equally accessible within the internal computer memory. Furthermore, computer programs could call up other computer programs immediately if required (subject to the constraint that all programs could fit in the computer memory at the same time), and programs could even modify other programs or themselves, to improve their processing beyond the bounds of imagination of their human creators. Von Neumann's idea, the concept of *stored program control*, was a very profound one and, more than any other person, he was responsible for computing as we know it today.

Although the future of computers was now assured, they remained large, unwieldy, expensive and unreliable machines until the valves were replaced by transistors. The transistor, originally invented in the late 1940s at Bell Laboratories, was the ideal device upon which to base a computer, being small, low in power consumption and very much more reliable than the valve it replaced. Its initial disadvantages, lower power output, lower voltage and higher noise, which delayed its acceptance in analogue applications, were unimportant in a computer where it was required to operate simply as a switching device.

Once computers began to be built using transistors another reliability problem emerged. As the complexity and processing power of computers increased, the limiting factor in reliability began to be the number of connections required between the components of the computer. This led to the idea of the integrated circuit, wherein the number of soldered connections was reduced by implementing larger and larger subsystems of the computer upon a single chip of silicon. The first integrated circuits began to appear in the early 1960s and from

ENIAC — Electronic Numerical Integrator and Calculator.

This interpretation of history has been disputed by Mauchly and Eckert, who suggest that they were the originators of the stored program concept. See Metropolis, N., Howlett, J., Rota, G.-C. *A History of Computing in the Twentieth Century* (Academic Press, 1980).

It is this facility more than any other which gives a computer its apparent intelligence, since it enables the computer to make logical decisions and to modify its action according to data fed into it.

The mechanisms for physically implementing the stored program control concept are considered in more detail in the sections *Computers — basic concepts* later this chapter and *Instruction execution — program control* in Chapter 4.

Bardeen, J., Brattain, W.H. *Physical Principles involved in Transistor Action*, Bell Systems Technical Journal, v. 28, pp. 239–277, April 1949.

then on it was only a matter of time until the complete computer could be fabricated on a single silicon chip.

## Computers since the 1960s

Computer development since the early 1960s has been characterised by three distinct phases, corresponding to the three different types of computer system which are currently in use. These can be categorised both by size and computing power (though the boundaries are fuzzy) into *mainframe* or centralised computing facilities, *minicomputers*, and *microprocessors* and *microcomputers*.

### *Mainframe and centralised computing facilities*

Mainframe computers represent the original concept of computers as embodied in machines like ENIAC. The size (room-size or bigger) and cost (£100 000 upwards) dictated that these machines could be owned only by the largest commercial and industrial organisations. At the same time the purchase and running costs of the machine meant that it was vital to ensure that it was used as efficiently as possible and did not stand idle. This led to considerable resources being expended on the development of efficient mechanisms for switching the machine from one program to another, either as each task was completed (*batch processing*) or in a time multiplexed fashion (*multi-user interactive processing*). The concept of mainframe computing was to maximise the efficiency of operation of the computer, sometimes at the expense of its users. Typical applications of mainframe computers are large data-base problems such as payrolls, banking, and stock control, and complex scientific problems requiring high processing power such as cosmology modelling, weather forecasting and some types of simulation.

### *Minicomputers*

In the late 1960s much smaller computers became available. The impetus for these machines was the increasing number of applications requiring *dedicated real-time* computing power; this coincided with the increasing availability of integrated circuits which reduced the physical bulk and the cost of the computer. Early 12-bit minicomputers such as the DEC PDP8 were only as powerful as today's 8-bit microprocessors, but the range of minicomputers has subsequently broadened and the more sophisticated machines now exceed the processing power of the mainframe computers of ten years ago. Costs range between about £20 000 and £500 000 for a machine typically the size of a filing cabinet. Applications in industry and science include control of numerical machine tools and chemical processes, and monitoring of scientific experiments, while in business applications these machines have enabled smaller companies which could not have afforded a mainframe computer to have local access to computing facilities for accounting, data-base manipulation and payrolls.

The major impact of the minicomputer has been to begin the change of attitudes in the use of computers which has continued and accelerated with the appearance of microprocessors. Minicomputers introduced, for the first time, the concept that a computer was cheap enough to be dedicated to a single task or user. This led to a trend away from the batch processing commonly used in

Although mainframe computers have been superseded for many applications by minicomputers and microprocessors, they still have many applications where high processing power or a very large memory are required. It should be borne in mind that each type of computer is developing all the time, and that today's microcomputer has the same processing power as a minicomputer ten years ago, or a mainframe computer twenty years ago.

*Dedicated* — use of a computer for a single fixed task (i.e. only one program is ever executed, even though the computer is in principal a general purpose machine). Dedicated operation is very common in microprocessors where the computer itself may form only a very small fraction of the total system cost. Conversely, mainframe computers are seldom dedicated to one task because this is not a cost-effective way to use them, except in the most expensive applications.

*Real-time* — use of a computer to interact with some external process at a rate governed by the external process. The

6

mainframe computers towards interactive processing where the user communicated with the computer directly via a visual display terminal (VDU). This was a profound change in emphasis, for it marked the beginning of a recognition that, in future, the most expensive part of the human–computer system was likely to be the human, and that one objective of the computer designer should henceforth be to maximise the efficiency of the human–computer dialogue, even if this resulted in less efficient use of the computer.

*Microcomputers, microprocessors and microcontrollers*

Strictly speaking, the microprocessor age dawned in 1971, with the development by a small semiconductor firm called Intel of a set of components which enabled a computer to be constructed on a single circuit board. The chip set (which had about the same computing power as the original ENIAC computer) was originally designed for a specific product (a Japanese calculator), but Intel was quick to realise its more general potential, and marketed it as the MCS-4 *microcomputer*. Though the complete computer required a whole board of electronics, the central processing unit (CPU), or brain of the computer, was contained on a single chip for the first time, and this chip became known as a *microprocessor*. The Intel 4004 CPU manipulated data only four bits (approximately one decimal digit) at a time, yet it found many applications before it was superseded in the mid-1970s by more powerful 8-bit microprocessors such as the Intel 8080 and 8085, the Motorola MC68000 (see Figure 1.2) and the Zilog Z80.

The present range of applications of microprocessors is enormous. At one end of the spectrum, microcomputers costing between £100 and £10 000 are used simply as smaller and cheaper general-purpose computers than have ever been available before. The bulk of microprocessor production, however, is not used in general-purpose computers but in dedicated microprocessor applications, where the microprocessor system acts as a microcontroller with a fixed program. Increasing levels of integration have now made it possible to include not only the CPU, but also the other components of the computer such as the memory on a

computer is required to respond to external stimuli at the rate these occur. Again this is very common in microprocessor applications.

The terminology used in this book is as follows:
*Microprocessor* — The central processing unit (CPU) of a microcomputer or microcontroller implemented on a single silicon chip.
*Microcomputer* — A complete general-purpose computer implemented using microprocessor technology. The computer may be implemented using a single chip or it may require a number of components connected together.
*Microcontroller* — a microcomputer programmed with one fixed program for a specific task. Again, the physical implementation may use only one or several chips.

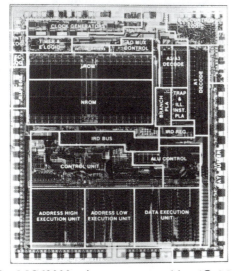

Fig. 1.2   MC68000 microprocessor chip. (© Motorola)

## Timer System

*Packed with features but easy to use, the M68HC11 timer architecture is widely recognised as the leader among 8-bit MCUs. Includes Input Capture, Output Compare, Real Time Interrupt, Pulse Accumulator and COP Watchdog. All unused timer pins may be configured as normal digital I/O.*

## CPU Core

*A powerfully enhanced version of the industry standard M6801 core, optimized for low power consumption and providing 91 new opcodes. Operating frequencies up to 4.0MHz for high performance, power-saving STOP and WAIT modes for economy. Six addressing modes, and a fully featured interrupt system.*

## Communications

*All versions of the M68HC11 include a Serial Peripheral Interface (SPI) and Serial Communications Interface (SCI) as standard. Both have software-selectable baud rates, and are designed to require minimum attention from the CPU to minimise processing overhead. The SPI operates at up to 2Mbits/sec.*

## EPROM

*The latest memory introduction to the M68HC11, the first Motorola MCU family to offer both EPROM and EEPROM. Provides a cost-effective, user-programmable ROM facility for small volume prototype and development runs. Optionally available in windowed packages for UV erasure and reprogramming.*

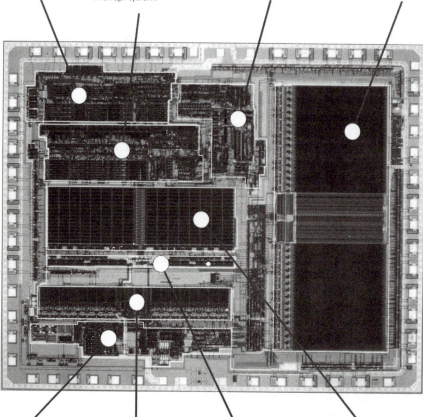

Die photo of the MC68HC711E9, the first MCU with on-chip EPROM and EEPROM.

## A/D System

*The interface to the real world; eight channels with either 8 or 10-bit resolution, based on a single successive approximation system using a charge redistribution technique to eliminate the need for an external sample-and-hold. Software selectable to provide single or continuous conversions.*

## EEPROM

*Non-volatile memory for storage of calibration, diagnostic, data logging and security information. EEPROM versions of the M68HC11 include an on-chip charge pump to provide the high voltage for the straight-forward programming procedure. Devices now available with up to 2K bytes of EEPROM.*

## ROM

*Mask programmed with the application software. M68HC11 devices are available with between 4K and 24K of ROM, and also in ROM-less versions for applications using only external memory. Every device includes an additional area of ROM containing Motorola bootstrap and test software.*

## RAM

*Uses a fully static design and is provided with a standby power supply pin for battery back-up. Available to the user software in all operating modes, the RAM is remappable to suit the hardware/software combination.*

Fig. 1.3   MC68HC11 microcomputer chip and its functional components. (© Motorola)

8

single chip, with the result that the 'computer on a chip' is finally a reality (see Figure 1.3). The cost of such a device may be as low as £1 for dedicated applications with large enough markets (100 000 devices or more).

In parallel with the development of single-chip microcomputers, increased chip packing densities have enabled the development of a third generation of microprocessors providing 16- or even 32-bit processing. These devices include the Intel 8086 family (widely used in the IBM Personal Computer), the Motorola 68000 family (used, for example, in the Apple Macintosh and many professional workstations) and the National Semiconductors 32000 family. All these devices are substantially more powerful than their 8-bit predecessors, and provide many new architectural features and instructions specifically geared towards larger processing tasks, such as programming in high-level languages.

The strong trend towards increased computing power on a chip and reduced chip cost continues to generate new applications for microprocessors. At one end of the spectrum the cheapest and simplest devices are being used to improve the performance of equipment where computerisation would never previously have been considered because of cost (for example, white goods, cars, cash registers, and weighing machines); at the other end of the spectrum the more powerful devices are creating completely new application areas (for example, speech synthesis and recognition, computerised communication and electronic mail, and robotics).

## CISC and RISC processors

Although current computers almost without exception employ the conventional 'von Neumann' architecture which this book describes, the development of applications requiring ever-increasing computing power continues to spur corresponding research into computer architectures. In the mainstream of this research at the moment is the current trend towards reduced instruction set computer (RISC) architectures.

The concept of RISC, originally investigated at IBM in the 1970s, and subsequently taken up at Berkeley and Stanford Universities in the 1980s, is based upon a reappraisal of the economic tradeoffs which underpinned the design of computers in the period 1950–1980. During this era, a key design issue was the cost (too high) and the speed (too slow) of memory. As a result, computer designers attempted to maximise the functionality per instruction in their designs, in order to minimise the amount of memory required and the number of memory accesses. This resulted in the development of progressively more complex instruction sets, leading to this class of processor being known as *complex instruction set computers* or CISCs.

The initial basis for research on RISC machines was the observation that, in practice, around 10% of the available CISC instruction set was used 90% of the time in typical applications, and more specifically, that high-level language compilers were usually unable to exploit the more esoteric machine language instructions. Following from this observation, it was then argued that if the redundant instructions were removed, the design of the instruction execution unit could be considerably simplified. This in turn would make it possible for the remaining reduced set of instructions to be executed much more rapidly than was previously possible, achieving improved performance overall. The two disadvantages of this scheme are, first, that faster execution of instructions

The *von Neumann bottleneck* results from the requirement that the CPU and memory communicate via a restricted bandwidth channel, the data bus (see the next section and Chapter 2), in any von Neumann computer.

The accuracy of these assertions can be determined by comparing representative current processors in each class. The Motorola MC68020 (CISC) contains 200 000 transistors, required 100 person-years of design effort and achieves a performance of 2 million instructions per second (MIPS); the Acorn ARM (RISC) contains 27 000 transistors, required 6 person-years of design effort and achieves 5 MIPS.

9

requires faster memory access, and second, that equivalent functionality requires more instructions (and hence more memory) because each individual instruction is simpler. However, these disadvantages become less significant by the year as memory densities and speeds increase, indicating that the benefits of RISC will progressively outweigh its disadvantages as memory technology develops.

In the period since about 1985, exactly this trend has been observed, with RISC processors increasingly outperforming their CISC counterparts. Although it seems likely that all future designs will now take RISC ideas as their starting point, this does not mean that CISC processors are obsolete. So much software has now been developed for the older CISC families of processors (particularly the Intel 80X86 series and the Motorola MC680X0 series), that these families will continue to be used for many years to come, and indeed, newer enhanced performance versions are still being designed.

### Parallel processing

The principal objective of parallel processing is to circumvent the von Neumann bottleneck of conventional computers (both CISC and RISC) by dividing up the processing into subtasks which can be executed in parallel and hence much faster. This requires both hardware configured to support parallel execution and software capable of recognising and suitably subdividing potentially parallel processes into their subordinate elements. In any configuration of parallel processors, key issues to be resolved concern the software and hardware mechanisms for communication and synchronisation between processors. These mechanisms are far from straightforward and are the subject of continuing research. As a result, parallel processing has so far remained a specialist niche of computing, although a principal long-term objective of researchers is to develop methods by which parallelism can be integrated with the mainstream of computing.

The transputer also embodies many of the RISC concepts discussed above.

To date, the most successful commercial approach to parallel processing has been the Inmos Transputer, one of the first microprocessors to be designed specifically for use as an element in a parallel processing system. Its key feature is the inclusion on the CPU chip of four serial communication links which can operate in parallel with normal processing. These links can be connected to other transputers to form a variety of different multiprocessor topologies, including chains, toruses, grids, trees and hypercubes. Inmos has also developed the programming language *Occam* specifically to support parallel processing, as well as developing versions of standard languages such as FORTRAN, C and PASCAL with parallel extensions.

### Computers — basic concepts

A computer can be defined as a machine which manipulates data according to a stored program executed within it. The data are often thought of as numbers, but can, with suitable processing, be any physical parameter which can be represented using binary numbers. Some of the more common types of computer data are examined in Chapter 3.

## Important features of a computer

The development process of the computer over the last 150 years has resulted in all computers containing a number of fundamental features:

*Stored program control:* The computer program, which is a sequence of instructions executed one by one to perform the required data manipulation, must be stored within the computer. This has important advantages over external program storage.

*Conditional branching:* One advantage of internal program storage is that the next instruction to be executed need not be the next in sequence since any instruction can be accessed as fast as any other (this is known as *random access*). The choice of which instruction to execute next can therefore be based upon the result of the previous operation or operations, giving the computer the ability to make decisions based upon the processing it performs.

*Loops and subroutines:* The ability of a program to execute a particular set of instructions repetitively when required can produce enormous savings in the storage needed for the program. Conditional branches can be made to loop back and repeat a set of instructions a number of times, and commonly required subtasks within a program can be called up from any other part of the program as required, without needing to include the instructions of the subtask in the main program every time it is called.

*Speed of electronics:* Even though the individual instructions available in a computer may be quite limited, because each instruction can be executed so fast, relatively powerful processing can be accomplished in what appears subjectively to be a very short time. (Compare this with the speed potential of Babbage's mechanical computer.)

> As an example, two ten-digit decimal numbers can be added together by the ARM 32-bit microprocessor in 0.1 $\mu$s.

*Cost:* The cost of computing power, and particularly the cost of computer memory is continually decreasing. It is now cheaper to store a computer instruction in an electronic memory than to store it on a card or a piece of paper tape.

*(Instructions can modify themselves):* Although this was one of von Neumann's original ideas embodied in the concept of stored program control, it has not been widely used since. One reason is that it is very difficult to keep track of what the computer is doing once the computer program has been modified from that originally written by the programmer. In microprocessors, in particular, this concept is avoided, because the implementation of a micro-controller with a permanently fixed program precludes any possibility of subsequent program changes.

> This area is still a subject of research, particularly in the areas of machine intelligence, and as part of the program to develop the 'fifth generation' of computers.

## A simple computer

Fig. 1.4 shows the structure of a simple computer. The computer can be split into a number of separate components, though the components shown do not necessarily represent the physical division between components in a real computer. For example, the control unit and arithmetic and logic unit (ALU) are generally implemented as a single chip, the microprocessor, in microcomputers. Similarly, the input and output unit may be combined into a single chip in some microcomputers. Nevertheless, Fig. 1.4 represents the conceptual structure of any computer from the smallest microcomputer to the largest mainframe computer.

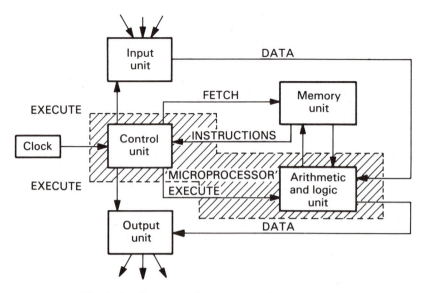

Fig. 1.4 Conceptual structure of a computer.

The first requirement of any computer is a mechanism for manipulating data. This is provided by the ALU, which can perform such functions as adding or subtracting two numbers, performing logical operations, incrementing and decrementing numbers and left and right shift operations. From this very basic set of operations, more complex processing functions can be generated by programming. Larger computers may provide additional more powerful instructions (for example, multiply and divide) within the computer instruction set.

Clearly, every computer must also include an input and an output unit. These provide the mechanism by which the computer communicates with the outside world. The outside world may consist of someone typing at a computer terminal and watching the response on a screen, or it may be some equipment, for example a washing machine, which is providing data inputs such as water temperature, water level and drum rotation speed, and is being controlled according to the program inside the computer, via computer outputs which switch on and off the water taps and heater, and alter the motor speed.

The computer must include an internal memory, which serves two functions. First, it provides storage for the computer program; second, it provides temporary storage for data which may be generated at some point during program execution by the ALU, but not be required until somewhat later. Such data *variables* must be able to be written into the memory unit by the computer, and subsequently read back when the data are required. The memory is organised as a one-dimensional array (or list) of *words*, and each instruction or data variable occupies one or more words in the memory. Each word is made up of a number of *bits* (binary digits) of storage in parallel.

The control unit of the computer controls the sequence of operations of all the components described above, according to the instructions in the computer program. Each instruction is fetched from the memory, and is then decoded by the control unit and converted into a set of lower-level control signals which cause the function specified by that instruction to be executed. When one instruction

All data and instructions within the computer are represented internally as binary numbers. Hence all computer components can be realised practically using two-state logic devices such as bistables and logic gates.

The number of bits in each word is defined by the designer of the computer, and is one measure of the computer's processing power.

execution has been completed the next instruction is fetched and the process of decoding and executing the instruction is repeated. This process is repeated for every instruction in the program and only differs if a branch instruction is encountered. In this case the next instruction to be fetched from the memory is taken from the part of the memory specified by the branch instruction, rather than being the next instruction in sequence.

The final component of the computer is a clock, or fixed-frequency oscillator, which synchronises the operation of all parts of the computer, and ensures that all operations occur in the correct sequence. The clock frequency defines the instruction execution speed of the computer and is constrained by the operating speed of the semiconductor circuits which make up the computer.

The computer is said to have a *two-beat* cycle because each instruction is first *fetched* from memory, and then *executed* to perform the function which the instruction specifies.

**Summary**

The objective of this introductory chapter has been to describe the range of computers which exist, and the range of applications which they address. The historical development of the computer has been described, with particular attention being drawn to ideas and concepts which subsequently proved to be fundamental in deriving the structure and operation of the computer as we know it today. The architecture and operation of a simple computer have been described, and its major components identified. In Chapters 2, 4 and 5 the detailed structure of these components will be explored, to give a full explanation of the hardware which makes up the present-day computer or microprocessor system.

# 2 Memory structure and architecture

**Objectives**
- ☐ To explain the structure and interconnection of registers within a computer central processing unit (CPU).
- ☐ To explain the structure of a computer main memory and show how a large number of memory locations may be uniquely accessed.
- ☐ To show how data can be transferred between registers in the CPU and to and from main memory.
- ☐ To describe the characteristics of different types of semiconductor memory.

*Compilers* and *interpreters* are examples of *system software* which is discussed in more detail in Chapter 9.

Within any computer, both instructions and data are stored internally in memory as binary numbers. This is because the computer can only understand and execute instructions coded in the binary machine language code appropriate to that particular type of computer. It may appear to the user that the computer is executing a program written in some other programming language, such as BASIC or PASCAL. In fact, in order to execute a program written in any other language, the program must first be converted to the computers' own machine language. This can either be done once and for all using a *compiler*, or as the program is executed using an *interpreter*.

Each instruction in the machine code instruction set of the computer is normally represented by one or more *words* in the computer memory. Each word is represented physically by a number of binary digits (*bits*) in parallel. Data are also stored as words within the computer memory and the word-length of the computer therefore defines the number of binary digits which the computer can manipulate simultaneously, since arithmetic manipulations are generally performed upon one memory word at a time. The number of bits per word is chosen by the designer of the computer, and is one measure of the processing power of the computer. At the present time, microprocessors typically use 8, 16 or 32 bits per word, minicomputers 16–32 bits per word and mainframe computers 32–64 or more bits per word.

Computer memory is implemented in a number of different ways. Semiconductor memory is the dominant technology at present, as a result of the revolutionary developments in integrated circuit technology over the last two decades. Several types of semiconductor memory are used, of which the two most important are *read/write memory* and *read only memory* (ROM). Other types of semiconductor memory, such as *electrically erasable programmable read only memory* (EEPROM) are also used in some specialised applications. Semiconductor memories are described as random-access memories because the time required to access a word from memory is the same, regardless of which word is to be accessed. Thus words can be read from the memory in any sequence without time penalty.

A useful general-purpose computer also normally has some type of *auxiliary* or back-up storage mechanism for long-term archiving of data or programs. The auxiliary storage can usually be completely detached from the computer, and is often some type of magnetic storage medium such as a tape or a floppy disk. The characteristics of auxiliary storage media are discussed in Chapter 8. Auxiliary storage devices generally provide *serial access* to data, in the same way as different pieces of music are stored serially on a cassette tape. In order to access data from such devices, a large time penalty must be tolerated; as a result, such devices are not usually used when fast random access is required.

### Semiconductor registers

There are two major types of semiconductor read/write memory, based on static logic devices and dynamic logic devices, and thus called *static memory* and *dynamic memory*. Static read/write memory is based upon the simple bistable storage element. The simplest bistable is the R-S flip-flop, which can store a single bit (binary digit) of information. A positive pulse on the S input stores a logical 0 at Q. The bistable is considered to be a memory device since by examining the state of the Q output at any time, one can determine whether the most recent pulse input was applied to S or R. The device is *volatile* since the memory is lost if power is removed. In practice, a slightly more complex flip-flop, the *clocked D-type*, is used as the basis of computer registers; data are transferred from the D input to the Q output on the rising or falling edge of the clock pulse. This has two advantages over the R-S flip-flop: first, the single D-input is compatible with the Q output, so that one memory device can drive another; second, the use of a clocked flip-flop enables the computer registers and memory to be designed as a synchronous system. This reduces the likelihood of the bistable being triggered by noise spikes transmitted through the power supply or by radiation, since the state of the input to the bistable can be sampled briefly by the clock pulse. More importantly, the use of a synchronised logic system makes it possible to eliminate race hazards.

The basis of dynamic memory is the capacitance of the gate input to an MOS (Metal Oxide Semiconductor) transistor. A charge can be stored in this capacitance and this causes the output transistor to be switched off or on to represent the two logic states depending on the value of the charge stored. Since the charge gradually leaks away, it is necessary to *refresh* the capacitors periodically (typically every few milliseconds) to maintain the charge, and hence the logic state, of the device. Refreshing is performed by reading the output of the device and feeding this back to the input to top up the charge on the capacitance. Thus the device is known as a *dynamic logic* device because the logic state is only maintained while the capacitance continues to be refreshed.

A single bit of storage, corresponding to one flip-flop, is of very limited use; the smallest unit of storage which a computer normally deals with is one word. In an 8-bit microprocessor, one word corresponds to eight binary digits or one *byte*, and a single byte thus allows numbers in the range 0 to 255 (0 to $2^8 - 1$) to be represented directly. By comparison, a 16-bit microprocessor allows numbers in the range 0 to 65 535 (0 to $2^{16} - 1$) to be represented in a single word, though most 16-bit microprocessors can also manipulate individual bytes of data.

Single words of storage are often required in the CPU of a computer to store

Disk storage systems are said to provide *semi-random access* because they employ two-dimensional media, which enable specific areas of data to be located much more quickly than with one-dimensional media such as tapes.

This section provides only a brief summary of the operation of static and dynamic memory. For a more detailed discussion, the reader is referred to: Stonham, T.J. *Digital Logic Techniques: principles and practice*, (Van Nostrand Reinhold, 1987) Chapter 7.

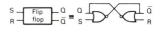

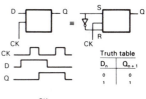

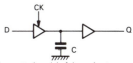

Conceptual model of dynamic storage cell

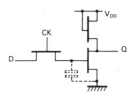

Physical implementation of dynamic storage cell

Note that the term *byte* invariably means eight bits, whereas the term *word* does not specify a fixed number of bits, but implies the word size of the computer currently being discussed.

The examples given below assume an 8-bit computer word for simplicity. This is representative of 8-bit microprocessors.

temporarily the results of arithmetic and logic operations carried out by the computer's ALU. These single words of storage are called *registers*, and almost every computer will have at least one register within its CPU. Sometimes, there may be several registers, each with a specific purpose, within the CPU. The term *accumulator* is then often used to describe a register specifically included to receive the results of arithmetic manipulations. Nevertheless, an accumulator is fundamentally identical in structure to any other kind of register; only its use may differ slightly.

The basic structure of the main computer semiconductor memory is conceptually identical to that of a register. The term *register*, however, is usually used to describe the limited number of words of storage accessed using the implied addressing mode (Chapter 7). The registers are often implemented as part of the CPU chip in microprocessor systems.

Fig. 2.1 shows the structure of a 8-bit register made up of eight D-type flip-flops in parallel. The clock input is common to all bistables since there is no requirement to deal with less than eight bits simultaneously. Hence the data at inputs $D_0$–$D_7$ are latched simultaneously into the eight bistables and appear at the outputs $Q_0$–$Q_7$ simultaneously on the negative edge of the clock pulse. After the clock pulse, $Q_0$–$Q_7$ are continuously available until the next clock pulse negative edge.

**Data transfer between registers**

If it is required to transfer the contents of a single source register to a single destination register, then this is achieved simply by connecting the Q outputs of the source register to the D inputs of the destination register and clocking the clock input of the destination register. In general, however, there will be more than one possible source register and more than one possible destination register. In this case, multiplexers and demultiplexers are used to identify the appropriate source register and select the appropriate destination register, respectively.

*Multiple sources — the multiplexer*

Consider first the requirement to select one from several source registers. Fig. 2.2 shows a circuit which enables one of four input bits a, b, c, or d to be selected and connected to the output x. The selection is achieved using two control bits $A_0$ and $A_1$, according to the binary code selected as shown in the truth table. The circuit can be extended to deal with words rather than bits by repeating the AND and OR gates within the dotted box for each bit of the word. Note that however many bits represent a word, only a single control circuit is needed to select the required source word, and this is connected to all sets of AND gates. For a large number of source registers with several bits per register word it becomes impractical to draw the full circuit, hence the simplified schematic shown in Fig. 2.2(c) is used.

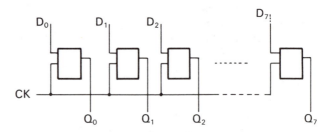

Fig. 2.1   Structure of an 8-bit register.

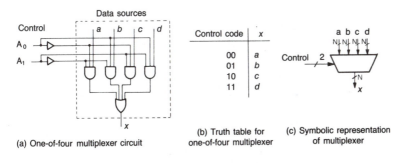

(a) One-of-four multiplexer circuit

(b) Truth table for one-of-four multiplexer

| Control code | x |
|---|---|
| 00 | a |
| 01 | b |
| 10 | c |
| 11 | d |

(c) Symbolic representation of multiplexer

The tick drawn through the input, output and control lines in the schematic is a shortform indicating that the line shown corresponds to several physical wires. The number next to the tick indicates how many.

Fig. 2.2   Data multiplexer circuit and function.

**Exercise 2.1**

Design and draw out a circuit which can select one of eight 2-bit words according to a 3-bit binary code applied to its control inputs.

## Multiple destinations — the demultiplexer

The demultiplexer performs exactly the reverse function of the multiplexer: given one source and several possible destinations it allows the required destination to be selected using the control inputs to the demultiplexer. Fig. 2.3 shows the circuitry of a demultiplexer which transfers a single bit source y to one of four destinations a, b, c or d, according to the control code specified by $A_0$ and $A_1$. Although it is possible to stack AND gates to form a word demultiplexer rather than the single-bit demultiplexer shown here, this is not generally required. Instead, the source data are connected to *all* possible destinations, but the *clock pulse* is distributed only to the required register using a single-bit demultiplexer, thus achieving the same effect with less circuitry.

This circuit is also known as an *address decoder* (see later this chapter) because an N-bit address applied to the control inputs is decoded to $2^N$ individual lines if y is permanently at logic 1.

## Data transfer using buses

For large numbers of registers when data may need to be transferred from any register to any other, a bus is normally used. Physically, the bus corresponds simply to N wires in parallel, where N is the number of bits in the particular computer word. Fig. 2.4 shows a typical arrangement, where a multiplexer is used to select from all the possible source registers. The output of the multiplexer then connects to the 8-bit bus (in this example) and thence to the inputs of all the possible destination registers. The required destination register is selected using a demultiplexer connected to each destination register's clock input. In this very general structure any register may be connected to any other, by applying

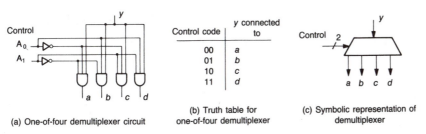

(a) One-of-four demultiplexer circuit

(b) Truth table for one-of-four demultiplexer

| Control code | y connected to |
|---|---|
| 00 | a |
| 01 | b |
| 10 | c |
| 11 | d |

(c) Symbolic representation of demultiplexer

Fig. 2.3   Data demultiplexer circuit and function.

17

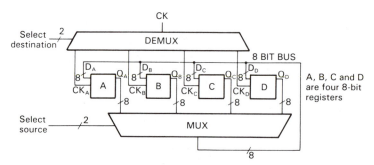

Fig. 2.4   Example register bus structure.

The register transfer language used throughout this book is defined in Appendix 2.

appropriate codes to the source select and destination select control lines. Thus, for example a function such as 'Transfer the contents of register A to register B':

$$(A) \rightarrow B$$

is easily implemented by selecting the source register A using the multiplexer, the destination register B using the demultiplexer, and pulsing the clock input.

To minimise the logic required to implement the multiplexer, the design shown in Fig. 2.2 is generally implemented using tristate logic. Fig. 2.5 shows a tristate logic implementation of Fig. 2.2. This particular implementation removes the need for the OR gates at the output and the multi-input AND gates at the input, which are replaced with single-input tristate buffers. In addition to the normal logic 0 and 1 outputs the tristate buffers can be put into a high-impedance output state; the demultiplexer driving the buffer control inputs ensures that all buffers except one are in the high-impedance state so that a single buffer drives the bus at any given time.

The high-impedance state is implemented in *transistor-transistor logic* (TTL) by arranging for both totem-pole output transistors to be switched off simultaneously.

The internal data buses on the ARM are 32 bits wide, but the internal bus on the MC68000 is 16 bits wide, even though its registers are 32 bits wide.

It is conventional to show the bus structure of a computer symbolically in computer documentation. As an example, Fig. 2.6 shows the structure of the Acorn ARM CPU. This device is shown as containing several internal buses which enable transfers to take place between a number of registers. Fig. 2.7 shows the register set available to the programmer on the Acorn ARM (the duplicate registers shown hatched are not available in the normal user mode of operation — see Chapter 5 for further details); Fig. 2.8 shows the corresponding register set for the MC68000, and Fig. 2.9 the (much smaller) set of registers on the MC68HC11. Examples below illustrate some of the machine code instructions which are provided in each device to support data transfers between registers.

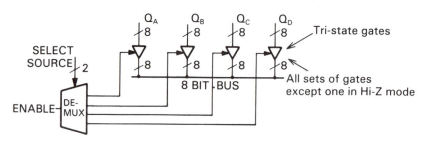

Fig. 2.5   Multiplexer using tristate logic.

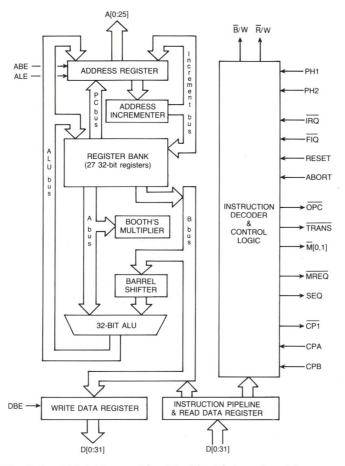

Fig. 2.6   ARM (Acorn Risc Machine) internal architecture.

| | user mode | svc mode | irq mode | fiq mode | |
|---|---|---|---|---|---|
| | R0 | | | | |
| | R1 | | | | |
| | R2 | | | | |
| | R3 | | | | |
| | R4 | | | | |
| | R5 | | | | |
| | R6 | | | | |
| | R7 | | | | |
| | R8 | | | R8_fiq | |
| | R9 | | | R9_fiq | |
| | R10 | | | R10_fiq | |
| | R11 | | | R11_fiq | |
| | R12 | | | R12_fiq | |
| | R13 | R13_svc | R13_irq | R13_fiq | |
| | R14 | R14_svc | R14_irq | R14_fiq | |
| | R15 (PC/PSR) | | | | |

Fig. 2.7   ARM register set.

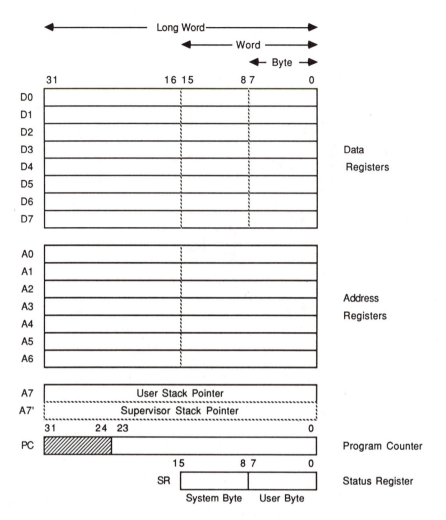

Fig. 2.8   Motorola MC68000 register structure.

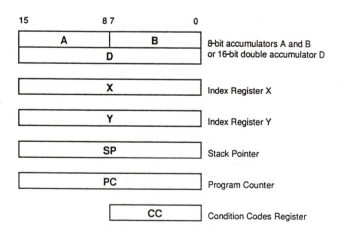

Fig. 2.9   MC68HC11 register set.

*Example Acorn ARM instructions*

| | | | |
|---|---|---|---|
| MOV | R12,R0 | (Transfer contents of R0 to R12) | $(R0) \rightarrow R12$ |
| MOV | R15,R14 | (Transfer contents of R14 to R15) | $(R14) \rightarrow R15$ |

*Example MC68000 instructions*

| | | | |
|---|---|---|---|
| MOVE.L | D0,D2 | (Transfer contents of data register D0 to data register D2) | $(D0) \rightarrow D2$ |
| MOVE.B | D1,D3 | (Transfer low-order 8-bit contents of data register D1 to data register D3) | $(D1) \rightarrow D3$ |
| MOVEA.W | D0,A1 | (Transfer low-order 16-bit contents of data register D0 to address register A1) | $(D1) \rightarrow A1$ |
| EXG | D6,D7 | (Exchange contents of data register D6 with data register D7) | $(D6) \rightarrow temp;$ $(D7) \rightarrow D6;$ $(temp) \rightarrow D7$ |

*Example MC68HC11 instructions*

| | | |
|---|---|---|
| TAB | (Transfer contents of A accumulator to B accumulator (8-bit)) | $(A) \rightarrow B$ |
| TSX | (Transfer contents of SP register to X register (16-bit)) | $(SP) \rightarrow X$ |

The mnemonics (e.g. MOV) used to describe the example instructions are defined by the device manufacturer, and are given in full in Appendices 3, 4 and 5.

Most MC68000 instructions can operate on bytes, words (16 bits) or long words (32 bits) of data: the data size to be used is specified by adding .B (byte) .W (word) or .L (long word) to the instruction mnemonic. If this extension is omitted a word (16-bit) operation is assumed.

The exchange instruction can only exchange all 32 bits of the specified registers. Note the need for a temporary register to enable the exchange operation to take place without corrupting either D6 or D7.

Note the lack of consistency between different manufacturer's instruction mnemonics, even when they are describing essentially the same operation!

Using the example register architecture of Fig. 2.4 show how an instruction *exchange registers A and B* could be implemented. How many clock pulses would be required?

**Exercise 2.2**

## Semiconductor read/write memory — main memory

In most general-purpose computers, the main computer memory is implemented using semiconductor read/write memory, in a similar way to registers. Whereas there are typically only a very few registers in a computer CPU however, the computer's main memory contains thousands or even millions of words. This immediately presents a problem of how to identify a single required word of memory.

As an example, consider a computer memory containing 4000 words, a very modest size by current standards. This 4000 word memory is equivalent to 4000 registers, and assuming an 8-bit word this corresponds to 32 000 bistables. Thus there are more than 64 000 connections required to access every bit of every word in the 4000 word memory (after allowing for 32 000 D inputs, 32 000 Q outputs and a number of clock inputs)! This presents a severe interfacing problem, since although it is feasible to put 32 000 bits of memory on a single silicon chip, it is quite impractical to have a 64 000 pin chip!

In order to resolve this problem, computer memory is organised as a list and accessed using a binary address which defines where in the list the required word lies, in exactly the same way as the numerical address of a house defines its position in a street. The list is an implicit rather than explicit structure, since the actual organisation of the memory words upon the chip is not a sequential list. For the 4000 word memory described above, a 12-bit binary address is sufficient

Read/write memory is often known as *random access memory* (RAM), but this is a misnomer, since *read only memory* (ROM) is also random access (see later this chapter).

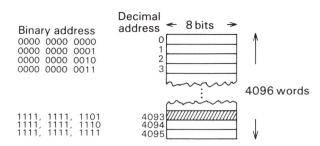

Fig. 2.10 Address structure of main memory.

to define uniquely any word within the memory (in fact, it allows a maximum of 4096 ($2^{12}$) unique addresses to be defined). Fig. 2.10 shows the structure of a 4096-word memory. Using this structure any 12-bit binary address uniquely identifies a single word within the memory (e.g. the binary code 1111 1111 1101 selects word 4093).

For a more detailed description of the internal structure of memory chips, refer to: Nichols, K.G., Zaluska, E.J. *Theory and Practice of Microprocessors* (Edward Arnold, 1982), Chapter 2.

To be useful, it must be possible both to read from and to write to the memory. Fig. 2.11 shows the address structure which is used to achieve this. Comparing this structure with Fig. 2.4, a number of points may be noted:

(*a*) The separate multiplexer and demultiplexer used for transferring data from one register to another have been replaced by a single demultiplexer which identifies the address of the required memory word. This is possible because it is assumed that it is not necessary to read from one address and write to another simultaneously, as was the case with register transfers (i.e. transfers are either from memory to a CPU register or vice versa, but not both simultaneously).

(*b*) As a result of (*a*) the addressing logic is much simplified; a single one-bit demultiplexer, used as an address decoder, is required. The read/write input is effectively combined with the clock pulse to the memory. For a *read* operation, the read/write line remains at logic 1 and acts as an enable signal to cause one of 4096 memory words to be connected to the data bus via tristate gates. For a *write* operation, the line pulses to 0, disabling the output from memory onto the data bus, and then back to 1, providing the clock pulse which latches data from the CPU into the memory word selected by the address decoder.

Fig. 2.11 shows the *conceptual* memory structure. In practice, memory chips are implemented as two-dimensional arrays with two orthogonal address decoders to minimise the address decoding circuitry.

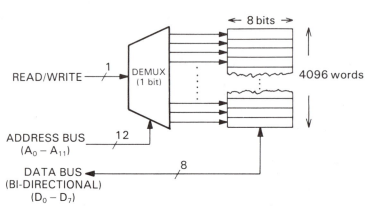

Fig. 2.11 Structure and addressing mechanism of a computer memory.

(*c*) Because data are not written and read simultaneously, a single *bidirectional* data bus can be used, i.e. data can pass either from the CPU to the memory on this bus, or in the opposite direction.

Using this structure, the 64 000 pins originally required to address 4000 words of memory can now be reduced to 21 pins, comprising 12 address inputs identifying the required memory word, eight bidirectional data lines which perform the actual data transfer, and a read/write line to define the direction of data transfer on the data bus and clock data into the memory when required. It should be noted, however, that the reduction in connections from 64 000 to 21 has not been obtained without imposing some restrictions; in particular, we can now access only one word at a time, whereas previously any number of words could be accessed simultaneously; furthermore, data transfers must now take place in only one direction at a time.

*Example transfers*

*Write*
    (*a*) Set $D_0$–$D_7$ to required binary pattern.
    (*b*) Set $A_0$–$A_{11}$ to address where data is to be stored.
    (*c*) Set read/write line to 0 (write).
    (*d*) After sufficient time for propagation delays, set read/write line to 1 (clock data into memory)

*Read*
    (*a*) Set $A_0$–$A_{11}$ to address to be read.
    (*b*) Read/write line should already be at 1.
    (*c*) After sufficient time for propagation delays, data stored in $D_0$–$D_7$ of the specified word can be read on the data bus.

The sequence of operations for read and write are similar, but no synchronising clock pulse is needed for the read operation.

As can be seen from Fig. 2.6, the bus structure of the Acorn ARM matches the model outlined above, except that the ARM has a 32-bit bidirectional data bus to perform data transfers between main memory and registers (and vice versa), and the ARM address bus is a 26-bit bus. There are also a number of control signals, including a read/write signal.

Although the ARM is a 32-bit microprocessor, and accesses to memory are therefore normally made in 32-bit chunks, the disadvantage of having such a large word size is that of representing much smaller units of data, such as characters, which only occupy a single byte each. To solve this problem, memory on the ARM microprocessor appears byte-orientated to the programmer, that is, every byte of memory has its own unique address. Although memory access still takes place in 32-bit words, it is possible to select any one of the four bytes from the word. The result of this is that whole word access can only be performed if the address of the word is divisible by four (e.g. $0000000_{16}$, $0000004_{16}$, $0000008_{16}$), while any address is valid for byte access. An attempt to specify a word address of $0000002_{16}$ is not permitted, as this implies that the required bytes are split between word 0 and word 1 of memory. This is illustrated in Fig. 2.12. Thus the 26-bit ARM address bus specifies a maximum addressing capability of $2^{26}$ bytes (or 64 Mbytes) of memory, and an additional control line ($\overline{\text{B/W}}$) is used to indicate whether a byte or word access to memory is intended.

The presence of a bar above a pin connection symbol is the conventional way of indicating that the signal is asserted when low rather than high.

| | Bit 31 | | | Bit 0 | |
|---|---|---|---|---|---|
| Location 0 | Byte 3 | Byte 2 | Byte 1 | Byte 0 | (Word 0) |
| Location 4 | Byte 7 | Byte 6 | Byte 5 | Byte 4 | (Word 4) |
| Location 8 | Byte 11 | Byte 10 | Byte 9 | Byte 8 | (Word 8) |
| Location 12 | Byte 15 | Byte 14 | Byte 13 | Byte 12 | (Word 12) |

Fig. 2.12   Memory organisation in the ARM microprocessor.

Although the MC68000 has 32 bit registers, its external data bus is only 16 bits wide. It has a 23-bit address bus and can thus address a maximum of $2^{23}$ words or 8 Mwords or 16 Mbytes. To support memory access of bytes, words (16 bits) and long words (32 bits), memory connected to an MC68000 is organised in a similar way to the ARM, as shown in Fig. 2.13.

The 23-bit address bus essentially accesses a word (16 bits) of memory at a time, using address lines A1–A23. An implied A0 (least significant bit) of the address bus, which is always zero, means that every word address is *even* and word addresses increment in twos rather than ones. In order to allow individual bytes of memory to be accessed when required, bit A0 of the address bus is replaced by two signals, $\overline{\text{UDS}}$ (Upper Data Strobe) and $\overline{\text{LDS}}$ (Lower Data Strobe). When $\overline{\text{LDS}}$ is asserted (set low) the lower data byte of the word is selected; when $\overline{\text{UDS}}$ is asserted the upper data byte is selected. Thus either byte can be read individually, or the full word may be read by asserting both lines simultaneously. Since the data bus and external memory are organised in words,

The MC68020, a full 32-bit implementation of the MC68000 architecture, has 32-bit data and address buses.

Long words can be specified on any even address, e.g. long word 6 comprises bytes 6, 7, 8 and 9.

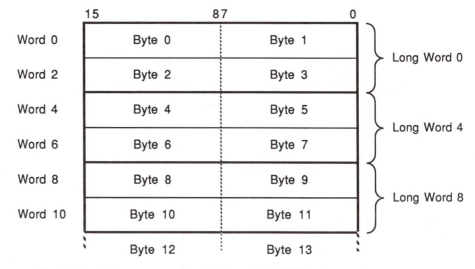

Fig. 2.13   Memory organisation in an MC68000 microprocessor system.

long words of 32 bits must be accessed 16 bits at a time. Hence a long word is stored in two successive memory words and is accessed via two successive read operations, between which the address must be incremented by two.

The MC68HC11 can be configured in a number of different operating modes, as explained in Appendix E. In the most general of these modes, *expanded multiplexed operating mode*, it has the capability of accessing a 64 kbyte (65 536 byte) address space using a 16-bit external address bus and an 8-bit bidirectional external data bus.

*Example Acorn ARM instructions*

| | | | | |
|---|---|---|---|---|
| LDR | R0,&1000 | (Load R0 with the 32-bit data in addresses 1000–1003 hexadecimal) | (&1000)→R0 | Note that 32-bit word accesses must be aligned on four byte boundaries, but byte accesses (signified by a B appended to the LDR or STR mnemonic) can be at any address. The & indicates a hexadecimal number in ARM assembly language. |
| LDRB | R1,&1003 | (Load R1 with the 8-bit data in address 1003 hexadecimal) | (&1003)→R1 | |
| STR | R1,&1004 | (Store the contents of R1 in addresses 1004–1007 hexadecimal) | (R1)→&1004 | |

*Example MC68000 instructions*

| | | | | |
|---|---|---|---|---|
| MOVE.W | 65534,D0 | (Load the contents of address word 65 534 into the least significant word of register D0) | (65534)→D0 | A 16-bit transfer: note that words always begin at an even address. |
| MOVE.B | 65535,D1 | (Load the contents of address byte 65 535 into the least significant byte of register D1) | (65535)→D1 | An 8-bit transfer: bytes can be accessed from odd or even addresses. |
| MOVE.L | 1000,D2 | (Load the contents of address words 1000 and 1002 into the most and least significant words of register D2 respectively) | (1000)→D2; (1002)→D2 | A 32-bit transfer, requiring two successive memory accesses to adjacent words. |

*Example MC68HC11 instructions*

| | | | | |
|---|---|---|---|---|
| LDAA | $1000 | (Load Accumulator A with the data in address 1000 hexadecimal) | ($1000)→A | The $ indicates a hexadecimal number in MC68HC11 assembly language. |
| STAB | $1004 | (Store the contents of accumulator B in address 1004 hexadecimal) | (B)→$1004 | |

*Registers versus main memory*

Because it is possible both to read from and to write into RAM, it can be used both for program and data variable storage. If data variables are stored in main memory, the memory is effectively being used in exactly the same way as registers, that is, as temporary storage for the intermediate results of data processing. Since registers and main memory are physically similar and logically identical, the question must arise as to why it is necessary to implement both within a computer.

In fact, it is quite possible to design a computer which contains no discrete general-purpose registers, but registers can significantly increase the processing speed of the computer. Registers are accessible more rapidly than main memory because a short address (typically only two or three bits) suffices to define a register uniquely. This reduces the time required for an instruction to access a register, since the instruction can be shorter, and stored in fewer memory words.

A few special-purpose registers are required in any computer (refer to Chapter 4).

For example, a 4-bit address would allow 16 unique registers to be accessed, as in the ARM microprocessor.

Furthermore, registers included on the CPU chip of a microprocessor are not bound by the same overall address and data bus timing constraints as the main memory, and hence register access speeds can be optimised as part of the CPU design process. In consequence, data processing performed using CPU registers is almost always faster than the same processing performed using data stored in memory locations. This advantage is lost if a very large number of registers is provided, hence a two-level structure, where registers are used for very short-term storage of a limited number of variables and main memory is used for less frequently accessed data, is found to be a good compromise.

Program instructions can also be stored in read/write memory. In general-purpose computers this is ideal, since the same computer memory is required to hold many different programs at different times; all that is needed is some auxiliary storage medium from which the program may be loaded into memory, and a means of transferring the program from the auxiliary storage medium to the computer's main memory. In contrast, the most common use of micro-processors is in dedicated applications where, for example, the microprocessor controls a point-of-sale terminal, a washing machine or a video game. In these dedicated applications, using RAM for the main program memory is impractical because the program would be lost every time power was removed from the system. Thus a non-volatile storage medium is required for dedicated micro-processor applications, such that the stored program may be executed imme-diately power is applied to the microprocessor system. Semiconductor ROM is used to store the program in this case.

### Semiconductor read only memory (ROM)

For further details of Read Only Memories refer to: Stonham, T.J. *Digital Logic Techniques: principles and practice* (Van Nostrand Reinhold, 1987) Chapter 6.

Although superficially very similar to RAM, ROM is in fact a combinational logic component wherein the data outputs of the ROM are simply a combina-tional function of the address inputs at any given time. Hence the name ROM arises because it is only possible for the microprocessor to read data from a ROM, and not (normally) to write to it. The method used to address a ROM is identical to that used for RAM; the only difference is that data can only be read, hence there is no requirement for a read/write control line in addition to the address and data buses. Several different types of ROM exist, and each has its own advantages and disadvantages:

See the illustration of the MC68HC11 in Fig. 1.3 for an example of how each of these types of memory is provided on a single chip.

*Mask-programmed ROM* is used in applications where a very large number (i.e. at least several thousands) of systems all require the same program. The required program is then specified by preparing a mask defining the binary program codes stored at each memory address. The required ROM is subse-quently fabricated using this mask. This process involves a substantial one-off development cost, hence it is impractical for small numbers of ROMs, but for large numbers of devices is the most economical solution.

*Programmable read only memory (PROM)* can be programmed once and for all by the user by fusing internal links to specify the data stored at each address. Since it is a one-off process, if any mistakes are made the device must be discarded and the process repeated with a new PROM. For this reason fusible-link PROMs are now obsolete, and instead EPROMs are used.

*Erasable programmable read only memory (EPROM)* may also be programmed by the user but makes use of isolated gate field effect transistors (FETs). The chip itself is visible through a quartz window, so that if it is desired to change the program, the complete program stored on the chip may be erased by exposure to ultra-violet light. Subsequently, the new or modified program may be stored in the device. This facility makes EPROMs very popular during the development of a microprocessor-based product, and for small production runs where the development cost of a mask-programmed ROM is not justified. For large numbers of identical devices, however, the unit cost of an EPROM is higher than that of a ROM.

*Electrically erasable programmable read only memory (EEPROM)* is sometimes used where it is required to provide memory with the characteristics of a non-volatile RAM. An example might be an electronic car speedometer/odometer which is required to retain the elapsed mileage even when the car battery is disconnected. Data are read in the conventional fashion, but individual addresses may be selectively erased and rewritten using extra control inputs to the memory and higher than normal voltages. The process of writing or erasing data is very much slower than the reading process. EEPROMs are considerably more expensive than other types of ROM, and would not therefore be considered unless these specific characteristics are required.

**Memory configuration in microprocessor applications**

In the example memory described earlier an arbitrary size of 4000 words was chosen. In practice, the memory can be any size, dependent upon the size of address bus used in the computer. For example, a 256-word memory would require an 8-bit address; a 4096-word (4-kword) memory would require a 12-bit address; a 65 536-word (64-kword) memory would require a 16-bit address; an 8 388 608-word (8-Mword) memory would require a 23-bit address.

Many 8-bit microprocessors use a 16-bit address bus, implying a maximum addressing range of 65 536 words, while 16–32-bit microprocessors use a 20-bit, 24-bit or 32-bit address bus, enabling them to access enormous amounts of memory. It is important to realise that although the number of bits which the address bus contains specifies the maximum amount of memory which the computer can directly address, no minimum is implied. Thus typical 8-bit microprocessor applications may not make use of the full 65 536 byte (64 kilobyte or 64 kbyte) addressing range possible with these devices.

This is illustrated in the memory map for a typical member of the MC68HC11 family, shown in Fig. 2.14, where only a small part of the available address space contains physical memory in the basic single-chip implementation (the remainder of the address space can, however, be used if additional external memory chips are added). A similar approach is commonly followed in computer systems based upon the ARM and MC68000 microprocessors, where only a small part of the total available address space will normally be populated with physical memory. All other addresses, though addressable by the microprocessor, would contain no physical memory, and would not be used.

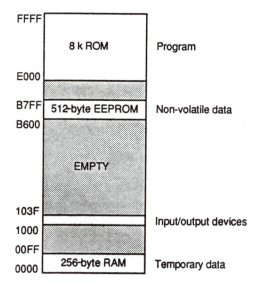

The addresses in Fig. 2.14 are expressed using the hexadecimal number format described in Chapter 3.

Fig. 2.14   Example MC68HC11 memory map.

**Summary**

This chapter has shown how the register and memory architectures of computers may be built up from standard combinational logic components and bistables. The use of multiplexers and demultiplexers to enable data to be transferred from one register to another has been introduced, together with the concept of a bus as a general-purpose data transfer path. The conceptual structure of a computer memory as a list accessed by means of a binary address has been shown, and a typical computer memory architecture derived. The major different semi-conductor memory technologies and their advantages and disadvantages have been explained. Finally, example instructions from the instruction sets of the ARM, MC68HC11 and MC68000 have been used to illustrate the data transfers which can typically be programmed using the machine language of a microprocessor.

**Problems**

2.1   Calculate the number of bits of memory in a computer memory with a 20-bit address and a 12-bit word.

2.2   A computer memory of at least 100 000 words is required for a particular application; what is the minimum address bus size which will allow each word to be uniquely addressed?

2.3   A 4096-word read/write memory is implemented physically using the list structure shown in Fig. 2.8. Calculate how many AND gates would be required in the memory address decoder, and how many inputs each AND gate would contain.

2.4 If the 4096-word memory was a ROM, how would the address decoder be modified?

2.5 The 4096 word memory is now redesigned as a two-dimensional array of $64 \times 64$ words. Calculate how many AND gates would now be required to address each word individually, and how many inputs each AND gate would contain.

# 3 Data representation in computers

**Objectives**
- ☐ To explain how to manipulate numbers in binary, octal, binary coded decimal, and hexadecimal formats.
- ☐ To describe the commonly used computer standard data formats, and the advantages and disadvantages of each format.
- ☐ To describe how alphanumeric data may be stored within a computer memory.
- ☐ To explain how computer instructions may be represented by means of binary codes.

In Chapter 2, the physical and conceptual structure of a computer memory was introduced, and it was explained how each word within the computer memory corresponds simply to a number of two-state memory elements, each capable of storing one bit (binary digit) of information. In order that information can be processed within the computer, it must be represented by a binary code which can be stored in the computer's memory and registers, since the computer can only understand binary data. The information that a computer can manipulate is not restricted simply to binary numbers. Any information which is capable of being represented by a binary code may be processed by a computer; as long as it is first converted to a digital format using an analogue-to-digital converter, even analogue information may be processed.

As an example, *word processors* are computers which process textual information which is coded by means of a standard text character code (see later this chapter).

Instructions which the computer executes (machine code instructions) are also represented by binary codes (see later this chapter).

In every case, computer programmers must make use of an *agreed code* to represent the data which they manipulate, so that once the data manipulation is complete, programmers can successfully interpret the results which the computer has produced. Several standard codes are widely used; these are introduced in this chapter and their advantages and disadvantages identified.

## Number systems

1 octal digit = 3 binary digits
1 hexadecimal digit = 4 binary digits

Within any computer, all numbers must be expressed in binary form. Humans are very poorly adapted to manipulating binary data directly and usually work either in *octal* (base 8) or *hexadecimal* (base 16). The advantage of these two bases is that in each case they can be converted very easily to true binary, while at the same time arithmetic is very similar to normal decimal arithmetic. Octal and hexadecimal both provide a relatively compact way of expressing numbers, whereas large numbers expressed in binary can quickly become unmanageable.

### The binary number system

The binary system uses only two separate symbols, 0 and 1, to represent numbers. In every other respect the conventions used are the same as for decimal arithmetic. In particular, the concept of *positional notation* is retained in binary arithmetic. Thus the least significant digit of a binary number represents the units ($2^0$), the next digit represents the twos ($2^1$), the next the fours ($2^2$) and so on in increasing powers of 2. Similarly, the fractional component of a number can be represented by digits to the right of the binary point, with each digit representing the next decreasing power of 2, i.e. one half ($2^{-1}$), one-quarter ($2^{-2}$), and so on.

Binary arithmetic is performed in exactly the same way as decimal arithmetic except that the rules are simplified because there are far fewer possible combinations of digits. For example, only eight possible input digit combinations can occur when adding two binary digits together allowing for a carry input and a carry output. These are shown in the truth table of a *1-bit full adder*, which is described in detail in Chapter 4.

A more detailed discussion of binary arithmetic may be found in Bartee T.C. *Digital Computer Fundamentals* (5th edition), (McGraw-Hill, 1981).

The binary point is similar to the decimal point in base 10 arithmetic.

*Examples*

| Decimal | Binary | Decimal | Binary |
|---|---|---|---|
| 14 | 01110 | 4.125 | 100.001 |
| + 19 | + 10011 | + 5.75 | + 101.110 |
| 33 | 100001 | 9.875 | 1001.111 |

| Decimal | Binary | Decimal | Binary |
|---|---|---|---|
| 27 | 11011 | 6.25 | 110.010 |
| − 15 | − 01111 | − 4.375 | − 100.011 |
| 12 | 01100 | 1.875 | 001.111 |

| Carry In | A | B | Sum | Carry Out |
|---|---|---|---|---|
| 0 | 0 | 0 | 0 | 0 |
| 0 | 0 | 1 | 1 | 0 |
| 0 | 1 | 0 | 1 | 0 |
| 0 | 1 | 1 | 0 | 1 |
| 1 | 0 | 0 | 1 | 0 |
| 1 | 0 | 1 | 0 | 1 |
| 1 | 1 | 0 | 0 | 1 |
| 1 | 1 | 1 | 1 | 1 |

*Truth table of a 1-bit full adder*

Work out the truth table of a 1-bit full subtractor.

**Exercise 3.1**

Perform the following addition and subtraction sums in binary:

**Exercise 3.2**

(a) 75 + 43      (b) 29 + 17      (c) 3.875 + 9.25      (d) 0.75 + 0.0625
(e) 48 − 17      (f) 95 − 62      (g) 8.625 − 4.875      (h) 0.625 − 0.375

Binary multiplication is particularly simple because every bit of the multiplier is either 0 or 1. Either the multiplicand is copied after shifting an appropriate number of bits if the multiplier bit is 1, or all zeros are copied if the multiplier bit is 0. Hence, the mechanism of binary multiplication is seen to be a repeated process of shifting the multiplicand by one bit and adding the result to the partial sum if the corresponding bit of the multiplier is 1.

*Examples*

| Decimal | Binary | Decimal | Binary |
|---|---|---|---|
| 10 | 1010 | 14 | 1110 |
| × 9 | × 1001 | × 7 | × 0111 |
| 90 | 1010 | 98 | 1110 |
|  | 0000 |  | 1110 |
|  | 0000 |  | 1110 |
|  | 1010 |  | 0000 |
|  | 1011010 |  | 1100010 |

Binary division is accomplished using the reverse process to binary multiplication. The divisor is compared with the dividend at the most significant bit position, and is subtracted if less with the most significant bit of the quotient being set. Otherwise the quotient bit is reset. The divisor is then shifted left and the process repeated as in conventional division.

*Examples*

| *Decimal* | *Binary* |
|---|---|

$$\begin{array}{r} 6 \\ 5\overline{)30} \\ 30 \\ \hline 0 \end{array} \qquad \begin{array}{r} 110 \\ 101\overline{)11110} \\ 101 \\ \hline 101 \\ 101 \\ \hline 0 \end{array}$$

| *Decimal* | *Binary* |
|---|---|

$$\begin{array}{r} 0.482\ldots \\ 7\overline{)3.375} \\ 2.8 \\ \hline .57 \\ .56 \\ \hline .015 \\ .014 \\ \hline .001\ldots \end{array} \qquad \begin{array}{r} 0.01111\ldots \\ 111\overline{)11.01100} \\ 1.11 \\ \hline 1.101 \\ .111 \\ \hline .1100 \\ .0111 \\ \hline .01010 \\ .00111 \\ \hline .000110\ldots \end{array}$$

**Exercise 3.3** Perform the following multiplication and division sums in binary:

(a) $9 \times 7$    (b) $13 \times 8$    (c) $4.5 \times 6$    (d) $3.25 \times 1.75$

(e) $77 \div 11$    (f) $132 \div 12$    (g) $25 \div 6.25$    (h) $12.5 \div 1.25$

## Octal (base 8) numbers

The octal number system is used to represent binary numbers in a form which is more readable to human beings. Each octal digit is equivalent to three binary digits, hence transformation from binary to octal and back is very easy. Most people find octal arithmetic little more difficult than arithmetic using the decimal system. One difficulty with octal, however, is that most computers tend to use word lengths which are multiples of four rather than three bits (for example, 8- and 16-bit microprocessors, 16 and 32 bit minicomputers). As a result data words cannot generally be expressed as an exact number of octal digits. This has led to the widespread use of the hexadecimal, or base 16, number system in microprocessors.

For example:

| | | |
|---|---|---|
| | 1111 1111 | Binary (255 Decimal) |
| = | FF | Hexadecimal |
| = | 377 | Octal |

**Exercise 3.4** Convert the decimal numbers given in Exercise 3.2 to octal, and perform the sums in octal.

## Hexadecimal (base 16) numbers

In the hexadecimal number system the numbers 0–9 are represented in the normal way, but the numbers 10–15 are represented by the letters A–F according to the Table in the margin. Each hexadecimal digit is thus equivalent to four binary digits so that an 8-bit word can be represented exactly by two hex. digits while a 16-bit word corresponds to four hex. digits. This advantage is offset by the fact that hexadecimal arithmetic is quite difficult. There seems to be a fundamental human conceptual problem in treating letters as numbers for arithmetic purposes, with the result that most people find it necessary to convert the letters A–F back to their decimal equivalent before they can manipulate them.

Convert the decimal numbers in Exercise 3.2 to hexadecimal and perform the sums in hexadecimal.

## Binary coded decimal (BCD) numbers

Binary coded decimal is a number system where four bits are used to represent each decimal digit. The binary codes corresponding to the hexadecimal digits A–F are unused in the BCD system. The advantage of this system is that BCD data may be readily converted back to decimal numbers simply by dividing the data word into 4-bit blocks which each correspond to one decimal digit. The disadvantage is that numbers cannot be coded as efficiently using the BCD system as they can using binary, since some binary codes are redundant in the BCD system. For example, an 8-bit word can represent a maximum of 256 different numbers (i.e. 0–255) using normal binary, whereas only 100 distinct numbers (i.e. 0–99) could be coded using BCD.

Within a computer, BCD calculations can be performed if numbers are adjusted to allow for the BCD format after normal binary arithmetic. Many computers have instructions which perform this adjustment automatically. As an example, consider the sum $9 + 3$ performed using the BCD format within a computer. The binary result is 12 (1100), a code which is unused in BCD. Thus, to detect BCD overflow, a binary result outside the range 0–9 must first be detected. This indicates a numeric overflow in the BCD format. To correct for this, the next more significant digit (the tens in this case) is incremented and 10 is subtracted from the less significant digit to correct it. For multi-digit numbers this process would be repeated for each digit, starting with the least significant digit.

*Hexadecimal numbering*

| Decimal | Hexadecimal |
|---------|-------------|
| 0–9 | 0–9 |
| 10 | A |
| 11 | B |
| 12 | C |
| 13 | D |
| 14 | E |
| 15 | F |

For those destined to perform a large amount of hexadecimal arithmetic, it is possible to buy hexadecimal calculators!·

**Exercise 3.5**

Most calculators, which are essentially pre-programmed 4-bit computers, use the BCD system. Each 4-bit data word corresponds to one decimal digit, and numbers are processed in a digit serial, bit parallel format.

The MC68HC11 microprocessor implements a 'Decimal Adjust Accumulator' instruction which performs this correction automatically on an 8-bit two-digit number stored in accumulator A. The MC68000 has separate instructions for BCD addition, subtraction and negation. There is no support for BCD arithmetic on the ARM.

## Examples

The following groups of numbers are all the same:

| 0101 1100 | Binary | | 1010 0011 0100 1011 | Binary |
|-----------|--------|--|---------------------|--------|
| 1   3   4 | Octal | | 1  2  1  5  1  3 | Octal |
| 5   C | Hex | | A  3  4  B | Hex |
| 9   2 ⎫ | BCD | | 4  1  8  0  3 ⎫ | BCD |
| 1001 0010 ⎭ | | | 0100 0001 1000 0000 0011 ⎭ | |

Express the following decimal numbers in binary, octal, hexadecimal and BCD.

**Exercise 3.6**

| | | | |
|---|---|---|---|
| (a) 11 | (b) 243 | (c) 7528 | (d) 35 289 |
| (e) 0.5 | (f) 5.125 | (g) 27.75 | (h) 178.625 |

## Standard numeric data formats

Several different number representations are commonly used inside computers depending upon the type of number which it is required to manipulate. In general, there is a tradeoff to be made between the complexity of the number representation used, the ease of performing numerical manipulations using that format, and the range and precision of numbers that can be represented. It makes no sense to use a very complex number representation (such as floating point, see later this chapter) to represent a simple integer number because this increases the complexity of the computer program required to manipulate the number and hence reduces the speed of any calculation.

### Unsigned integer

The unsigned integer format is the simplest possible number representation within the computer. One word is assumed to represent the required binary number directly. The *range* of numbers which can be represented using the data format is defined by the word length of the computer, for example

8 bits allows unsigned integers in the range 0–255, and
16 bits allows unsigned integers in the range 0–65535

to be represented. Numerical manipulation of numbers in the unsigned integer format is quite straightforward, because all computers have instructions which enable numbers in this format to be added, subtracted, shifted, and so on. The disadvantage of this format is the restriction it places upon numbers which can be represented; using the unsigned integer format, it is not possible to represent negative numbers or fractions, and the range of numbers is restricted by the size of the computer word.

### Negative numbers; sign plus absolute magnitude

Two methods are commonly used to represent negative numbers. The simplest conceptually is to use one bit of the computer word to represent the sign of a number while the remainder of the word represents its absolute magnitude. The convention most commonly used is that the most significant bit of the word is the sign bit, and that:

m.s.b. = 1 implies a negative number
m.s.b. = 0 implies a positive number.

Thus an 8-bit computer word allows numbers in the range $\pm 127$ to be expressed, while a 16-bit word enables numbers in the range $\pm 32\,767$ to be specified. In practice, it is found that this is not the most useful representation of negative numbers for ease of computer manipulation. Instead, the most commonly used method of representing negative integers in computers is the 2s complement format.

### Negative numbers; 2s complement

In the 2s complement numeric format, using an N-bit word, the number $- A$ is represented as $2^N - A$. This means that, as with sign plus absolute magnitude numbers, the most significant bit becomes the sign bit and if the most significant bit is set, this corresponds to a negative number. By inspection, it can be seen that

---

The different numeric data formats are reflected in computer programming languages such as BASIC, FORTRAN, and PASCAL, which allow different *types* of numeric constant and variable to be defined, for example *integer* and *real*. The different data types are coded differently in the computer.

In practice, a number greater than 255 can be represented using an 8-bit word by splitting it into two or more bytes and storing each byte as a separate memory word. However, this significantly increases the complexity of arithmetic processing.

Note that the number zero has two valid representations in this format:

+0  i.e.  0000 0000
−0  i.e.  1000 0000

an 8-bit computer word allows numbers in the range $-128$ (1000 0000) to $+127$ (0111 1111) to be represented, and that the number zero now has a unique representation (0000 0000). The number $-1$ now becomes 1111 1111.

At first sight the advantages of the 2s complement system are not obvious. The first point to note is that, in practice, a negative number $-A$, represented by $2^N - A$, is most easily found by *complementing* and then *incrementing* the original positive number A. Thus the number $-57$ would be found as follows:

$$\begin{array}{rl} & \textit{sign bit } 0 = \textit{positive} \\ & \downarrow \\ 57 = & 0011\ 1001 \\ \text{Therefore} - 57 = & 1100\ 0110 \\ & + 1 \\ = & 1100\ 0111 \quad \textit{sign bit } 1 = \textit{negative} \end{array}$$

Note also that the format is consistent since $-(-57) = +57$:

$$\begin{array}{rl} - 57 = & 1100\ 0111 \\ \text{Therefore} - (-57) = & 0011\ 1000 \\ & + 1 \\ 57 = & 0011\ 1001 \end{array}$$

which is the same number as at the start.

One advantage of this process is that the sign bit is generated automatically by the 2s complement process. Any number can thus be determined by first examining the sign bit. If it is 0, the number is positive and the remaining bits in the word represent simply the positive integer value of the number; if it is 1, the number is negative and the modulus of its value may be found by performing the 2s complement operation to yield the required positive integer.

To *complement* a number, each bit of the number is inverted. To *increment* it, one is added to the number. Both these functions are invariably available in the instruction set of any computer. The name '2s complement' arises because the complementing process is strictly known as the *1s complement* and 1 is then added to the 1s complement.

Express the following decimal numbers in the 2s complement data format assuming a 12-bit word length:

**Exercise 3.7**

(a) 1025    (b) $-782$    (c) 2040    (d) $-1652$
(e) $-1025$    (f) 782    (g) $-2040$    (h) 1652

Convert the following 2s complement numbers to signed decimal equivalents:

**Exercise 3.8**

(a) 0101 1110    (b) 1001 1111
(c) 1000 0110 1101    (d) 1110 0000 1111
(e) 1011 1100 0100 1011    (f) 0111 1110 1111 0000

A further important advantage of the 2s complement numeric format is that both addition *and* subtraction may be performed using only the addition operation: to subtract a number one simply adds the 2s complement of the number. Some examples should clarify this operation.

*Examples*

| Decimal | Binary | | Decimal | Binary | |
|---|---|---|---|---|---|
| 57 | 0011 1001 | | 57 | 0011 1001 | |
| + 43 | + 0010 1011 | | − 43 | 1101 0101 | (2s complement 43) |
| 100 | 0110 0100 = 100 | | 14 | 1 0000 1110 | = 14 |
| | ↑ | | | ↑ ↑ | |
| | *positive* | | | *positive* | |

carry (ignored)

35

| Decimal | Binary | |
|---|---|---|
| 43 | 0010 1011 | |
| − 57 | 1100 0111 | (2s complement 57) |
| − 14 | 1111 0010 | 0000 1110 = 14 *Result* = − 14 |
| | ↑ | |
| | negative | |

| Decimal | Binary | |
|---|---|---|
| − 43 | 1101 0101 | (2s complement 43) |
| − 57 | 1100 0111 | (2s complement 57) |
| − 100 | 1 1001 1100 | 0110 0100 = 100 *Result* = − 100 |
| | ↑ ↑ negative | |
| | carry (ignored) | |

As can be seen from these examples, the most important advantage of 2s complement arithmetic is that the sign of any arithmetic operation is calculated automatically. By contrast, compare how the operation 43 − 57 would be performed using data stored in the sign plus absolute magnitude format:

(*a*) Strip off sign bits
(*b*) Perform the trial subtraction 43 − 57. This causes an underflow, indicating that the result must be negative.
The result is not − 14, however, but 114 (*i.e.* 128−14)

Operations (c) and (d) are only performed if underflow occurs on the trial subtraction.

(*c*) To get the correct result reverse the two numbers and perform the subtraction, 57−43 = 14
(*d*) Invert the sign bit to indicate the negative result.

There is one further problem in dealing with numbers stored in the 2s complement format; again this should be obvious from the examples given above. How can numeric overflow be detected when the carry bit clearly has no significance in 2s complement arithmetic? Examination of some examples suggests the solution:

*Examples*

| Decimal | Binary | |
|---|---|---|
| 57 | 0011 1001 | |
| + 75 | 0100 1011 | |
| 132 | 1000 0100 | 0111 1100 = 124 |
| | ↑negative | *Result* = − 124 XX |

| Decimal | Binary | |
|---|---|---|
| − 57 | 1100 0111 | |
| − 75 | 1011 0101 | |
| − 132 | 1 0111 1100 | = 124 XX |
| | ↑ carry (ignored) | |

In both these examples the result is incorrect owing to numeric overflow. If the conditions required for overflow to occur are considered it should become clear that:

(a) *The signs of the two numbers to be added must be the same* (i.e. we must add two positive or two negative numbers). If the signs of the two numbers differ then the value of their sum must lie between the two numbers, and hence must be within the range of numbers which can be expressed.

(b) *Overflow has occurred if the sign of the sum differs from the sign of the two numbers.* If two positive numbers are added, the result should also be positive; similarly the result of adding two negative numbers should be negative.

These conditions can be expressed as the Boolean function:

$$\text{overflow} = C_S.\overline{A_S}.\overline{B_S} + \overline{C_S}.A_S.B_S$$

where $C_S$ = sign of sum after addition
$A_S$ = sign of A before addition
$B_S$ = sign of B before addition.

Computers generally provide a mechanism for detecting overflow after 2s complement arithmetic operations in addition to overflow of unsigned integers.

So far the numeric data formats examined have been integer data formats, hence it has not been possible to represent numbers greater than $2^N - 1$ or less than 1 using a single N-bit word. Two further formats are used if it is wished to represent numbers outside this range.

The example microprocessors all contain *status* bits C and V. C is set by an unsigned integer overflow, while V detects 2s complement overflow (see next chapter).

### Fixed point numbers

In a fixed point number format, the decimal point is assumed to be at a fixed position in the computer word. This position is chosen to be convenient for the calculation taking place. If the decimal point is chosen to be after the least significant bit of the word then the number is simply an integer number. Signed fixed point numbers can also be formed using either the sign plus absolute magnitude format or the 2s complement format. The major disadvantage of the fixed point format, however, is that *range* is traded against *resolution*. Thus if an 8-bit word length is considered with the decimal point after the least significant bit, data with a range of 0–256 and a resolution of 1 can be represented. If, however, the decimal point is before the most significant bit the resolution is increased to 1/256 (0.003 906) but with a range of only 0–1. Thus if both high resolution and a large range are required, a further numeric format is used; this is the *floating point* number format.

Example fixed point word:
8 bits

Binary point

### Floating point numbers

Floating point numbers are defined in the format $\pm A \times 2^{\pm B}$, where A and B are each specified as separate fixed point 2s complement numbers. A particular problem with the floating point format is that there is no universal standard for the number of bits used to represent A and B. Varying the number of bits used to represent A alters the resolution of the floating point number which can be expressed, while varying the number of bits which represent B alters the range of numbers. In addition, A can, in principle, be an integer or a fraction. Floating point numbers are inherently redundant because the number $1 \times 2^{+10}$ could equally well be represented as $0.5 \times 2^{+11}$, $2 \times 2^{+9}$, and so on. The convention, therefore, is that the mantissa A is normalised to be a fraction with no leading zeros.

A is called the *mantissa*, and B is called the *exponent* or *characteristic*.
In some floating point formats a base other than 2 is used; however, the base is always a power of 2, such as 4, 8 or 16.

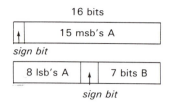

As an example, one possible floating point format used in some 16-bit minicomputers manufactured by IBM, Digital Equipment Corporation (DEC), Hewlett-Packard and Data General represents each number using two 16-bit words. The mantissa A is represented by a 24-bit 2s complement fraction, while the exponent B, also in 2s complement form, occupies the remaining eight bits of the 32-bit format. This enables numbers to be represented with a resolution of 1 in $2^{23}$, corresponding to about 7 decimal digits' precision, and a range of $2^{\pm 128}$ or approximately $10^{\pm 38}$.

**Exercise 3.9**  Compare the range and resolution of a 32-bit floating point number and a 32-bit 2s complement integer.

**Exercise 3.10**  How are the range and resolution of a 32-bit floating point numeric format altered if the exponent is expressed in base 16 rather than base 2? Suggest an advantage of the base 16 format.

The obvious advantage of the floating point numeric format is that a very wide range of numbers may be expressed with good precision; such a facility is often required in scientific computing. Against this, however, must be weighed the disadvantage that numeric manipulation using the floating point format is much more complex than simple integer arithmetic. This means either that lengthy software (both in execution time and program size) must be written to perform floating point calculations, or that special (and expensive) floating point hardware must be built into the computer. Hence the floating point format is only used where normal integer arithmetic provides insufficient range and resolution.

**Text formats — the ASCII character code**

It has been estimated that for every number manipulated by a computer ten alphabetic characters are processed. Text processing is not restricted only to word processors, but is also a requirement of any general-purpose computer, since in every computer language, program instructions are initially coded using alphanumeric characters. The text strings corresponding to each instruction are subsequently converted into executable machine code instructions.

In the same way as different codes exist to represent different numeric formats, several standard codes have been defined which are used to represent alphanumeric characters. The most widely used codes are ASCII and EBCDIC. The full ASCII code is given in Appendix 1, and is used almost universally in microcomputers and computer peripheral equipment. Each character is represented by an 8-bit code, which is very convenient for 8-bit microprocessors. Six bits of the code define 64 characters including 52 lower and upper case letters. A seventh bit allows a further 64 characters to be defined; these include the numbers 0–9, punctuation, and a number of non-printing control codes which are used to perform control functions such as carriage return, line feed and backspace on printers and terminals. The eighth and final bit in the ASCII format is often used as a *parity* check during data transmission (for example, from a computer to a terminal), to allow errors to be detected. Either *even parity* or *odd parity* may be chosen, or the parity bit may be set to 1 and ignored.

ASCII    — American Standard Code for Information Interchange

EBCDIC   — Extended Binary Coded Decimal Interchange Code

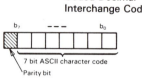

7 bit ASCII character code

Parity bit

*Examples*

| | |
|---|---|
| 0100 0001 ASCII | character A — even parity |
| 0111 1010 ASCII | character Z — odd parity |
| 1011 0101 ASCII | character 5 — odd parity |
| 1000 1000 ASCII | character *backspace* — even parity. |

## Instruction words

So far only the representation of numbers or text as memory words has been considered. In addition, however, computer *instructions* are stored in memory; this is the stored program concept introduced by John von Neumann.

Like every other type of information, instructions must be represented within the computer as binary codes. In general, every different type of computer has its own set of machine instructions, which are chosen by the manufacturer of the computer and reflect the architecture of the particular computer design. Thus a set of binary machine code instructions written to execute a specific program on one type of computer are unlikely to be executable if transferred to another type of computer unless it has been specifically designed to execute the same instruction set.

The number of different instructions which can be represented in the instruction set of a particular computer is constrained simply by the number of bits which are allocated to define the instruction. As an example, a 2-bit instruction code might be used to define four instructions as follows:

| | |
|---|---|
| 00 | could be ADD |
| 01 | could be SUBTRACT |
| 10 | could be LOGICAL AND |
| 11 | could be LOGICAL OR |

These are instructions commonly found in the instruction set of almost any computer.

Similarly, a 4-bit instruction code would allow up to 16 unique instructions to be defined, while an 8-bit code would enable up to 256 unique instructions to be specified. In general, as more bits are made available to define instructions, a larger repertoire of instructions can be included in the instruction set, and consequently the processing power of the computer increases.

In most computers, the same memory is used to store both data and instruction words; the number of bits available to define instruction codes is therefore usually the same as the data word-length of the computer. Thus an 8-bit microprocessor manipulates data in units of eight bits, and also executes instructions which are stored as 8-bit words, giving the possibility of 256 different instructions. Each different type of instruction (for example, ADD, SUBTRACT, AND, OR, etc.), is given a unique binary code to identify it. This code is called the *operation code* or *opcode*.

It is not generally sufficient for an instruction to consist of an opcode alone; the opcode specifies only the type of operation, not the data on which the instruction operates. This additional information must be specified where necessary by an instruction *operand*, which identifies which numbers are to be ADDed, SUBTRACTed, etc. The instruction operand can specify the data on which the instruction operates in one of several different ways: the operand itself can be the data, or the operand can specify the address in memory of the data on which

This is not universally true: some computers have completely separate (i.e. separately addressed) program and data memories. In this case instruction word-length and data word-length can each be separately optimised to suit the computer. As an example, the Texas Instruments TMS 1000 family of single-chip microcomputers, commonly used in calculators and simple electronic games, use an 8-bit instruction word and a 4-bit data word.
In 8-bit microprocessors, the instruction operand occupies one or more additional bytes following the opcode.

the instruction will operate. If the operand specifies the address where the data are to be found, this address may be specified directly, or it may be calculated in one of several ways from the instruction operand. The different ways of specifying an instruction operand are described in detail in Chapter 7 and are known as the *addressing modes* of the instruction.

---

**Worked Example 3.1**    It is required to add the contents of the memory word at address 100 hex. to the contents of the memory word at 180 hex. and store the result at address 200 hex. using the Motorola MC68HC11 processor. Show the machine code which would be stored in memory to perform this task.

The sum can be represented in register transfer language as:

$$(0100_{16}) + (0180_{16}) \rightarrow 0200_{16}$$

The following are instructions from the instruction set of the MC6809 which would be used for this example:

(*a*)  Load accumulator A with the contents of address 100 hex.
   $(100_{16}) \rightarrow A$
(*b*)  Add the contents of address 180 hex. to accumulator A.
   $(180_{16}) + (A) \rightarrow A$
(*c*)  Store the contents of accumulator A in address 200 hex.
   $(A) \rightarrow 200_{16}$

For the MC68HC11, the example above would be translated into machine code as follows (refer to Appendix E for a complete list of MC68HC11 instructions and their machine code equivalents):

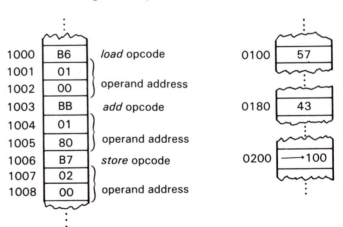

---

The address in memory where the instructions are stored is arbitrary in these examples; the data addresses are fixed. It is very important, however, that instruction execution should commence at the correct address (1000 hex. in this case). If, for example, the instructions were executed starting from 1001 hex., then operands would be interpreted as opcodes and vice versa, leading to unpredictable results! In this case the high byte of the first operand (01) would be executed as an opcode: unfortunately no MC68HC11 instruction is defined for this opcode. Thus the response of the microprocessor beyond this point would be uncertain. Note that the number of operand bytes which follow the opcode is defined by the opcode itself, so that instructions of variable length are possible in most computers. This point is discussed in more detail in Chapter 7.

**Exercise 3.11**

Repeat Worked Example 3.1 using appropriate instructions from the instruction set of the MC68000.

The example instructions given above are typical of the instructions which would be available in the instruction set of an 8-bit microprocessor. They are called *single-address* instructions because each instruction is capable of specifying only one address in memory. Larger CISC computers using bigger word-lengths may have *double-address* or even *triple-address* instructions: these computers will be capable of executing instructions which specify two or three different memory addresses, respectively. For example, a computer with triple address instructions would be capable of executing the example above using the single instruction: 'Store the sum of the contents of addresses 100 hex. and 180 hex. in address 200 hex.' Obviously, double- or triple-address instructions will require more operand storage space in memory than single-address instructions, thus offsetting to some extent the advantage of the more powerful instruction.

In this area, RISC philosophy is significantly different from CISC philosophy. In RISC processors nearly all the instructions are *zero-address* instructions: this means that most instructions can only operate on data stored in CPU registers, and cannot access memory at all. Typically, the exceptions to this will be *load* and *store* instructions which are used to move data between memory and registers. This approach has three advantages. First, the zero-address instructions can be kept short since no memory address need be included in the machine code for the instruction (the objective is generally for every instruction to be one word long). Second, since every instruction is the same length, the design of the instruction decoder is considerably simplified in comparison with CISC architectures where the instructions are typically of variable length. Finally, the simplification of the instruction decoder and the fact that no data have to be fetched from memory to execute the instruction means that instruction execution is much faster for typical RISC instructions than for their CISC equivalents. This advantage is partially offset by the fact that, typically, more instructions are required to implement a particular function in a RISC processor than for the equivalent CISC processor, as illustrated in Worked Example 3.2.

The MC68000 has a limited double-address instruction capability: the MOVE instruction can move data directly from one memory address to another. All other MC68000 instructions can only specify a single memory address (any further addresses specified within the instruction will be register addresses).

The ARM microprocessor has only four instructions which access memory: LDR (load), STR (store), LDM (load multiple register) and STM (store multiple register). All 18 ARM data processing instructions are zero-address instructions (see Appendix D).

See the sections *Instruction interpretation and control* (Chapter 4) and *Instruction size* (Chapter 7), for further details.

---

**Worked Example 3.2**

Determine the ARM instructions required to implement Worked Example 3.1.

For the ARM microprocessor, it is not possible to add the contents of a memory location directly to a register in the CPU, since only load and store instructions can access data in memory. Therefore, this operation must be broken down into two separate components, the first of which loads the second operand from memory into a CPU register, and the second then adds the contents of the two registers together. Thus the following are instructions from the ARM instruction set which would be used to implement this example:

(*i*)   Load register R0 with the contents of address 100 hex.
        $(100_{16}) \rightarrow R0$

(*ii*) Load register R1 with the contents of address 180 hex.
$(180_{16}) \rightarrow R1$

(*iii*) Add registers R0 and R1, and store the result in R2
$(R0) + (R1) \rightarrow R2$

(*iv*) Store the contents of register R2 in address 200 hex.
$(R2) \rightarrow 200_{16}$

Note that this requires four instructions compared with the three instructions which would be needed for the MC68HC11 or MC68000.

## Summary

Data and instructions are stored in a computer memory as a series of binary words. These binary words can represent numbers, alphanumeric data, computer instructions, or indeed any other physical parameter which can be represented by means of a binary code. A number of standard data codes are very widely used in many different types of computer: for example, the 2s complement code for representing positive and negative integer numbers, floating point codes for representing real numbers and the ASCII code for representing alphanumeric information. Instruction codes unfortunately tend to be defined uniquely for each different type of computer; thus machine code programs for one type of computer can seldom be executed on any other type of computer. Once a program has been coded into binary for storage in the computer memory it is very difficult to tell which binary codes represent instruction opcodes, which represent operands, and which represent data. The computer determines how to interpret each binary code by assuming that the first word encountered is an opcode, and that each opcode defines how many operand words follow it. If an attempt is made to execute binary codes which correspond to data as if they were program instructions, the results will be unpredictable!

## Problems

3.1 Computer memory size is normally expressed in kilobytes (kbytes) and megabytes (Mbytes) where 1 kbyte is 1024 bytes and 1 Mbyte is 1024 kbytes. What are the hexadecimal, decimal and octal equivalents of the following memory sizes expressed in bytes?

(*a*) 1 kbyte    (*b*) 4 kbytes    (*c*) 16 kbytes    (*d*) 64 kbytes
(*e*) $\frac{1}{4}$ Mbyte    (*f*) 1 Mbyte    (*g*) 4 Mbytes    (*h*) 16 Mbytes

3.2 Calculate the address bus size required to address each of the memories specified in Problem 3.1.

3.3 Perform the following sums in binary using the BCD code and show how the result must be adjusted to take care of the BCD format in each case.

(*a*) 38 + 47    (*b*) 19 + 68    (*c*) 372 + 429
(*d*) 655 + 187    (*e*) 4792 + 1836    (*f*) 5019 + 2994

3.4 IBM 360/370 series computers use either a 32 bit or a 64 bit floating point format as follows:

| 32-bit | 31 | 30 | 24 | 23 | | 0 | |
|---|---|---|---|---|---|---|---|

sign exponent    mantissa

| 64-bit | 63 | 62 | 56 | 55 | | 0 |
|---|---|---|---|---|---|---|

The exponent is expressed as a power of 16 and is a 7-bit signed integer, and the most significant bit gives the sign of the whole number. For each format estimate the range and resolution which is available.

3.5 The binary code below is stored in the memory of an MC68HC11 microcomputer system, but it is not known whether the code represents numeric data, alphanumeric characters, computer instructions, or some other type of information. For each set of data, try to interpret the data according to the following data formats:

(a)  8-bit unsigned integer
(b)  16-bit 2s complement integer
(c)  two-digit BCD
(d)  floating point format as on page 38
(e)  ASCII alphanumeric data
(f)  MC68HC11 machine code instruction

In each case, can any conclusions be drawn about the probable intended format of the data?

*Binary Code*

| (i) 0100 1111 | (ii) 1011 0110 | (iii) 1100 1000 |
|---|---|---|
| 1011 0111 | 0111 0000 | 0100 0101 |
| 0001 0000 | 0000 0100 | 0100 1100 |
| 0000 0000 | 1011 0111 | 0100 1100 |
| | 0111 0000 | 0100 1111 |
| | 0000 0000 | 1010 0001 |

# 4 Data processing

**Objectives**
- [ ] To show the structure and operation of a computer central processing unit (CPU) or microprocessor unit (MPU).
- [ ] To describe the two-beat (fetch and execute) computer cycle.
- [ ] To show the structure and operation of the arithmetic and logic unit (ALU) of a computer.
- [ ] To show the mechanisms for implementing conditional program execution and looping, through the use of program status flags and branch or jump instructions.
- [ ] To describe how a program instruction may be decoded to the primitive register and combinational logic control signals which execute the function specified by the instruction.

In Chapter 2 the structure of a computer memory was introduced, and in Chapter 3 it was shown that computer data and instructions could be stored in this memory using a number of predefined data formats. Registers provide short-term storage for data variables, and are one of the components found in the computer CPU.

In this chapter the remaining CPU components are introduced, and the mechanism by which the CPU controls execution of the computer program will be explained. It will be shown that the CPU comprises a number of registers, some with special purposes, and two additional components, the *arithmetic and logic unit*, and the *control unit*, which were introduced in Chapter 1. These components together are often encapsulated as a single integrated circuit, known as a *microprocessor*.

Some microprocessor systems use a different functional division between the chips making up the complete microcomputer; the division suggested here is not essential.

### The function of the central processing unit

The arithmetic and logic unit (ALU) of a computer may be thought of as the heart of a computer since this is the component which performs the data manipulation operations which are essential in any data processing task. Similarly the control unit may be likened to the brain of the computer since its function is to control the program execution according to the sequence of instructions encoded as the computer program. The control unit does this by *fetching* the instructions one by one from the memory and then *obeying* the data manipulation which each instruction specifies. Thus each instruction execution may be seen to require a two-beat cycle, where the first beat always fetches the instruction and the second beat executes the function specified by the instruction. The fetch operation is invariant for all instructions, but the execute operation varies according to the instruction fetched and may, for example, cause the addition of the contents of two registers, the clearing of a memory location or the transfer of data between a register and a memory location. Except where an operand is already held in a CPU register, additional clock cycles are required to fetch the operand from memory.

The computer central processing unit or microprocessor unit must therefore perform three tasks, each of which is examined in more detail below:

(a) *Communication with memory* (see following section). The CPU must provide a mechanism for fetching instructions from memory prior to execution, and it must also provide a means of fetching and storing data which may be temporarily saved in memory.

(b) *Interpretation of instructions* (see later this chapter). The CPU must include logic which decodes the operation code of each instruction to generate the low-level control signals which perform the data manipulation specified by the instruction. These control signals are typically register and memory write and select signals, and signals which specify the operation to be performed by the ALU. They also include control signals which read additional instruction operand words from memory when this is required.

(c) *Execution of instructions* (see later this chapter). The CPU must provide a mechanism for performing the data manipulations required by the instruction set of the computer. Many instructions simply transfer data from one place to another within the computer; this can be achieved simply by providing suitable data buses for data transfer, together with appropriate address and control lines. The fundamental feature of a computer, however, is the ability to process data and hence generate new information from it; this is accomplished by the ALU, according to control signals generated by the decoded instruction. Additionally, instructions are required which alter the sequence of program execution according to the results of calculations performed in the ALU; conditional *branch* and *jump* instructions fulfil this requirement.

In the following sections each of these requirements will be examined in more detail and solutions developed using the Motorola MC68000 microprocessor as the primary example. Additional examples based upon the ARM and MC68HC11 microprocessors will be given where these devices illustrate features not found on the MC68000.

## CPU communication with memory

Data are communicated between the CPU and the memory of a computer using *buses*; similarly, communication between the registers in a computer CPU occurs via buses internal to the CPU. Conceptually there is no difference between these two types of bus, but in microprocessors the *external buses* connecting to memory are brought out to the pins of the microprocessor while the *internal buses* exist only on the silicon chip, and are inaccessible externally (Fig. 2.6).

In order for the CPU to be able to access instructions or data stored in the main memory, the CPU must first of all supply the address of the required memory word using an *address bus*. When this address has been specified, the required instruction or data can be read into the CPU using the *data bus*.

In the case of data it may also be necessary to *write* data into the memory from time to time as well as to *read* data from the memory. One way to do this would

Because the microprocessor external buses connect to other system components such as memory and input/output interfaces, their characteristics (e.g. voltage levels, timing requirements, fan-out) must be carefully defined. This is not necessary for buses internal to a chip.

In expanded multiplexed operating mode, the MC68HC11 provides a 16-bit external address bus and an 8-bit external data bus, enabling a maximum of 64 kbytes to be uniquely addressed.

The MC68000 has a 24-bit
address bus and a 16-bit data
bus, allowing up to 16 Mbytes
of memory to be addressed,
one byte or one 16-bit word at
a time.

The ARM has a 26-bit address
bus and a 32-bit data bus,
allowing up to 64 Mbytes of
memory to be addressed, one
byte or one 32-bit word at a
time.

The read/write (R/W) control
signal is one of a number of
lines making up the *control bus*.

The MC68HC11 has a 16-bit
program counter, enabling it to
address any byte in memory.
The MC68000 has a 32-bit
program counter for
compatibility with other 68000
family processors, but only 24
bits of this are connected to the
external address bus (see
Fig. 2.8). The ARM's program
counter is also 24 bits long (the
other eight bits store ALU and
processor mode status
signals—see p. 56). The two
least significant bits of the
26-bit ARM address bus are
always 0 for instruction word
accesses, since all instructions
are 32 bits long and must be
aligned with a 32-bit word
boundary (see p. 61).

The MC68HC11 uses a form of
synchronous bus
communication in its expanded
multiplexed operating mode,
though the timing is more
complicated than shown here
because the data bus and least
significant byte of address bus
are multiplexed on the same
pins.

be to have two separate data buses, one for reading data from the memory into the CPU, and one to write data back into memory. To minimise the number of pins required on a microprocessor CPU chip, however, it is common to multiplex the data read and data write buses into a single bus with a separate *read/write control line* which specifies the direction of data transfer.

If a bidirectional data bus is used, it is impossible to read and write data simultaneously, hence temporary data storage in the form of registers must be provided on the CPU. The registers provide a means of storing data between one instruction execution and the next, as, for example, in the program which adds two numbers together in the previous chapter. Subsequently, the numbers may be written back into the main memory.

A further requirement of the CPU is a register to keep track of which instruction is being executed, so that instructions can be executed in sequence. This register is called the *program counter* (also sometimes known as the instruction counter), and acts as a pointer to the next instruction to be executed. It is incremented immediately after each instruction is accessed from memory, and also after accessing every instruction operand or operand address if the operand is stored in a separate word of memory. Each time that it is required to read the next instruction word from memory, the output of the program counter is connected via the address bus to the memory, thus supplying the address of the next instruction. After allowing an appropriate time for propagation delays the instruction word can be read into the CPU from the data bus.

It is also possible for the program to load a completely new value into the program counter; this causes the next instruction to be fetched from the new address in the program counter, implementing a program *branching* or decision-making capability (see later in this chapter).

The timing of computer operations is controlled by a single clock oscillator, so that all operations occur synchronously with respect to each other. The maximum clock frequency is defined by the propagation times within and between the various components of the computer system. If a computer system is implemented using only static logic, then the computer can be used at any clock frequency from the maximum down to d.c. Most microprocessors, however, use dynamic logic to maximise the chip packing density and hence the processing power of the device. In this case, there is also a minimum clock frequency below which the computer will not work correctly because the dynamic logic devices which it contains are not being refreshed sufficiently frequently.

The design of the CPU to meet clock frequency requirements is the responsibility of its manufacturer, but where the CPU is interfaced to an external component such as memory or an input/output device, it is the responsibility of the computer hardware design engineer to ensure that the external component(s) meet the timing requirements of the CPU and its clock. There are two common approaches to achieve this, *synchronous bus communication* and *asynchronous bus communication*.

Fig. 4.1 shows the timing of a typical synchronous memory read cycle. The clock frequency is chosen to allow sufficient time for a valid memory address output on the address bus to propagate down the bus, through the memory, and cause a valid data output to appear on the data bus. The trailing edge of the clock pulse can then be used to latch the contents of the data bus into the CPU. Obviously, if too high a clock frequency is chosen, insufficient propagation time

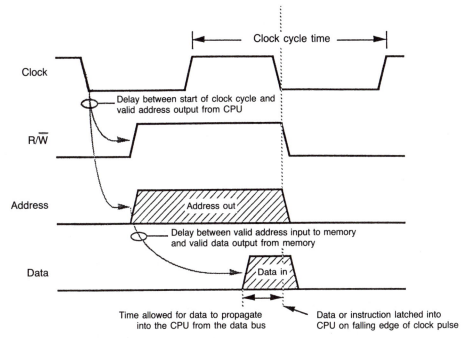

**Fig. 4.1  Synchronous memory read cycle timing.**

Labels within the figure:

Clock cycle time

Clock

Delay between start of clock cycle and valid address output from CPU

R/$\overline{\text{W}}$

Address

Address out

Delay between valid address input to memory and valid data output from memory

Data

Data in

Time allowed for data to propagate into the CPU from the data bus

Data or instruction latched into CPU on falling edge of clock pulse

is allowed, and corrupt data may be latched into the CPU.

Asynchronous bus communication is rather more complex than synchronous bus communication, and is based upon the use of a *handshake* mechanism to synchronise the CPU and memory devices. This has the advantage that the CPU can communicate successfully whatever speed of memory or input/output device is used, and indeed can adjust its operation to match different propagation delays for different memory components within the same system.

The principle of asynchronous bus communication is illustrated in Fig. 4.2. The CPU generates a valid address and signals this by asserting the *address strobe* control line. When the memory detects the address strobe, it places data on the data bus and signals that the data are valid by asserting a *data acknowledge* signal. The processor then in turn detects the data acknowledge signal, latches the data, and then negates its address strobe line to indicate that it has read the data. Finally, the memory negates its data acknowledge signal to complete the handshake.

Although every instruction executed will require at least one memory access during the instruction fetch cycle, many instruction execution cycles will not involve further memory accesses. This is particularly the case for the ARM processor, where all data processing instructions operate on registers only (see Chapter 2).

In addition to the address and data buses, microprocessors generally require a number of other control signal connections to external components. These signals are grouped together under the common title of the *control bus*, but in fact vary significantly from one type of computer to another, although there are some common elements.

Handshake mechanisms are often used to synchronise asynchronous input/output devices to the computer: see Chapter 8 for an example.

Asynchronous bus communication is commonly used on higher-performance processors such as the MC68000 and ARM.

Note that additional logic is required in the memory system to implement the data acknowledge signal.

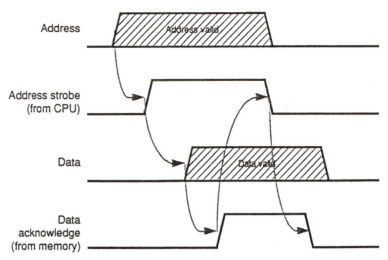

Fig. 4.2   Asynchronous memory read cycle timing.

The MC68000 and ARM microprocessors have control signals which allow DMA devices to be connected to them, but the exact implementations vary and are beyond the scope of this book.

One of the control bus signals common to all microprocessors is the read/write line described above. Another group of signals which is commonly provided is a set of *bus control lines* which allow another device to take control of the buses from the microprocessor. This type of operation is also usually implemented using a handshake mechanism and thus requires at least two lines, which are generally connected to and from direct memory access (DMA) input or output devices, as described in Chapter 5. If the microprocessor uses a separate input/output address space, then one or more control signals is required to differentiate between memory and input/output addresses.

Other control bus signals are provided to support specific features of different processors. For example, both the MC68000 and the ARM have several control signals which support hardware error detection facilities such as an attempted access to an invalid address. In contrast, whereas the ARM implements its address bus directly using 26 address lines A0–A25, the MC68000 replaces the least significant address bit, A0, by a pair of control signals $\overline{\text{UDS}}$ (upper data strobe) and $\overline{\text{LDS}}$ (lower data strobe), which allow access to individual bytes within a word, as described in Chapter 2.

Summarising and generalising these points, it can be seen that any computer requires three buses to enable data transfers to take place between the CPU of the computer, the computer memory, and its external input and output interfaces. These buses are:

(a) an *address bus* to specify the required address;
(b) a *data bus* to enable bidirectional data transfers to take place;
(c) a *control bus* to provide various clock and control signals.

In addition, at least one register (accumulator) is required to provide short-term local data storage in the CPU, and a program counter is required to indicate the next instruction to be executed. Exact CPU architectures vary considerably from one computer or microprocessor to another, and depend among other things upon the level of integration which was possible at the time the computer was designed.

All of the example processors comfortably exceed these minimum requirements.

*Example*

Consider the execution of the MC68HC11 instruction LDAA $100 (load accumulator A with the contents of address 100 hex.), expressed in register transfer language as:

$(100_{16}) \rightarrow A$

It is possible now to surmise the data transfers which must take place in order to fetch and execute this instruction. Clock cycle by clock cycle, they are as follows:

*Clock cycle 1:*  The contents of the program counter are connected via the address bus to the address inputs of the memory. On the falling edge of the clock pulse the output from the memory (which will be the LDAA opcode, B6 hex.) is latched into the CPU. The program counter is then incremented. Hence the first clock cycle is used to fetch the instruction opcode from memory.

*Clock cycle 2:*  After decoding the instruction opcode, the CPU now knows that the operand address (100 hex.) must be fetched from the next two consecutive bytes in memory. The program counter output (which now points to the next word after the opcode) is therefore connected once again to the address bus, and the most significant byte of the operand address is read in exactly the same way as the opcode was read during the previous clock cycle. The program counter is then incremented as before, so that it now points to the least significant byte of the operand address.

*Clock cycle 3:*  Using exactly the same mechanism as in cycles 1 and 2, the least significant byte of the operand address is read into the CPU.

*Clock cycle 4:*  The full 16-bit operand address which has now been assembled in the CPU is connected to the address bus. The operand itself is read into the CPU and latched into accumulator A on the falling edge of the clock pulse.

Write down the sequence of events, clock cycle by clock cycle, during execution of the remainder of the example program given on page 40.

The dollar sign ($) is used by Motorola to indicate a hexadecimal number in MC68HC11 assembly language.

Notice that the requirement to store the operand address from cycle 2 to cycle 4 of the instruction implies that a 16-bit address storage register exists somewhere within the MC68HC11 CPU, even though this register is not explicitly mentioned by Motorola.

Because the program counter is again incremented automatically at the end of cycle 3, it is left pointing to the opcode of the next instruction when execution of 'LDAA $100' is completed.

**Exercise 4.1**

**Instruction execution — data manipulation**

If it were only possible to use a computer to transfer data backwards and forwards between registers and memory, the computer would be of very little practical use; its power lies in its ability to manipulate and process information so that new information can be generated from data which already exists. The arithmetic and logic unit (ALU) is the component of a computer system which performs the task of data manipulation. Generally it is adequate to consider the ALU as a black box with two one-word-wide data inputs, and one one-word-wide data output. In addition, the ALU contains a number of control inputs which specify the data manipulation function to be performed. The ALU is a combinational logic circuit, whose output is an instantaneous function of its data and control inputs; it has no storage capability. Thus the result of any ALU operation must be stored in an accumulator. The following are typical of the functions which the ALU must perform:

Add  
Subtract  } Arithmetic operations

Logical AND  
Logical OR  
Exclusive OR  
Complement } Logical operations

Shift left  
Shift right  
Select input word A  
Select input word B

Multiply  
Divide

In practice, although add and subtract are regarded as fundamental operations of the ALU, they are made up using the Boolean AND/OR/INVERT operations, as is shown below.

All of these functions (except perhaps multiply and divide) are likely to be provided on even the simplest computer or microprocessor, since they form a basic set of operations from which more complex processing may be constructed. For example, most early 8-bit microprocessors did not include multiply and divide instructions because these two functions, though very useful, require a large increase in the complexity of the ALU logic circuits. Multiplication and division can, however, be accomplished by repeated shift and add operations (see Chapter 3), so the lack of specific instructions did not prevent these functions being included in a program. It did, however, result in much slower program execution compared with a CPU which includes these instructions within its instruction set.

The MC68HC11 includes a restricted 8-bit multiply instruction which multiplies together the contents of the A and B accumulators and stores the 16-bit result in the D register (concatenated A and B registers). It also includes fractional and integer 16-bit divide instructions.

For example, division by 5 could be achieved by dividing by 8 (shift right 3 bits) and then multiplying by 8/5 (1.6).

The ARM microprocessor includes general 32-bit multiply and multiply with accumulate instructions, but has no corresponding division instructions. If required, division must therefore be performed by dividing by an appropriate power of 2 (which is achieved by shifting the operand right the corresponding number of bits), and then multiplying by an appropriate scaling factor.

The MC68000 implements signed and unsigned multiply and divide instructions with a full range of memory addressing modes, reflecting its CISC design.

*Arithmetic and logical operations*

Most of the example functions mentioned above can be implemented using simple logic circuits, and it is fairly obvious that a number of different functions can be combined within the ALU by using the control inputs to select the source of the ALU output data from among the various possible functions. As an example, Fig. 4.3 shows how a 2-bit control code could be used to select between logical AND, OR, exclusive OR (XOR) and Complement operations performed on two 8-bit input words.

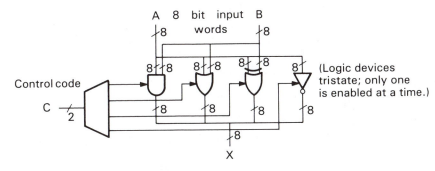

Fig. 4.3 Example ALU providing four logic operations. (The complement operation ignores the B inputs).

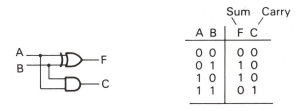

Fig. 4.4 1-bit half adder and truth table.

Of the basic operations mentioned above, the most complex to implement are the add and subtract operations. It is therefore worthwhile to examine in detail how these functions can be implemented, and to build up the logic circuitry of an 8-bit *adder/subtractor unit*, as might be included in the CPU of an 8-bit microprocessor.

The basic building block of any adder/subtractor circuit is the 1-bit *half adder*, shown in Fig. 4.4. This can most easily be implemented using a single XOR gate and an AND gate (other logic implementations are also possible). The sum, F, is set if either of the inputs is 1, while the carry output (C) is set if both inputs are 1.

Though this circuit is adequate for the least significant bit of any multi-bit addition, all the other bits require an additional carry input connected to the carry output of the adjacent less significant bit of the sum. To implement this function, a 1-bit *full adder* is required; this can be constructed from two half adders as shown in Fig. 4.5. Circuit operation is exactly the same as for the previous half adder if the carry input is 0, but if it is 1 the sum and carry outputs are increased by one from their previous values, to reflect the carry input from the adjacent less significant bit. Thus an 8-bit full adder could be constructed using eight full adders to give one adder for each bit of the output. The carry output of each bit would be daisy-chained to the carry input of the next more significant bit, so that carrys could ripple through the adder when two 8-bit numbers were added. The carry output from the most significant bit and the carry input to the least significant bit would enable multi-byte additions to be performed one byte at a time if required (Fig. 4.6).

A further requirement is the ability to carry out subtraction as well as addition

It should be noted that when two binary numbers are added, the propagation time of the addition is dominated by the time taken for the carry to ripple from the least significant to the most significant bit. For this reason *carry look-ahead* units are often used to speed up this process. These units contain logic functions which anticipate the carry outputs of an N-bit binary addition operation (an example TTL device is the SN74LS182).

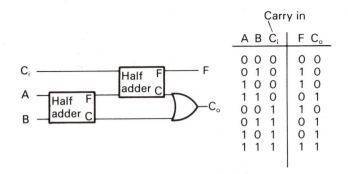

| A | B | $C_i$ | | F | $C_o$ |
|---|---|---|---|---|---|
| 0 | 0 | 0 | | 0 | 0 |
| 0 | 1 | 0 | | 1 | 0 |
| 1 | 0 | 0 | | 1 | 0 |
| 1 | 1 | 0 | | 0 | 1 |
| 0 | 0 | 1 | | 1 | 0 |
| 0 | 1 | 1 | | 0 | 1 |
| 1 | 0 | 1 | | 0 | 1 |
| 1 | 1 | 1 | | 1 | 1 |

Fig. 4.5   1-bit full adder and truth table.

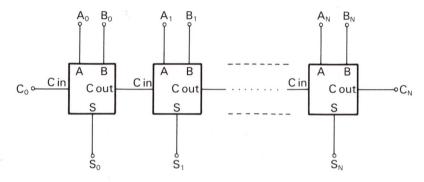

Fig. 4.6   Connection of an N-bit full adder.

operations. This can be achieved by modifying the full adder as shown in Fig. 4.7, so that it contains an additional control input which is used to select between addition and subtraction operations. Subtraction is performed by complementing the B input to the adder, and setting the carry input to the least significant bit of the sum, so that the B input is converted to its 2s complement. An 8-bit full adder/subtractor can be constructed by obvious parallel extension.

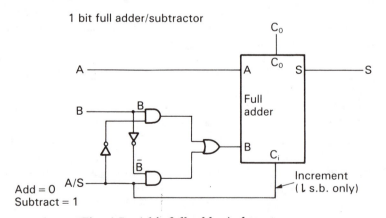

Fig. 4.7   1-bit full adder/subtractor.

**LOGIC SYMBOLS**

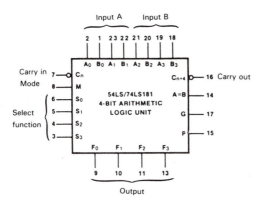

**LOGIC DIAGRAM**

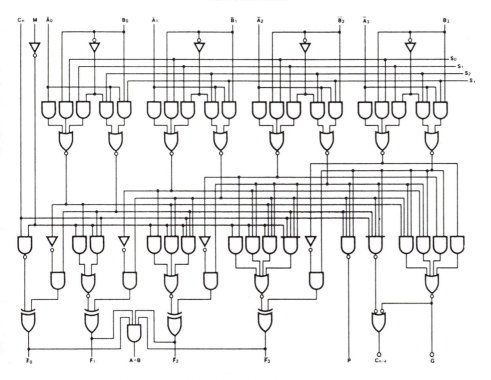

Fig. 4.8   TTL 74LS181 4-bit ALU/function generator.

Because the ALU of a computer is simply a component of the computer CPU, it is uncommon for manufacturers to publish detailed logic circuits describing the device. However, some insight can be gained by examining a discrete ALU chip, such as the TTL 74LS181 ALU/function generator. Some details of this device are given in Fig. 4.8, which is reproduced from the Fairchild TTL data book. As can be seen, the full logic circuit is quite complex, requiring a total of nearly 70 gates of different types, and little insight is gained by examining the detailed circuit diagram. If, however, the ALU is considered simply as a black box, then it can be seen that it provides two 4-bit inputs $A_0$–$A_3$ and $B_0$–$B_3$ which correspond to the data inputs, a 4-bit control code input $S_0$–$S_3$ and a mode control input M. The mode control input selects between logical and arithmetic operations (M = 1 logic; M = 0 arithmetic) while the four control inputs allow up to 16 different operations of each type to be selected. In practice there are fewer operations than this required, and some of the functions indicated in the function table either are duplicates or are meaningless functions which are generated by default.

The ALU also includes a carry input ($C_n$) and a carry output ($C_{n+4}$) which are the ripple carry signals described earlier. The carry input has no effect during logic operations (M = 1), but during arithmetic operations if the carry input bit is high, the outputs $F_0$–$F_3$ are incremented by one from the values shown in the function table. Finally, the circuit includes logic which performs a 4-bit carry look-ahead (carry generate (C) and carry propagate (P)); carry look-ahead for larger words can be accomplished by connecting these outputs to the 74LS182 carry look-ahead chip mentioned above.

Combining all these features, the 74LS181 provides the following functions:

| | |
|---|---|
| Logic: | $A.B$ $\quad$ $\overline{A.B}$ |
| | $A + B$ $\quad$ $\overline{A+B}$ |
| | $A \oplus B$ $\quad$ $\overline{A \oplus B}$ |
| Arithmetic: | A plus B |
| | A plus B plus 1 |
| | A minus B |
| | A minus B minus 1 |
| Increment: | A plus 1 |
| Decrement: | A minus 1 |
| Set: | $1111_2$ |
| Clear: | $0000_2$ |
| Select: | $A$ $\quad$ $\overline{A}$ |
| | $B$ $\quad$ $\overline{B}$ |
| Shift: | A plus A |
| | (equivalent to shift left one bit; in practice shift left and right are usually implemented using a separate shift register.) |

It would also be possible to provide these same arithmetic and logic functions using a ROM. To duplicate the logic functions of the 74LS181 would require a ROM with the following inputs:

| | |
|---|---|
| Function select | 4 bits |
| Mode | 1 bit |
| Carry in | 1 bit |
| A inputs | 4 bits |
| B inputs | 4 bits |
| Total | 14 bits |

The following outputs would also be required:

| | |
|---|---|
| F outputs | 4 bits |
| Carry output | 1 bit |
| A = B output | 1 bit |
| Carry generate | 1 bit |
| Carry propagate | 1 bit |
| Total | 8 bits |

As technology develops and design effort becomes more expensive, while silicon area becomes more plentiful, this approach becomes more attractive (i.e. larger chips can be successfully formatted at lower cost).
Refer to: Stonham, T.J. *Digital Logic Techniques: principles and practice* (Van Nostrand Reinhold, 1987) Chapter 6.

These same functions could be implemented using a ROM rather than random logic; as the margin note shows, however, this approach is not very resource-effective and would in this case require a 16-kbyte ROM. A further alternative is to make use of a *programmable logic array* (PLA); this can be considerably more efficient than a ROM since the *don't care* inputs and outputs which must be included in the ROM substantially reduce the complexity of the PLA.

The material above serves to give a feel for the components which make up the ALU of a computer. On this basis it may be surmised that any 8-bit microprocessor will contain an ALU which has the general structure shown in Fig. 4.9. It will contain two 8-bit inputs A and B, and a single 8-bit output F. In addition, there will be a number of control inputs, which will allow the ALU function to be

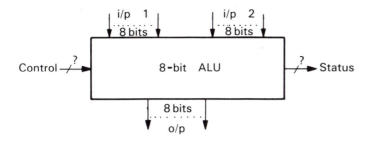

Fig. 4.9   General structure of an 8-bit ALU.

selected, and will be generated by the computer control unit when it has decoded the computer instruction. The control inputs also include a carry input from a previous arithmetic operation.

*ALU status signals — the status register*

There will also be a number of *status* outputs from the ALU; these indicate the result of the current operation. This information is subsequently stored in a *status register* so that it may be used to determine how processing will continue (see next section). Each status bit provides a single piece of binary information about the previous arithmetic or logical operation, for example, whether the last operation resulted in a carry output, whether the A and B inputs to the ALU were equal, etc. These status signals are an essential feature of any von Neumann computer, because they make it possible for the computer to perform a *conditional branch* based upon the results of the previous operation. Thus the computer has a decision-making capability based upon the results of the processing which it carries out.

To implement a conditional branching mechanism in any computer requires the following hardware features:

(a) A number of *status* or condition outputs from the ALU, each of which is a binary indicator of some aspect of the data manipulation just performed by the ALU.

(b) Temporary storage (a *status register*) for the status outputs from the ALU, so that the status result of the ALU operation can be accessed by subsequent conditional branch operations.

(c) *Conditional branch* instructions based upon the binary value of an individual status bit.

The status registers of the MC68HC11 and MC68000 are shown in the marginal notes, while the ARM status register, which is combined with the program counter to form a single 32-bit register (R15), is shown in Fig. 4.10.

Details of the status register will vary from one computer to another, depending upon its complexity, but although the exact bit allocation varies, all three of the example processors provide very similar status functions. The status bits common to all three example processors are:

*Carry/Borrow (C)*. This bit indicates an overflow condition during unsigned integer arithmetic. It is set if a carry results from an arithmetic operation and is reset otherwise.

The MC68HC11 and MC68000 status registers are described as *condition code* registers by Motorola.

*MC68HC11 condition code register*

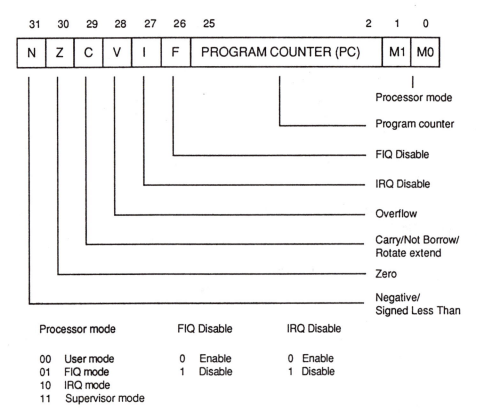

Fig. 4.10   The ARM Program Counter and Status Register (R15).

*Overflow (V)*. This bit indicates an overflow condition after a 2s complement arithmetic operation. It is set if an operation causes a 2s complement overflow and reset otherwise. Note that this condition is not identical to the carry/borrow status condition (refer to previous chapter).

*Zero (Z)*. The zero flag is set if the result of an arithmetic or logical operation is zero, and is reset if the result is not zero.

*Negative (N)*. The negative bit is set if the result of a 2s complement arithmetic operation is negative, and is reset otherwise. In effect, the negative bit is a copy of the m.s.b. of the ALU data output word.

Other status flags support specific freatures of each example microprocessor. They are identified below:

*MC68HC11*. The half-carry (H) flag is set if a carry occurs from bit 3 to bit 4 during MC68HC11 addition operations. This status bit is used by the *Decimal Adjust Accumulator* instruction to determine whether any adjustment of the result is required after an arithmetic operation on a BCD coded number. The *interrupt* (I), *non-maskable interrupt* (X) and *stop* (S) flags are all associated with control of interrupt requests from input or output devices and are not used directly by conditional branch instructions. The subject of interrupts is covered in detail in Chapter 5.

*ARM*. A notably unusual feature of the ARM is that status register bits are *only* affected by the result of a data processing operation if the suffix 'S' (for status)

*MC68000 condition code register*
(User byte of MC68000 status register only shown. System byte not shown.)

The MC68000 effects BCD arithmetic using specific BCD arithmetic instructions. The ARM has no BCD arithmetic capability (note this illustration of CISC versus RISC philosophies).

The exceptions to this rule are the instructions CMP, CMN,

TEQ and TST, which *always* set the status register bits.

The MC68000 system byte contains similar information.

is added to the instruction mnemonic. Thus the programmer has explicit control over the contents of the status register.

The *interrupt* (I) and *fast interrupt* (F) flags are associated with control of interrupts and are discussed in Chapter 5. The *mode* bits (M1, M0) define the current mode of operation of the processor, and form part of the protection mechanism used by the processor in multi-tasking applications (a full description of this mechanism is beyond the scope of this book).

*MC68000.* The *extend* bit (X) is used as a carry for multiple precision arithmetic. It is identical to C for arithmetic operations, but is unaffected by data movement operations, which reset the carry bit.

The MC68000 16-bit status register is subdivided into 2 bytes, a *user* byte combining the condition codes, and a *system* byte containing interrupt and supervisory information not available to normal programs (see Chapter 5).

By testing the binary value of a status bit stored in the condition code register, a conditional branch instruction can determine whether or not a specific program branch should be executed.

Estimate the size of ROM required to implement the MC68HC11 ALU. (*NB*: the MC68HC11 ALU is actually implemented using random logic.)

**Exercise 4.2**

Estimate the size of ROM required to implement the ARM ALU (*NB*: the ARM ALU is actually implemented using random logic.)

**Exercise 4.3**

*Further miscellaneous instructions*

Referring to the instruction sets of the example processors in Appendices 3, 4 and 5, it can be seen that a large proportion of the instructions deal with arithmetic or logical manipulation of data. Most of the instruction types have been explained already in this and preceding chapters, but it is worthwhile identifying a few additional ALU functions which have not previously been mentioned.

(*a*) *Arithmetic and logical shift operations.* There are two types of shift operation depending upon whether a signed number or an unsigned integer or logical value is being manipulated. In the case of a signed 8-bit integer, it is commonly required to shift the number but retain the sign bit in its most significant bit position. The *arithmetic shift right* (ASR) instruction does this, whereas the *logical shift right* (LSR) instruction shifts a zero into the most significant bit, and is thus used for shifting unsigned integers.

(*b*) *Rotate left and right.* Rotate instructions operate in exactly the same way as shift instructions except that bits which are shifted out of one end of the word are loaded back into the word at the other end. The carry bit of the status word is also included in the rotate operation; this is very useful if it is required to test whether an individual bit of a word is set.

Note that shift and rotate operations are implemented rather differently on the ARM, reflecting the position of the barrel shifter in the ARM CPU (see Fig. 2.6). Since this barrel shifter can shift or rotate any operand supplied to the right-hand input of the ALU, shift or rotate operations can be appended to operand 2 for any of the ARM's data processing operations, rather than being represented as separate instructions as is the case for the MC68HC11 and MC68000.

(*c*) *Compare.* Compare instructions are used to test the value of a variable; they do this by setting the bits in the status register as if a subtraction had been performed, but without altering the value of the variable. For

A single-bit right shift has the effect of dividing a binary number by two; a single-bit left shift multiplies by two. Shift operations are also useful for serial to parallel and parallel to serial data conversion.

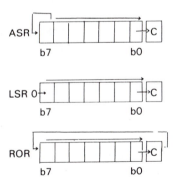

example, if the MC68HC11 A accumulator and memory location 55 both contain the same binary value then the instruction *Compare memory location 55 with A* (CMPA 55) will set the zero flag, without altering A or the memory location.

### Instruction execution — program control

It is the ability to perform branches which enables a computer to make decisions on the basis of the data which it manipulates, and hence to appear 'intelligent'.

*Program branching*, the ability of the computer program to alter the sequence of program execution, is a facility fundamental to every computer. By this means the computer is able to make logical decisions based upon the results of computation. In order to implement branching, the computer's instruction set must include instructions which control the sequence of instruction execution. These instructions do not manipulate data and are thus fundamentally different from all the other instructions which have so far been considered. Referring to Appendices C, D and E, it may be seen that the instruction sets of the example microprocessors contain a number of *jump* and *branch* instructions (the distinction between these two terms as used by Motorola will be made clear shortly). The branch instructions include both unconditional branches and conditional branches which are based upon a number of conditions determined by examination of the condition code register. Thus, for example, the MC68HC11 *branch if carry set* (BCS) instruction would be executed if a previous arithmetic operation had resulted in the condition code register C flag being set, whereas if the C flag was not set the next sequential instruction would be executed as normal.

An interesting feature of the ARM architecture is that *all* instructions can be conditional, not just branch instructions: any instruction is converted to its conditional equivalent by appending one of 16 condition mnemonics to the basic instruction mnemonic (see Appendix E).

**Exercise 4.4**   What status condition would be required for the following MC68HC11 branches to be executed:
- (*a*) Branch if equal to zero (BEQ)?
- (*b*) Branch if plus (BPL)?
- (*c*) Branch if less than or equal to zero (BLE)?
- (*d*) Branch if greater than zero (BGT)?
- (*e*) Branch always (BRA)?

The basic purpose of any branch instruction is to alter the contents of the program counter so that the next instruction to be executed will not be the next in sequence. There are several different ways by which this can be achieved, however, and each method has its own advantages and uses.

### The absolute jump instruction

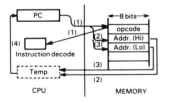

The *absolute jump* instruction contains the address to which instruction execution is to be transferred in the word(s) immediately following the jump operation code. The margin Figure shows the instruction format which is used in the MC68HC11 microprocessor, and this is also typical of many other 8-bit microprocessors. The instruction execution sequence is as follows:
- (*a*) The contents of the program counter are output on the address bus and, after allowing for propagation delays, the operation code is read into the CPU and decoded. The program counter is incremented.

(*b*) After decoding the operation code, the CPU knows that the instruction is a jump instruction, and that the operation code is followed by a 16-bit address stored in the two bytes which contiguously follow the operation code. The program counter contents are therefore output once again on the address bus, and the first byte of the jump address is read into the CPU. The program counter is then incremented again.

(*c*) The program counter contents are output on the address bus for a third time, and the second byte of the jump address is read into the CPU. The program counter is incremented for a third time.

(*d*) Finally, the jump address is loaded into the program counter where it overwrites the previous contents of the program counter. As a result, during the fetch cycle of the next instruction, when the program counter contents are output onto the address bus, the instruction fetched is not the next instruction in sequence.

*Example 1: MC68HC11*

The MC68HC11 instruction set includes the instruction *jump* (JMP), which is a 3-byte instruction conforming to the format shown in the margin Figure above. Note that this format means that the instruction can be used to jump to any address in the MC68HC11 64 kbyte address space. The instruction is unconditional; this means that the jump is always executed regardless of any status condition. (The MC68HC11 instruction set does not include any conditional jumps; these are implemented using the branch mechanism described below.)

*Example 2: MC68000*

The MC68000 instruction set includes an unconditional *jump* (JMP) instruction which is identical to the MC68HC11 except that the operand can be either a 16-bit (word) or 32-bit (long word) address. Like the MC68HC11, conditional jumps are not available; these are implemented via *branch* instructions.

*Example 3: ARM*

In keeping with the RISC philosophy of providing a minimal functional instruction set, the ARM has no jump instruction, and relies entirely upon branch instructions (see below).

*The relative branch instruction*

Whereas the absolute jump instruction simply overwrites the current program counter contents with a new value, the relative branch instruction constructs the new program counter contents by adding an offset to the current program counter contents. The offset is stored in the word(s) immediately following the operation code. The margin Figure shows the format of the instruction for the MC68HC11, and again this is common to many other 8-bit microprocessors. The program counter offset, stored as the instruction operand, is usually held in a 2s complement form, since this allows both positive and negative offsets to be specified. Thus a branch may be either forwards or backwards in the program from the current program counter value. The instruction is executed in the following sequence:

The 16-bit address allows a jump to be made anywhere in the MC68HC11 address space; this is not possible with the MC68HC11 branch instruction.

Note that the first byte of the jump address cannot be loaded directly into the program counter since it would alter the program counter contents and prevent the second jump address byte being accessed correctly. An additional temporary storage register must therefore exist on the MC68HC11 CPU chip.

One application of the unconditional jump instruction is for applications where a program is to be executed indefinitely. The unconditional jump instruction is used to jump back to the beginning of the program when the end is reached.

Notice that the terms *branch* and *jump* are usually used interchangeably; Motorola uses the term 'jump' *exclusively* for absolute jumps, and the term 'branch' *exclusively* for relative branches. This distinction is also maintained in this book.

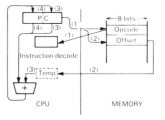

(*a*) The contents of the program counter are output on the address bus and the operation code is read into the CPU, where it is decoded. The program counter is incremented.

(*b*) The CPU now knows that the instruction is a relative branch instruction, and that the operation code is followed by a single-byte offset. The program counter is therefore output on the address bus and the offset is read into the CPU. The program counter is incremented again.

(*c*) The least significant byte of the program counter contents is added to the offset read from memory, and the result stored back in the lower eight bits of the program counter.

(*d*) The most significant byte of the program counter contents is added to any carry which may have occurred during the previous addition and the result is stored back in the eight most significant bits of the program counter.

Because the offset is specified as a 2s complement 8-bit number, the branch can be $-128$ to $+127$ bytes from the current program counter value. At the time this calculation is made, however, the program counter has already been incremented twice to fetch the opcode and the offset. Thus the branch can in fact be $-126$ to $+129$ bytes from the address of the instruction opcode.

There is no specific reason why the offset must be only a single byte. Motorola (and most other 8-bit microprocessor manufacturers) have chosen to implement the branch instruction this way because it decreases the instruction size, and hence makes the program more compact, and because programming statistics indicate that the majority of program branches lie within the range offered by a single-byte offset.

*Example 1:MC68HC11*

Where a larger offset is required the unconditional jump instruction must be used.

The MC68HC11 unconditional branch instruction (BRA) is a 2-byte instruction stored in exactly the format shown above. It allows program branches to transfer program execution $-126$ to $+129$ bytes from the current program address.

The MC68HC11 also provides a wide range of conditional branch instructions. For all of these instructions, if the specified condition is met, the program branch is executed, otherwise program execution continues with the next instruction in sequence.

*Example 2: MC68000*

This facility is essential for writing *position-independent* code, that is, code which will run unaltered at any address in memory (see Chapter 7).

Where an offset larger than 32 kbytes is required, the unconditional jump instruction must be used.

The MC68000 implements conditional branches in exactly the same way as the MC68HC11, and uses identical mnemonics for the instructions, except that the 8-bit offset is encoded along with the opcode in a single 16-bit instruction word. Because it is clear that sometimes conditional branches will be required over a greater distance than $\pm 128$ bytes, an alternative binary coding of the branch instruction is also possible, where the opcode word is followed by a second operand word, which contains a 16-bit offset. The required offset size and appropriate instruction size are evaluated automatically by the assembler program. This provides the capability to branch up to $\pm 32$ kbytes from the current program address.

*Example 3: ARM*

Like the MC68000, and as with all ARM instructions, the ARM branch instruction (B) occupies a single word (in this case, a 32-bit word). Since the opcode itself only requires eight bits, 24 bits are available for specifying the 2s complement offset. Furthermore, since branches must be to addresses on 32-bit word boundaries, bits 0 and 1 of the branch address will always be 0, and hence the 24-bit offset is sufficient to specify any address in the 26-bit (64 Mbyte) address space of the ARM processor. Note that, since instruction execution is carried out in a three-stage pipeline on the ARM, although the branch instruction is only one word long, the program counter will be two instructions further on from the branch instruction by the time the branch is executed, leading to an offset adjustment of − 2, which is allowed for automatically by the assembler.

Offsets wrap around at the top and bottom of the address space: this happens automatically as a result of ignoring overflow and underflow in the 2s complement address caculation.

*Branch/jump to subroutine*

When any computer program is written, the fundamental approach which should be taken is to use a *top-down*, or structured, design strategy. The objective is to define the program first in broad outline terms, and then to refine the program by specifying the task in terms of a number of subtasks each of which implements a subset of the problem. The subtasks are then themselves further divided into sub-subtasks, and this process of stepwise refinement is continued until the problem is fully specified in terms of computer instructions. At each greater level of refinement, more task-specific detail is introduced, so that this detail does not obscure the overall structure of the program unnecessarily. One corollary of this approach is that it is commonly found that the same subtask is required at a number of different places in the program. It would be possible to duplicate the required subtask code in the program every time the subtask was executed, but this is a very inefficient use of the computer memory. It would also be possible to have a single copy of the subtask code stored in memory, as shown in the margin Figure, and to branch or jump to this code every time the subtask function was to be executed. This also is not satisfactory, however, because once the subtask is complete, there is no way of knowing at what point the main task was suspended.

A much fuller discussion of the concepts of *structured programming* will be found in: Attikiouzel, J. *Pascal for Electronic Engineers* (Van Nostrand Reinhold, 1984).

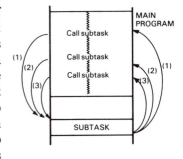

What is required is a way of getting back to the main program once the subtask has been completed, and continuing program execution from that point. To do this it is necessary to store the contents of the program counter at the time the branch to the subtask is made, so that this value can subsequently be reloaded back into the program counter when it is desired to resume execution of the main program. Notice that because the program counter is normally incremented immediately after every fetch cycle, the program counter contents already point to the next instruction in the main program at the time that it is stored.

Using this mechanism the sequence of operations to execute a subtask or *subroutine* would be:

(a) *Execute 'call subroutine' instruction.* The subroutine address is specified either as an absolute address or as a relative offset in exactly the same way as the jump and branch instructions described earlier. In addition, however, the *call subroutine* instruction includes a mechanism which saves the current program counter contents before modifying the program counter value. At this time the program counter contents point to the instruction immediately after the subroutine call, which is where execution of the main program continues when the subtask is complete.

(b) *Execute the subtask.* The instructions comprising the subroutine are executed in the normal way. They are terminated by . . .

(c) *Return from subtask.* This is a special instruction which restores the previously stored value of the program counter.

(d) *Continue main program.* The main program can now be continued in the normal fashion.

The only problem with this mechanism is how to store the program counter contents. Several methods are used in different types of computer. Among the most common are:

(a) *Programmed instructions.* Programmed instructions which store the contents of the program counter in memory are executed before the subroutine is called. The subroutine is called simply by executing a jump or branch instruction. On completion of the subroutine, the previous program counter contents are restored using programmed instructions which reload the program counter from the address where it was stored in memory. Though simple conceptually, the disadvantage of this scheme is that it is inefficient because an additional instruction is needed to store the program counter contents before branching to the subroutine. Furthermore, the mechanism is unwieldy from the programmer's point of view.

This very simple mechanism was used in the TMS1000 family of 4-bit single-chip microcomputers, as well as on the ARM.

(b) *Dedicated CPU register.* A dedicated register is provided in the computer CPU; the program counter contents are loaded into this register when the subroutine is called. This scheme is simple in hardware terms, and the call and return instructions can be executed rapidly because no memory accesses are needed. The major disadvantage is that if *nested* subroutines occur (i.e. within the first subroutine there is a call to a further subroutine) the contents of the register are overwritten by the second subroutine call, and the main program continuation address is lost.

A dedicated CPU register, R14, known as the link register (LR), is the basic mechanism provided by the ARM for implementing a branch to subroutine. The branch to subroutine is executed using the BL (branch with link) instruction which decrements the current program counter value (to allow for the instruction pipeline) and then stores the result (the subroutine return address) in the link register. No special instruction is required to implement the return from subroutine, since this is effected simply by copying the contents of R14 back into R15 (MOV R15, R14 or MOV PC, LR).

Note that, like any ARM instruction, BL can be conditional, leading to a full set of 16 possible conditional branch to subroutine instructions.

To allow for subroutine nesting, an explicitly programmed *memory stack* is used (see below): the programmer includes an instruction which copies the link register (and any other registers which must be preserved through the subroutine call) at the start of the subroutine, and a corresponding instruction to unstack the registers at the end.

This appears to be less efficient than the autonomous stack described below, but in fact, where a *stack frame* is used, it can be more efficient (see Worked Example 7.3, Exercise 7.6 and Problem 7.5).

This mechanism has been used in a number of Intel microprocessors, such as the 4004 and 4040 4-bit microprocessors (now obsolete) and the 8048 series of 8-bit single-chip microcomputers.

(c) *CPU register stack.* The CPU register stack is structured as a last-in first-out (LIFO) store. As each subroutine is called the current program counter contents are stored in the next vacant register. Then when a return from subroutine is executed the most recently stored program counter contents are reloaded from the register stack. Using this mechanism subroutines can be nested to a maximum level corresponding to the number of registers in the stack. An attempt to nest beyond this level corrupts the stack and prevents the main program being resumed.

(*d*) *Memory stack*. A memory stack is used in exactly the same way as the CPU register stack described above, but is implemented using the computer's main read/write memory. As a result the stack can be as large as necessary, within the constraints of the maximum memory available. For practical purposes, unlimited subroutine nesting is possible. In order to identify the area of memory which is to be used as the stack, a special CPU register is required; this register is called the *stack pointer* because it always points to the next free memory location into which a subroutine return address can be stored, as is shown in the margin figure on the next page.

Almost all general-purpose 8- and 16-bit microprocessors use a memory stack for subroutine return address storage, but other mechanisms are quite common in mainframe and minicomputers.

The stack pointer in the MC68HC11 is a 16-bit register which can point to any address in the 64 kbyte address space. On the MC68000, address register A7 is designated as the stack pointer, and since it is a 32-bit register, it can point to any address within the MC68000 address space. On the ARM, it is conventional to use register R13 as the stack pointer. Recent 16- and 32-bit microprocessors like the MC68000 and ARM in fact generally allow any general-purpose register to be used as a stack pointer, because this mechanism is extensively used by block-structured languages such as Pascal not only for subroutine linkage, but also for parameter passing to functions and procedures, and for local variable storage within functions and procedures (see below).

This convention is used because it results in separate stack pointers (and link registers) being available in each of the ARM execution modes (see Fig. 2.7).

Because each memory word on the MC68HC11 is only eight bits in length, subroutine return addresses are stored as two bytes in adjacent memory locations. Similarly, on the MC68000 the 24-bit return address is stored as two consecutive 16-bit words (the highest byte is set to zero). On the ARM, the 24-bit return address can be stored in a single 32-bit word.

The sequence of operations to save the current program counter contents when a subroutine is called during execution of an MC68HC11 program is as follows:

$$(PC_L) \rightarrow (SP) \qquad (SP) - 1 \rightarrow SP$$
$$(PC_H) \rightarrow (SP) \qquad (SP) - \rightarrow SP$$
$$\text{Subprogram address} \rightarrow PC$$

This sequence is identical regardless of whether the subroutine address itself is specified as an offset (BSR), or as an absolute address (JSR).

The stack pointer is decremented automatically after each byte of information is stored through it, so that after the program counter contents have been stored, the stack pointer is left pointing to the next free address in the memory stack. When it is desired to return from the subroutine, the reverse operation takes place thus:

$$(SP) + 1 \rightarrow SP \qquad ((SP)) \rightarrow PC_H$$
$$(SP) + 1 \rightarrow SP \qquad ((SP)) \rightarrow PC_L$$

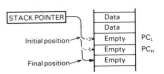

*Subroutine return address storage on memory stack*

Notice that when data are removed from the stack, the stack pointer must be incremented before the stack is accessed, otherwise data are not retrieved from the correct address.

Unfortunately, there is no standardisation between different types of processor as to the order in which bytes or words are pushed onto the stack (i.e. whether the high byte or low byte is stored first). Nor do all processors post-decrement the stack before pushing data onto it and pre-increment it after taking data off it. For the three example processors in this book, the following rules apply:

*MC68HC11*: As illustrated above, the return address is stored *least significant*

In practice, the programmer does not need to know the order of stacking bytes/words and whether a pre-decrement or post-decrement mechanism is used when calling subroutines, since the mechanism is autonomous. When subroutine calls are mixed with data storage on the stack, however (see below), this knowledge is vital to avoid possible *stack corruption*.

*byte* first. The stack is *post-decremented* before the return address has been pushed onto the stack, and is *pre-incremented* after the return address is pulled off the stack.

*MC68000*: The return address is stored *least significant word* first. The stack is *pre-decremented* before pushing the subroutine return address, and *post-incremented* after pulling the subroutine return address.

*ARM*: The ARM does not implement any autonomous mechanism for saving the contents of the program counter on a memory stack; it simply copies the program counter contents to the link register. However, where an explicitly programmed memory stack is used to preserve the contents of the link register across nested subroutine calls, the stack can have any one of four structures, as outlined in the next section.

**Exercise 4.5**  Indicate the data transfers which take place using the MC68HC11 data and address buses when the following instructions are executed:

(*a*) Jump to subroutine (JSR)

(*b*) Branch to subroutine (BSR)

(*c*) Return from subroutine (RTS)

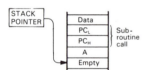

*Subroutine return address storage on memory stack*

RTS executed without pulling A off the stack causes program execution to continue at address A.PC$_H$ instead of address PC$_H$.PC$_L$!

In more recent microprocessor designs (for example, the MC68000 and ARM) separate *user* and *system* stack pointers are often provided to eliminate the possibility of stack corruption.

The stack pointer mechanism has two other uses apart from its use for saving subroutine return addresses mentioned above. One use is to save the program status (i.e. register contents) during an interrupt request: this is described in the next chapter. The other use is as a means of providing a temporary LIFO data store in memory for other CPU registers. To support this use, programmed instructions in the MC68HC11 instruction set is provided which enable any register to be saved and retrieved on the memory stack. The mechanism of operation of these instructions is exactly the same as for the autonomous subroutine mechanism.

The push and pull instructions are often found to be very useful for preserving the value of data within registers while a subroutine is executed. Thus the accumulator is *pushed* onto the stack before the subroutine is called, and is retrieved from the stack using the *pull* instruction after the program has returned from the subroutine. Notice that it is very important that the number of pull operations exactly matches the number of push operations within a subroutine; if this requirement is not observed, the subroutine return address may be accessed from an incorrect position on the stack, with the result that program execution continues from an incorrect address. This problem is called *stack corruption* and is caused by mixing the autonomous function of the stack pointer with its use by programmed instructions. The margin Figure helps to clarify the problem. A final point concerning the use of a stack pointer is that instructions are obviously required which can initialise the stack pointer to a suitable address in memory. It is also the responsibility of the programmer to ensure that sufficient memory is available for the stack requirements.

**Exercise 4.6**  In what other way could stack corruption take place?

*Example 1: MC68HC11*

The MC6809 push and pull instructions can save any MC68HC11 register on the stack, for example:

PSHA

will push the 8-bit A accumulator onto the stack, and

PULX

will pull the next two bytes off the stack and store them in the 16-bit X register.

*Example 2: MC68000*

The MC68000 has two stack pointers, known as the *user stack pointer* (USP or A7) and the *supervisor stack pointer* (SSP or A7'). Subroutines and interrupts use the supervisor stack pointer, but the division between the two stack pointers is rigidly enforced, and usually program instructions cannot access the supervisor stack pointer at all. The equivalent of the MC68HC11 push and pull instructions are implemented on the MC68000 using the *move multiple registers* instruction (MOVEM). For example:

MOVEM.L   D0–D3/A1/A4,–(SP)

would copy registers D0–D3 and A1 and A4 to the user stack, pre-decrementing the user stack pointer for each word of each register, while the converse operation of reloading the registers from the stack would be specified as:

MOVEM.L   (SP)+ ,D0–D3/A1/A4

(Here, the dash (–) is used to indicate an inclusive range of registers, and the slash (/) to delimit additional register terms.)

*Example 3: ARM*

The ARM has four stack pointers (R13, R13_svc, R13_irq and R13_fiq), one for each of the four modes in which the processor can operate. Like the MC68000, program instructions can normally only access the stack pointer available in the current mode. The ARM provides extensive support for memory stacks using the LDM (load multiple register) and STM (store multiple register) instructions. Four possible stack formats are supported, each of which can be specified using an appropriate two-character acronym appended to the LDM or STM instruction mnemonic. The four different stack formats are illustrated in Figure 4.11, and arise as a result of the interaction of two binary variables. First, the stack can be a *full* stack or an *empty* stack: a full stack is one in which the stack pointer points to the last data item written to it; an empty stack is one in which the stack pointer points to the first free slot in the stack. Second, the stack can be an *ascending* stack or a *descending stack*: an ascending stack is one which grows from low memory addresses to high ones, whereas a descending stack grows in the opposite direction. Combining these options leads to the four stack types illustrated in Figure 4.11. As the four stack types are functionally equivalent, only one is usually needed for any specific piece of software. For consistency with the MC68000 microprocessor, the *full, descending stack* (equivalent to a pre-decrement stack) is used in the examples below. For this stack type, registers are stored on the stack using an instruction of the format:

STMFD   SP!, {register list}

*Stack addressing* is also available as a general addressing mode (see Chapter 7) on both the ARM and MC68000, but not the MC68HC11.

The use of user and supervisor stack pointers in the MC68000 and ARM is associated with two specific modes of operation, *user mode* and *supervisor mode*. These two modes provide hardware support for using the MC68000 and ARM in multi-tasking operating systems (see Chapter 9). In general, programs running in user mode cannot access supervisor mode facilities, but supervisor mode programs (for example, the operating system kernel) can access user mode facilities. A detailed discussion of advanced MC68000 and ARM facilities is beyond the scope of this book.

The *move multiple registers* instruction can operate on words or long words, but not bytes. This is because it is required to maintain alignment of the stack pointer on word boundaries.

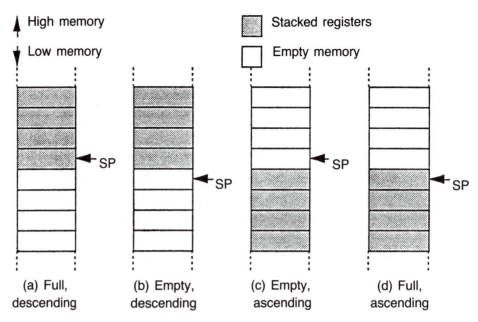

High memory

Low memory

Stacked registers

Empty memory

SP

SP

SP

SP

(a) Full,
descending

(b) Empty,
descending

(c) Empty,
ascending

(d) Full,
ascending

Fig. 4.11  Stack types supported by the ARM.

In ARM assembly language the exclamation mark is used to indicate that, after stacking the registers, the updated value of the stack pointer is written back to it. The curly brackets are used to indicate a list of registers.

Note that registers are stored on the stack in a fixed order which is independent of the order in which they are specified in the instruction.

Note that unstacking direct into the program counter avoids the need for a separate MOV PC, LR instruction.

and loaded from the stack back into registers using the instruction:

    LDMFD   SP!, {register list}

where the register list is a list of registers separated by commas. Thus, for example, at the start of any subroutine, the link register (into which the program counter contents have been copied) must be saved on the stack, along with any other registers which should not be altered by the subroutine, e.g.

    STMFD   SP!, {R0, R1, LR}; stack R0, R1, return address

To terminate the subroutine and simultaneously restore previous register values, the following instruction would be used:

    LDMFD   SP!, {R0, R1, PC}; unstack regs. and return

The LDM/STM instructions can, like other ARM instructions, be modified to be conditional on the status register, e.g. LDMMIFD, LDMEQFD, etc.

**Instruction interpretation and control**

Many CISC computers use a rather more complex control structure than that described here. These computers are said to be *microprogrammed* because each instruction is made up of a sequence of elemental *microinstructions* each of which performs a small part of the complete instruction.

A final aspect of the CPU to be considered in this chapter is the mechanism for converting the instruction opcodes into the low-level control signals which cause the operation specified by the opcode to be executed. This is the function of the *control unit* of the computer. Because the instruction sets of different types of computer differ, so, too, do the control units differ in the way that they decode the operation codes to elemental control signals for the rest of the computer. Nevertheless, some observations may be made about the general structure of computer control units.

When the instruction opcode is loaded into the CPU from the computer's memory, it is stored in the *instruction register*. This register provides temporary storage for the opcode while it is applied to the inputs of an *instruction decoder*, which converts the opcode to the required low level control signals. The instruction decoder is a combinational logic component, and may be implemented using random logic, a PLA, or even using a ROM, though this tends to be rather inefficient in this application. In any event the instruction decoder may be considered as a black box which takes as its input the instruction opcode, the outputs from the status register and the clock signals, and produces as its output a set of combinational logic control signals and a set of register and memory write signals. The margin Figure shows the general structure of the MC68HC11 control unit.

The *combinational logic control signals* are connected to all the combinational components in the computer, such as the ALU function and mode select inputs, and multiplexer and demultiplexer control inputs. The timing of the signals applied to these units is unimportant, so long as sufficient time is allowed for data and control signals to propagate through all components. In some instructions, however, a particular component of the computer may be used several times, and in this case the *sequence* of operations is obviously important. An example would be the use of the 8-bit ALU twice during calculation of the address to which program execution is transferred by a branch instruction.

The *register control* outputs of the instruction decoder are connected to the write (latch data) inputs of all the CPU registers, and to the memory read/write line of the control bus. The timing of these signals is important because it controls when data are written into the CPU registers or memory. This must only occur when the register data inputs are known to be valid (i.e. after sufficient time has been allowed for all propagation delays to die away). This can be achieved by gating the register control signals with a suitable clock phase, so that data are latched into the required registers on the falling edge of the clock signal.

Microprogramming is, however, outside the scope of this book; refer instead to:
Nichols, K.G., Zaluska, E.J. *Theory and Practice of Microprocessors* (Edward Arnold, 1982), Chapter 13. This covers microprogramming and the control structure of microprocessors in more detail than can be attempted here.

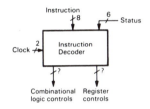

## Summary

The CPU of a computer or microprocessor contains an arithmetic and logic unit (ALU), a control unit and a number of registers. The ALU provides the means for performing arithmetic or logical manipulation of data stored in the computer's main memory or registers, and thus enables the computer to perform general data processing tasks. Status outputs from the ALU provide binary indications of several conditions which may result during arithmetic or logical operations. These status signals are stored in a status register and may be used to determine subsequent processing using conditional branch or jump instructions.

Most CPUs contain a number of general-purpose registers which provide short-term storage for the results of arithmetic and logical processing. In addition, however, there are often a number of special-purpose registers with dedicated functions within the CPU. One such register is the program counter, which provides a pointer to the next instruction in the program. The program counter is automatically incremented after every instruction memory access. Another common CPU register is the stack pointer, which is used as a pointer to a last-in first-out (LIFO) store in memory which preserves the program return address when a subroutine is being executed.

The control unit converts the machine code instructions fetched from the computer's main memory into the actual control signals required to execute the function specified by the instruction. The mechanism for doing this varies significantly from one computer to another, and may use a ROM, a PLA, random logic circuits or microprogramming.

## Problems

4.1 Describe the sequence of events, clock cycle by clock cycle, when the following MC68HC11 instructions are executed.

(*a*) Load the stack pointer from the contents of addresses 100 hex. and 101 hex. (LDS $100).

(*b*) Jump to subroutine at address 3F80 hex. (JSR $3F80).

(*c*) Branch to subroutine with address offset F0 hex. (BSR $F0).

(*d*) Return from subroutine (RTS).

4.2 Write the algorithm for a program to multiply two 8-bit unsigned integers stored in addresses 0 and 1, and to store the result in addresses 2 and 3, assuming a microprocessor with no explicit multiply instruction.

It is recommended that algorithms should be written using a *structured high-level language* such as PASCAL. Refer to earlier comments, and to Chapter 10.

4.3 Write assembly language code for the program described in Problem 4.2.

4.4 Modify the algorithm written in Problem 4.2 so that it can be used to multiply two 2s complement numbers.

4.5 Write assembly language code for the program described in Problem 4.4 for the processor of your choice.

4.6 Estimate the time taken to execute the programs written in Problems 4.3 and 4.5, and compare this with the time taken to add two 8-bit numbers.

# Input and output interfaces 5

**Objectives**

☐ To describe the computer hardware interfaces required to enable input and output of data to and from a computer.
☐ To explain the techniques which implement computer input and output and their applicability.
☐ To describe the facilities provided by typical microprocessor interface chips.
☐ To explain how to design interfaces for computers and microprocessor systems.

The hardware implementation of all the blocks within the basic computer structure introduced in Chapter 1 has now been explained in detail, except for the input and output interfaces. These interfaces are most important, for without them data cannot be input to the computer from the outside world, nor can the results of computation be transmitted back from the computer.

The following general references are useful for this chapter:
Peatman, J.B. *Microcomputer Based Design* (McGraw-Hill, 1977), Chapter 5.
Osborne, A. *An Introduction to Microcomputers, Volume 1: Some Basic Concepts* (2nd edition) (Osborne/McGraw-Hill, 1980), Chapter 5.

## Characteristics of input and output devices

Computers need to be interfaced to a very wide range of different devices. Table 5.1 shows some examples, ordered according to the complexity of the required interface. The more complex devices may well require much more complex interfaces than simple devices such as switches or lamps. Nevertheless, the basic computer hardware interface is quite simple, and four general techniques suffice to deal with any interface device, however simple or complex the device may be.

Microprocessors are generally connected to a much wider range of devices than larger computers, because their range of applications is much wider.

**Table 5.1  Examples of input and output devices**

| Input | Output | Complexity |
|-------|--------|------------|
| Switches | Lamps | Simplest |
| Transducers | Servos | |
| Counters | Alphanumeric displays | |
| Paper tape | | |
| Magnetic tape | | |
| VDU terminals | | |
| Disk units | | Most complex |

Using Table 5.1 as an example, we can group the interface devices according to several different characteristics:

The characteristics of analogue-to-digital and digital-to-analogue converters are discussed in detail in Stonham, T.J. *Digital Logic Techniques: Principles and Practice* (Van Nostrand Reinhold, 1987), Chapter 7.

Compare a torch bulb with a large d.c. motor.

If the data are only valid at a particular time, the interface must be able to detect this.

All the example processors use the memory-mapped input/output technique.

An 8-bit computer word and a 16-bit address bus are assumed for all examples in this chapter.

(1) *Analogue/digital:* If the device uses a digital data format, this simplifies the interface to the computer, but most real signals occur naturally in an analogue form. In this case it is necessary to process the signal using an analogue-to-digital converter (input) or a digital-to-analogue converter (output) in order to connect the computer to the outside world.

(2) *Electrical characteristics:* The electrical characteristics of the device to be interfaced to the computer may vary enormously; nevertheless, any device can be connected to the computer's inputs or outputs if a suitable electrical interface is designed.

(3) *Operating speed:* The speed of operation of the device affects the interface design. Two factors are particularly important: first, the computer's *response time* when an input device supplies data or an output device signals its readiness to receive data; second, the *data rate* when a stream of successive data input or output operations is performed.

(4) *Data availability:* The interface may be able to provide or receive data continuously, or data transfer may be restricted to discrete time intervals.

(5) *Data timing:* Data may need to be transmitted to, or received from, the computer at regular time intervals (*synchronously*) or irregularly (*asynchronously*).

In general, the first two problems outlined above influence the design of the electrical interface to the computer, while the last three problems are solved by suitable design of the program which inputs or outputs data to the computer.

**Memory-mapped input and output**

The simplest possible way of connecting a computer to an external device is to make the external device look like a memory location to the computer. Then, if data are written into this special memory location, they are output to the external device, and if data are read from the location they are input from the external device. Hence, to the computer the data input and output locations (often called input and output *ports*) look like memory, but to the external device they look like inputs and outputs to the computer.

Fig. 5.1 shows the simplest possible input interface to a computer. The eight data lines $D_0$–$D_7$ connect to the external device which is assumed to provide input data in an 8-bit parallel TTL (Transistor-Transistor Logic)-compatible format. (If it does not, additional interfacing circuitry is required to convert the data to this format.) The external device inputs $D_0$–$D_7$ connect to eight tristate transmission gates which enable input data to be connected to the computer data bus if a logic-1 output occurs from the address decoder. The address decoder will only give a logic-1 output for one specific address within the address space of the computer. Hence, if data are read from this address, they are effectively read from the external device.

An obvious problem with this interface is that external data must be continuously available, otherwise an incorrect value may be input. If the data are not continuously available, a more complex interface, described later in this chapter, is required.

A similar technique can be used to provide an output interface to the computer.

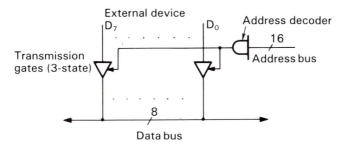

Fig. 5.1   Simple computer input interface.

Fig. 5.2 shows a simple output interface, again configured to appear as a memory location to the computer. In this case, a register is required rather than simple tri-state transmission gates, so that data can be available continuously to the outside world, even though they appear only momentarily on the data bus. Using this configuration, data are continuously available until overwritten by a subsequent data output operation.

*Address decoder — minimal address decoding*

An address decoder is needed for both the input and output interface, to ensure that the interface appears on the data bus only for one specific memory location; otherwise *memory contention* could occur between data or program memory and input or output ports. One disadvantage of this is that significant logic circuitry is needed to select one unique memory location from the 64 kbyte address space of a typical 8-bit microprocessor. In a memory-mapped input/output computer, this circuitry can be minimised by a technique known as *minimal address decoding*, which makes use of the fact that, in typical dedicated microprocessor applications, only a small part of the complete address space is used.

For a more detailed discussion of minimal address decoding, refer to the design example in Chapter 10.

Memory contention occurs when more than one physical component occupies a particular memory address. This should not happen if the system is designed correctly.
Note that the same technique can be used to minimise the address decoding of the program and data memories.

Choose a suitable memory allocation to minimise the input and output port address decoding for an application requiring a program of 4 kbytes plus two input ports and two output ports.

**Worked Example 5.1**

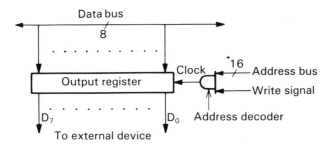

Fig. 5.2   Simple computer output interface.

*Solution*

Since the program occupies only 4 kbytes it can be stored within the bottom 32 kbytes of memory. Hence address line A15 will be logic-0 for any access of program or data made by the computer. Thus A15 = 1 can be used to select the input and output interfaces. For example, each interface can be uniquely selected if A15 = 1, and A0 and A1 are decoded to select one from four possible interfaces. Address lines A2–A14 are not connected to the input and output interfaces.

The interfaces thus appear at addresses:    $8000,   $8001,   $8002,   $8003
and are also replicated at:              $8004,   $8005,   $8006, ...
                                         ... $FFFD, $FFFE, $FFFF

> Note that this solution is not unique: the program and input/output port addresses could equally well be reversed.

The replication of addresses at which the ports appear is unimportant because there is no program or data memory occupying any of these addresses. Hence in this example only three address lines need to be decoded rather than the full sixteen.

**Exercise 5.1**    Show how the addressing of the program memory in Worked Example 5.1 could be minimally decoded if it is implemented using 2 kbyte ROMs.

### Input and output via a separate address space

> The 80x86 family use a separate input/output address space: only the least significant eight address lines are connected to the input/output ports.

> It is possible to have an input/output address space using completely separate address and data buses, but this duplication would require too many external pin connections on a microprocessor CPU chip.

An alternative way of reducing the address decoding required for input and output ports is to provide a separate input and output port address space. This can be much smaller than the memory address space, since only a few input and output ports are required in most computer applications. Hence fewer address lines are required to identify a specific port uniquely. In computers using this scheme (Fig. 5.3), the data bus commonly connects to both address spaces, and a subset of the address bus lines is connected to the input/output address space. One or more additional control signals are provided to indicate whether a data transfer from the CPU should access the memory address space or the input/output address space. Effectively, these control signals function as a 17th address line.

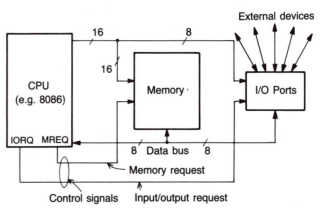

Fig. 5.3   Separate input/output address space.

In a memory-mapped computer, the same instructions which perform load and store operations when accessing memory locations, become input and output operations when they address input and output ports. If a separate address space is provided, however, it must be supported by specific input and output instructions in the instruction set of the computer.

Thus the 80X86 family of microprocessors includes a number of instructions which are designed to access input or output ports rather than memory. The most important of these are IN (input from a port) and OUT (output to a port).

Conversely, if a computer has specific input and output instructions in its instruction set, it will also have a separate input output address space.

## Direct transfer

*Direct transfer* is the simplest form of data input or output which a computer can use, and is chosen when the timing of the input or output operation is unconstrained and the data are continuously available. Thus a direct transfer input (output) operation corresponds simply to a read input (write output) instruction.

As an example, consider an input interface from eight latching push-buttons, and an output interface to eight LEDs. Data are continuously available at the input interface, so that a simple read input instruction executed at any time will load the current value of the eight push-button switches into the computer. Similarly, the LEDs can accept data output from the computer at any time, and a simple write output instruction is all that is needed to output data from the computer.

More commonly, input data are not continuously available from the input device, or the output device cannot accept data output at any time. In these cases direct transfer input/output is not possible, and a more complex mechanism, known as *test and transfer*, is used instead.

## Test and transfer

Consider the case of data input to a computer. If data are not continuously available, how can the computer tell when they are valid? The incoming data may be synchronous, that is, they may occur at fixed intervals, or they may be asynchronous and occur randomly. If the data are synchronous it may be possible for the computer to predict when the data will be available, but this is not straightforward and is seldom attempted in practice. A much better solution is to make use of a continuously available status signal provided by the data input device to tell the computer when valid data are available. This status signal then also becomes an input to the computer, but because it is *continuously available* it can be read at any time using the direct transfer technique.

The status input to the computer requires only a single bit within an input port, though in practical microprocessor interface chips there may be several different status signals provided, which are aggregated together in a *status port*. In a typical implementation the status signal might be defined as follows:

Also sometimes known as *programmed data transfer*; this is a misnomer because *direct transfer* and *interrupt transfer* (see following section) also use programmed instructions to perform data transfers.

Status signals are also sometimes known as *flags*; the two terms are synonymous.

|  |  |  |
|---|---|---|
| STATUS = 1 | Data available | (Data can be read) |
| STATUS = 0 | Data not available | (Data not valid) |

Fig. 5.4*a* shows how the computer program can now make use of the status input to determine whether valid input data can be read, and hence ensure that

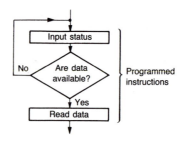

Fig. 5.4a Test and transfer loop.

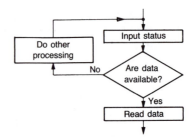

Fig. 5.4b Test and transfer with
other processing.

data are only read from the peripheral device at the appropriate time. A similar technique can be used to provide test and transfer data output, but in this case the status signal tells the computer whether the output device is ready to accept data transferred to it from the computer.

**Exercise 5.2** Write a subroutine using MC68HC11 (or ARM, or MC68000) instructions to perform a test and transfer input from a data port at address 80 hex. The status bit is configured as the most significant bit of a status port at address 81 hex., and is a logic 1 when data are available.

Most of the computer peripheral devices described in Chapter 8 can be interfaced to the computer using the test and transfer technique. A detailed example of interfacing using the test and transfer method is given in Chapter 8.

Test and transfer is the most common method used for implementing data input/output in computers, because it is simple to program, requires relatively little additional hardware beyond the data interface itself, and can accommodate input and output devices with widely varying data rates. Nevertheless, there is a significant disadvantage to the method. This occurs when the method is used to connect the computer to a slow input or output device, when a considerable amount of processing time may be wasted in the loop which continually tests the status signal. If, for example, test and transfer is used to input a string of bytes representing characters from a VDU terminal, even the most proficient typist cannot type faster than about 10 characters per second. The computer may therefore spend nearly all of its processing time executing the status loop while it waits for the next byte of data to become available. This is clearly a very inefficient way of using the computer's processing power, but in many applications this may not matter. If no data processing can be done until all the characters of a line have been typed (representing the input of a command to the

74

computer perhaps), then there is no disadvantage in 'wasting' the time spent executing the status loop.

Sometimes, however, it is desired to do other processing while waiting for the data to become available. One possibility would be to test the status signal, and, upon finding that data are not yet available, to perform some other processing while waiting for the data to arrive (Fig. 5.4*b*). Unfortunately this introduces a further problem, because a decision now has to be made about when to test the status signal again. If the data are only briefly available, they may be missed completely if the computer tests the status signal at infrequent intervals.

An alternative input technique is therefore needed which allows the computer to continue with its normal processing, but nevertheless ensures that data can reliably be input or output to the computer when required. This technique is called *interrupt transfer* and is described in the next section.

### Interrupt transfer

The basic concept of interrupt transfer is quite straightforward: a hardware mechanism in the computer CPU allows an external device to signal to the computer that it wishes to input data to the computer (or that it is ready to accept data output from the computer). Immediately this signal is received in the CPU, the computer stops the program currently being executed, and executes a special program, the *interrupt service subroutine*, which performs the data input or output required by the interrupting device. On completion of the interrupt service subroutine, the computer resumes execution of the previous program from where it left off.

This sequence of events is depicted diagrammatically in Fig. 5.5, and can be split into several distinct stages:

(*a*)  The normal program is being executed.

\*\*\*  An interrupt is requested by the external device.

Typically, a signal equivalent to the status signal used for test and transfer input is used to signal the interrupt request: instead of being a normal input to the computer, this is connected to a dedicated input on the CPU. Special hardware is provided within the CPU which responds to a transition of this line by stopping execution of the current program and initiating the interrupt service subroutine.

(*b*)  The interrupt request is ignored until the current instruction has been completed.

A very common use of the interrupt mechanism is to implement a *real-time clock*. The clock consists of a counter which counts pulses from a fixed-frequency clock oscillator, and interrupts the normal computer processing at preprogrammed time intervals (for example, once every second). The interrupt service routine resets and restarts the counter, and updates variables stored in RAM which represent the time of day. This information may then be used to time-stamp any data manipulated in the main computer program.

This event occurs asynchronously with respect to normal program execution; thus the interrupt can occur at any time during execution of an instruction.

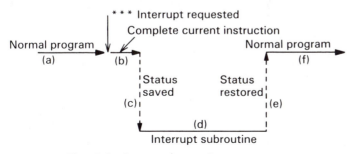

Fig. 5.5   Interrupt transfer sequence.

This is necessary so that execution of the normal program can be stopped and later restarted in a predictable manner, without any instructions being missed out or any intermediate data being lost.

(*c*)  The current program *status* is saved.

The interrupt service routine will use the same CPU registers as the normal program, and the contents of these registers must, therefore, be saved in memory before the interrupt service routine is executed, because these registers will be overwritten during the interrupt service routine. Otherwise, when normal program execution is resumed the registers will contain different data from when execution was stopped, and errors will result in the main program.

(*d*)  The interrupt service subroutine is now executed.

This will generally perform data input or output associated with the interrupting device.

(*e*)  On completion of the interrupt service subroutine, the original program status is restored (i.e. the values when normal program execution was stopped are reloaded into the CPU registers).

(*f*)  Normal program execution is resumed from the instruction immediately after the last instruction to be completed before servicing the interrupt.

*Status retention*

Whenever an interrupt service subroutine is executed, the contents of the program counter must be saved so that normal program execution can subsequently be resumed at the correct instruction. In addition, any register used within the interrupt service subroutine must be saved to avoid corrupting data in the normal program.

Registers can either be saved by an autonomous method (i.e. hardware on the CPU automatically stores the CPU registers in memory), or using programmed instructions executed at the start of the interrupt service routine. An example of the autonomous method is provided by the MC68HC11 microprocessor, which uses the memory stack mechanism introduced in previous chapter as a method of automatically stacking all CPU registers in memory when an interrupt occurs (Fig. 5.6). (The stack pointer register itself is not saved since it is needed in order to retrieve the other registers later.) Each byte stored upon the stack requires one clock cycle, and in addition the address of the interrupt service subroutine must be loaded into the program counter before execution can begin, so that in practice, there is a delay of several microseconds between the interrupt request and the start of execution of the interrupt service subroutine.

If an autonomous mechanism is not provided, the program counter contents (and perhaps the status register) will still be saved automatically, but program instructions must be executed at the start of the interrupt service subroutine to save registers which are overwritten during the interrupt service subroutine.

Because it has so many more registers than the MC68HC11, it does not make sense to save all these registers automatically when an interrupt occurs on the MC68000. Instead, only the program counter and status register are stacked. Further registers can then be stacked as necessary using *move multiple register* instructions within the interrupt service routine. The MC68000 also changes from

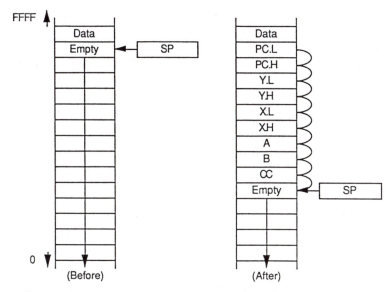

FFFF

Data
Empty ← SP

0

(Before)

Data
PC.L
PC.H
Y.L
Y.H
X.L
XH
A
B
CC
Empty ← SP

(After)

Fig. 5.6  MC68HC11 memory stack used for status retention.

its user mode to its supervisor mode when an interrupt occurs, but the implications of this change are beyond the scope of this book.

The ARM uses a different philosophy for status retention during interrupts, based upon providing duplicates of some of the CPU registers which are used when an interrupt occurs, thus avoiding corruption of the original register contents. The duplicate registers are shown hatched in Fig. 2.7. When an interrupt is signalled on the IRQ pin, the ARM processor goes into mode 2 (the IRQ mode) which has two private registers, R13__irq and R14__irq. The program counter (R15) is saved in the private link register (R14__irq) so that R14 will not be corrupted, and R13__irq provides a private stack so that the normal stack pointer (R13) will be unaffected. Any other registers which are used in the interrupt service subroutine must have their previous values preserved by saving them on the stack at the start of the interrupt routine, and restoring them at the end, otherwise normal program execution will be corrupted.

When an interrupt is signalled on the FIQ pin, the ARM processor goes into mode 1 (the FIQ mode). This is similar to mode 2, except that it has seven private registers mapped to R8–R14 (R8__fiq–R14__fiq). A fast interrupt will therefore not alter any of the user mode registers R8–R14, and no additional stacking of registers is required within an FIQ interrupt service subroutine unless registers R0–R7 are used within the routine.

At the end of the interrupt service subroutine, all registers must be restored to their original values. If an autonomous mechanism was used to save the CPU registers, a special *return from interrupt* instruction is used to unstack all registers from memory automatically in the reverse order in which they were stacked. This is the function of the RTI instruction in the MC68HC11 instruction set. Similarly, the MC68000 RTE instruction (*return from exception*) causes both the status register and program counter to be unstacked. Since the instruction MOV PC,LR on the ARM has the effect of restoring both the previous program counter and status register (including mode bits) values, this instruction is used on the ARM for returning from an interrupt routine as well as from a subroutine.

The interrupt request can normally be inhibited using special instructions which prevent interrupts from occurring at undesirable times in program execution. This is achieved by setting the interrupt bit(s) in the status register. The MC6809 and MC68000 provide instructions which allow an operand to be logically ANDed or ORed with the status register, allowing full control over all the condition codes bits. On the ARM, since the status register is part of register R15, it is accessible in the same way as any other register, and the individual interrupt bits can be set or reset using ORR and AND instructions. The interrupt bit(s) are also set when an interrupt request is received, and reset when the return from interrupt instruction is executed, to prevent a further interrupt while the first is serviced.

**Vector mechanisms**

When an interrupt is serviced, the start address of the interrupt service subroutine (the *interrupt vector*) must somehow be specified. In a normal subroutine, the address to be loaded into the program counter is specified as part of the instruction which calls the subroutine. The interrupt is initiated by an external event, however, hence some other mechanism for specifying the interrupt vector must be provided. In fact, as is illustrated below, *vectoring mechanisms* are required for a number of other reasons in computers, in addition to their use for supplying the start address of an interrupt service subroutine.

*Interrupt vectors stored in memory*

One method (used in the MC68HC11 processor) is to store the address of the interrupt service routine in dedicated locations in memory. Fig. 5.7 shows a memory map of the top 64 locations in the address space of the MC6809 microprocessor, which are dedicated to specifying 32 vectors. Each vector (or address) requires two bytes of storage in memory. The interrupt request vector is stored at addresses FFF2 hex. and FFF3 hex. When an interrupt request occurs, after stacking the CPU registers in memory, the contents of address FFF2 hex. are loaded into the high byte of the program counter, and the contents of FFF3 hex. into the low byte.

The MC68000 has a similar, but more extensive, set of vectors (known as *exception vectors*) stored in the bottom 1 kbyte of memory (see Fig. 5.8). Unlike the MC6809, which has a single interrupt request input, the MC68000 has three interrupt inputs. These allow up to eight separate levels of interrupt to be specified by an external device, by encoding the required interrupt level on the three interrupt inputs. (A code of 0 represents the 'no interrupt' condition, level 1 is the lowest interrupt level and level 7 the highest interrupt level). Corresponding to these seven interrupt levels are seven vectors (described as *autovectors* in Fig. 5.8) which allow the addresses of seven corresponding interrupt routines to be specified in exactly the same way as for the MC68HC11. The only difference is that since MC68000 family components can specify a 32-bit address, each vector occupies four bytes rather than two.

| Vector Address | Interrupt Source | CC Register Mask | Local Mask |
|---|---|---|---|
| FFC0, C1 | Reserved | — | — |
| • | • | | |
| • | • | | |
| • | • | | |
| FFD4, D5 | Reserved | — | — |
| FFD6, D7 | SCI Serial System | I Bit | See Table 9-3 |
| FFD8, D9 | SPI Serial Transfer Complete | I Bit | SPIE |
| FFDA, DB | Pulse Accumulator Input Edge | I Bit | PAII |
| FFDC, DD | Pulse Accumulator Overflow | I Bit | PAOVI |
| FFDE, DF | Timer Overflow | I Bit | TOI |
| FFE0, E1 | Timer Output Compare 5 | I Bit | OC5I |
| FFE2, E3 | Timer Output Compare 4 | I Bit | OC4I |
| FFE4, E5 | Timer Output Compare 3 | I Bit | OC3I |
| FFE6, E7 | Timer Output Compare 2 | I Bit | OC2I |
| FFE8, E9 | Timer Output Compare 1 | I Bit | OC1I |
| FFEA, EB | Timer Input Capture 3 | I Bit | OC3I |
| FFEC, ED | Timer Input Capture 2 | I Bit | OC2I |
| FFEE, EF | Timer Input Capture 1 | I Bit | OC1I |
| FFF0, F1 | Real Time Interrupt | I Bit | RTII |
| FFF2, F3 | IRQ (External Pin or Parallel I/O) | I Bit | See Table 9-4 |
| FFF4, F5 | XIRQ Pin (Pseudo Non-Maskable Interrupt) | X Bit | None |
| FFF6, F7 | SWI | None | None |
| FFF8, F9 | Illegal Opcode Trap | None | None |
| FFFA, FB | COP Failure (Reset) | None | NOCOP |
| FFFC, FD | COP Clock Monitor Fail (Reset) | None | CME |
| FFFE, FF | RESET | None | None |

Fig. 5.7 MC68HC11 interrupt vectors (© Motorola).

ARM exception vectors are shown in Fig. 5.9 and are organised in a slightly different way from those on the MC68HC11 and MC68000. All exceptions cause the contents of the PC to be saved in the appropriate R14 register, M1 and M0 to be set to the specified mode and the F and I status bits to be set according to the mode (reset and FIQ set both F and I; all other exceptions set I only). The specified address is then loaded into the PC. The vector table should contain a set of branch instructions to exception routines which carry out appropriate processing corresponding to each exception.

Note the difference compared to the MC68HC11 and MC68000: the specified address contains a branch instruction rather than a vector to be loaded into the program counter.

Clearly the interrupt vectors must be initialised before the first interrupt request occurs, otherwise an incorrect address will be loaded into the program counter. Hence these vector tables must either be implemented physically using non-volatile memory (e.g. ROM), or initialised in the program before interrupts are enabled.

*Interrupt vectors supplied by the interrupting device*

An alternative approach is for all, or part, of the interrupt vector to be supplied by the interrupting device. This approach is more flexible than the one described above, because it allows several possible interrupt sources to use the same interrupt input to the CPU, yet to specify different interrupt service routines. On the other hand, it implies additional complexity both in the logic of the interrupting device, and in the CPU. If the interrupting device is to supply an interrupt vector (normally via the data bus) it must be told when to do so: this is achieved by the provision of an *interrupt acknowledge* control bus output from the CPU which connects to any possible interrupt source. On receipt of this signal, the

## Exception Vector Assignment

| Vector Number(s) | Dec | Address Hex | Space | Assignment |
|---|---|---|---|---|
| 0 | 0 | 000 | SP | Reset: Initial SSP[2] |
| 1 | 4 | 004 | SP | Reset: Initial PC[2] |
| 2 | 8 | 008 | SD | Bus Error |
| 3 | 12 | 00C | SD | Address Error |
| 4 | 16 | 010 | SD | Illegal Instruction |
| 5 | 20 | 014 | SD | Zero Divide |
| 6 | 24 | 018 | SD | CHK Instruction |
| 7 | 28 | 01C | SD | TRAPV Instruction |
| 8 | 32 | 020 | SD | Privilege Violation |
| 9 | 36 | 024 | SD | Trace |
| 10 | 40 | 028 | SD | Line 1010 Emulator |
| 11 | 44 | 02C | SD | Line 1111 Emulator |
| 12[1] | 48 | 030 | SD | (Unassigned, Reserved) |
| 13[1] | 52 | 034 | SD | (Unassigned, Reserved) |
| 14 | 56 | 038 | SD | Format Error[5] |
| 15 | 60 | 03C | SD | Uninitialized Interrupt Vector |
| 16–23[1] | 64 | 040 | SD | (Unassigned, Reserved) |
| | 95 | 05F | | — |
| 24 | 96 | 060 | SD | Spurious Interrupt[3] |
| 25 | 100 | 064 | SD | Level 1 Interrupt Autovector |
| 26 | 104 | 068 | SD | Level 2 Interrupt Autovector |
| 27 | 108 | 06C | SD | Level 3 Interrupt Autovector |
| 28 | 112 | 070 | SD | Level 4 Interrupt Autovector |
| 29 | 116 | 074 | SD | Level 5 Interrupt Autovector |
| 30 | 120 | 078 | SD | Level 6 Interrupt Autovector |
| 31 | 124 | 07C | SD | Level 7 Interrupt Autovector |
| 32–47 | 128 | 080 | SD | TRAP Instruction Vectors[4] |
| | 191 | OBF | | |
| 48–63[1] | 192 | 0C0 | SD | (Unassigned, Reserved) |
| | 255 | 0FF | | — |
| 64–255 | 256 | 100 | SD | User Interrupt Vectors |
| | 1023 | 3FF | | — |

NOTES:
1. Vector numbers 12, 13, 16 through 23, and 48 through 63 are reserved for future enhancements by Motorola. No user peripheral devices should be assigned these numbers
2. Reset vector (0) requires four words, unlike the other vectors which only require two words, and is located in the supervisor program space
3. The spurious interrupt vector is taken when there is a bust error indication during interrupt processing
4. TRAP in uses vector number 32 + n
5. MC68010 only. See Return from Exception Section.
   This vector is unassigned reserved on the MC68000 and MC68008

Fig. 5.8   MC68000 exception vectors (© Motorola).

| Address (hex.) | Function | Mode | Return Mechanism | |
|---|---|---|---|---|
| 00 | Reset | 11 (SVC) | (n/a) | |
| 04 | Undefined instruction | 11 (SVC) | MOVS PC,R14 | ;SVC's R14 |
| 08 | Software interrupt (SWI) | 11 (SVC) | MOVS PC,R14 | ;SVC's R14 |
| 0C | Prefetch abort | 11 (SVC) | SUBS PC,R14,4 | ;SVC's R14 |
| 10 | Data abort | 11 (SVC) | SUBS PC,R14,8 | ;SVC's R14 |
| 14 | Address exception | 11 (SVC) | SUBS PC,R14,4 | ;SVC's R14 |
| 18 | IRQ interrupt | 10 (IRQ) | SUBS PC,R14,4 | ;IRQ's R14 |
| 1C | FIQ interrupt | 01 (FIQ) | SUBS PC,R14,4 | ;FIQ's R14 |

Fig. 5.9   ARM exception vectors.

device which interrupted can then output its interrupt vector on the data bus, implying additional logic within the device to accomplish this task.

An indirect vector-by-device mechanism is available on the MC68000. In this case, on receipt of an interrupt acknowledge from the MC68000 CPU, the interrupting device supplies a vector number which is multiplied by four (shifted two places left) and then used as an offset into the table of MC68000 *user interrupt vectors* which starts at address 100 hex. (see Fig. 5.8). After saving the program counter and status register, the vector pointed to by the interrupting device is then loaded into the program counter as the start address of the interrupt service subroutine.

*The MC68000 autovector mechanism is intended primarily for interfacing MC6800 family 8-bit peripheral chips, which are not capable of supplying a vector number: most MC68000 family devices include logic to supply a vector number on receipt of the interrupt acknowledge signal.*

Estimate the minimum time required for the MC68HC11 microprocessor to respond to an interrupt request (assume a 1 MHz clock).

**Exercise 5.3**

*Other vectors*

As is obvious from Figs 5.7–5.9, the vectoring mechanism is used for a wide range of purposes in addition to the interrupt mechanism described above. These different uses increase the flexibility of the device, and the applications which it can address. For example, the extensive range of exception vectors provided on the MC68000 are intended to support application of this processor to multi-tasking and multi-user operating systems such as Unix, which are beyond the capabilities of simple devices such as the MC68HC11. Some of the simpler additional facilities which make use of vectoring are described below:

*The MC68000 family of microprocessors have been used extensively in engineering workstations, most of which use the Unix operating system.*

(a) *Reset*: When power to a computer is first switched on, all CPU registers, and in particular the program counter, will contain arbitrary values. Thus a mechanism is required to initialise the program counter so that program execution begins at the first program instruction. One method is simply to clear the program counter and to ensure that all programs start at address 0. A more flexible mechanism is to allow program execution to start at any address by providing a *reset vector* which is loaded into the program counter on receipt of a transition on the reset line of the CPU. This mechanism is exactly comparable to the interrupt request except that it is initiated by the reset input to the microprocessor rather than by the interrupt request input. In the MC68HC11, the reset vector is stored in addresses FFFE hex. and FFFF hex. In the MC68000, both the system stack pointer and program counter are loaded on reset: the stack pointer initial value is stored in addresses 0–3, and the program start address in

*This mechanism is used on the ARM.*

addresses 4–7. These addresses must be implemented in non-volatile memory since they cannot be initialised as part of the program! No registers are saved when a reset is executed, since the registers will contain arbitrary values when power is first applied to the system. Any other interrupt request inputs are automatically inhibited by a reset in case the interrupt vector(s) must be set up during the initialisation routines in the program.

(b) *Non-maskable interrupt* (XIRQ on the MC68HC11; level 7 interrupt on the MC68000): This operates in exactly the same way as the normal interrupt request input, but (once enabled) cannot be inhibited.

(c) *Software interrupts* (MC68HC11) and *traps* (MC68000): These terms are both used to describe a single-word program instruction which is equivalent to a subroutine call. By using the vector mechanism, no call address need be specified in the instruction itself. In the MC68HC11, the SWI instruction causes all registers to be stacked, as well as vectoring to a special service routine. In the ARM and MC68000, execution of the SWI or TRAP instruction causes the processor to switch to the supervisor mode, and thus provides an orderly mechanism by which user programs can access the supervisor mode and the privileged operating system resources which are normally only accessible in this mode.

A common use for these instructions is to implement a mechanism for user programs to access hardware resources in a computer system, for example input/output devices such as terminals, printers and disks.

*Interrupt prioritisation*

Where more than one source of interrupts can occur, some kind of *interrupt priority* must be assigned to define the relative importance of the interrupt sources. The MC68HC11 implicitly assigns highest priority to the highest interrupt vector address. Hence a reset occurring during an interrupt service routine would cause the MC68HC11 to be reset, but an interrupt request would be ignored during the non-maskable interrupt routine.

The MC68000 has roughly the same prioritisation of exceptions as the MC68HC11; reset has the highest priority followed by external interrupts, with the traps instruction having lowest priority. Where multiple external interrupts occur, level 7 interrupts have highest priority and level 1 lowest. The interrupt acknowledge mechanism also makes it possible for external hardware to define the relative priorities of multiple interrupt sources. This is commonly done by a technique known as *daisy-chaining*, where interrupt requests are relayed from one device to another in a chain and the interrupt acknowledge is relayed back in the opposite direction as shown in Fig. 5.10. The nearest device to the CPU then has highest priority, and can inhibit interrupts occurring from any lower-priority device simply by not passing incoming interrupt requests on to the CPU. Similarly, any device further down the chain can inhibit devices with lower priority, but not those with higher priority.

Note the disadvantage of this technique: it may take several instructions before the interrupting device is identified, thus increasing the response time before the interrupt is serviced.

Finally, if several devices are all logically ORed to the same processor interrupt input, and thus all cause vectoring to the same interrupt service routine start address, prioritisation can be accomplished by software: the interrupt service routine simply tests each possible interrupting device in sequence, starting from the highest priority device, until it discovers the source of the interrupt. This technique is known as *interrupt polling*.

As is illustrated by the three example processors, the general principles of

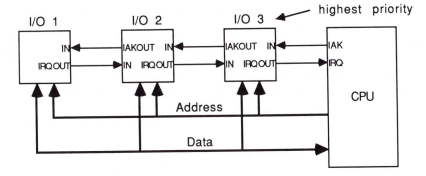

Fig. 5.10 Hardware prioritization of interrupts using a daisy-chain.

interrupt transfer are common to all computers, but the details of status retention and interrupt vectoring differ significantly from one processor to another. The reader is referred to the references at the start of the chapter, and also to manufacturers' documentation, for more specific details.

### Autonomous transfer (direct memory access)

In the vast majority of applications, test and transfer or interrupt transfer provide a satisfactory means of communication between the computer and the outside world. Where the fastest data transfer rates are required, however, data must be transferred direct between the peripheral device and memory, so that the overhead associated with fetching and executing a loop of instructions for each data word transferred is avoided.

In autonomous transfer, therefore, the computer buses are used to transfer data between the peripheral and memory, but the transfer is controlled by a special-purpose input/output controller known as a direct memory access (DMA) controller. The DMA controller replaces the CPU as the device which controls data transfers between the computer and its interfaces, and while a data transfer is taking place, the CPU is tristated so that the DMA controller can control the computer buses instead.

Fig. 5.11 shows the general structure of a DMA controller, and indicates how it

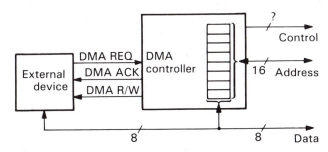

Fig. 5.11 Direct memory access controller.

is interfaced to the external device and the computer's data, address and control buses. The controller contains a number of internal control and status registers which are configured as addresses within the memory space of the computer. These registers can therefore be accessed by normal program instructions which allow the characteristics of the data transfer to be defined. For example, the number of words of data to be transferred, and their source and destination, can all be specified. In addition, these registers specify the mode of data transfer, and the current status of the DMA controller (such as whether it is active or inactive at any given time).

Once initiated, the transfer takes place by periodically stopping normal program execution for one clock cycle so that a word of data can be transferred between the interface device and a memory address specified by the DMA controller. The rate at which transfers can take place is generally limited by the speed of the interface, and if this can operate fast enough, the CPU may be shut down completely until the transfer is complete. Because the data transfer mechanism involves the use of some clock cycles which would otherwise be used to execute program instructions, the mechanism is known as *cycle stealing*.

Direct memory access is commonly required to interface hard disks which may communicate at rates in excess of 1 Mbyte/sec (see Chapter 8).

Since autonomous transfer requires considerable additional hardware compared with the mechanisms previously described, its use is seldom contemplated unless it is unavoidable because a very high data transfer rate is required.

**Example microprocessor input/output devices**

All the common input/output mechanisms used by computers have now been discussed. This section shows how the hardware to implement these techniques is effected in typical microprocessor interface chips. The examples chosen are the MC6821 Peripheral Interface Adaptor (PIA), which is a general-purpose parallel interface, and the MC6850 Asynchronous Communications Interface Adaptor (ACIA), which is a serial interface designed for driving terminals, printers and other common character-orientated computer peripherals. Both devices are part of the Motorola MC6800 family of components and therefore interface directly to the bus structure of the MC68HC11 microprocessor. They can also be easily connected to the MC68000 microprocessor, which includes a number of control lines designed specifically to interface to Motorola 8-bit peripheral chips. Other devices in the same range include counter/timers, DMA controllers, combination chips (containing both serial and parallel interfaces, for example) and more specialised devices which interface to raster-scan video displays, floppy disk drives, and other computer peripherals. A similar range of devices is produced by Acorn to support the ARM microprocessor.

For an example application of the MC6850, see Chapter 8.

For details refer to the Motorola 8 bit microprocessor and peripheral data handbook.

*Example 1 — MC6821 Peripheral Interface Adaptor*

A full description of the MC6821 PIA is given in the Motorola 8-bit microprocessor and peripheral data handbook.

The MC6821 PIA contains the following basic components: two 8-bit parallel data ports; two 8-bit data direction registers; and two 8-bit control/status ports. Fig. 5.12 shows the architecture of the device and Fig. 5.13 shows a programming model of half the PIA. (The complete device is essentially two duplicate parallel input/output ports together with their appropriate control logic.)

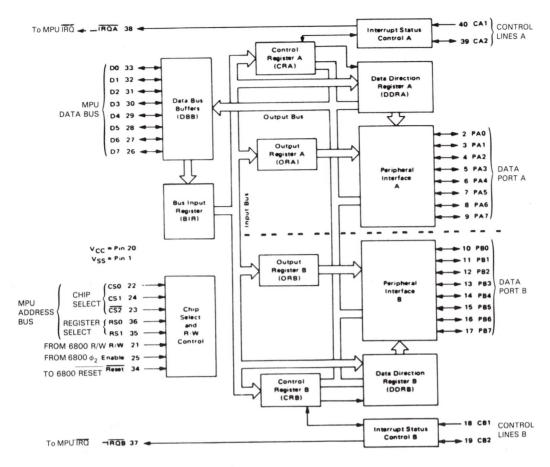

Fig. 5.12   Architecture of the MC6821 PIA (© Motorola).

*Configuration*

The control/status ports and data direction registers are initialised by the program to configure the PIA to suit the particular application. Each of the 16 bits in the two data ports can be individually defined as an input or output using corresponding bits in the two data direction registers. Referring to Fig. 5.12, RS0 and RS1 connect to A0 and A1, respectively, to select one of the four memory locations which the PIA occupies within the microprocessor address space. Three chip select lines are provided to reduce the amount of external address decoding logic required. (In many applications, no external address decoding will be required, if the technique of minimal address decoding is used.) Although the PIA contains six registers, these only occupy four memory locations because each peripheral interface register occupies the same memory address as its associated data direction register: selection between them is accomplished using bit 2 of the appropriate control register (see Fig. 5.13). The control registers also allow the user to specify how the external status and control lines CA1, CA2, CB1, and CB2 are connected.

For example, see the design example in Chapter 10.

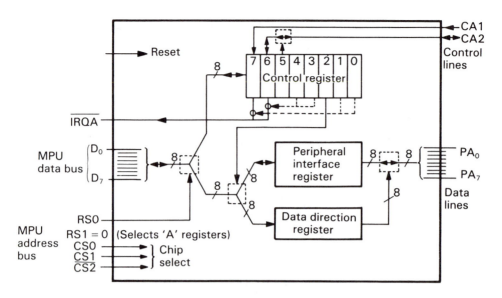

Fig. 5.13   Functional details of half the MC6821 PIA.

Thus:

HARDWARE    RS0  → A0
            RS1  → A1
            CS0  ⎫
            CS1  ⎬  address decoding — address X
            CS2  ⎭

SOFTWARE    Address X = ⎫ Peripheral interface register A
                        ⎭ Data direction register A
               X + 1 =    Control register A
               X + 2 = ⎫ Peripheral interface register B
                        ⎭ Data direction register B
               X + 3 =    Control register B

Select between peripheral interface register and data direction register using bit 2 of appropriate control register:

   0 selects data direction register
   1 selects peripheral interface register

Individual bits in the peripheral interface register are configured as inputs or outputs by appropriate bit coding of corresponding bits in the data direction register:

   0 = input
   1 = output

CONTROL REGISTER must be initialised to determine the action of CA1 and CA2 (CB1 and CB2), and to enable or disable interrupts.

CRA7/CA1 (status input only) function specified by CRA1, CRA0

    CRA1: $0 \rightarrow$ CRA7 set on negative transition of CA1
            $1 \rightarrow$ CRA7 set on positive transition of CA1
    CRA0: $0 \rightarrow$ IRQ output to MC6800 disabled (for test and transfer)
            $1 \rightarrow$ IRQ output to MC6800 enabled (for interrupt transfer)

CRA6/CA2 (status input or strobe output) function specified by CRA5, CRA4, CRA3

    CRA5: $0 \rightarrow$ CA2 = input
            $1 \rightarrow$ CA2 = output

    CRA4, CRA3: if CA2 = input, function as CRA1, CRA0
                    if CA2 = output, specify various output strobe pulses

Once the initial configuration of the PIA has been defined, data transfer can be performed via the device using either test and transfer or interrupt transfer. (If direct transfer were possible a simple 8-bit output latch or tristate input gate would probably be used since no additional control logic would be required.)

## Input of data

(a) Data presented at PA0–PA7, appears at D0–D7
(b) 'Data ready' pulse from peripheral device on CA1 (or CA2) sets flag in control register (CRA7 or CRA6).
(c) Program (i) interrupts, or
           (ii) jumps out of waiting loop which is inspecting CRA7 (CRA6).
(d) Program reads contents of memory address where peripheral interface register is configured. (*NB*: This must occur before the data disappears.)
Optional:
(e) Send pulse on CA2 to peripheral device to indicate that data has been read (handshake).

The handshake mechanism and its use are discussed in Chapter 8.

## Output of data

Either:
(a) Load data into memory address where peripheral interface register is configured.
(b) If required, set bit 3 of control register (CRA3) to give output data ready pulse on CA2; reset CRA3 to complete pulse.
or
(a) The peripheral device can request data by a pulse on the CA1 line. This will cause either (i) an interrupt, or
                        (ii) a jump out of a waiting loop.
(b) Load data into memory address where the peripheral interface register is configured.
(c) Provide handshake on CA2 if necessary.

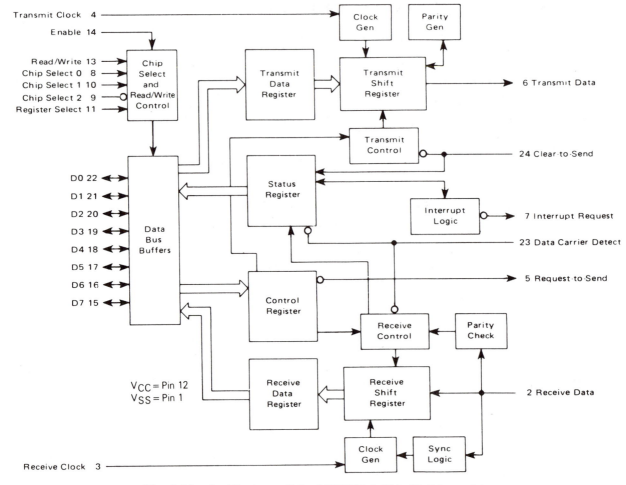

**Fig. 5.14** Architecture of the MC6850 ACIA (© Motorola).

*Example 2 — MC6850 Asynchronous Communications Interface Adaptor*

A full description of the MC6850 ACIA is given in the Motorola 8-bit microprocessor and peripheral data handbook.

The MC6850 ACIA (see Fig. 5.14) contains the following components: an 8-bit write-only serial data transmit register; an 8-bit read-only serial data receive register; an 8-bit write-only control register; an 8-bit read-only status register; and additional logic for clock division, synchronisation, parity generation and detection, etc.

*Configuration*

The MC6850 ACIA is often used to implement the RS232 serial communication protocol: see Chapter 8 for an example.

From the processor's point of view, the ACIA appears as two memory locations within the microprocessor's address space. If the register select line (RS) is high, the data transmit and data receive registers are selected; if RS is low, the control and status registers are selected.

The control register is used to define the characteristics of the data transfer operation: for example, the divide ratio between the external clock inputs and the transmit/receive serial data rate; the data format (number of data bits, parity, number of stop bits); and the interrupt configuration (enabled or disabled for various data transfer events).

The status register contains information on the status of serial data transfers as they proceed: for example, it defines when the transmit data register is empty or the receive data register full; it contains information on any serial transmission errors which may have occurred (such as *framing errors*, *parity errors* or *overrun errors*); it includes an interrupt bit to allow the device to be polled by software where several devices are connected to a single interrupt request input; and it provides a means by which the processor can read external control lines such as *data carrier detect* (DCD) (used when the device is connected to a modem) and *clear to send* (CTS).

For definitions of these terms, see below.

CTS is one of the handshake lines in the RS232 protocol (see example in Chapter 8).

Thus:

HARDWARE   RS   → A0
           CS0 ⎫
           CS1 ⎬   address decoding — address Y
           CS2 ⎭

SOFTWARE   Address Y   ⎫ (input)Status register
                       ⎬ (output)Control register
           Address Y + 1 ⎫ (input)Receive data register
                         ⎬ (output)Transmit data register

CONTROL REGISTER must initially be used to reset the ACIA (there is no separate reset input), and subsequently to define the serial data transfer rate and data format, and to enable interrupts, if appropriate, before data transfers begin.

CR1/CR0 reset the device (code 11) and select the divide ratios between the external receive and transmit clocks and the respective receive and transmit data rates.

00 → divide by 1
01 → divide by 16
10 → divide by 64

CR4/CR3/CR2 define the serial data format:

See the example in Chapter 8.

CR4: 0 → 7 data bits
     1 → 8 data bits
CR3: 0 → 2 stop bits
     1 → 1 stop bit
CR2: 0 → even parity
     1 → odd parity

The exceptions to this coding are codes 100 and 101 which specify two and one stop bit, respectively, but with no parity in either case.

CR6/CR5 define whether the ACIA IRQ output to the processor is enabled for data output, and provide control over the request to send (RTS) output. The most important codes are:

RTS is the other line used for handshaking in the RS232 protocol.

89

00 → interrupt disabled for data output
01 → interrupt enabled for data output
10 → RTS line goes high (low for 00 or 01)

CR7 defines whether the ACIA IRQ output to the processor is enabled for data input:

0 → interrupt disabled for data input
1 → interrupt enabled for data input

STATUS REGISTER defines the status of data transmission and reception. This includes status bits for test and transfer operations, a handshake input bit, an interrupt input bit, and various error flags.

ST0 is the *receive data register full* (RDRF) flag, and is set when received data are transferred from the receive shift register to the receive data register. It is reset when the processor reads the data register (or when the ACIA is reset).

ST1 is the *transmit data register empty* (TDRE) flag, and indicates that the data in the transmit data register has been transferred to the transmit shift register, and that new data may be loaded into the transmit data register.

ST2 is the *data carrier detect* (DCD) flag and is only of interest if the ACIA is being used to transfer data down a telephone line via a modem.

ST3 is the *clear to send* (CTS) bit, and provides a handshake input to the modem. The external device can use this line to indicate whether it is ready to receive data from the ACIA (if the CTS input is 0) or not (if the CTS input is 1).

ST4, ST5 and ST6 are used to indicate various kinds of serial data transfer error.
ST4 indicates if a *framing error* (FE) occurs. This happens if a received character is improperly framed by its start and stop bits, as defined by control register bits CR4, CR3 and CR2. Such an error might occur if the ACIA data receive rate was different from the transmit rate of the device to which it was connected, or if the ACIA was expecting a different data format (in terms of number of data or stop bits).
ST5 indicates if a *receiver overrun* error (OVRN) occurs. This happens if a received character is not read from the receive data register before it is over-written by the next received character. In this case, characters are obviously lost.
ST6 indicates if a *parity* error (PE) occurs, as discussed in Chapter 2. Even, odd or no parity can be selected: the ACIA includes logic to test the parity of incoming data, and to generate a parity bit for outgoing data.
ST7 is the *interrupt request* (IRQ) bit, and is simply a copy of the IRQ output to the processor. It is provided to enable interrupts to be polled, in the case of more than one possible interrupt source.

As for the PIA, once the ACIA has been initialised, data transfers can be carried out using either the test and transfer techniques, or using interrupt transfer.

*Input of data*

(a) Data presented serially in the specified format at the receive data input are shifted in at the specified clock rate and transferred into the receive data register.

(b) This causes the *receive data register full* (RDRF) flag to be set.

(c) Program (i) interrupts, or
   (ii) jumps out of the waiting loop which is inspecting RDRF.

(d) Program reads contents of memory address where receive data register is configured (*NB*: this must happen before the next character of data is received or an overrun error will occur), and repeats loop from step (a) if necessary.

*Output of data*

(a) Load data into memory address where transmit data register is configured.

(b) When character has been shifted out and ACIA is ready for next character, *transmit data register empty* (TDRE) bit will be set.

(c) Program (i) interrupts, or
   (ii) jumps out of the waiting loop which is inspecting TDRE, and repeats loop from step (a) if necessary.

In fact, TDRE will be set as soon as the character can be transferred to the shift register: this is known as *double buffering*.

**Summary**

The external interface to a computer provides its means of communication with the outside world. The interface hardware consists of input buffers and output registers configured to appear either as memory locations or as addresses in a separate input/output address space. In general, a status and control interface is needed in addition to the data interface to ensure that transfers only occur when valid data are available.

Four methods, direct transfer, test and transfer, interrupt transfer and direct memory access (DMA), are used to implement data input and output. The first three methods use programmed instructions to perform data transfers and the data rate is therefore limited by the data transfer program loop execution time. DMA makes use of the computer buses to perform the data transfer direct between the peripheral device and memory, but the transfer is controlled by a dedicated DMA controller. This allows very rapid data transfers but substantially increases the complexity of the interface.

When DMA is not required, direct transfer is used if data are continuously valid. Otherwise, test and transfer can be used unless the execution time wasted testing the status input would be unacceptable.

**Problems**

5.1 Write a program for the MC68HC11 (or ARM or MC68000) microprocessor to read eight latching push-button switches and copy them to eight LEDs. What assumptions does your program make?

5.2 Estimate the maximum time required to respond to a change in the input status signal for the program developed in Exercise 5.2. What clock rate are you assuming?

5.3 A printer with an 8-bit parallel data interface is to be connected to an MC68HC11 microprocessor system using an MC6821 PIA. The printer also provides a status signal which is a logic 1 when the printer is busy and a logic 0 when it is ready to receive data. All printer connections are TTL-compatible. The PIA is configured at a base address of 8000 hex. Write a program to initialise the PIA for test and transfer data output to the printer.

5.4 Write a subroutine to transfer a byte of data stored in accumulator A to the printer described in Problem 5.3.

5.5 For the system described in Problem 5.3, explain how the initialisation program would be modified if data output were to be initiated by an interrupt request caused by the *printer ready* signal. If two similar printers were both controlled by a single MC68HC11 and MC6821 using interrupt transfer, how would the interrupt lines be connected to the microprocessor, and how could the processor distinguish the source of an interrupt?

5.6 Design the hardware of a real-time clock which interrupts an MC68HC11-based microcomputer system at intervals of 0.1 second and show how it would be connected to the computer (use standard 74 series TTL components). The clock should be derived from the MC68HC11 1 MHz clock.

5.7 The real-time clock of Problem 5.6 is required not only to interrupt the computer at intervals of 0.1 second, but also to provide a 6-BCD digit input to the computer specifying the time in tens of hours, hours, tens of minutes, minutes, tens of seconds, and seconds. Show how the clock could be connected so that the interrupt service routine can read the time every time an interrupt occurs.

(NB. Problems 5.1–5.7 could all be implemented using the MC68HC11 on-chip input/output facilities. Refer to the MC68HC11 HCMOS single-chip microcontroller manual for all details of its input/output capabilities.)

# Programming computers and microprocessors  6

---

☐ To introduce the concept of programming computers in machine code, and explain the limitations which make machine code programming impractical.
☐ To explain how a mnemonic assembly language may be used to write computer programs.
☐ To explain how programs written in assembly language are converted into executable machine code programs using an *assembler* program.
☐ To introduce *assembler directives* as a method for specifying additional information to the assembler about the program which is being assembled.
☐ To examine the limitations of assembly language as a computer programming medium and consider the advantages and disadvantages of programming in high-level languages.

**Objectives**

---

The stage has now been reached where the basic structure of a computer and the format of the computer's instructions should be understood. Each instruction is represented within the computer as one or more computer words coded by means of a string of binary digits. The instruction sets of three typical microprocessors have been examined, and some example instructions illustrated. The next requirement is to consider the techniques which are used to build up complete programs using these instructions.

Computers may be programmed using a variety of programming *languages*. At one end of the scale, the binary coded machine instructions are a programming language which the computer can understand and execute directly; human beings find it very difficult to program directly in machine code, however, and consequently prefer to write programs in languages which mean more to the programmer. In practice this means programming languages which are closer to the English language. Although it is not possible to program computers directly in English, some programming languages are sufficiently problem-orientated that the programmer need know nothing about the detailed structure of the computer at all. Other languages reflect the architecture of the computer much more closely. These are known as *machine-orientated* languages. Each type of language has advantages and disadvantages, and one objective of this chapter is to compare and contrast the different types of programming language.

Unless the computer program is written directly in binary machine code it is necessary to convert it from the *source code* format (generally a string of ASCII characters representing each line of text in the program) into machine code which can be loaded into the computer memory and then executed. In principle, this conversion could be done by hand, but in practice it is always done using a computer program written specifically to convert the source program to its executable machine code equivalent. The conversion program forms part of the computer

The electronic components making up the computer are commonly known as the computer *hardware*, while the programs written to run on the computer are known as computer *software*. The term *firmware* is also sometimes used to describe a program stored in a programmable read-only memory (PROM).

A useful general reference for this chapter and introduction to high-level programming languages is:
Attikiouzel, J. *Pascal for Electronic Engineers* (Van Nostrand Reinhold, 1984).

These languages are called *high-level languages*. Commonly used examples include BASIC, PASCAL and FORTRAN.

*Assembly language* is the principal machine-orientated language. Since each different type of computer has a different architecture, however, they also have different assembly languages.

*system software*, which is described in more detail in Chapter 9. Regardless of the original programming language used, the conversion program must generate as its output a binary machine code program for the specific type of computer on which the program is intended to run. Often this machine code program is stored on a backing storage medium such as a floppy disk so that it can subsequently be loaded into the computer memory when required and executed. Alternatively, the machine code program could be copied into a PROM so that it can reside permanently in memory, ready to be executed at any time. In this case, no backing storage medium is required, since the PROM provides permanent storage.

In order to execute a program, the machine code program must be stored as a sequence of binary words in the computer memory. The addresses at which the program resides can be chosen at the programmer's convenience, but may be constrained by the particular architecture and configuration of the computer. Similarly, data variables and constants used in the program can reside anywhere in memory that is convenient. To begin execution of the program, the program counter must be preset with the address of the first instruction in the program. The computer then sequentially obeys consecutive instructions of the program unless the instruction specifies otherwise (for example, halt, jump or branch instructions). In a dedicated computer system the same program may continue to be executed indefinitely until power is removed from the system. Alternatively, several different programs may concurrently reside in different parts of the computer memory. Any of these programs may be executed simply by jumping to the execution start address of the program from the program currently being executed.

The program can be stored in PROM or RAM, but data variables must reside in RAM.

General-purpose computers nearly always have two or more programs resident in different parts of memory simultaneously. One example of this is given later in this chapter, and the issue is considered in more detail in Chapter 9.

### Machine code programming

Machine code is the native binary code used to represent the instruction set of the computer. The machine code instruction set is defined by the designer of the computer and constrained by the architecture chosen. Thus exact details of the instructions developed for each different type of computer differ although the general features of all computer instruction sets (e.g. addressing modes, arithmetic and logic operations, CPU registers) are conceptually similar. As a result, machine code programs cannot normally be transferred between one type of computer and another.

For example a program written in MC68000 machine code could not be executed on an ARM microprocessor.

To avoid confusion, the remainder of this chapter is based around examples using the MC68HC11 microprocessor only: equivalent examples based upon the ARM and MC68000 microprocessors are given in Appendix F.

Since machine code instructions are the actual binary code which is stored in the memory of the computer, a machine code program can be loaded into the computer's memory and executed directly. Machine code is the only language for which this is possible, and as a result machine code programming has some attractions as a method of initially learning how a computer works. Once the basic operations of the computer have been mastered, however, and larger programs are attempted, machine code becomes increasingly tedious.

Machine code programs are normally loaded into the computer memory using a simple *monitor* program (see Chapter 8).

Machine code programs are normally written using either hexadecimal or octal format notation. This simplifies conversion to the final binary format, while at the same time being much easier for the human programmer to deal with than a long string of binary digits. CISC computers generally use variable-length instructions, the length of the instruction depending upon the addressing mode used and the type of instruction. Hence each binary code stored in memory could potentially represent an instruction operation code, an instruction operand, an operand address, or even a data variable which is accessed by the program. Thus a programmer confronted with a sequence of binary codes stored in a computer memory cannot easily determine what the original program was. If it is desired to *disassemble* a program, this can normally only be achieved by knowing the execution start address of the program and sequentially decoding each instruction to determine the original program.

*Disassembler* programs can sometimes be obtained to perform this task automatically. However, the assembly language program so produced will not be commented, and thus will still be very cryptic.

### Example MC68HC11 machine code program

It is desired to write a very simple computer program to control a set of eight lights according to the setting of eight SPST (Single Pole Single Throw) switches. The eight switches are configured to appear as a single memory location within the address space of the MC6809 (at address 7004 hex.), while the eight lights occupy memory location 7000 hex. Thus the switches appear as a read-only memory word, while the lights are a write-only memory word.

The choice of addresses of the input and output ports is arbitrary, but some guidelines which can be used to minimise the address decoding logic required are given in Chapter 10.

The algorithm for implementing this program might be written down as:

(a) Load the contents of the switch memory location into an accumulator.
(b) Store the accumulator in the memory location corresponding to the lights.
(c) Repeat the complete operation indefinitely.

This example is almost trivially simple, and could be coded directly, but in general it is necessary to write down an *algorithm* which expresses the proposed solution to the problem before attempting to code the solution.

The program might then be coded as follows:

```
                                        Hex. machine
     Coding            Register transfers  code
Load switches to Acc.A ($7004) → A    B6  70  04 ⎫ operand
Store Acc.A in lights    (A) → ($7000) B7  70  00 ⎭ addresses
Branch back to start                   20  F8 ←——— 2s complement
                        Hexadecimal    ↑           program
                                operation codes  counter offset
```

Thus the program would be stored in memory in the following binary format (the hexadecimal equivalent of each binary word is also shown for comparison):

| Binary | Hexadecimal |
|---|---|
| 1011 0110 | B6 |
| 0111 0000 | 70 |
| 0000 0100 | 04 |
| 1011 0111 | B7 |
| 0111 0000 | 70 |
| 0000 0000 | 00 |
| 0010 0000 | 20 |
| 1111 1000 | F8 |

Even though the example is trivial a number of important points are illustrated. First, it is quite difficult to determine what the function of the program is simply by looking at the binary or hexadecimal codes. Furthermore, even if the codes are disassembled to reveal what the original instructions were, the purpose of the program is still unclear unless it is also known that address 7004 hex. corresponds to a set of switches, and address 7000 hex. to a set of lights. Second, the programmer is required to do some rather tedious — and indeed error-prone — 2s complement arithmetic to determine the correct offset which should be added to the program counter so that the branch instruction correctly transfers program control back to the first instruction in the sequence. A final interesting point is that this program is inherently *position-independent*, that is, the program executes correctly wherever it is stored in memory. By contrast, the equivalent program implemented using the MC68HC11 jump instruction would require an absolute jump address to be specified, and hence would only execute correctly if the program were loaded with the first instruction corresponding to this address.

It is possible to write quite long and complex programs in machine code; the problems which are evident even in a small program such as the example above become much more pronounced in larger machine code programs, however. Essentially these problems all boil down to the fact that a machine code program contains no *documentation* which helps to explain the purpose of the program. There are no mnemonics or other ways of memorising the instructions in the program, and all program addresses must be calculated explicitly by the programmer. Hence machine code programming is long-winded and error-prone, and is impractical except as a vehicle for learning how a computer works. For realistic programming tasks, a *programming language* which is meaningful to the programmer, but can be easily converted to machine code, is required.

**Exercise 6.1** Write an MC68HC11 (or ARM or MC68000) machine code program to shift a single logic-1 bit from l.s.b. to m.s.b. of the lights at address 7000 hex. with a delay of 0.1 seconds between each shift. The program should cause the cycle to repeat indefinitely by transferring the single bit from m.s.b. to l.s.b. when the m.s.b. is reached.

**Assembly language programming**

Assembly language is a symbolic language in which mnemonic codes are used to represent the machine code instructions available in the computer's instruction set. Thus there is a one-to-one correspondence between the mnemonic instruction codes and the actual machine codes. So that the programmer does not have to calculate addresses and allocate memory by hand, *labels* are used to represent addresses in assembly language programming. When the program is converted to its final machine code equivalent, the labels are replaced by appropriate addresses. The features of assembly language programming are best illustrated by considering a simple example program written in MC68HC11 assembly language.

*Example MC68HC11 assembly language program*

First of all, a *program specification* is required. In this case, the program to be written is a modification to the machine code program described earlier. The program must read the setting of the eight SPST switches and output this setting to the eight lamps with a delay of five seconds.

An algorithm which implements the program specification must now be produced. This algorithm may be written using a high-level computer language (see below), or a flow chart may be used. Note that an immediate problem arises in

---

The ability to write programs using position-independent code has significant advantages, particularly for large, modular computer programs. As a result, more recent microprocessor designs such as the ARM and MC68000 contain a wide range of relative addressing modes to support position independence (see Chapter 7).

The importance of good program documentation is emphasised throughout this chapter, and cannot be too strongly stressed.

A *label* is simply a mnemonic character string defined by the programmer which is used to represent an address in a program. Thus the assembly language code BRA START might be used to indicate a branch to the instruction tagged with the label START. (See example below.)

The vagueness of this program specification illustrates a common problem in computer programming.

If flow charts are used, some care is needed to retain a good program structure (see Chapter 10).

interpreting this specification. One possible interpretation of the specification would be the following algorithm (left-hand side):

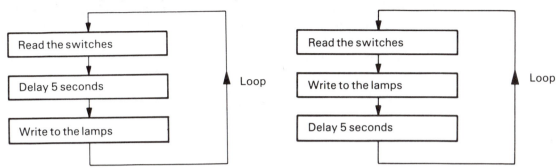

but this algorithm produces a variable delay between five and ten seconds because the switch setting is normally changed during the five-second delay loop, and a delay of up to five seconds subsequently occurs before the switches are sampled again.

An alternative algorithm which might be considered is shown on the right, but again this produces a variable delay, this time of up to five seconds. That even quite a simple specification can be interpreted in a number of different ways serves to highlight the importance of producing an accurate and complete specification for any programming task before attempting to implement a solution. Very often, the definition of the specification can prove to be a significant part of the total project; conversely, many projects fail to achieve the required objective due simply to a failure to specify the project requirements accurately.

In this case, neither of the algorithms described so far implements the function originally intended in the specification. The following algorithm (written in *pseudo-PASCAL*) implements a program which compares the switch setting with the switch value previously stored as a variable in the computer memory, and when a change is detected, inserts a delay of five seconds and then updates the lamp display.

```
Program Displayswitches (switches, lamps);
var switchstored: integer;
begin
    repeat forever
        while switches = switchstored do        read switches and compare
        begin                                   with stored value.
            read (switches)
        end;
        for i: = 1 to 50 do
        begin
            for i: = 1 to ? do                  nested delay loop to give a
            begin                               5 second dclay. (The
            end;                                question mark indicates a
        end;                                    value which is defined by
        switchstored: = switches;               the time taken to execute
        write (lamps)                           a loop of the delay loop
end.                                            routine.)
```

Pseudo-PASCAL is a non-rigorous representation of the language PASCAL which retains its control structures, and may be used for expressing an algorithm which subsequently is programmed in another language.

The technique of writing program algorithms in a structured high-level language such as Pascal is highly recommended even when the program is subsequently coded in assembly language. It helps to ensure that the program is well structured and hence readable and modifiable. If the algorithm is complex, it should be simulated and proved in a high-level language in any case before coding in assembly language.

Note that even this algorithm does not fully implement the specification; consider, for example, what happens when a second change in the switch settings occurs within five seconds of the first change. Full implementation of the specification requires quite a complex program.

If the coding process is not a straightforward conversion from pseudo-PASCAL or flow chart, the algorithm should be further refined before coding is attempted.

The $ prefix is used by Motorola to indicate a hexadecimal number. Address $100 provides temporary storage for the variable *switchstored*.
Note the use of a label to indicate symbolically the branch address.
The # prefix is used by Motorola to indicate the immediate addressing mode. A number not prefixed by a $ symbol is a decimal number.
The inner delay loop takes a total of 6 μs to execute; thus executing it 16 666 times produces a total delay of 0.1 s. The outer loop is executed 50 times, giving a total delay of 5 s.
Note how the loop testing instructions appear at the end of the loop in assembly language, but at the beginning in many high-level languages. This is one factor which reduces the readability of assembly language.

Note that the algorithm is now significantly more complex because of the need to detect a *change* in the value of the switches.

The algorithm can be coded using MC6809 assembly language instructions. The task of coding is quite straightforward because the required algorithm has already been developed in pseudo-Pascal, thus it is not (and should never be) necessary to develop the algorithm at the same time as the assembly language code is written down. The required assembly language code is:

| Label | Opcode | Operand/Operand Address | |
|-------|--------|------------------------|---|
| START | LDAA | $7004 | |
| | CMPA | $100 | |
| | BEQ | START | |
| | LDAB | #50 | |
| LOOP1 | LDX | #16666 | |
| LOOP2 | DEX | | (3 cycles) |
| | BNE | LOOP2 | (3 cycles) |
| | DECB | | |
| | BNE | LOOP1 | |
| | STA | $100 | |
| | STA | 7000 | |
| | BRA | START | |

**The assembler program**

The assembly language program above could be converted into the equivalent machine code instructions by hand, but this task is essentially a mechanical process, and as such can most easily be accomplished by using a computer program known as an *assembler*. The assembler takes as its input an assembly language program which has previously been typed into the computer using some type of *text editor* (see Chapter 9) and produces as its output the equivalent machine code program. In addition, an *assembler listing* is normally produced which correlates the original assembly language program with the machine code produced by the assembler. This assembler listing is essential for debugging algorithm errors in the assembly language program.

A *text editor* is a program which enables a user to input and manipulate text files within a computer via a VDU terminal. The text files are stored and coded within the computer as ASCII characters.

The assembler program reads each line of source assembly language code as a string of ASCII characters terminated by a carriage return. It then allocates memory for the equivalent machine code by looking up each mnemonic instruction in a table which indicates both the required opcode and the number of operand or operand address words (if any) which must follow the opcode. The example in the margin shows how this process would take place for the assembly language program described above. In some cases it may be necessary for the assembler to examine the operand field of the source text line in addition to the opcode field in order to determine how many words should be allocated for the complete instruction. As an example, the addressing mode of a memory reference instruction in MC68HC11 assembly language is indicated in the operand field (the same instruction mnemonic is used for all instructions of the same basic type), and hence this field must be examined before either the exact opcode or the number of operand bytes can be determined.

The operand field may contain some type of arithmetic expression requiring evaluation by the assembler in order to determine the actual operand or operand address. One example would be the conversion between base 10, base 16, base 8 and base 2 required to convert an address or immediate operand to the format required in the actual machine code. Most assemblers also allow rather more complex arithmetic constructs within the operand field of the instruction.

Another important requirement of the assembler is the ability to evaluate symbolic labels into the intended address references. If the label refers backwards to an instruction which has already been allocated an address, then this presents no problems, but if the reference is forward to an instruction or data variable which has not yet been assembled, then it is not possible to fill in the correct address in the space allocated for that address after its opcode. For this reason, assemblers normally require two passes through the source file to generate the final machine code program. The first pass sets up a symbol table containing all the label references in the program, while the second pass allocates memory, fills in unresolved references and generates the assembler listing.

An obvious problem with any assembly language (or indeed high-level language) program is that *syntax errors* may occur in the program. These errors may be caused by the programmer incorrectly formatting the source program, or by attempts to use incorrect mnemonics or invalid addressing modes, or even by simple typing errors. Whatever the reason, the source program will contain statements which cannot be meaningfully assembled. Thus, another task of the assembler program must be to check and verify that the source program is syntactically correct, and this task must precede any attempt to produce the machine code program.

A feature of most assembly languages which has not been illustrated in the example above, but is nevertheless a common requirement, is the ability for the programmer to include informative comments in the program without the assembler attempting to interpret these comments as instructions. Comments are often identified by preceding them with a special character such as an asterisk (*) or a semi-colon (;), or simply by assuming that any text which appears after the operand field but before the carriage return in an instruction line is a comment. Though these comments are ignored by the assembler, they are often the most important part of the program from the programmer's point of view, since they provide a mechanism for annotating the program to explain its operation in more detail. This is of particular importance in an assembly language program, because the program algorithm may well be obscured by the detail of the assembly language. Good assembly language programs may contain up to three comment lines for every line of code, and this level of commenting is needed if the program is to

The memory allocation for the program described above would be as below. Note that the program base address could be anywhere in memory, and does not have to be 0000. All numbers are hexadecimal.

| Address | Code | Notes |
|---|---|---|
| 0000 | B6 | Load opcode |
| 0001 | 70 | 16-bit switch |
| 0002 | 04 | address |
| 0003 | B1 | Compare opcode |
| 0004 | 01 | 16-bit |
| 0005 | 00 | variable address |
| 0006 | 27 | Branch opcode |
| 0007 | F8 | 8-bit branch offset |
| 0008 | C6 | Load opcode |
| 0009 | 32 | Immediate operand |
| 000A | CE | Load opcode |
| . | . | . |
| . | . | . |

and so on.

Every programming language has a rigid *syntax* or grammar which defines allowed words, grammatical constructions and source text format.
Note that a program which is syntactically correct may still contain faults in the program algorithm. The syntax check simply verifies that the program contains meaningful instructions; the instructions may not constitute a sensible program, however!

Extra time spent documenting an assembly language program may at first sight seem to be wasted; the student should remember, however, that most programmers are employed to maintain and update programs, rather than to write new programs. Attempting to modify a poorly documented assembly language program can be a salutary experience!

Remember that documentation should include not only comments in the program, but also a written explanation of program operation, and a formal description of the algorithm (written in a high-level language as above).

be readily understood by someone other than the original programmer. An example of the way in which the comment facility of an assembly language can be constructively used is shown in Fig. 6.1, which shows the assembler listing of the program described above.

The output of the assembler program comprises the machine code program and the assembler listing. The assembler listing may be output to a printer directly, or it may be stored on some backing storage medium such as a floppy disk or a tape (see Chapter 8). Similarly, the machine code program may also be stored on a backing storage medium, or alternatively it may be loaded directly into memory. In this case the program could subsequently be executed directly by jumping to the program starting address. Since programs commonly contain faults in their algorithms when first written, however, it is more usual at this stage to enter a debugging phase where program execution can be examined in detail. The characteristics of *monitor* or *debug* programs which are provided to help in this task are discussed in more detail in Chapter 9.

**Exercise 6.2**  It is required to use the MC68HC11 microcomputer containing the eight switches and eight lamps described previously as a reaction timer. Five seconds after starting program execution the timer will illuminate all the lights to indicate the start of the reaction time measurement. The program then counts the time delay between the lights being lit and the user depressing a switch, in units of 10 ms. When the switch is depressed the result should be displayed on the lights in binary (i.e. reaction time between 0.01 and 2.55 seconds). When the switch is released, the whole program should be repeated.

(a) Write down a program algorithm in a suitable high-level language.
(b) Implement the algorithm in MC68HC11 machine code.
(c) Modify the program to insert a random time delay instead of a five-second time delay when the switch is released.

**Assembly language directives**

Fig. 6.1 shows the assembler listing output of a typical assembler for MC68HC11 assembly language. All text to the right of and including the vertical row of semi-colons was typed in as the MC68HC11 assembly language source file. (Each line which starts with a semi-colon is a comment line.) The numbers in the three columns to the left of the text are generated by the assembler. The first column is simply a source program line number. This is followed by a four-digit hexadecimal address specifying the 16-bit memory addresses allocated for each instruction. The third column contains a two-digit hexadecimal opcode and this is followed by a one- or two-byte operand address or operand as appropriate. In the case of branch instructions, the branch address is specified as a 2s complement offset.

It can be observed that the assembler listing contains a number of lines which have the same format as instruction lines, yet the opcodes specified in these lines are not legitimate MC68HC11 instructions. These lines contain program *directives* or *pseudo-opcodes* which provide additional information to the assembler program to enable the program to be correctly assembled. The type of information which may be required is best illustrated by considering some example program directives.

The directives available in an assembly language are defined by the designers of the assembler program.

100

```
 1    ;=====================================================
 2    ;Program to display switch settings on LEDS
 3    ;after a delay of five (5) seconds.
 4    ;=====================================================
 5    ;
 6    ; A.C.Downton
 7    ;
 8    ;-----------------------------------------------------
 9    ;
10    ;Define processor type:
11    ;
12    .PROCESSOR      M68HC11              ;MC68HC11 processor
13    ;
14    ;-----------------------------------------------------
15    ;
16    ;Define constants:
17    ;       Time delay = 1/2 second
18    ;       Switch address = 7004H
19    ;       LEDS address = 7000H
20    ;
21    .DEFINE DELAY    = 16666             ;(16666*6us=0.1 sec.)
22            SWITCH   = 7004H,            ;switch port address
23            LEDS     = 7000H             ;LEDs port address
24    ;
25    ;-----------------------------------------------------
26    ;
27    ;Set program base address
28    ;
29            .ORG     100H                ;data origin
30    ;
31    ;Temporary storage for switch settings
32    ;
33    SWSTRD: .BYTE[1]                     ;allocate 1 byte
34    ;
35    ;*****************************************************
36    ;
37    ;Main program:
38    ;Reads switches and compares with previous stored
39    ;value. If different inserts a 5 second delay and
40    ;then outputs new value to LEDs. Also updates
41    ;previous stored value.
42    ;
43  0101  B67004    START:  LDAA    SWITCH
44  0104  B10100            CMPA    SWSTRD       ;Has setting changed?
45  0107  27F8              BEQ     START        ;Branch if no change
46                  ;
47                  ;5 second time delay
48                  ;
49  0109  C60A              LDAB    #50          ;outer loop, 50*0.1 sec.
50  010B  CEF424    LOOP1:  LDX     #DELAY       ;inner loop, 0.1 sec.
51  010E  09        LOOP2:  DEX                  ;decrement inner loop
52  010F  26FD              BNE     LOOP2        ;branch if <0.1 sec.
53  0111  5A                DECB                 ;decrement outer loop
54  0112  26F7              BNE     LOOP1        ;branch if <5 secs.
55                  ;
56                  ;Output to LEDs and modify stored value
57                  ;
58  0114  B70100            STAA    SWSTRD       ;modify stored value
59  0117  B77000            STAA    LEDS         ;output switches to LEDs
60                  ;
61                  ;Repeat complete loop
62                  ;
63  011A  20E4              BRA     START
64                  ;
65                  ;*****************************************************
66                  ;
67                  ;Define execution start address
68                  ;
69                          .END    START
70
```

This assembler listing was actually produced by an MC68HC11 cross-assembler running on a DEC minicomputer under the Unix operating system (see Chapter 9). Several versions of the cross-assembler are available for different processors including the MC6809, Z80 (see Appendix F), 8085, 6502 and various other 8-bit microprocessors. As such, although it uses standard MC68HC11 mnemonics, the directives differ slightly from those defined by Motorola and described in the text. Table F.1 in Appendix F gives the equivalent directives for standard Motorola MC68HC11/MC68000 assembly language and standard ARM assembly language. Differences from the directives discussed in the text are noted below.

.DEFINE is equivalent to EQU

.ORG is equivalent to ORG

.BYTE[1] is equivalent to RMB 1

.END is equivalent to END

Fig. 6.1   MC68HC11 assembly language program assembler listing.

Although the specific examples given here are taken from the Motorola MC68HC11 assembler, similar features are found in any other assembly language. The exact directive names may vary from one assembly language to another (see Appendix F).

*Example program directives*

(a) *Program origin address*: The program origin address directive allows the programmer to specify the initial address for memory allocation of the program. Thus the program may reside anywhere in memory that is convenient for the programmer and the particular application. If a program origin address is not specified, then the assembler normally defaults to a program origin address such as 0.

*MC68HC11 Example*

|           | ORG | $80 |
|-----------|-----|-----|

sets the program origin address to 80 hex.

(b) *Program end point*: The program end point directive tells the assembler that no more instructions follow, and that the end of the source file has been reached. The END directive can also be coupled with an address label if desired. In this case the label identifies the address at which program execution is to begin when the machine code program is executed. The same label must also appear in front of the relevant instruction. If the END directive appears in the program with no label following it, the assembler assumes that the program start address should be the same as the program origin address. Often this is not the case because data tables or storage for variables may precede the first instruction. The assembler listing shows a typical example of the use of this feature.

*MC68HC11 Example*

|     | END | START |
|-----|-----|-------|

terminates the source file and indicates that program execution should begin at the address labelled START.

(c) *Reservation of storage locations*: Most programs make use of data variables which must be stored at specified addresses in read/write memory. When the assembly language program is assembled, storage for these variables must be allocated by the assembler, even though the data variable memory locations are not coded with any specific values. The MC68HC11 assembler uses the reserve memory byte(s) (RMB) directive to allocate storage locations for data variables. The directive is normally preceded by a label which references the address at which the data variable is stored, and may be followed by a number which indicates the number of bytes of memory to be allocated for the specified variable. The example assembler listing shows how the data variable *switchstored* (SWSTRD) has been allocated a byte of memory immediately before the start of the program. It would be possible to arrange for data variables to be stored in a completely separate area of memory (if, for example, the program were to be stored in ROM and the data variables in RAM) by preceding the RMB directive with an ORG directive specifying the storage address for data variables, and then preceding the program itself by another ORG directive specifying the address of the first program instruction. The program and data variable origins could then be selected according to hardware memory configuration criteria.

Even if the actual addresses chosen for variable storage are unimportant, explicit memory must still be allocated for each variable.

*MC68HC11 Example*

|       | LABEL | RMB | 1 |
|-------|-------|-----|---|

reserves one byte of memory at the address specified by the symbolic label LABEL.

(d) *Specification of program data*: Another common programming requirement is for the programmer to be able to specify data values which can be stored in memory and accessed by the assembly language program. Such data might include ASCII messages to be output to a terminal or printer, tables of data values, or individual data bytes required by a program. The MC68HC11 assembler allows data bytes to be specified using the form constant byte (FCB) directive. Like the RMB directive, FCB is normally preceded by a label which identifies the address of the data byte or table of bytes. The operand field following the FCB directive contains the value(s) to be stored in the data locations. The number of bytes of data is implied by the number of data values specified after the FCB directive. ASCII character strings can be specified using the form constant character (FCC) directive. The character string is specified directly in the operand field, surrounded by suitable delimiters, such as single quotes.

*MC68HC11 Examples*

        MASKS        FCB            $80,$40,$20,$10

specifies four bytes of data containing the values 80, 40, 20 and 10 hex., and stored at symbolic addresses MASKS, MASKS + 1, MASKS + 2 and MASKS + 3 respectively.

        MSG1        FCC            'Hello World'

specifies a string of 11 bytes containing the ASCII characters corresponding to the text 'Hello World'. The first character (H) is stored at symbolic address MSG1 and subsequent characters are stored in sequential addresses after this.

(e) *Equate symbol to value*: The equates directive (EQU) is simply used to equate a label appearing in the address field of the directive with the value specified in the operand field. The directive does not cause any memory to be allocated nor does it directly specify the contents of any memory location, as can be seen by reference to the example program listing. The EQU directive has two purposes; first, it enables physical data values and addresses which are in themselves not very memorable to be equated to mnemonics which are much more easily remembered. Thus, for example, the use of the mnemonic SWITCH to identify the address of the memory location which corresponds to the set of eight physical switches immediately reminds the programmer that this is the physical significance of address 7004 hex. Whenever the label SWITCH subsequently appears in the program, the assembler substitutes the value specified in the EQU directive. Thus, the mechanism provides an *aide-mémoire* feature, and improves the readability of the program. A second advantage of the EQU directive is that it can very much simplify retrospective changes in an assembly language program. A typical example might occur during the development of a microprocessor application requiring the design of both hardware and software. By using the EQU directive each port assignment can be defined once only at the start of the program. If the port assignment is subsequently altered, only a single change is required to the program, instead of changing every instruction which contains a reference to the modified port address.

*MC68HC11 Examples*

$$\text{SWITCH} \qquad \text{EQU} \qquad \$7004$$

equates the symbolic label SWITCH to the physical address 7004 hex. (which represents the switch input port).

Fig. 6.1 shows how most of the directives described above are used in an actual assembly language program. In addition to the examples given, most assemblers contain many other directives, providing features such as *conditional assembly* and *macros*, which are beyond the scope of this introductory discussion, but are discussed briefly in Chapter 9. Directives are also required to specify cross-references between separately assembled source programs which are to be linked together to produce a final machine code program. This task, and the required directives, are described in detail in Chapter 9.

### High-level languages

Example languages which come under the broad heading of high-level languages are FORTRAN, COBOL, PASCAL and ADA. All these languages are *compiled* (see below) to produce the required machine code program. There are also many other compiled high-level languages, some developed for specific application areas.

Though infinitely preferable to programming in machine code, assembly language programming, even with good diagnostic and debugging software and a user-friendly text editor, is tedious and prone to errors. The fundamental problem is that any computer assembly language is a low-level language strongly based upon the register architecture of the computer being programmed. As a result, individual assembly language instructions execute only a very small part of the programmed task, and the programmer becomes bogged down with detailed hardware and architectural considerations, rather than being able to concentrate upon his program algorithm. For most programming applications, a much better solution is to program in a *high-level language* which is specifically orientated towards the programming problems which need to be solved, rather than towards the architecture of the computer.

To illustrate this point, compare the readability of the pseudo-PASCAL and uncommented assembly language programs earlier in this chapter.

Industry figures show that a typical programmer produces about ten lines of fully debugged and documented code per day. This figure is more or less independent of programming language, hence the programmer working in a high-level language has a very much higher productivity than the assembly language programmer.

High-level languages have a number of advantages over assembly language from the programmer's point of view. It is much easier to achieve good program structure and readability using high-level languages because these languages (particularly the so-called 'structured' languages such as PASCAL and ADA) have been designed with this specific objective in mind. The programmer writes his program using English-like statements rather than mnemonics, and these statements provide a good deal of *self-documentation*. Because the high-level languages are problem-orientated rather than processor-orientated, the typical student can master a high-level language much more rapidly than an assembly language, and in many cases need know nothing about the detailed architecture of the computer in order to write programs. Furthermore, the same high-level language may be used on many different types of computer, so that having mastered a single language the programmer is not restricted to a single type of computer. Perhaps the most important advantage of high-level language programming is the reduced development time required for an application programmed in a high-level language compared with the same application programmed in assembly language. This arises because a single line of high-level language source code implements functions equivalent to many lines of assembly language code, so that a high-level language source program implementing a particular function is very much shorter than the assembly language source program implementing the same function.

Given the advantages of high-level languages, it may seem surprising that assembly language programming is ever even considered. Unfortunately, high-level languages have limitations as well as advantages. One disadvantage is that the machine code generated by a high-level language program is generally less efficient than the machine code generated from an equivalent assembly language program, because the task of conversion from the high-level language source program to machine code is performed mechanically by a *compiler* (see below). As a result, the high-level language version of the program may typically occupy 50–100% more memory than its assembly language equivalent. A related problem is that the larger high-level language machine code program normally executes more slowly than its assembly language equivalent, and this may cause problems in time critical applications. Finally, some types of programming tasks are not suited to some high-level languages, because the language lacks a particular facility required for the specific application. As an example, one might consider the problems of implementing complex logic functions using a language such as FORTRAN, which contains only elementary Boolean functions, compared with the relative simplicity and efficiency of implementing the same functions using assembly language, which contains a wealth of Boolean and bit manipulation instructions.

The languages described above are often described as *applications programming languages* because they are specifically designed to simplify the writing of applications programs for computers. By contrast, a further class of programming languages which may be considered are the so-called *system programming languages*. These languages provide the facilities needed for writing *system software* (Chapter 8), which may be thought of as computer programs which are the tools used in the development of application programs. The assembler program described in the previous section is an example of system software. A particular characteristic of system software is that it must interact closely with the specific hardware of the computer system on which the software runs, such as a VDU terminal, a printer and backing storage media such as floppy disks or tapes. As a result, system programming languages must be capable of directly accessing the hardware of the computer and manipulating it at the bit level, in the same way as is possible with assembly language. In addition, however, system programming languages provide the same sort of high-level program control structures (for example, conditional statements, repetitive execution loops and procedures) as are available in high-level languages. System programming languages thus combine the low-level control capability of an assembly language with the high-level structure of applications languages, and hence are sometimes thought of as high-level assembly languages. Against this, most system programming languages do not provide the full range of facilities expected in an applications programming language. For example, they might include only integer arithmetic facilities rather than floating point arithmetic and a full range of trigonometrical and scientific functions.

Example system programming languages are PL/1 (developed for programming IBM computers), BCPL and C. Several variations of PL/1 have been developed for smaller microprocessor based systems. These include PL/M (for Intel microprocessors), PL/Z (for Zilog microprocessors) and MPL (for Motorola microprocessors).

System programming languages are often a good compromise for the engineer who may need close access to the system hardware.

## High-level language compilers

Like assembly language, high-level languages cannot be directly executed on the computer. Thus a source program written in a high level language must first of all be converted into an executable machine code program. This may be achieved either by the use of a *compiler* which converts the source program into machine code executing the functions specified in the program, or by an *interpreter* program, whose operation is described in the next section. The compiler operates in a way which is broadly analogous to an assembler, in that source code written in the particular high-level language is read by a compiler for that language, the program syntax is checked, and a machine code program implementing the functions specified in the source program is generated. This machine code program may subsequently be loaded into the computer's memory and executed, or it may be stored for later use on a backing storage medium. The main difference between the high-level language compiler and an assembler from the user's point of view is that whereas the assembler produces one machine code instruction for each assembly language instruction, the compiler may produce many machine code instructions to implement each high-level language statement. Thus although the machine code implementing a particular function in a high-level language may be 50% or 100% longer than the machine code produced by an equivalent assembly language program, the source code of the high-level language program is invariably very much shorter than the equivalent assembly language program.

The compiler often produces assembly language as an intermediate stage of the compilation process.

## High-level language interpreters

The most commonly available interpreted high-level language is BASIC, which is incorporated into nearly all small personal and business computers.

A high-level language interpreter is a program which is co-resident in the computer memory at the same time as the source program. The interpreter executes the source program by taking each source program statement in turn and executing machine code instructions which implement the function specified by the source code. Thus the interpreter is said to *interpret* the source program. This technique has both advantages and disadvantages when compared with compilation.

The most important difference between a compiler and an interpreter is that the interpreter does not produce a separate machine code program which can be executed directly. The source program must be interpreted by the co-resident language interpreter. This has a number of important corollaries. First, it means that an interpreted high-level language cannot be used to develop the software for a dedicated microprocessor application unless the designer is prepared to build both the high-level source code program and the language interpreter into his final hardware. In most cases such a solution would require very much more memory than the machine code program alone. Second, interpreted programs execute many times more slowly than the equivalent compiled or assembled programs, because in effect the interpreted program source statement must be converted to machine code each time the source statement is executed (and this may be many times if the statement is embedded within a program loop). By comparison, the source statement is converted to machine code once and for all by a compiler, and there is thus no execution time overhead associated with converting source code to machine code when a compiled program is run.

Language interpreters have one significant advantage, however, compared

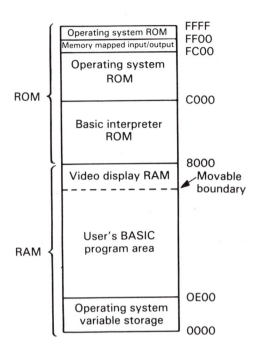

| | | FFFF |
| Operating system ROM | | FF00 |
| Memory mapped input/output | | FC00 |
| Operating system ROM | | |
| | | C000 |
| Basic interpreter ROM | | |
| | | 8000 |
| Video display RAM | | Movable boundary |
| User's BASIC program area | | |
| | | 0E00 |
| Operating system variable storage | | |
| | | 0000 |

Fig. 6.2  A typical small microcomputer memory map.

with compilers. Because both the source program and the interpreter are resident in memory simultaneously, the source program may be executed as soon as it has been written. There is no delay while the program is compiled to executable machine code. Furthermore, the interpreter can check the syntax of a program statement immediately that statement has been typed in, so that syntax errors can be corrected by the programmer without first having to compile the program to identify these errors. For this reason, programs can generally be developed more rapidly using a language interpreter than using a compiler, and interpreters are generally considered to be more *user-friendly* than compilers, hence their widespread application in home computers. As an example, Fig. 6.2 shows the memory map of a typical small microcomputer (the BBC microcomputer) which contains a ROM-resident BASIC interpreter.

**Summary**

This chapter has introduced a number of different ways of programming computers. At the lowest level, computers can be programmed directly in machine code, but this is very tedious, error-prone, and impractical except as a vehicle for learning how the computer works. Assembly language is a programming language in which the machine code instructions are represented using mnemonics; in addition, labels are used to represent addresses and directives enable data variables and constants to be defined within the assembly language program. In consequence, assembly language programming is very much easier than machine code programming, while retaining a one-to-one relationship between the assembly language instructions and the machine code instructions produced when the source program is assembled to produce machine code. For many applications, specific detailed knowledge of the computer hardware is not required and in this case programs can be written using a variety of high-level languages. Programs can generally be developed much faster using high-level languages than using assembly language, but this advantage may be offset by increased program size and slower execution time. High-level source code programs may be compiled to produce directly executable machine code programs, or they may be interpreted using a co-resident language interpreter.

### Problems

(Although these problems may be tackled simply as theoretical exercises, it is strongly recommended that the student should program them on an actual computer system if at all possible. This provides the opportunity to test and debug the programs in a realistic way, and will verify the student's suggested solution. The problems are described in terms of an MC68HC11 implementation but can equally well be written in ARM or MC68000 assembly language (or indeed in any other assembly language).)

6.1 Modify the program written in Exercise 6.2 so that the reaction time displayed on the eight lamps is indicated in BCD (i.e. a reaction time between 0.01 and 0.99 seconds can be displayed).

6.2 Modify the program described in Problem 6.1 so that if the reaction time exceeds 0.99 seconds, all the lamps flash on and off three times per second.

6.3 *Duck Shoot* — A simple microprocessor-controlled game.
'Duck Shoot' makes use of the program written in Exercise 6.1, where the lamps are illuminated in sequence at intervals of 0.1 seconds. A lit lamp represents the duck and the objective of the player is to press the corresponding switch while the particular lamp is illuminated. When this is achieved the appropriate lamp should remain permanently lit. The objective of the game is to shoot all eight ducks in the minimum possible time.

(i) Develop an algorithm to implement 'Duck Shoot' using an appropriate high-level language.

(ii) Write a program which implements your algorithm in MC68HC11 assembly language.

Hint: In order to detect that a switch has been depressed while the appropriate lamp is lit, the program must check that the switch is *not* depressed when the lamp is first illuminated, but *is* depressed when the lamp is switched off, and the next lamp illuminated.

6.4 As part of a particular MC68HC11 application, three ASCII decimal digits representing a number in the range 0–255 are stored in three successive locations in the MC68HC11 address space. Write a subroutine which will convert the three ASCII digits into an 8-bit unsigned binary integer. The subroutine should be called with the index register pointing to the first digit and should return the 8-bit binary number in the A register. Provide full documentation of the program, including an explanation of the algorithm written in a suitable high-level language. Indicate how the program could be modified to detect when the ASCII number is greater than 255. (The ASCII digits 0–9 are coded as the hexadecimal numbers 30–39, respectively.)

6.5 (Uses material from Chapter 5 as well as Chapter 6.)
A microprocessor system consisting of a Motorola MC68HC11 micro-

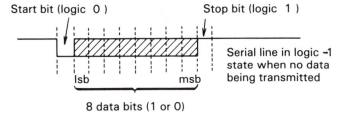

Fig. 6.3　Serial data format for Problem 6.5.

See also Problem 6.6.

processor with associated memory and a 1 MHz crystal controlled clock is to be interfaced to a printer. The printer has an asynchronous serial interface which is connected to the least significant bit of an MC6821 Peripheral Interface Adaptor data port configured at address 4000 hex. An assembly language subroutine is required which takes as its input an 8-bit data word held in accumulator A, and produces a serial output at 300 baud (accurate to $\pm 5\%$), with the format shown in Fig. 6.3.

(a) Write assembly language code to initialise the PIA for the data transfer.

(b) Write an algorithm in a suitable high-level language to show how programmed instructions can provide a one-bit serial data output.

(c) Code the algorithm developed in (b), and show how the timing constraints specified above can be accommodated.

6.6 Repeat Problem 6.5 using an ACIA. Give the assembly language code required to initialise the ACIA, and write an assembly language subroutine which takes as its input an 8-bit data word held in accumulator A, and outputs it via the ACIA at 300 baud. (Assume the ACIA is configured at address 5000 hex.) Compare and contrast the solutions to Problems 6.5 and 6.6.

6.7 Add directives to the programs written in Problems 6.1–6.6 so that in each case the program origin is at 8000 hex., the data origin is at 80 hex. and other program directives introduced in Chapter 6 are used as appropriate.

# 7 Instruction size and addressing modes

**Objectives**

☐ To explain why CISC computers generally use instructions of variable length, while RISC computers use fixed-length instructions.

☐ To explain why several different addressing modes are provided in any computer.

☐ To describe how and when to use the different addressing modes provided in the instruction set of a computer.

## Instruction size

The format of a computer machine code instruction has already been introduced in Chapter 3. In general every instruction must contain:

(*i*) an *operation code* which specifies the type of operation to be executed;

(*ii*) an *operand* which specifies the data upon which the instruction operates.

A few instructions have no operand, for example, the MC68HC11 no operation (NOP) instruction.

For an 8-bit microprocessor such as the MC68HC11, the use of a single 8-bit word to represent an instruction would allow up to $2^8$ or 256 instruction types to be specified, but this allocation would leave no bits in the word available to identify the operand.

In fact, the MC68HC11 includes a number of instructions whose opcode consists of two bytes rather than a single byte. This is a consequence of the fact that this microprocessor is an upgrade of a previous simpler microprocessor: the Motorola MC6800. It was not found possible to include all the required additional instructions and addressing modes in the upgraded processor using only the remaining unused opcode binary codes; thus the few available unused codes were 'expanded' by defining some of these codes to require a second opcode byte. Typically, the second byte is used to define registers on which the instruction operates, examples of which are given later in the chapter.

This mechanism is not commonly found in 8-bit microprocessors; it is a side-effect of developing a compatible upgrade to an earlier microprocessor.

To provide the full 64 kbyte addressing range required for the MC68HC11 microprocessor would require a 3-byte instruction in which the first byte identified the type of operation, and the remaining two bytes the address of the operand. The second and third bytes would be concatenated to form a 16-bit address.

Several other possibilities also exist. As is shown in the following section, one requirement is to provide instructions which specify data directly within the instruction, for example 'Load accumulator A with the data 99' expressed in register transfer language as

$$99 \rightarrow A$$

This instruction could be stored in two bytes by allocating the first byte for the operation code of the instruction while the second contained the operand itself, 99.

110

Finally, some instructions manipulate data stored in CPU registers. For these instructions no memory address need be specified. Thus an instruction of the type 'Transfer the contents of accumulator A to accumulator B' or

$$(A) \rightarrow B$$

could be coded using a single byte instruction. Note that in this case, although no explicit external memory address is required, the addresses of the accumulators A and B are implicit in the operation code.

The worst-case requirement in an 8-bit microprocessor like the MC68HC11 is for 3-byte instructions which allow us to identify an address anywhere in memory. To simplify the control logic of the CPU, one design approach would be to make all instructions three bytes long, and ignore the unnecessary bytes where appropriate. This would be very inefficient since it would not only increase the size of any program but also slow program execution since there would be many memory accesses for bytes which would subsequently be ignored. To avoid these problems CISC computers are generally designed to use *variable-length* instructions. This increases the complexity of the control logic as the computer must first fetch and decode the operation code of each instruction before it can determine how many further words must be accessed in order to load the instruction operand. The advantage is that programs are more compact and execute more quickly.

Assuming that all instructions are *single-address* instructions.

This is one of the simplifications made in RISC processor design. The execution time inefficiency is avoided by using a much larger word size (e.g. 32 bits) so that every instruction is one word rather than three

The same general arguments concerning instruction size also apply to the MC68000 microprocessor, but there are two significant differences. First, the MC68000 uses a 16-bit data bus, hence operation codes are 16 bits long rather than eight bits. Instructions consist of between one and five 16-bit words, and since each instruction always has a single 16-bit opcode, the operand length in MC68000 instructions can vary between zero and four words. Second, although (like the MC68HC11) most MC68000 instructions are single-address instructions, the MC68000 MOVE instruction has a double address capability. It is to support this capability that the maximum MC68000 instruction word length is five words, since the four-word operand allows the instruction to specify two 32-bit addresses in memory. All other MC68000 instructions have a maximum length of three words.

For example, the MC68000 instruction:

MOVE 100000,200000

would occupy five words and would move the contents of address 100000 to address 200000.

The design philosophy of RISC machines such as the ARM differs in several ways from the CISC examples described above. First, a large instruction word size (e.g. 32 bits or even 64 bits) is chosen, so that it is feasible to encode both the opcode and operand within a single instruction word. This makes it possible to design the processor so that all instructions are one word long, which in turn simplifies the design of the instruction decoder, which speeds up instruction execution time. Second, because it is feasible to put a significant number of registers on the CPU chip, most instructions can be constrained to operate only on registers, with only the load and store instructions having to specify full memory addresses. This has the advantage that the data processing instructions, which do not access operands in memory, can be executed very fast, and further simplifies the instruction decoder design.

The penalty for these design choices is that the fixed instruction length makes it difficult to support two of the most commonly used addressing modes (*direct* and *immediate* addressing, as used in the example program in Chapter 6, and described in detail in the next sections). This has disadvantages for the assembly

With a fixed-length instruction word, there are unfortunately insufficient bits available to implement direct and immediate addressing modes in full.

language programmer, but fortunately these disadvantages can be overcome by careful compiler design, and so are not normally observed when programming in high-level languages.

### Addressing modes

Consideration must now be given to the addressing modes which are required to produce a useful computing device. An obvious requirement is to be able to address the whole of the computer memory, but in practice statistical studies of computer programs show several common patterns in the way that data memory is accessed. Different addressing modes can be defined to support these characteristic patterns, and hence to improve the efficiency and execution speed of the computer program and simplify programming. For example, most instructions reference words in arrays or tables of data shorter than 256 words (and thus addressable using an 8-bit address). Also, data variables are generally stored in contiguous areas of memory to minimise the amount of read/write memory required in the computer system. Finally, 80–90% of branch instructions refer to addresses less than 128 words away from the current program counter address. Hence, although it is sometimes necessary to specify a full absolute address, it can often be more convenient and more economical of memory to express an address as an offset to an array base address, or relative to the current program counter value.

An individual instruction *type* may be able to make use of several different *addressing modes*. The different modes will correspond to different machine codes, but usually the same assembly language mnemonic will be used for all instructions of the same basic type. Whereas it was once thought that the best way to increase the processing power of a computer was to increase the number of instruction *types* available to it, this has now been generally recognised as an undesirable objective, and has been one of the major threads leading to the development of reduced instruction set computers (RISCs). Instead, the aim in designing current general-purpose CISC microprocessors is to provide what are known as *orthogonal* or *regular* instruction sets, where a fairly small number of basic instruction types are available, but each instruction type can be used with all meaningful addressing modes which the processor supports. This approach has two advantages: first, it substantially eases the problem of memorising and using the computer's instruction set for the assembly language programmer; second, it simplifies the implementation of high-level language compilers for use with the processor.

The three example microprocessors illustrate this change of thinking in their instruction set design. The MC68HC11, though introduced in the mid-1980s, has a CPU architecture derived from the Motorola MC6800 general-purpose 8-bit microprocessor which was introduced in 1974. The MC68HC11 has a total of 145 different instructions, many of which can use one of four memory addressing modes (*immediate, direct, extended direct*, and *indexed*). Many of the remaining instructions are unique mnemonics defining operations on registers in the CPU.

The MC68000 (designed in about 1979) has far fewer basic instruction types, 56, than the MC68HC11. However, it supports 14 distinct addressing modes, and introduces a further dimension of orthogonality, in that its instructions can operate on three main data types: bytes, words (16 bits) and long words (32 bits). In addition, special instructions support operations on bits and BCD digits.

The ARM RISC processor, introduced in the late of 1980s, has even fewer instructions (only 25). Rather than attempting to make every instructions as orthogonal as possible, the instruction set is subdivided into two main groups: data processing instructions and memory reference (load and store) instructions. The data processing instructions can only operate on data in CPU registers, while only the load and store instructions can use a full range of memory addressing modes. Thus data processing on variables stored in memory must be implemented by subdividing the processing into components which transfer the variable(s) between registers and memory, and a component which performs the data manipulation within CPU registers.

Summarising, it may be seen that the range of addressing modes available to a particular computer will influence not only program size and execution speed but also the programming convenience of the computer. These points should be borne in mind as the addressing modes most commonly provided in mini-computers and microprocessors are examined.

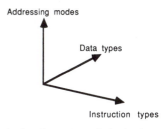

*Instruction set regularity in the MC68000.*

Compare Worked Examples 3.1 and 3.2.

Compare the number of discrete instruction types and addressing modes for the three example processors. Which assembly language is likely to be easiest to learn?

**Exercise 7.1**

## Implied addressing

*Implied addressing* describes instructions which manipulate data stored in CPU registers or accumulators. An implied address instruction does not access locations in the main computer memory. Typically there will only be a small number of CPU registers, hence only a few bits are needed to identify each register uniquely. Thus the bits which encode the register identification information can often be included within the operation code itself, leading to a single word instruction. The name *implied* arises because the register address(es) is (are) implied by the operation code. There are also a few instructions with no address specified at all, such as MC68HC11 NOP instruction. These are strictly known as zero-address instructions, but are often grouped together with implied address instructions.

Whereas implied addressing is one of several possible generally available addressing modes for CISC computers, and operations which can be carried out in registers can usually also be executed in memory locations, on the ARM, the 18 data processing instructions can *only* operate on registers. Since any of the 16 accessible registers in the ARM CPU can be uniquely specified using a 4-bit code, 12 bits are required to specify two source registers and one destination register. The second source register can optionally have an arbitrary shift or rotate operation applied to it before it reaches the ALU (see Fig. 2.6). Five bits in the instruction word are used to specify the amount of shift or rotation (0–31 bits) and a further three bits identify the type of shift or rotation (logical or arithmetic shift right or left; rotate right with or without extend). Thus a total of 20 out of the 32 bits in the instruction word are used to specify up to three implied address operands, leaving the remaining 12 bits to identify the instruction type.

Beware of variations in the terminology used to describe addressing modes: some differences for the example processors are noted in the text.

*Example 1: MC68HC11*

| | | | |
|---|---|---|---|
| MUL | (Multiply A and B accumulators) | (A)*(B) | →D |
| ASRA | (Arithmetic shift right A) | (A)/2 | →A |
| TAB | (Transfer accumulator A to B) | (A) | →B |

*Example 2: MC68000*

These instructions are called *register direct* instructions in the MC68000 literature.

| | | | |
|---|---|---|---|
| MOVE.W D0,D1 | (Move l.s. word of D0 to D1) | (D0) | →D1 |
| EXG D5,A5 | (Exchange D5 and A5 registers) | (D5) | →Temp |
| | (always a 32-bit operation) | (A5) | →D5 |
| | | (Temp) | →A5 |
| CLR.B D3 | (Clear l.s.byte of D3) | 0 | →D3 |

*Example 3: ARM*

| | | | |
|---|---|---|---|
| MOV | R1, R2, LSL#4 | (Shift contents of R2 4 places left and transfer result to R1) | (R2) ≪ 4→R1 |
| SUB | R7, R3, R5 | (Subtract contents of R5 from contents of R3 and store result in R7) | (R3)−(R5)→R7 |
| ADD | R0, R1, R2, ROR#2 | (Rotate contents of R2 right 2 places and add to R1, storing result in R0) | (R2) ≫ 2 + (R1)→R0 |

It should be noted that many CISC addressing modes which access external memory locations also make use of implied addressing to define either a source or a destination CPU register.

```
        b7      b0
Address X   | OPCODE |
Address X+1 |  DATA  |

        b15  b8 b7    b0
Address X | OPCODE | DATA |
```

The # symbol immediately in front of the operand is used to indicate the immediate addressing mode in MC68HC11 assembly language (see Chapter 6).

**Immediate addressing**

A common requirement is to provide an addressing mode where the instruction itself can specify the data to be operated on. Typical uses might be to specify the number of times a loop of instructions is to be executed, or to initialise a variable. This function is supported using the *immediate addressing* mode, where the data immediately follow the operation code. In an 8-bit microprocessor this instruction might require two bytes (a single-byte operation code followed by one data byte) or three bytes if a 16-bit operand is to be specified, as may be the case if a 16-bit register is to be initialised. For a larger computer such as the MC68000 where the opcode requires less than a complete word, it may be possible to combine the opcode and the immediate data within separate fields of the same word.

*Example 1: MC68HC11*

| | | | |
|---|---|---|---|
| LDA | #99 | (Load accumulator A with data 99) | 99→A |

| | | |
|---|---|---|
| ADDB #64 | (Add 64 to accumulator B) | (B) + 64→B |
| LDS #4095 | (Initialise the stack pointer) | 4095→SP |

*Example 2: MC68000*

| | | | |
|---|---|---|---|
| MOVEQ #99,D0 | (Load register D0 with data 99) | 99→A | |
| ADDI.B #64,D1 | (Add 64 to 1.s.b. of D1) | (D1) + 64→D1 | |
| MOVEA #4094,A7 | (Initialise the stack pointer) (default is 16-bit operand) | 4094→SP | A7 (alternatively SP) accesses the *user* stack pointer. The *supervisor* stack pointer is only accessible in supervisor mode. |

On the ARM a limited form of immediate addressing is implemented as an extension of implied addressing, thus unlike the remaining ARM addressing modes described in the following sections, immediate addressing can be applied to any of the ARM data processing instructions.

ARM immediate addressing is achieved by making operand2 an *immediate operand*, or constant value. Immediate operands are indicated by a '#' prefix followed by the number, instead of specifying a register for operand2. For example, to move the number '100' into register R0, the instruction

> ARM immediate addressing is distinguished from other ARM addressing modes because the operand is part of the instruction, and thus the addressing mode does not make any further references to memory after the instruction fetch.

| | | |
|---|---|---|
| MOV R0,#100 | Move 100 into register R0 | 100→R0 |

can be used. To add '1024' to the value of register R1, we can use the instruction:

| | | | |
|---|---|---|---|
| ADD R1, R1,#&400 | Set R1 = R1 + 1024 | (R1) + 1024→R1 | The & symbol indicates a hexadecimal number in ARM assembly language. |

To perform a logical AND between register R4 and the binary value %111, setting all but the least significant three bits of R4 to zero and placing the result in R0, we can use:

| | | | |
|---|---|---|---|
| AND R0, R4,#%111 | Set R0 = R4 AND %111 | (R4)∩7→R0 | The % symbol indicates a binary number in ARM assembly language. |

However, these seemingly straightforward immediate addressing operations conceal the underlying complexity of the mechanism used by the ARM to implement immediate addressing. It was mentioned earlier that every instruction on the ARM processor occupies one 32-bit word: there is a penalty which must be paid for this simplicity. After allocating bits for the instruction opcode, the register number and so on, it is impossible to include a 32-bit immediate data field in the instruction. In practice, only 12 bits are allocated for the immediate data field in the data processing instructions (see ARM summary instruction set, Appendix E).

If all 12 bits of the field were used to store the binary representation of the immediate constant, then only numbers in the range 0–4095 could be represented. This would make it extremely difficult to load a register with a 32-bit quantity. To allow more flexibility, the 12-bit immediate operand is split into an 8-bit data field and a 4-bit shift field. The 4-bit field specifies one of 16 different positions in a 32-bit word at which the data in the 8-bit field should be placed. This is summarised in Fig. 7.1.

```
       BIT 31                          BIT 0            Position

       ......................76543210                      0
       10....................765432                        1
       3210..................7654                          2
       543210................76                            3
       76543210..............                              4
       ..76543210............                              5
       ....76543210..........                              6
       ......76543210........                              7
       ........76543210......                              8
       ..........76543210....                              9
       ............76543210..                             10
       ..............76543210                             11
       ...............76543210........                    12
       .................76543210......                    13
       ...................76543210....                    14
       .....................76543210..                    15
```

Fig. 7.1   The position system used in ARM immediate operands.

---

**Worked Example 7.1**   Suppose it is required to represent the number 175. In pure binary, this is:

%00000000000000000000000010101111

This can be represented as a data field of 175 (%10101111) and a position shift of zero (%0000). It would appear as:

Immediate operand:   %0000 10101111

Suppose the number 4992 is to be represented. In binary, the number is:

%00000000000000000001001110000000

This corresponds to the data value 78 (%01001110) shifted left six places (equivalent to multiplying by 64). This would be represented by a shift number of 13. The full number would therefore be represented as:

Immediate operand:   %1101 01001110

This scheme allows 7- or 8-bit quantities to be placed anywhere within the 32-bit range (because the position field is only four bits wide, it is only possible to select seven bits between bit 1 and bit 9, bit 3 and bit 11, etc.). If it is necessary to load a full 32-bit word, this must be done by breaking it down into four groups of eight bits. The first byte can be loaded with a simple MOV instruction, the remaining bytes must be loaded with ADD instructions, using immediate operands shifted 8, 16 and 24 bits.

To minimise the inconvenience caused by this problem, the ARM assembler includes additional directives specifically to assist in implementing immediate address instructions.

Fortunately, when using immediate operands, the number required is specified to the assembler in the usual way. The assembler then tries to generate appropriate data and shift numbers. If this is not possible (with 257, for example), then an error is produced at assembly time.

## Direct addressing

In any computer it must be possible to access data stored within any location of the memory address space. The *direct addressing* mode is normally used to achieve this, and in 8-bit microprocessors a 3-byte instruction is usually required, where the first byte is the opcode and the remaining two bytes specify a 16-bit operand address. The MC68HC11 supports this type of operation, which is called *extended* addressing in Motorola's literature. By analogy, the equivalent addressing mode in the MC68000 will typically require a three-word instruction, where the first word is the opcode and the remaining two words allow an address of up to 32 bits to be specified. In the MC68000, this addressing mode is known as *absolute long addressing*.

*Example 1: MC68HC11*

| LDAA 4095 | (Load accumulator A from address 4095) | $(4095) \rightarrow A$ |
|---|---|---|
| STD 1024 | (Store 16-bit D register in addresses 1024 and 1025) | $(A) \rightarrow 1024$ $(B) \rightarrow 1025$ |

*Example 2: MC68000*

| MOVE 65536,D0 | (Load D0 from address 65536) | $(65536) \rightarrow D0$ |
|---|---|---|

The MC68HC11 and MC68000 also include variations of direct addressing which are more restrictive in their addressing range, but result in shorter instructions. The advantage of these schemes is that they permit the programmer to choose the appropriate direct addressing mode to optimise the size and execution speed of his program.

In addition to absolute long addressing, the MC68000 also supports *absolute short addressing*, where the opcode is followed by a single word address, which can specify an address within a range of 64 kbytes.

*Example 3: MC68000*

| MOVE 4094,D0 | (Load D0 from address 4094) | $(4094) \rightarrow D0$ |
|---|---|---|

MC68HC11 *direct addressing* is similar to extended addressing except that only one byte of address follows the opcode. This byte specifies the lower eight bits of the address to be used, and thus the MC68HC11 direct addressing mode addresses only the bottom 256 bytes of the 64 kbyte address space. The same mnemonic is used for both the MC68HC11 direct and extended addressing modes, but different opcodes are generated by the assembler, depending on whether the operand address lies within or outside the bottom 256 bytes of memory.

Typically, addresses are identified using labels rather than explicit addresses in assembly language. The examples below use numerical values purely for clarity.

| Address X | OPCODE |
|---|---|
| Address X+1 | ADDRESS (HI) |
| Address X+2 | ADDRESS (LO) |

MC68000 addresses are limited in practice to 24 bits, but full 32-bit addresses can be specified on the MC68020.

On the MC68HC11 and MC68000, direct addressing is indicated by the lack of any prefix to the operand address or label.

| Address X | OPCODE |
|---|---|
| Address X + 1 | ADDRESS |

No distinction is made in MC68000 assembly language between absolute short and absolute long addressing: absolute short addressing is chosen if the assembler can identify that the specified address lies within the top or bottom 32 kbytes of address space.

If data variables can be stored within the area of memory accessible to the MC68HC11 direct addressing mode (or MC68000 absolute short addressing mode), they can be accessed using the shorter, faster version of the direct addressing instruction. Where necessary, however, the MC68HC11 extended direct addressing mode (MC68000 absolute long addressing mode), although generating longer, slower instructions, can be used to access any address in memory.

*Example 4: MC68HC11*

> LDAA 48  (Load accumulator  (48) → A
> A from address 48

**Exercise 7.2**  Write down the cycle-by-cycle sequence of data transfers which takes place when the following MC68HC11 (or MC68000) instructions are executed using the immediate and direct addressing modes:
(*a*) Logical AND a register
(*b*) Store a register in memory
(*c*) Load the stack pointer register
Verify your solution by comparing it with the data in Appendices C and/or E.

To be able to specify a full direct address for ARM load and store instructions would require a 26-bit address field in the instruction. Unfortunately, after allocating bits for the instruction opcode, the register addresses, etc., there are simply not enough bits left for an operand address! Therefore, this mode of memory access is not available on the ARM. Although this appears at first sight to be a major limitation in programming the ARM, the *appearance* of supporting direct addressing (for small programs) can be given by using *program counter relative addressing* (see the section on relative addressing later in this chapter).

Where program counter relative addressing cannot be used, the function of direct addressing has to be achieved by breaking the memory reference down into two stages. The first stage is to load the required memory address into a register, using immediate addressing. The second stage is then to access the data in the required memory address using *register indirect addressing*, as described in the next section.

**Register indirect addressing**

For the addressing modes examined so far, the address which the instruction accesses is explicitly defined in the instruction. This definition occurs at the time the program is written and assembled, and is thus fixed during program execution.

In practice, it is often desirable to be able to change the address which a particular instruction accesses as the program executes. For example, the programmer may wish to write a program loop which steps through a predefined contiguous block of memory, one word at a time, initialising each word to a specific value (for example, 0). The obvious way of doing this is to write a simple loop of code which is repeated for each word initialised. A method of *address modification* is therefore required such that each execution of the program loop, though executing the same set of instructions, steps through memory accessing words sequentially.

This is achieved by using a register to specify the required address: the register can then be incremented (or decremented) for each iteration of the loop.

The addressing mode is known as *register indirect addressing* because the address of the operand is given, not directly within the instruction, but indirectly via an implied register address within the instruction. All computers implement some form of register indirect and/or indexed addressing (an extension of register indirect addressing which is discussed in the next section) because the requirement to be able to define an operand address at run time (i.e. dynamically) rather than only at the time the program is written (i.e. statically) is essential for any practical computer.

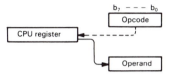

---

An MC68000 microprocessor application needs to initialise a 100-byte block of memory at 1000 hex. to zero as part of the initialisation phase of a program. How can this be coded efficiently?

**Worked Example 7.2**

Clearly the solution is *not* a list of 100 consecutive instructions of the form:

| | | |
|---|---|---|
| CLR.B | D0 | initialise D0 to zero |
| MOVE.B | D0,$1000 | initialise first address |
| MOVE.B | D0,$1001 | initialise second address |
| MOVE.B | D0,$1002 | initialise third address |

The solution is to use register indirect addressing, by initialising a suitable register to point to the start of the specified area of memory, and a counter to count the required number of iterations round the loop:

| | | | |
|---|---|---|---|
| | MOVEA.L | #$1000,A0 | initialise A0 to point to first address |
| | MOVE.L | #100,D1 | initialise D1 as a loop counter |
| | CLR.B | D0 | initialise D0 to zero |
| LOOP1 | MOVE.B | D0,(A0) | copy D0 into address pointed to by A0 |
| | ADDQ.L | #1,A0 | increment A0 to next address |
| | SUBQ.L | #1,D1 | decrement loop count |
| | BNE | LOOP1 | repeat loop if count not zero |

These two instructions can be replaced by the single instruction below.

---

Worked example 7.2 illustrates the use of *address register indirect addressing* (Motorola's terminology) in the MC68000. Any of the registers A0–A7 can be used as the address register, though A7 is normally reserved for use as the user stack pointer. The MC68000 also supports two variations of register indirect addressing which allow the register to be automatically post-incremented or pre-decremented. In this case, the size of the increment or decrement (1, 2 or 4 bytes) is specified implicitly by the operand data (byte, word or long word, respectively). Thus the following instruction could be used to replace the separate register indirect address instruction and register increment instructions in the above example:

| | | |
|---|---|---|
| MOVE.B D0,(A0) + | (copy D0 into address pointed to by A0 and then increment A0) | (D0)→(A0); (A0) + 1→A0 |

The MC68HC11 also includes two 16-bit index registers X and Y, which can be used for register indirect addressing.

*Example 1: MC68HC11 Register Indirect Addressing*

STAA 0,X  (store contents of A at address    (A)→((X))
pointed to by X register)

In the absence of direct addressing, register indirect addressing is one of the most important addressing modes available on the ARM microprocessor. Like all other memory addressing modes, however, it is only available on the load and store insructions.

*Example 2: ARM register indirect addressing*

STR  R0,[R1]  (Store contents of R0          (R0) → (R1)
at address pointed to by R1)
LDR  R2,[R3]  (Load R2 with the contents     ((R3)) → R2
of the memory address
pointed to by R3)

**Indexed addressing**

*Indexed addressing* is designed to assist the programmer in accessing multiple tables or arrays of data. A common programming requirement is to be able to perform some sort of arithmetic manipulation upon arrays of data by successively accessing elements of each array and manipulating them individually. This requirement is rather similar to that described in the previous section, except that rather than accessing a single array, the mechanism is now generalised so that a single address register can deal efficiently with corresponding elements of several arrays.

To do this, all that is required is to add a *base address*, specified within the instruction, to the address in the register. The register is now known as an *index register* because, rather than supplying the full address of the operand, as was the case for register indirect addressing, it now supplies only an *offset* or *index* from the base address specified in the instruction. The *effective address* of the operand is thus given by:

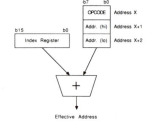

Effective address, EA = base address + (X)

where the base address is the base address of the array and X is the index register.

---

**Worked Example 7.3**   Consider a program which is required to add together two arrays A and B which each contain N elements, so as to produce an array A + B. The arrays might be stored in memory as follows:

| Address | Element | Address | Element | Address | Element |
|---------|---------|---------|---------|---------|---------|
| 0       | A1      | 40      | B1      | 80      | A1 + B1 |
| 1       | A2      | 41      | B2      | 81      | A2 + B2 |

| Address | Element | Address | Element | Address | Element |
|---------|---------|---------|---------|---------|---------|
| 2 | A3 | 42 | B3 | 82 | A3 + B3 |
| . | . | . | . | . | . |
| . | . | . | . | . | . |
| . | . | . | . | . | . |

On the MC68HC11, using only the direct addressing mode, the code required would be:

```
LDAA  0  ⎫
ADDA 40  ⎬ Repeated N times for N array elements (N < 40)
STAA 80  ⎭
LDAA  1
ADDA 41
STAA 81
   .
   .
   .
```

If the same program is now implemented as a program loop using the indexed addressing mode, the base address of each array can be specified within the instruction, and the offset which identifies the address of the required array element can be computed using the index register. The index is computed by incrementing the index register once each time the program loop is executed. Thus the program structure is:

(a) load the index register (initialisation)
(b) perform array element manipulation
(c) increment the index register
(d) compare index register with number of array elements (loop comparison to enable termination at the end of the loop)
(e) branch to (b) if end of array not reached.

Hence the program instructions would be:

```
LDX   #0        *initialise index register
LDAA  0,X       *load array element from array A
ADDA  40,X      *add array element from array B
STAA  80,X      *store result in array A + B
      INX       *increment index register
CPX   #N        *N is the number of array elements
BNE   LOOP      *repeat if last element not reached
```

Two specific points should be noted about this program. First, the use of three different base addresses allows three different tables to be accessed using the same index register offset. Second, although the program is much more compact than the same program implemented using direct addressing (especially if N is large), it executes more slowly than a comparable sequence of direct address instructions, because of the loop execution time overhead caused by the increment, compare, and branch instructions.

Most computers implement a range of different variations of indexed addressing; it is therefore worthwhile studying the simplest form of indexed addressing as implemented on each of the example processors before going on to examine more complex variations which may be provided.

*Example 1: MC68HC11*

The MC68HC11 includes two 16-bit index registers, X and Y, within its register architecture. These can be used as shown in the previous example to implement indexed addressing. However, the base address (which is included as an operand in the instruction) is restricted to eight bits, which means that, in practice, any table of data to which the indexed addressing mode is applied must have its base address within the bottom 256 bytes of memory. This is a significant restriction, and arises because although Motorola describe this addressing mode as indexed addressing in their literature, the mode actually primarily implements *based addressing*, a very similar addressing mode which is described in the next section.

*Example 2: MC68000*

The MC68000 also does not have a true indexed addressing mode which allows a 32-bit base address to be specified within the instruction. It does, however, allow a 16-bit base address within the instruction. Strictly, this mode should be regarded as based addressing as described below, and indeed Motorola's litera-ture calls the mode *address register indirect with displacement* which is an accurate (though less than concise!) definition of based addressing. The 16-bit address included in the instruction is in signed 2s complement form; its sign is extended to the m.s.b. of the effective address. Hence a displacement of $-32\,768$ to $+32\,767$ bytes from the address contained in the specified address register is possible, and thus for small applications using 64 kbyte or less memory, it is possible to treat this mode as true indexed addressing. For larger applications indexed addressing must be achieved by using the MC68000 *based indexed* addressing mode described below.

> MOVE 1022(A2),D2  (Load D2        $(1022 + (A2)) \rightarrow D2$
> with data at
> address 1022 + A2)

The MC68000 *based indexed addressing mode* (called *address register indirect with index* by Motorola) computes the effective address by adding together a base address in an address register, an index in a data or address register, and an 8-bit offset (which could be zero) from the instruction. The index can be 16 or 32 bits. Since both the base and the index can be 32 bits, it is possible to use this mode for true indexed addressing over the full 16 Mbyte addressing range of the MC68000, once the base register has been initialised.

*Example 3: ARM*

Since the immediate offset is a 12-bit 2s complement signed integer, it can take any value in the range $-2048$ to $+2047$.

The nearest approximation to indexed addressing as described above on the ARM is *pre-indexed addressing with an immediate offset*. Again, this mode is primarily intended to implement based addressing, but if the offset is used to define the base address, it can also implement indexed addressing. Example instruction:

            LDR   R0,[R1,#40]   (load R0 from the address        ((R1) + 40)→R0
                                given by contents of R1 + 40)

Full indexed addressing can be achieved in a similar way to the MC68000, by using an effective address made up from a base address and index, both stored in registers, for example:

            LDR   R0,[R1,R2]   (load R0 from the address  ((R1) + (R2))→R0
                               given by contents of R1 +
                               contents of R2)

In addition, the index can be given as the contents of a register to which a shift operation has been applied (as with the data processing instructions). This mode is useful when accessing word data from a table, since to access the nth entry in the table, it is necessary to access the 4nth byte in the table, as each entry occupies four bytes. This is conveniently achieved by appending a 2-bit left shift to the index register, as follows:

            LDR   R0,[R1,R2,LSL#2]             ((R1) + (R2)*4)→R0


Write an MC68HC11 (or ARM or MC68000) program which uses the indexed addressing mode to read a list of ten data elements, data 1 to data 10, stored from address 20 hex. upwards, and produces a second list, result 1 to result 10, stored from address 40 hex. upwards, where result 1 is given by data 1, result 2 by data 1 + data 2, result 3 by data 1 + data 2 + data 3, and so on.

**Exercise 7.3**

Repeat Exercise 7.3 using register indirect addressing rather than indexed addressing. What can you learn from comparing the two solutions?

**Exercise 7.4**


## Based addressing

A common requirement in programming is to be able to access a set of related parameters which are stored contiguously in memory; it is often most convenient if these parameters can be accessed by specifying different offsets from a fixed base address, rather than having to identify each parameter individually. The addressing mode required to do this is known as *based addressing*. Typical applications of based addressing include:

(a) accessing items in a stack frame (see Worked Example 7.4);
(b) accessing data in a parameter area whose base address is passed to a subroutine (see the section on inter-task communication in the design example of Chapter 10);
(c) accessing a particular field of a linked list element: the base address register holds the start address of the element and the instruction specifies an offset to the required field of the element.

All of these examples are commonly encountered in structured high-level languages such as PASCAL, C, BCPL, ADA and MODULA 2, hence any microprocessor which is intended to support high-level language compilers must in turn provide based addressing.

If you have not yet encountered *structured data types* and *pointers* in a high-level language, this example will mean nothing at present! Review it when you are familiar with these concepts.

**Worked Example 7.4**

It is common in high-level languages such as PASCAL and C to pass parameters to a procedure or function using the processor stack. Before calling the procedure or function (which corresponds to a subroutine in assembly language) the required parameters are pushed onto the stack using push instructions of the type introduced in Chapter 4. Unfortunately, since the subroutine call causes the subroutine return address to be stacked immediately below any parameters, the parameters cannot simply be pulled off the stack within the subroutine, without removing the return address at the same time. It is possible to access the parameters by assuming that they are at fixed offsets away from the address in the stack pointer register, but this address may not remain constant throughout the subroutine if it is also required to push and pull register values onto the stack during the subroutine. The solution commonly adopted is to set up a stack *frame pointer*, where the frame pointer is simply another address register like the stack pointer, and is initialised to the current stack pointer value at the start of the subroutine. Regardless of any further stack usage within the subroutine, the frame pointer will continue to provide a reference address from which the parameters can be accessed as fixed offsets (see the margin Figure).

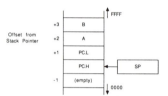

*Stack pointer position after MC68HC11 subroutine call*

The following MC68HC11 program instructions illustrate how parameters can be passed to a subroutine and accessed within the subroutine using a *stack frame*.

Within the main program, all that is required is to push the parameters onto the system stack before calling the subroutine:

```
PSHB          Push B then A onto the system stack
PSHA          (contents of A and B are two parameters to pass)
JSR   SUB1    Jump to subroutine
INS           Restore the stack pointer to its original position
INS
```

The first part of the subroutine would have the following format;

```
SUB1  TSX         (S)→X address register (X is the frame pointer)
```

(some intervening instructions, which might include pushes)

```
LDAA 2,X     Restore parameter pushed 2nd to A
LDAB 3,X     Restore parameter pushed 1st to B
```

---

**Exercise 7.5**  In Worked Example 7.4, the parameters are loaded into accumulators A and B before being transferred onto the stack. Why bother with the complexity of a stack frame, when the parameters will still be available in A and B after the subroutine has been called?

**Exercise 7.6**  What limitation does Worked Example 7.4 have, and how could it be resolved? (*Hint*: consider nested subroutines.)

As Worked Example 7.4 shows, although based addressing and indexed addressing are used in different ways, no distinction is commonly made between their representations in assembly languages.

On the MC68HC11, register indirect, indexed and based addressing as described in this chapter are lumped together by the manufacturer as parts of indexed addressing. If the offset is zero, the mode corresponds to register indirect addressing; if the offset can be expressed within eight bits ( $\pm$ 128 bytes) the mode is the equivalent of based addressing. If the base address lies within the botton 256 bytes of memory, then the mode can implement true indexed addressing.

On the MC68000, *address register indirect with displacement* corresponds to based addressing as described above. The same mode can, however, also be used for indexed addressing in small systems with less than 64 kbytes of memory. If a base address requiring more than 16 bits is needed, the MC68000 *based indexed* (*address register indirect with index*) mode is used.

On the ARM, *pre-indexed addressing with an immediate offset* corresponds to based addressing as described above, and can be used under some circumstances to implement indexed addressing. Full indexed addressing is implemented by using pre-indexed addressing with a register-defined base address.

## Indexed addressing versus based addressing

As may be apparent from the previous two sections, the distinction between indexed and based addressing is subtle, and the two are easily confused. Essentially, this distinction depends upon which component of the effective address is *dynamic*, i.e. required to vary at run time, and which is *static*, i.e. defined at assembly time. Indexed addressing is used where the base address of a data structure is known at assembly time, but arbitrary components must be accessed at run time; this is commonly the situation in array manipulation problems. Based addressing is used when the relative position of an element in a data structure is known at assembly time, but the base address of the structure is not. This situation arises frequently when manipulating dynamic data structures in high-level languages, and when passing parameters via a stack or using a pointer.

The confusion is not helped by the differing terminology used by different microprocessor manufacturers, nor by the fact that some of them apparently do not understand the distinction between based and indexed modes themselves (or did not when the chips were designed)!

## Relative addressing

In *relative addressing* the address at which the required data are found is specified with respect to the current program counter contents. Thus the operand address specified within the instruction represents an offset from the present program counter value.. In the MC68HC11, and in most early 8-bit microprocessors, the relative addressing mode is restricted to branch instructions, and uses an 8-bit 2s complement offset which allows branches backwards or forwards 128 bytes from the current instruction. For the 80–90% of program jumps which lie within this range, the branch instruction reduces the memory requirement by one byte compared with a jump instruction specifying a full 16-bit address.

For the MC68HC11, the *effective address* is given by:

$$EA = (PC) + 2s \text{ complement offset}$$

It should be noted that, at the time that this calculation is made, the program counter points to the instruction immediately after the branch instruction since the program counter is automatically incremented every time a program byte is fetched from memory.

Note that the terms *branch* and *jump* have specific distinct meanings in Motorola literature, but are often used interchangeably elsewhere.

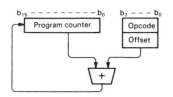

125

BRA −2 has the effect of
stopping program execution
since the instruction branches
back to itself.

*Example 1: MC68HC11*

    BRA    −2 (Branch back 2 bytes)
    BNE    40  (Branch forwards 40
                     bytes if zero flag not set)

The MC68000 provides a more extensive range of relative addressing options. It implements relative branches with an 8-bit offset, exactly like the MC68HC11, but also offers the possibility of specifying a 16-bit offset, allowing branches of up to $\pm 32\,768$ bytes away from the current program counter value. The assembler automatically chooses the appropriate offset size depending on whether the branch offset is greater or less than 128 bytes.

*Example 2: MC68000*

    BRA    −2 (Branch back 2 bytes)     $(PC) - 2 \rightarrow PC$
    BNE    254 (Branch forwards 254   $(PC) + 254 \rightarrow PC$
                     bytes if zero flag not set)

The ARM includes a 24-bit offset within its branch instruction and thus can branch to any word address within its 26-bit address space, by wrapping around where necessary at the top and bottom of the address space.

BRA −2 also has the effect of
stopping program execution,
because the ARM instruction
pipeline means that the program
counter is two instructions
ahead of the execution unit.

*Example 3: ARM*

    BRA    −2 (Branch back 2 words)    $(PC) - 2 \rightarrow PC$
    BNE    10 (Branch forwards 10 words  $(PC) + 10 \rightarrow PC$
                   if zero flag not set)

Whereas in the MC68HC11, relative addressing is restricted to branch instructions, on the ARM and MC68000 it is a generally available addressing mode. As was illustrated in the machine code example program in Chapter 6, the principal advantage of relative addressing is that it allows the construction of *position-independent code* which can execute anywhere in the address space of the processor without modification.

In practice, the requirement for position independence is a common one, particularly in *multi-tasking* computer systems (see Chapter 9), and in order to support position independence fully, not only branch instructions but all memory reference instructions must be made relative to the program counter. Worked Example 7.5 illustrates how relative addressing can be used to provide position independence for a normal memory reference instruction.

---

**Worked Example 7.5**

Consider a program where it is required to output to a VDU a message stored as a string in memory. The most convenient way to do this is to use register indirect addressing, which requires that the address register be initialised to point to the first character (byte) in the string, and subsequently incremented to point to each following character in turn. Outline MC68000 code to accomplish this requirement would be as follows:

           LEA       MSG,A0  Point to message
  LOOP   MOVE.B (A0),D0  Load character from message

```
              CMP.B    #0,D0     Is character zero?
              BEQ      NEXT      Branch out of loop if so
              BSR      PCHAR     Otherwise, print character
              ADDQ     #1,A0     Increment to next character in string
              BRA      LOOP      Repeat for next character
                                  .
MSG           FCC      'An example text string'
                                 (stored as a string of bytes)
              FCB      0         Identifies the end of the string
                                  .
   NEXT                .          (next part of program)
```

All the branches in the above code are relative to the current value of the program counter, so it may appear at first sight that the program is position-independent. However, the instruction 'LEA MSG,A0' uses the direct addressing mode to load the address corresponding to the label 'MSG' into the A0 address register. Thus, when the code is assembled, this address is specified absolutely, and will not be valid if the code is moved elsewhere in memory.

The solution to this problem is simply to use program counter relative addressing for the LEA instruction, so that 'MSG,A0' is replaced by 'MSG(PC),A0'. The effect of this will be that the effective address loaded into the A0 address register will become:

$$EA = (PC) + MSG - (PC)$$

where MSG – (PC) is the offset stored in the instruction itself, and represents the distance from the LEA instruction to the address MSG. This is the same wherever the program is loaded in memory, hence the instruction address is now specified in a position-independent manner.

---

The MC68000 can specify only a 16-bit offset in relative address instructions which are called *program counter with displacement* instructions in MC68000 literature. However, the MC68000 also supports two variations of relative addressing which form the effective address by adding an 8-bit offset specified in the instruction to the current program counter value, and then adding either a 16- or 32-bit index from a data or address register. This mode is described as *program counter with index* in MC68000 literature, and is effectively a combination of indexed addressing and relative addressing. As such, it may be useful when trying to access arrays of data in a program which is intended to be position-independent.

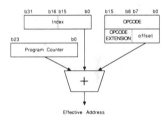

*MC68000 program counter with index addressing*

Note that the *Load effective address* instructions load the address of the operand rather than the operand itself into the specified register.

*Example 4: MC68000*

```
LEA    15(PC),A3   (Load A3 with the     (PC) + 15 → A3   47FA   (opcode)
                   current contents of the                000F   (offset)
                   PC plus 15)
```

On the ARM, program counter relative addressing is a special case of pre-indexed addressing, using the program counter, PC or R15, as the index register. The program counter can thus be referred to using the pre-indexed addressing mode previously described. Since no direct addressing mode is provided on the

127

ARM, program counter relative addressing is very widely used to substitute for direct addressing. The ARM assembler therefore allows a simpler format, which has the appearance of direct addressing, to be used to express program counter relative address instructions. Within the 32-bit instruction word, 12 bits are allocated to encode the 2s complement offset, restricting the offset range to $\pm 2048$ bytes.

*Example 5: ARM*

The first two examples would be identical if executed with a program counter value of 0.

| | | | |
|---|---|---|---|
| LDR | R0,[R15,#1000] | (Load R0 from address (PC) + 1000) | (PC) + 1000→R0 |
| LDR | R0,&1000 | (Load R0 from address 1000) | |
| LDR | R0,TABLE | (Load R0 from the address given by the label 'TABLE') | |

**Stack addressing**

See also Worked Example 7.4.

The concept of a *stack* has already been introduced during the discussion of subroutine mechanisms (Chapter 4). Exactly the same mechanism can, however, be used as an explicit addressing mode which provides a short-term last-in first-out (LIFO) store in memory. As has already been pointed out, stack addressing is functionally equivalent to register indirect addressing with auto-increment or decrement, but it is mentioned explicitly here because most computers also provide special-purpose instructions to access the system stack (the area of memory pointed to by the stack pointer register, SP). Examples of these special purpose instructions are given below.

*Example 1: MC68HC11*

| | | |
|---|---|---|
| PSHA | (Stack accumulator A) | (A)→(SP) |
| | | (SP)-1→SP |
| PULX | (Unstack register X) | (SP) + 1→SP |
| | | ((SP))→X.H |
| | | (SP) + 1→SP |
| | | ((SP))→X.L |

Note that the 16-bit register is stored/retrieved one byte at a time; the most significant byte is stored at the lower memory address.

*Example 2: MC68000*

| | | |
|---|---|---|
| MOVEM D0/A0, – (A5) | (Push D0 and A0 onto a stack formed by A5) | (A5) – 1→A5 |
| | | (D0)→(A5) |
| | | (A5) – 1→A5 |
| | | (A0)→(A5) |

A word operation is assumed (.L mnemonic extension gives a long word operation). Any address register can act as a stack, and any or all of the 16 general purpose registers can be stacked.

*Example 3: ARM*

| | | |
|---|---|---|
| STMFD SP!,{R0,LR} | Stack R0 and the Link register (R14)) | (SP)-4→SP |
| | | (R0)→(SP) |
| | | (SP)-4→SP |
| | | (R14)→(SP) |

Note that only complete 32-bit registers can be stacked on the ARM: there is no provision to stack a byte or word as on the MC68000.

Extreme care must be taken in using stack addressing during subroutines and interrupts, since a failure to remove data stored on the stack during a subroutine before the end of the subroutine will cause an incorrect address to be loaded into the program counter when the subroutine return instruction is executed. This is known as *stack corruption* and occurs because the stack pointer register is used both by autonomous hardware mechanisms within the microprocessor such as subroutine calls, and at the same time as an explicit addressing technique. In the MC68000 the problem can be avoided by reserving the system stack purely for autonomous functions and using any other address register for providing LIFO storage.

### Operation code fields

Close examination of the binary codes used to represent computer instructions often shows that these codes can be split up into smaller *fields* which individually define some aspect of the instruction, such as the addressing mode used for the CPU register(s) implied by the instruction. An example of this is shown in Fig. 7.2, where the binary codes of all the MC68HC11 ADD instructions are given. These instructions are all memory reference instructions (signified by bit 7 being set) and can, therefore, use the four common MC68HC11 memory addressing modes. These are coded using bits 4 and 5 of the opcode, while bit 6 indicates whether the instruction implies accumulator A or B as the operand destination. Note that for all instructions bits 0–3 are identical. These bits define the basic operation as an ADD operation. Similar fields within instruction opcodes can also be identified in the other two example processors.

| Mnemonic | Addressing mode | Hex. | Binary |
|----------|-----------------|------|-----------|
| ABA      | Implied         | 1B   | 0001 1011 |
| ADDA     | Immediate       | 8B   | 1000 1011 |
|          | Direct          | 9B   | 1001 1011 |
|          | Indexed         | AB   | 1010 1011 |
|          | Extended        | BB   | 1011 1011 |
| ADDB     | Immediate       | CB   | 1100 1011 |
|          | Direct          | DB   | 1101 1011 |
|          | Indexed         | EB   | 1110 1011 |
|          | Extended        | FB   | 1111 1011 |

1 = memory reference, 0 = others ⟍ ADD code
0 = accumulator A 1 = accumulator B
00 = immediate, 01 = direct, 10 = indexed, 11 = extended

Fig. 7.2   Opcode fields in MC68HC11 ADD instructions.

The ARM microprocessor encodes most opcode information in explicit fields (see Appendix D). This indicates how simple the instruction decoder logic is on the ARM as compared with the other example processors.

### Summary

Variable-length computer instructions are commonly used on CISC computers to allow several different addressing modes to be provided within the instruction set, while at the same time ensuring that instructions are coded efficiently in memory. On RISC computers, in contrast, the objective of simplifying the instruction decoder design to maximise execution speed is achieved by constraining all instructions to be one word long. This design choice imposes some limitations on the addressing modes available on RISC processors.

Current CISC computer designs attempt to provide regular and orthogonal instruction sets so that each basic instruction type can be used with every addressing mode which is meaningful. RISC computers, on the other hand, typically subdivide the instruction set into load and store instructions which access memory and can use a variety of addressing modes, and data processing instructions which are constrained to operate only on CPU registers.

Different addressing modes provide alternative techniques for accessing the instruction operand. The techniques provided are related to common programming requirements and the needs of high-level language compilers. They are intended to enable instructions to be compact and efficient, and to simplify programming of the computer.

The most commonly used addressing modes are:

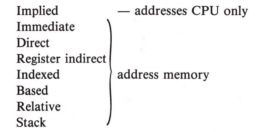

Implied   — addresses CPU only
Immediate
Direct
Register indirect
Indexed   address memory
Based
Relative
Stack

Many more complex variations of these addressing modes may also be found. Recent microprocessor designs tend to have more addressing modes than older 8-bit devices, but in general:

(a) All CISC processors have *immediate* and *direct* addressing modes, but it is more difficult to support these modes on RISC processors, because of the limited number of instruction word bits available to specify the data (immediate) or address (direct). RISC processors therefore rely more heavily on *register indirect* addressing to access arbitrary addresses in memory.

(b) All processors have some kind of addressing mode which allows *address modification* within the program at run time. There are several ways of supporting this requirement, each optimised for different data manipulation tasks. The most commonly provided modes allowing address modification are *register indirect, indexed* and *based*.

(c) *Relative addressing* is essential to write *position independent code*.

(d) *Stack addressing* and *implied addressing* may be supported by special instructions in addition to or instead of being generally available addressing modes.

(e) In most assembly languages, the mnemonic defines the instruction *type* and the required addressing mode is identified in the operand field.

**Problems**

7.1 For the three example microprocessors, identify any special-purpose implied address instructions.

7.2 Write down the cycle-by-cycle sequence of operations which takes place when the ARM instruction STMFD SP!,{R0–R3, LR} is executed.

7.3 Write down the cycle-by-cycle sequence of operations which takes place when the MC68000 instruction MOVEM.L A2/D2–D5/SP/D0 is executed.

7.4 How might a memory indirect jump instruction be used?

7.5 Extend the example given in Worked Example 7.4 so that it provides a full parameter passing mechanism using the stack. In particular, the solution should:

(*a*) enable a functional result parameter to be returned via the stack (cf. functions in PASCAL);

(*b*) maintain separate frame pointers associated with each subroutine call through nested subroutines;

(*c*) support re-entrant and recursive code.

# 8 Computer systems

**Objectives**  ☐ To explain the differences between general-purpose and dedicated computer systems.
☐ To discuss the methods by which data and programs may be entered into a computer.
☐ To describe typical computer peripherals and backing storage media, explain their purposes, and compare and contrast their performance.
☐ To explain how digital data may be represented as flux changes on magnetic media and compare alternative representations.
☐ To describe the data structures used for storing data on magnetic disks.
☐ To examine the additional computer facilities required to enable development and debugging of microprocessor hardware.

Much of the material in the preceding chapters has been orientated particularly towards the design of computer and microprocessor applications where the final product is a dedicated system in which the computing device executes a single program residing permanently in ROM. This reflects the fact that many engineering design projects incorporate computers or microprocessors to acquire and process data, to control equipment, or to maintain displays. In addition, however, most engineers and scientists need to use computers as a tool for calculation, simulation and data analysis even if their main activity is unconnected with computers. As a result the general-purpose computer is a familiar sight in most laboratories.

Thus in considering the application of computers, one must be aware of two distinct classes of computer system; on the one hand are dedicated computer applications, which are a particularly common way of using microprocessors because of their cheapness and flexibility; on the other are the general-purpose computer systems capable of executing a wide range of programs and thus requiring backing storage facilities so that these programs may be loaded into the computer memory when required.

In the early days, nearly all computers were of the general-purpose type, simply because their cost was too great for them to be dedicated to a single application; this is still generally the case with mainframe and minicomputers. Nowadays, while microprocessors are widely used in dedicated computer applications, the demand for cheap computing facilities has generated a large market also for microprocessor-based general-purpose computers which are simply scaled down versions of the larger mini- and mainframe computers.

A particularly important application of the general-purpose computer which is considered in this chapter is as a development tool used for developing other (dedicated) microprocessor applications.

In this chapter the hardware facilities required to produce a useful general-purpose computer system are considered; the corresponding software facilities are examined in Chapter 9.

## Program and data input/output

In Chapter 6, it was observed that the simplest way of writing a program is directly in binary code. Even if the program is available in this form the further problem of loading it into the computer's memory remains. This problem is perhaps most easily perceived by considering the dilemma which faced the builders of the first electronic computers in the 1940s. Although they could build the hardware of their computers and could write programs in abstract form on pieces of paper, they required a mechanism which would enable them to load the binary numbers representing their programs into the memory of the computer. A very simple way of doing this, employed in the earliest machines and still used today on many computers, is to make use of a set of switches and lamps connected directly to the data, address and control buses of the computer.

Another method used on very early computers was to implement memory using a plug-board matrix. The presence or absence of a plug then represented a logic 1 or logic 0, respectively.

### Switch registers and lamps

The switch register and lamps are perhaps the most recognisable part of any computer, though they have been rendered obsolete by the introduction of non-volatile permanent computer memory (ROM) over the last decade. A typical computer switch register consists of a set of binary switches corresponding to each bit of the data and address buses, together with a number of control function switches which enable the user to stop and start program execution, load data into a specified memory location, increment the memory address, load the program counter and so on. Since the computers which contained switch registers were generally implemented using SSI (Small Scale Integrated) and MSI (Medium Scale Integrated) circuits, it was easy to add additional logic to enable such operations to take place. Thus a program could be loaded into the computer memory and then executed using the following sequence:

(a) Stop program execution (if the computer was previously executing a program).
(b) Set the binary address of the first instruction on the address switches.
(c) Set the required binary value on the data switches.
(d) Press the *load* button (this would effectively pulse the write line so that the data on the data switches were loaded into the specified address in memory).
(e) Increment the address.
(f) Repeat until all instructions have been loaded into memory.
(g) Set the program counter to point to the first instruction in the program.
(h) Start program execution.

The advantage of such a mechanism for loading programs is that it can be entirely hardware-based; no pre-existing computer-resident software is required in order to load the program into memory. This is in contrast to every other method of loading programs which is described in this chapter, and for this reason it was one of the first methods used for loading programs into early computers. Switch registers continued to be used throughout the era of magnetic core memory to recover from program 'crashes' which overwrote the whole of memory, but are not required now because software to read other programs from magnetic tape or disk can be permanently (and non-erasably) resident in computer memory using ROMs.

A switch register is a very slow method of inputting a program to a computer since every bit must be specified individually; furthermore, mistakes can very easily be made. In practice, even on the early computers, the switch register was used simply as the first stage in inputting a program unless the program was extremely short (say, less than 20 words). For longer programs, the switch register would be used to input a short program which would then itself read the longer program into memory from a storage device such as a magnetic tape reader.

This process is known as *bootstrapping*, and is described in more detail in Chapter 9.

### Keypad and numeric display

The modern equivalent of the switch register is the hexadecimal keyboard and seven-segment display often found on simple microprocessor *evaluation kits*, which are used for learning about the architecture and instruction set of a microprocessor. The keyboard and display are generally combined with a simple *monitor* program stored in a ROM which forms part of the memory of the evaluation kit. This monitor, together with the keyboard and display, allows the user to input machine code programs and data to read/write memory. In addition, facilities are provided so that programs input in this way may be executed, memory and CPU registers may be examined, and program errors may be found using simple debugging facilities such as *breakpoints* and *single-stepping*. Instructions and data are normally specified in hexadecimal format rather than directly in binary, and conversion to binary within the evaluation kit may be performed by the monitor program or by hardware. In essence the evaluation kit and monitor provide a mechanism for writing and debugging very simple machine code programs of the sort which may be required when learning about the microprocessor.

A *breakpoint* is a point in a program, set by the user, at which control is passed back to the monitor program. The user may then examine memory, registers, and so on, to determine whether the program is operating correctly. *Single-stepping* is a facility whereby control is passed back to the monitor program after execution of each instruction, so that the user can examine program execution in detail.

### Visual display unit (VDU) or printing terminal

A much more flexible general-purpose input/output device for use with a computer is a VDU or a printing terminal producing hard-copy output. Since such devices can display a full range of alphanumeric characters, they can be used not only to input programs in a binary or hexadecimal format but also for textual input and output of programs as source code. Visual display terminals normally communicate with a computer using one of several possible serial asynchronous protocols.

The most commonly used protocols are RS232, in which a logic 0 is represented as a positive voltage of nominally 12 V and a logic 1 as a negative voltage of the same magnitude, and 20 mA current loop where positive and negative current flows are used to represent logic 1 and 0. In each case the data format is as represented in Fig. 6.3. Each 8-bit ASCII character is framed by a logic 0 start pulse and one or two logic 1 stop pulses. If another character is not transmitted immediately after the first character, the data line remains at logic 1. The next character can then be synchronised by detecting the transition to logic 0 of its start pulse.

Many terminals and printers can accept either protocol; RS232 is more widely used, but 20 mA current loop can be used over longer distances.

A number of different data rates are used to cope with varying physical characteristics of different types of terminal. The slowest data rate commonly used is 110 baud, which is required for teletypes capable of printing only 10 characters per second. The data format for 110 baud serial transmission includes one start bit and two stop bits, so that each character requires a total of 11 bits to be trans-

baud = bits/second

mitted, resulting in a data rate of 10 characters per second. In general, VDUs can operate at very much higher speeds than printing terminals because no mechanical operations are required, and a terminal may often be interfaced at a data rate of 9600 baud or faster. A single start and stop bit are used at this speed so that 9600 baud corresponds to 960 characters per second. Other commonly used data rates lie between these extremes and are powers of two slower than 9600 baud (i.e. 4800 down to 300 baud).

At the computer, the interface to the serial line requires conversion to appropriate logic levels and may then be accomplished either by software which performs serial-to-parallel and parallel-to-serial conversion within the computer (see Problem 6.5) or by a dedicated input/output device containing shift registers and control logic to perform the same function, such as the Motorola MC6850 ACIA introduced in Chapter 5.

The required logic levels depend upon the type of computer. Most microprocessors are MOS devices and use TTL-compatible logic levels. There are also a number of CMOS (Complementary Metal Oxide Conductor) microprocessors, and large computers may use high-speed ECL (emitter coupled logic) logic.

### Serial communication with a terminal

It is required to connect a terminal which communicates via an RS232 interface at 9600 baud to an MC68000 microprocessor system via an interface based upon an MC6850 ACIA. This will require serial communication both from the microprocessor to the terminal (data output to the screen) and from the terminal to the microprocessor (data input from the keyboard). These two interfaces are independent in software terms, but both can be supported by a single MC6850, which contains both a serial input and a serial output port. It is assumed that the ACIA is configured at a base address of 8000 hex., with the ACIA data input and output registers, therefore, at 8001 hex.

Since the routines for inputting a character and outputting a character are independent, the problem can be subdivided by initially considering just one of these routines, for example, the character input routine. A test and transfer subroutine is required which simply tests whether bit 0 (the receive data register full (RDRF) bit) of the ACIA status register is set, and reads in the received character if it is. This would require the following code:

**Worked Example 8.1**

The second part of this worked example is a solution to Problem 6.6. (There is no difference from the microprocessor's point of view between a printer and a terminal connected via a serial communication line.)

```
| Subroutine to read one character of data from a terminal
| via an RS232 serial line. Data are returned in register D0.
| No error checking is performed.
|
READCH  BTST.B   #0,$8000   | test status port, bit 0 (RDRF)
        BEQ      READCH     | loop if bit 0 not set
        MOVE.B   $8001,D0   | data is valid: read data port
        RTS                 | return from subroutine
```

Reading the data port causes the RDRF bit to be reset.

The program which calls this subroutine can deal with the character of data returned as appropriate to the application. For example, if the program were reading in a character string making up a command entered by the user of the program, the characters would simply be stored in an array until an appropriate terminating character such as <carriage return> or <space> was received. After executing the specified command, the program would be ready to read the next character from the terminal.

The subroutine which outputs a character to the terminal is very similar to the character input subroutine. In this case bit 1 (transmit data register empty (TDRE)) of the status register is tested to determine whether the previous character has finished being shifted out. The TDRE status flag is set high if the transmit data register (TDR) is empty. Thus the required code is:

```
|
| Subroutine to write one character of data to a terminal
| via an RS232 serial line. Data are passed to the subroutine
| in register D0. No error checking is performed.
|
WRTCH   BTST.B   #1,$8000   | test status port, bit 1 (TDRE)
        BEQ      WRTCH      | loop if bit 1 not set
        MOVE.B   D0,$8001   | TDR is empty: output char.
        RTS                 | return from subroutine
```

**Exercise 8.1**

Worked Example 8.1 above assumes that the ACIA has already been suitably initialised. Assuming that the terminal operates at 9600 baud, with one stop bit, seven data bits and odd parity, and that a divide-by-16 ratio of the ACIA clock input is needed for 9600 baud operation, write a subroutine which initialises the ACIA for the required serial data format.

**Exercise 8.2**

Error checking is an important part of asynchronous serial data transmission since correct data reception requires careful synchronisation of the transmitting and receiving devices.

The data input subroutine above does not carry out any error checking of the input character to verify that it has been correctly received. The ACIA includes logic to check whether a *framing error, overrun error* or *parity error* has occurred during reception; these conditions are identified by setting bits 4, 5 and 6 of the ACIA status register, respectively. Add code to the input subroutine to check whether any transmission error has occurred. This information should be passed back to the calling program in register D1. If an error has occurred, bit 7 of D1 should be set, and bits 6, 5 and 4 should contain a copy of the equivalent bits of the ACIA status register. Otherwise, register D1 should contain 0.

**Computer backing storage media**

The main computer memory provides random access to any memory location: this is a fundamental requirement to permit branch and loop operations. Ideally, electromechanical backing storage media should also provide fast random access. In practice, the mechanical characteristics result in serial access if one-dimensional media are used, and semi-random access if two-dimensional media (such as disks) are used.

Unlike the early computers which used magnetic core memories, modern general-purpose computers use semiconductor read/write memory (RAM) to store programs. When the computer is switched off, any memory-resident program is therefore lost. Although this problem can be avoided by storing programs in ROM, this solution is not acceptable in a general purpose computer where the fundamental requirement is to be able to run a wide range of different programs. This problem is resolved by providing every general purpose computer with one or more non-volatile backing storage media from which programs can be loaded into memory, and on which programs can be permanently stored when the computer is switched off. A wide variety of media is available, and their characteristics in terms of data access speed and storage capacity vary by several orders of magnitude. Some storage media provide *serial* access to data, while others provide *semi-random* access. The most commonly used media at present are based upon magnetic storage techniques, but in the past cards and paper tape were widely used, and laser-based optical storage systems are now becoming available even for small microcomputers.

## Digital magnetic recording techniques

The vast majority of currently used computer backing storage media are based upon magnetic storage techniques, because these provide compact storage, large capacities, high data access rates, and in the case of disk memories semi-random access. Although the accessing characteristics of the various magnetic storage media vary greatly, in nearly all cases the same basic digital recording techniques are used to store information on the magnetic medium.

Logic 1s and 0s are encoded on the magnetic medium as flux changes induced by applying pulses to the write head, which is in close proximity to the storage medium surface. When the pulse applied to the head terminates, a flux pattern remains on the magnetic surface in one of two polarities depending upon the polarity of the magnetising pulse, as is shown in Fig. 8.1. In choosing a format for encoding digital data, two conflicting requirements must be addressed: one objective is to obtain the maximum possible data packing density on the medium; the other is to maximise the reliability of data storage. A number of possible alternative data encoding formats are examined below, to illustrate the techniques which are used and the problems which occur.

*Return-to-zero encoding*

Return-to-zero data encoding is perhaps conceptually the simplest data format, since a logical 1 is encoded by means of a positive pulse to the write head, while a logical 0 produces a negative pulse. In between each pulse, the drive to the write head returns to 0, as shown in Fig. 8.2(a), thus giving rise to the name of the encoding format. The recorded flux pattern on the magnetic surface after the sequence of pulses shown in Fig. 8.2(a) is shown in Fig. 8.2(b), where the horizontal axis represents position along the surface of the medium, rather than time. If this surface is drawn past a read head, the magnetic flux is coupled into the core of the read head, and induces a voltage in the winding proportional to the rate of change of flux on the magnetic surface, as shown in Fig. 8.2(c). The original data can then be recovered by gating the output of the read head with an accurately timed strobe signal recorded on a parallel clock track of the recording medium, as shown in Fig. 8.2(d).

An obvious disadvantage of this data encoding method is that a timing track is required in addition to the data track in order to recover the recorded information. By contrast, some of the data formats introduced later are inherently *self-*

One advantage of storing data as flux changes is that the magnetic medium does not necessarily have to be read at the same speed as it is written. Compare this with the frequency shift keying system used for storing data from microcomputers on audio cassette recorders (p. 142)

The recorded pulse is a distortion of the original data pulse because of fringing effects around the write head.

Notice that the waveform of the recovered data at the output of the read head is not a copy of the input pulse waveform, nor is it the same as the flux pattern on the magnetic medium.

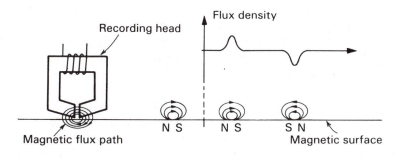

Fig. 8.1   Digital data storage using magnetic flux changes.

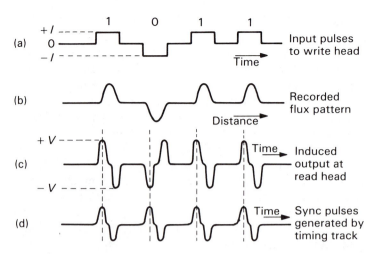

Fig. 8.2   Return-to-zero data storage and recovery.

*clocking*, resulting in potentially higher data packing densities. A more serious problem with the return-to-zero format occurs when it is desired to rerecord over previously recorded data. Because the recorded flux returns to zero between each pulse, any later recording must be aligned exactly with the previous recording to ensure that each previous pulse is overwritten and erased by the corresponding new pulse. Insufficiently accurate alignment of the pulses results in a previous pulse remaining on the medium between two new pulses, and causes a corresponding data error when the medium is read. In practice, it is quite difficult to achieve a timing accuracy sufficient to eliminate all errors, and alternative encoding techniques, based upon non-return-to-zero data formats, are generally used instead.

It is also difficult to ensure that the magnetic material remains demagnetised between pulses, since any stray flux tends to magnetise it.

### Return-to-bias encoding

A simple way of eliminating the problem of erasing previously recorded data is to ensure that current flows in the recording head at all times, so that all previous data are overwritten when the medium is rerecorded, regardless of the timing relationship between the new and old recordings. This can be achieved by using the data encoding scheme shown in Fig. 8.3, where current flows permanently in the write head, so that the whole length of the storage medium is magnetised in one direction or the other. In this particular example the data format differs from return-to-zero encoding only because the signal level transmitted to the write head when no pulse is being written is at the same level as a logic 0 pulse. Other examples of non-return-to-zero encoding formats also exist, and indeed the phase and frequency modulation encoding formats described below are both non-return-to-zero codes.

When return-to-bias data are read back from the magnetic medium, the output signal from the read head contains pulses corresponding to each logic 1 data bit but no pulses at all corresponding to logic 0. Thus a clock track is again essential in order to recover the data correctly, though in this case the timing requirements are much less stringent.

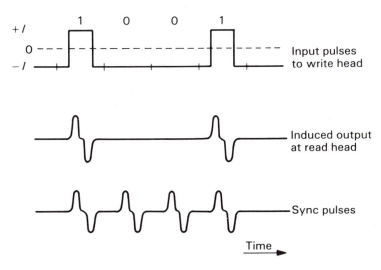

Fig. 8.3   Return-to-bias data encoding.

In many applications it is desirable (in some cases essential) to be able to recover data without the use of a clock track. In these cases a self-clocking code is used which not only codes the required serial data stream, but also provides sufficient transitions in the signal output to enable a free-running clock within the data recovery circuit to synchronise itself to the data waveform. To do this, self-clocking data formats must provide at least one logic transition per bit period, regardless of the data sequence which is being represented. Furthermore, as the clock cannot become synchronised instantaneously, the data sequence must be preceded by a *preamble* or *synchronisation pattern* to allow clock frequency synchronisation.

Fig. 8.11 shows how data are stored on a floppy disk, and illustrates the use of a synchronisation pattern.

### Phase modulation or biphase encoding

Phase modulation essentially represents a logic 0 by means of a positive transition and a logic 1 by means of a negative transition as shown in Fig. 8.4. Since each transition leads to a pulse in the read head when the medium is read, output pulses appear at a frequency which lies between the input data rate and twice the input data rate. A constant stream of logic 1 or logic 0 data bits causes output pulses to occur at twice the data input rate, while alternate 1s and 0s produces output pulses at the same rate as the data input. The output pulse sequence produced by the read head for biphase encoded data is quite complex, and some effort is required to recover the original pulse train from this signal. This is the penalty which is paid for using a compact self-clocking data format.

### Frequency modulation

A rather simpler self-clocking data format is the frequency modulation (FM) encoding format used on single-density floppy disks, which is shown in Fig. 8.5. In this format a logic 0 is represented by a single pulse, while a logic 1 requires two pulses. In effect, each data bit is preceded by its own clock bit. The FM data

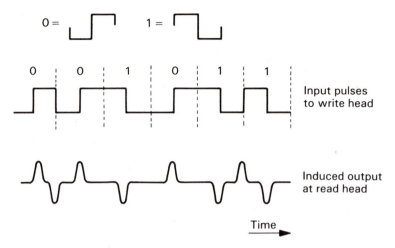

Fig. 8.4   Phase modulation data encoding.

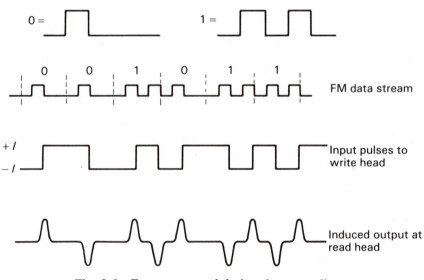

Fig. 8.5   Frequency modulation data encoding.

stream is divided by two before applying it to the write head, hence a logic 0 results in a single flux change at the write head while a logic 1 produces two flux changes. The output from the read head thus contains two pulses per bit time for a logic 1 and one pulse per bit time for a logic 0. This signal is filtered and smoothed by the read electronics, and then differentiated to produce a zero-crossing for each peak of the smoothed signal. The input data stream can then be recovered by generating an output pulse for each zero crossing.

*Modified frequency modulation*

The disadvantage of the FM format described above is that the data encoding is only about 50% efficient, since for every data bit a clock bit is also recorded. If a

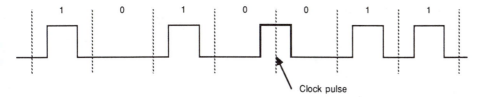

Fig. 8.6   Modified frequency modulation data encoding.

more efficient coding system could be used, for a given maximum density of flux reversals per inch, a higher data density would be achieved. The basic idea of modified frequency modulation (MFM) is to reduce the number of clock bits coded in the bit stream without losing the self-clocking capability of the code.

In examining the FM data format of Fig. 8.5, three observations may be made:

(a) No clock bit is required if the data bit is 1, since the data bit acts as its own clock bit in this case.

(b) No clock bit is required if a single 0 data bit occurs between two 1 data bits.

(c) The only circumstance under which a clock bit is essential is where a stream of more than one successive 0 data bits occur.

Thus the MFM encoding scheme is derived from FM by removing all clock bits except in case (c) above: in this case a clock pulse is inserted at any boundary between two successive 0 bits, as shown in Fig. 8.6. The effect of this change is to double the actual data density obtainable for a given bit density on the recording medium; the disadvantage is that the format is significantly more difficult to decode than simple FM, because it relies on phase differences between data and clock pulses to distinguish them.

**Cassette, cartridge and reel-to-reel tape**

These three magnetic storage media can be grouped together since they all provide serial access backing storage. As might be expected, the performance which can be obtained in terms of data rate and storage capacity depends upon the amount of money which one is prepared to spend. Reel-to-reel tape provides the highest data rates and capacities, but at a cost which is an order of magnitude greater than cartridge or cassette tape. Table 8.1 summarises typical performance characteristics of these three media.

**Table 8.1   Typical performance characteristics of magnetic tape media**

| Tape system | Storage capacity (bytes) | Data rate (bits/s) | Tracks |
|---|---|---|---|
| Reel-to-reel | $10^8$ | $10^6$ | 7 or 9 |
| Cartridge | $10^7$ | $5 \times 10^4$ | 1, 2 or 4 |
| Cassette | $10^6$ | $2.5 \times 10^4$ | 1 or 2 |
| Mini-cassette* | $5 \times 10^4$ | 1500 | 1 |
| Audio cassette | $10^6$ | 1200 | 2 or 4 |

* These devices are similar to normal digital cassette systems but use smaller cassettes similar to those used in dictation systems.

Eight of the nine tracks are
used to record the data; the
final track is a clock track for
synchronising data on the other
eight tracks.

There are several reasons why reel-to-reel tape transport systems are expensive. One is that the data are recorded in a bit-parallel byte-serial format using nine parallel tracks. Thus nine read/write heads are required, rather than a single head as is the case with cassette transports which store data in a bit-serial format. Cartridge tape transports are available in formats which allow one-, two- or four-channel recording.

A second source of expense in a tape system is the tape transport mechanism. For reasons which are explained in the next section, data are generally recorded on tape in discrete blocks which are delimited by blank tape. In order to search for a particular block as fast as possible a high tape speed must be employed, but at the same time the tape transport must be capable of very rapid stopping and starting within the inter-block gaps so that the amount of tape wasted within these gaps may be minimised. On reel-to-reel tape, the large inertia of the reels means that the tape passing the head must be isolated from the reels so that the required start-stop characteristics can be achieved. Long lengths of tape are laced through tensioning arms to provide this isolation. On cartridge and cassette transports, the lower inertia of the tape transports and media simplifies the transport design considerably.

Some mention should also be made of the audio cassette data storage systems used in many home microcomputer systems. Since these make use of standard domestic recorders rather than commercial data recorders, information must be coded using audio tones rather than flux changes to represent logical 1s and 0s. The most commonly used formats represent logic 1s and 0s as 2400 Hz and 4800 Hz audio tones, using a frequency shift keyed (FSK) data encoding scheme. This enables data to be recorded reliably at data rates up to 1200 baud. The performance of audio cassette data storage systems is also restricted because the low speed employed by audio cassette recorders ($1\frac{7}{8}$ inches/second) results in very slow searching of the tape compared with digital tape storage systems.

By comparison, digital cassette
and cartridge mechanisms can
read and write data at tape
speeds of up to 30
inches/second, and search for
inter-block gaps at up to 90
inches/second.

### Physical data structures on magnetic tape

Given a backing storage system of the type described above based upon magnetic tape, the information stored is, in principle, chosen entirely at the convenience of the programmer. An obvious example would be to use such a system for storing machine code programs, which could subsequently be loaded into the computer memory and executed.

In practice, a loader program (see Chapter 9) designed to read a machine code program into memory would require some additional information apart from the string of machine codes constituting the program. First, the machine code instructions on tape would need to be preceded by data indicating the address in memory at which the program was to be loaded, and possibly the start address as well if this was not the same. Second, some effort would have to be made to detect, and if possible correct, errors in the string of machine codes read into memory, since a single bit read in error would cause the program not to run correctly.

A common method of providing a rudimentary error detection facility is to make use of a *checksum*. The machine code program is split up into blocks of, for example, 128 or 256 bytes (the choice of block length is arbitrary), and associated with each block of code is a checksum which represents the arithmetic sum of all the bytes of data in the block, ignoring overflows. The checksum is itself written onto the tape at the end of the block of data. When the machine code program is subsequently read back into the computer, the loader performs an identical summation process on each block of machine code program, and compares the resulting checksum with the checksum read from the paper tape. Any difference between the two checksums indicates that an error has been made in reading the tape, since any error will change the checksum value.

Another common use for the backing storage medium is to store programs in their source code format. In this case the program would be stored as a string of alphanumeric characters coded using the ASCII code, and each character would occupy one byte on the magnetic tape. Again, the text data would be split up into fixed-size blocks and a checksum appended to each block to allow errors to be detected.

*Example block structure — Intel HEX records and Motorola S records*

Intel HEX records and Motorola S records are a means of representing machine code as a series of records (or blocks) using only printable ASCII characters. These formats are primarily intended for transferring machine code programs across serial lines and character-only communication media. They can also be used for storing programs on magnetic tape, however, and were originally developed for storing machine code on paper tape, which could be generated and read by teletype terminals. (Such terminals were commonly used instead of VDUs with early microprocessor systems.) The Motorola S record format is as follows:

(*record header information*)
- start of record symbol
  (ASCII character 'S')
- the record type
  (ASCII character '9' — end of file; ASCII character '1' — data block)
- the length of the record
  (in bytes, coded as 2 hex. digits (i.e. record length of 0–255 bytes))
  (The record length is the length of all of the remaining bytes in the record, i.e. the load address (2 bytes), data and checksum (1 byte))
- the load address for the record
  (2 bytes, represented as 4 hex. digits, specifying a 16 bit address)
(*record data*)
- the machine code
  (each byte of code is represented as 2 hex. digits)
(*record tail*)
- a checksum on the record
  (1 byte, represented as 2 hex. digits, representing the 1s complement of the sum of all bytes in the record except the initial characters)

The format of Intel HEX records is very similar:
(*record header information*)
- start of record symbol
  (ASCII character ':')
- record length
  (1 byte, coded as 2 hex. digits)
- load address
  (2 bytes, coded as 4 hex. digits)
- record type
  (1 byte, coded as 2 hex. digits:
    00 — data record;
    01 — end of file.)
(*record data*)
- data
  (each byte represented as 2 hex. digits)
(*record tail*)
- checksum
  (1 byte, represented as 2 hex. digits, representing the 2s complement of all bytes in the record except the initial start marker character)

*Interfacing a magnetic tape reader*

A reel-to-reel magnetic tape system is to be interfaced to an MC68000 microprocessor system using an MC6821 PIA configured at a base address of 6000 hex. The interface electronics in the tape transport contains an 8-bit output

**Worked Example 8.2**

port and associated 'data valid' status output bit (1 is valid); an 8-bit input port and associated 'data valid' status input bit (1 is valid); a tape start/stop control line (0 is stopped, 1 is started) and a 'tape valid' signal which is 1 when the tape reaches normal running speed and 0 otherwise. All signals are TTL-compatible. Write software to allow the MC68000 to read data from the tape system, assuming that the data are stored in Motorola S record format as given above, and represent a machine code program which should be loaded into the MC68000 memory at the load address(es) specified in the record header(s).

This problem should strictly be tackled in a top-down fashion, but this is only possible once it is recognised what subroutines are required at the lowest levels to effect character input from the magnetic tape. Initially, therefore, the lowest-level character input subroutine is considered.

The hardware interface between the peripheral interface adaptor and the magnetic tape system is very simple. Considering only the tape reader interface, the eight data outputs from the tape system would be connected directly to the eight data lines PA0–PA7 (or PB0–PB7) on the PIA. The 'data valid' output from the tape reader would interface to the CA1 (or CB1) control input to the MC6821 and would be configured to set bit 7 of the control register on a positive transition of the sensor line (i.e. as the 'data valid' signal goes to its 'valid' state). The interrupt request output from the PIA would be disabled. It is assumed initially that the magnetic tape is permanently running.

A test and transfer subroutine which simply tests whether bit 7 of the control register is set, and reads data from the PIA port if it is, can now be written as follows:

```
| Subroutine to read one byte of data from magnetic tape.
| Data is returned in register D0.
| No error checking is performed.
|
READ    BTST.B    #7,$6001    | test control port, bit 7
        BEQ       READCH      | loop if bit 7 not set
        MOVE.B    $6000,D0    | data is valid: read data port
        RTS                   | return from subroutine
```

The program which calls this subroutine must obviously deal with the byte of data returned as appropriate. For example, if the byte of data is a hex. digit representing one nibble of a byte of machine code, it must be converted to the appropriate 4-bit binary number, concatenated with the other nibble of the same byte, and stored in the appropriate address in memory. This address would be defined by a pointer register initialised to the load address of the code and incremented for each successive byte of machine code. After performing the required function, the program would be ready to read the next character from the magnetic tape.

At this stage, a potential synchronisation problem begins to become apparent. The data processing performed on each byte of data read from the magnetic tape, and the movement of tape under the tape head, are two simultaneously occurring but asynchronous events. Depending upon the speed at which the tape is driven and the amount of processing to be performed upon each byte of data, two possibilities exist:

1 nibble = 4 bits (½ a byte)

(*a*) The time taken to process the data may be short compared with the time taken to move the tape sufficiently for the next byte of data to appear at the data outputs of the tape system.

(*b*) The data processing time may be longer than the time taken to move the tape to the next data byte.

In either of these cases it is necessary to consider how (if at all) the data input program should be modified to ensure that each byte of data is read successfully.

If the data processing time is short compared with the time taken for the next data byte to become available, there is no possibility that data bytes from the tape will be missed completely. It may be, however, that when the data input subroutine is next called, the previous byte of data is still present at the tape system data outputs. Using the configuration of the PIA described above, this does not matter because the status bit (control register bit 7) is set by the positive-going edge of the 'data valid' pulse, and is reset when data is read from the data register in the PIA. Thus the status bit is not set again until the positive transition of the next 'data valid' pulse, and the subroutine simply waits in the program loop until this occurs.

**Exercise 8.3**

A magnetic tape reader interface to an MC68HC11 is configured as described in the example above, except that the 'data valid' input is connected to data input PB7. Write a subroutine to read data from the magnetic tape reader, ensuring that there is no possibility of data bytes being read more than once, if the processing time for each data byte is much shorter than the time taken for the next byte to become available.

Given the amount of processing required to convert the Motorola S record format data to machine code and load it into memory, it may not be possible to carry out all the processing for each byte within the time interval available between reading one byte and the next byte becoming available. The solution to this problem would then be to copy each byte of the record directly into an array in memory without carrying out any intermediate processing. When the checksum character indicating the end of the record is received, the tape would be stopped, and all of the processing required for the whole block could be carried out. Since the tape is stationary at this point, there are no constraints on the time available for carrying out this task.

Operating the tape system in this way requires two further signals: first, a motor on/off control signal, and second, a status signal ('tape valid') to indicate when the tape has reached normal running speed and it is valid to look for data at the data port. These two signals could be interfaced via additional lines on the PB data port of the PIA: for example, PB0 could be configured as a data output for controlling the motor, and PB1 as a data input for testing whether the tape was up to speed.

The control output and status input provide what is known as a *handshake* between the computer and the tape system. The purpose of the handshake is to synchronise fully two mutually asynchronous processes. In general this can be achieved by the use of two control lines between the devices. One line is a data request output from the device which wishes to read data (in this case the computer), while the second line is a data available output from the second device indicating when the data can be read. The timing sequence is shown in Fig. 8.7 and is arranged so that there is no possibility of any data being missed during the

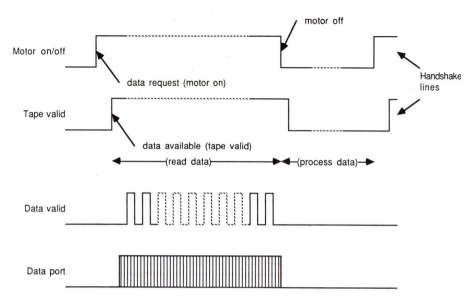

Fig. 8.7 Handshake transfer timing sequence.

transfer. The data available signal is generated as a response to the data request signal, and the next data request signal is not generated until the data read in response to the data available signal has been processed. In the particular application of reading data from the magnetic tape system, the data request signal corresponds to the tape motor control line, and the data available signal corresponds to the 'tape valid' status line.

The handshake concept can now be applied to the particular application being considered in this example, and an algorithm for reading S records from magnetic tape can be deduced:

(*1*) Start tape motor (set control output)
(*2*) Wait for 'tape valid' input (test status input)
(*3*) Read complete S record, and copy into memory array
      (including record header, data and tail)
(*4*) Stop tape motor (reset control output)
(*5*) Process complete S record
(*6*) Repeat complete loop until end of file reached

The algorithm can now be further refined by subdividing steps (*3*) and (*5*) into smaller parts. In particular, step (*3*) will contain within it the routine developed already for reading an individual character from the tape, and step (*5*) will require a subroutine to convert two hex. digits to 8 bit binary format.

**Exercise 8.4**    Complete the design and coding of the problem outlined above.

---

**Magnetic disk systems**

The fundamental disadvantage of all the backing storage systems described so far is that they are one-dimensional media which require data to be accessed in a sequential format. In many computer applications random or semi-random access is required, both for data files which may be manipulated by the computer program, and for overlays to large programs which normally reside on backing storage media, but may be loaded into memory and executed when required. One way to overcome this problem is to use a two-dimensional storage medium, such as a disk, on which the data can be stored in a number of concentric tracks. Rather than winding a long tape past the heads to find the required data, the head can then be moved orthogonally across the tracks until the required track is found.

Disk memories make use of rigid disks coated with magnetic oxide for storage. Since the disk surface is flat, a number of disks may be stacked together within the disk storage system to produce large storage capacities within a fairly compact device. Fig. 8.8 shows the structure of a rigid disk system. Each disk contains a large number of concentric tracks on which data can be recorded, and one or both sides of the disk can be used. A single read/write head is used for each disk surface, and the heads are moved backwards and forwards to access different tracks using mechanical actuators. Unlike tape systems, the heads on hard disk systems do not directly contact the magnetic medium, but are supported a few micrometres above its surface by laminar air flow. This means that there should be no wear of the magnetic medium, and hence no gradual degradation of its performance.

The maximum time required to access a specific word of data stored on a disk is made up of two components: the time required to position the read/write head at the appropriate track, and the time elapsed before the required word of data moves past the read/write head. This second component is defined by the rotational speed of the disk, and in the worst case is given by the reciprocal of the speed in revolutions per second. This time corresponds to the condition where the required word has just passed the read/write head when the device is accessed, and the computer then has to wait for a full revolution of the disk. A commonly quoted parameter for disk storage systems is *average rotational latency*, which is half the maximum access time, since on average it will be necessary to wait half a revolution for the required word to be read. The performance characteristics of

*Overlays* are generally used when a program is too large to be fully memory-resident. The program is segmented, and different segments are loaded from backing storage as necessary during execution.

This type of storage medium is said to provide *semi-random* access as it gives much faster access than serial access media such as tapes, but does not provide true random access.

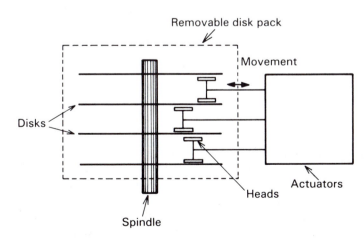

Fig. 8.8 Rigid magnetic disk memory.

**Table 8.2  Performance characteristics of typical Winchester disk systems**

| Characteristic | Specification | |
|---|---|---|
| Drive type | Hitachi DK515C-78 | Rodime RO-652 |
| Disk size | 5.25 in. | 3.5 in. |
| Unformatted capacity | 780 Mbytes | 25.5 Mbytes |
| Formatted capacity | 670.5 Mbytes | 21.3 Mbytes |
| Rotational speed of disk | 3600 r.p.m. | 2746 r.p.m. |
| Number of tracks/surface | 1356 | 306 |
| Number of surfaces | 14 | 4 |
| Track density | 1296 tracks/in. | 600 tracks/in. |
| Bit density of inner track | 40 210 bits/in. | 14 700 bits/in. |
| Data transfer rate | 2.458 Mbytes/s | 0.937 Mbytes/s |
| Seek speed (including settling time) | | |
| Minimum | 4 ms | 18 ms |
| Average | 16 ms | 85 ms |
| Maximum | 40 ms | 180 ms |
| Approximate price (1991) | £1200 | £250 |

Apart from the difference in storage capacity and data transfer rate, the main difference between the two example devices is in the type of head position actuator used. Low-cost drives designed for single-user microcomputer systems usually use a stepper motor actuator, whereas high-performance drives use a rotary actuator or voice coil to obtain very high seek speeds. The latter are essential to obtain adequate response times for multi-user minicomputer systems.

two example disk memories are summarised in Table 8.2. The physical data storage formats used for storing information on hard disks are very similar to those used for floppy disks, described in the next section.

Hard disk systems are available in a variety of configurations and sizes, and two main types exist. One type is the *removable disk system* commonly used on large minicomputers and mainframes, and illustrated in Fig. 8.8. These systems typically use large disks with diameters up to 14 inches. With the development of microcomputers generating a need for smaller, cheaper hard disk systems, *Winchester disks* have become widely used. These devices contain non-removable disks within a fully sealed enclosure, and are typically much smaller than removable disk systems. Early examples used 8 inch disks, but current devices are mostly based upon 5¼-inch and 3½-inch disks and are housed in packages of the same size as equivalent floppy disk systems, so that they can be readily built into microcomputer systems. The figures in Table 8.2 compare two Winchester disk systems, one of which is intended for use in workstations (the Hitachi DK515C-78) and one of which is designed for use in small microcomputer systems (the Rodime RO-652).

Winchester disks are fully sealed to prevent dust entering the disk enclosure and causing the read/write head to touch the disk surface. Conventional disk systems with removable disks employ air filters to ensure that all dust particles are removed from the disk enclosure.

**Floppy disks**

Floppy disks operate in very much the same way as fixed disks, but make use of cheaper media and provide smaller capacities and slower access than fixed disks. The medium was first invented by IBM as a semi-random access storage device for small computer systems where the cost of a rigid disk system could not be justified. As microcomputers have become more and more widely used this medium has expanded enormously and spawned a variety of different floppy disk standards. The original floppy disk (see Fig. 8.9) was 8 inches in diameter, but

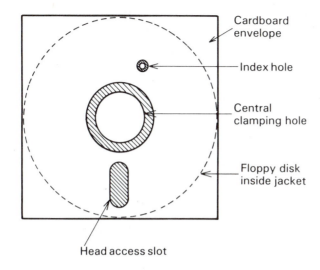

Cardboard envelope

Index hole

Central clamping hole

Floppy disk inside jacket

Head access slot

Fig. 8.9 Floppy disk and envelope.

8-inch and 5¼-inch disks have cardboard envelopes as shown in Figure 8.9: 3-inch and 3½-inch disks are mounted within rigid plastic, and have a retractable cover over the head access slot. They are therefore physically much more robust than the larger floppy disks.

5¼-, 3½- and 3-inch disks are now also widely used, and the 8-inch disk is obsolete.

The floppy disk consists of a thin disk of magnetic material on a plastic backing which is supported and protected within a cardboard or plastic envelope. The disk is clamped into the drive through a hole at the centre and rotates within the envelope. A slot is cut from the envelope along a radius from the centre to allow the disk read/write head to access the magnetic material and traverse from track to track. The disk drive contains either one or two read/write heads, depending upon whether single- or double-sided disks are used. In contrast to the rigid disk described previously, the read/write head is actually in contact with the medium when data are being read or written. To minimise the wear associated with reading and writing data, either the read/write head is unloaded from the disk surface when data is not being accessed, or alternatively the disk drive motor is stopped. In either case this leads to an additional source of delay in accessing information from the floppy disk by comparison with rigid disks.

Typical figures for read/write head life and media life are 15 000 and 3000 contact hours, respectively. (Note that media life may be sharply reduced if wear is not evenly spread over the whole disk.)

**Physical data structures on floppy and hard disks**

Like data on tapes, data stored on disks are split up into fixed-size blocks. An address is normally recorded as part of the header information of each block, since random access to blocks on a disk is commonly required, unlike tapes where access is usually sequential. One reason for storing data in blocks on the disk is the ability to detect errors in reading the data as described earlier. Another reason is that the majority of time required to access a data word from a disk is associated with positioning the read/write head at the correct place on the magnetic surface. Having achieved the correct head position there is an almost negligible overhead in reading a large block of words rather than a single word; furthermore, in most computer applications strings of contiguous words need to be accessed.

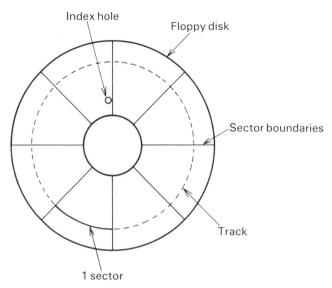

Index hole

Floppy disk

Sector boundaries

Track

1 sector

8 sectors, 512 bytes/sector format shown

Fig. 8.10    Floppy disk data format.

Soft-sectored disks can be reformatted to change the number of sectors on a track. This is not possible with hard-sectored disks because the number of sectors is defined by the number of physical sector marks.

The IBM soft-sectored floppy disk format is used as an illustration because it is the most widely used 5¼-inch floppy disk format. Many other formats also exist.

*NB*: The physical bit density increases on the inner tracks because the physical length of a sector decreases.

The inter-field gaps are made large enough to allow for tolerance variations between different disks and different disk drives, so that a disk recorded on one disk drive can be read on another.

On a disk, the blocks of data are called *sectors* and are subdivisions of a track as shown in Fig. 8.10. Within each track, sectors are identified using an index mark or hole on the floppy disk. The sector which is encountered immediately after the index mark is numbered 1, and other sectors follow in sequence up to the last sector. Most floppy disks use a *soft-sectored* format where sectors are identified simply by counting elapsed time from the index mark. *Hard-sectored* formats can also be used, however, and in this case sectors are uniquely defined by physical sector holes on the disk.

A typical floppy disk format, such as the format used for IBM PC compatible floppy disks, allows eight sectors per track with each sector capable of storing 512 bytes of data. The IBM format uses 40 tracks per side of a double-sided 5¼-inch disk with a density of 48 tracks per inch, and thus gives a total capacity per disk of 320 kbytes. Data are represented using the MFM encoding scheme described earlier in the chapter. Since this format was defined in the early 1980s, developments in floppy disk technology have resulted in higher track densities becoming possible, such that 5¼-inch disks with a density of 96 tracks per inch and 640 kbytes capacity are now commonly used. Similarly, 3½-inch disks with the same number of tracks and storage capacity per track are also common in many IBM PC compatibles: these have an even higher track density of 135 tracks per inch. Table 8.3 gives some specifications for typical 5¼- and 3½-inch disk systems.

Each sector is further subdivided into an identification field, which contains the sector address, and a data field which contains 512 bytes of data. Some details of the exact format are given in Fig. 8.11. Each field is delimited by a gap which allows fields to be written selectively without overwriting adjacent fields. For example, when data are written to the floppy disk, only the data field is normally rewritten; the address field remains unchanged and is simply used to identify the correct sector to be written. Following a data gap the first recorded information is

**Table 8.3  Performance characteristics of typical 5¼- and 3½-inch floppy disk drives**

| Characteristic | Specification | |
|---|---|---|
| Drive type | Mitsubishi M4853 5¼ in. | Teac FD35F 3½ in. |
| Unformatted capacity | 500 kbytes (FM) | 500 kbytes (FM) |
| | 1000 kbytes (MFM) | 1000 kbytes (MFM) |
| Formatted capacity | 327.68 kbytes (FM) | 327.68 kbytes (FM) |
| | 655.36 kbytes (MFM) | 655.36 kbytes (MFM) |
| Rotational speed of disk | 300 r.p.m. | 300 r.p.m. |
| Number of tracks/side | 80 | 80 |
| Number of heads | 2 | 2 |
| Track density | 96 tracks/in. | 135 track/in. |
| Radius of inner track | 1.3438 in. | 0.9129 in. |
| Bit density of inner track | 5922 bits/in. | 8717 bits/in. |
| Seek speed | 3 ms/track | 3 ms/track |
| Head settling time | 15 ms | 15 ms |
| Head loading time | 50 ms | 50 ms |
| Motor start time | 250 ms | 400 ms |
| Approximate price (1991) | £150 | £150 |

Compare the track density and bit density of floppy disks with that of hard disks: much higher densities are possible for hard disks because the rigid disk has a surface which is manufactured to much higher tolerances.

always a synchronising field which allows the data clock to synchronise itself to the incoming data rate. In the identification field the synchronising information is followed by a 4-byte address which identifies both the track and the sector which is being accessed. Thus, errors in seeking the correct track on the disk can be identified from the track address read within the sector. The address is followed by 3-byte cyclic redundancy code (CRC) which allows any error in reading the address field to be detected. In the data field the synchronising information is followed by 512 bytes of data, and this is again followed by a 3-byte cyclic redundancy code which enables errors in reading the data field to be detected.

Cyclic redundancy codes are another technique used for detecting errors in blocks of transmitted data, and are used in a similar way to checksums. The CRC is created by dividing the transmitted block of data by a predefined polynomial.

*Estimation of disk performance*

**Worked Example 8.3**

Given the disk performance characteristics of Table 8.3, estimate:
  (*a*) the maximum time to access a sector on the disk;
  (*b*) the maximum data rate when data are read from the disk;

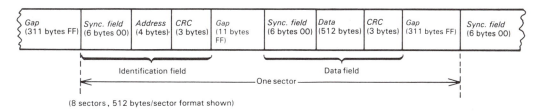

Fig. 8.11  Data fields on a floppy disk.

(*c*) the average data rate when several contiguous sectors are read (not including initial access time).

(*a*) The maximum access time is given by adding together the time required to seek the requested track, the head settling time, the head loading time, and the rotational latency. The maximum seek time occurs when a seek from the outer to the inner track, or vice versa, is requested. Using the figures given, for either of the example floppy disk drives, the maximum access time would be:

| | |
|---|---:|
| Seeking from outside to inside track (80 × 3 ms) | 240 ms |
| Head settling time | 15 ms |
| Head loading time | 15 ms |
| Rotational latency (maximum) | 200 ms |
| *Total* | 470 ms |

(*b*) The maximum data rate can be estimated from the disk rotational speed and dimensions, making use of the information given as to the density of bits stored on the magnetic surface. Thus at the inner track, the data rate is given by the rotational speed in revolutions/second multiplied by the circumference of the inner track multiplied by the data density.

$$\text{Data rate} = 5 \times 2\pi \times 0.9129 \times 8717$$
$$= 250 \text{ kbits/s}$$

(*c*) The data rate calculated in (*b*) above is the data rate when the data field within the sector is being transferred to the computer. When the address or synchronising fields, or the CRC codes are being read, however, the data rate is zero. Thus if a number of contiguous sectors are read, the average data rate is given by averaging the data rate to include both the periods when data are being read, and also periods when other sector information is being read. Since the number of data bytes in a sector (512) and the number of sectors on a track (8) are known, the average data rate may be estimated simply by estimating the ratio between the data stored on a track, and the total storage capacity of a track, and multiplying this by the peak data rate calculated above.

| | |
|---|---|
| Total data bits per track | $= 8 \times 512 \times 8$ bits |
| | $= 32\ 768$ bits |
| Total storage capacity per track | $= 2\pi \times 0.9129 \times 8717$ bits |
| | $= 50\ 000$ bits |
| Thus, average data rate | $= 250\ 000 \times 32\ 768 \div 50\ 000$ |
| | $= 163\ 840$ bits/s |
| | $= 20.48$ kbytes/s |

A particular computer system uses a disk structure in which accessed sectors are *interleaved* by a factor of six, i.e. the next logical sector to read is physically the sixth sector after the sector currently being read. Estimate the average data rate for reading data from a disk using this format.

## Microprocessor hardware development facilities

The components described so far in this chapter enable a complete general-purpose computer system comprising processor, memory, backing storage media and terminals to be constructed. Such a system can be used for applications programming, data analysis and many other commonly required functions. For the electronics engineer, one particular use of a general-purpose computer is for developing applications programs for dedicated microprocessor applications. In this case an additional requirement is to have available suitable tools for developing and debugging the hardware of the microprocessor system as well as the software. These tools turn out to be very different form the traditional engineer's debugging tools of oscilloscopes and meters, because the hardware environment of a microprocessor system is quite dissimilar to traditional analogue or digital electronics.

The type of tool required can best be perceived by considering the design process which occurs when a microprocessor-based product is developed. The design can be split into two parts, software design and hardware design. The hardware design should be relatively straightforward, except perhaps for specialised input or output interfaces, because the designer is designing using a standard set of components configured in a standard way. By using a microprocessor instead of (for example) random logic, the designer is transferring the design complexity from hardware to software. The general purpose computer can be used for developing the microprocessor software, to the point where the final program has been written and debugged or simulated within the environment of the computer.

At this stage, the machine code program can be copied into PROMs using a PROM programmer, the PROMs can be plugged into the prototype hardware and the complete prototype tested. The prototype may not work (or may work incorrectly) for two reasons:

(*a*) there may be a fault in the prototype hardware design which has not previously been detected, or

(*b*) a fault may exist due to an unexpected interaction between the hardware and the software within the product.

In either case, the problem may not be detected until a fairly late stage in development because the hardware and software are each developed in isolation. Several development tools have been introduced to assist the hardware development of microprocessor-based products, and in particular to help to resolve problems which occur when hardware and software are first integrated together.

### In-circuit emulation

The term *in-circuit emulation* was first coined by Intel to describe a hardware debugging facility built into its proprietary microprocessor development systems

**Exercise 8.5**

*Interleaving* is a way of matching the average incoming data rate from a disk with the rate at which data can be processed by the computer. The interleave factor is chosen so that rotational latency is minimised for the required computer processing time (see Figure below).

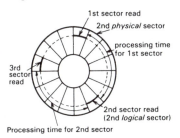

1st sector read
2nd *physical* sector
processing time for 1st sector
3rd sector read
2nd sector read (2nd *logical* sector)
Processing time for 2nd sector

To minimise the chance of a hardware fault, the designer should develop test software which exhaustively tests the prototype hardware, in addition to the actual product software.

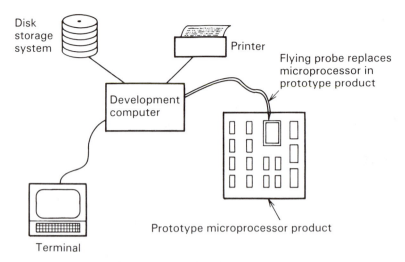

Fig. 8.12   In-circuit emulation.

(which are in other respects standard general purpose computers). The facility has since gained wide acceptance and is now a recognised feature of all microprocessor manufacturers' development systems, and is also available as a separate add-on facility for other general-purpose computers. Fig. 8.12 shows the concept of an in-circuit emulator and illustrates its use.

The emulator is generally implemented by removing the target microprocessor chip from its socket on the hardware prototype, and replacing it with a flying probe connected by means of an umbilical cable to the computer. This allows the computer to access and control the buses on the hardware prototype. The computer can then *emulate* the target microprocessor, and execute the prototype software while overall control still resides within the development computer. Thus facilities for setting breakpoints, single-stepping, and examination of memory and CPU registers can be provided in an analogous way to the monitor facilities described earlier in this chapter and in Chapter 9, but with all functions being monitored in the environment of the prototype hardware. Diagnostic information can be displayed on the computer terminal or printed on a printer for subsequent analysis.

The emulator can also be used as a method of down-line loading software into the memory of the prototype, prior to emulation. If the prototype does not contain sufficient RAM to store the program, memory within the development computer can simulate the product memory. Thus emulation does not need to be a once-and-for-all operation undertaken when software development is nearly complete, but can be performed at any stage during development, even before the hardware design is complete. In this way, the possibility of the hardware and software of the prototype being incompatible can be minimised.

A final requirement of emulation, which may be needed to identify obscure interface timing problems when the prototype software is run, is the ability to trace program execution as the program is run in real time. Monitoring a program using single stepping or breakpoints interrupts program execution every time control is passed back to the monitor program, and this may make it impossible to verify the correct operation of time-critical input and output operations. Since the computer has access to the prototype buses, however, if suitable additional hardware is used, the state of these buses can be recorded for each clock cycle during full-speed program execution using a separate memory. The bus states can subsequently be examined to determine whether the program was correctly executed. Normally the user specifies a *window* of bus states to be recorded, data acquisition being triggered by a specified initial bus condition.

## Logic analysers

Logic analysers are self-contained diagnostic tools which perform much the same functions within the microprocessor environment as an oscilloscope performs in examining analogue circuit operation. They contain probes which are connected to the microprocessor buses (sometimes a clip is provided which mounts directly on top of the microprocessor chip), and allow bus activity on the product to be monitored. Data are acquired from the buses in real time and displayed to allow program execution to be verified. The display can be of logic states (*logic state analysis*), where the bus states on successive clock cycles are monitored and displayed in binary, hexadecimal or even as instruction mnemonics, or alternatively a reconstituted multi-channel oscilloscope display (*logic timing analysis*) can be produced so that bus timing, input/output timing or asynchronous events can be monitored.

*NB*: The emulator is an *active* device (the probe replaces the microprocessor chip) and can control and modify program execution, whereas the logic analyser is a *passive* device which simply monitors the bus activity of the microprocessor within the prototype hardware.

## Signature analysers

Whereas logic analysers and in-circuit emulators are used to debug a microprocessor-based product during its initial development, signature analysers are designed for fault-finding in mature microprocessor products. They enable *continuity checks* on circuit nodes to be made by comparing the digital data stream at a particular node with the expected data stream for a correctly operating product. This is analogous to analogue fault-finding by measuring node voltages and comparing them with expected node voltages specified on a circuit diagram.

In order to use a signature analyser, a standardised test stimulus must first be provided on the microprocessor buses, and this is usually achieved by building a very short test program sequence into the product software. The test sequence is selected by putting the product into a *test* mode using a switch or alternative external input. The signature analyser is now connected to a suitable clock source (normally the microprocessor system clock), and the single probe input can then monitor individual data, address or control bus lines. The serial bit sequence acquired from the monitored line is compressed into a hexadecimal four-digit code which is displayed on a four-digit seven-segment display, and can be compared with an expected reference code (the actual codes are irrelevant since the test is a simple pass/fail test). By examining each bus line in turn, faults such as open or short-circuit lines or lines shorted together can be found very rapidly.

The four-digit code is generated in much the same way as a cyclic redundancy code.

## Summary

This chapter has examined the components beyond the computer itself which are needed in order to construct a useful general-purpose computer system. These components include terminals and printers used for inputting data and programs to the computer, and backing storage media, used for providing permanent non-volatile storage when power to the computer is removed. Some consideration has been given to the methods of interfacing such devices to the computer, in particular the problem of synchronising the peripheral device with the computer to ensure correct data transfer. A number of data structures for storing information on backing storage media have also been examined, to illustrate the techniques used to identify required blocks of data and detect errors in data transfers. Finally, the particular requirements of microprocessor applications development have been considered, and some additional tools used for microprocessor hardware debugging introduced.

## Problems

(These problems are written with an MC680HC11 implementation in mind, but with small changes could be treated as problems for the ARM or MC68000.)

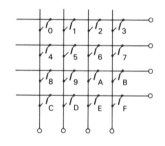

8.1 A set of 16 key-switches are connected as a 4 × 4 matrix as shown in the margin figure. Explain how an MC6821 PIA could be configured to detect the depression of a key, and write an assembly language subroutine which scans the key-switches and returns with the A and B accumulators containing a 16-bit binary code indicating which key has been depressed. (It may be assumed that only one key will be depressed at a time.)

8.2 The 16 key-switches are coded with the hexadecimal numbers 0–F as shown. Write an assembly language program which returns an ASCII code in the A accumulator corresponding to the key which has been pressed.

8.3 In Problem 8.1, it is desired to initiate keyboard scanning via an interrupt when a key is pressed. Explain how this can be achieved, and what extra hardware would be needed.

8.4 It is required to develop software to output data to the magnetic tape system described in Worked Example 8.2, using a further MC6821 PIA.

    (*a*) Explain how the interface to the tape input port could be implemented using the MC6821, to output data using the test and transfer method.

    (*b*) Write a routine in MC68HC11 assembly language which can be called repetitively by the main program to output a block of data to magnetic tape. The subroutine should be called once to output each data byte, which will be passed from the main program in accumulator A.

    (*c*) How could the software be modified to perform the required data transfers under interrupt control?

8.5 The software which calls the magnetic tape output routine of Problem 8.4 outputs data as a block of 256 bytes made up as follows:

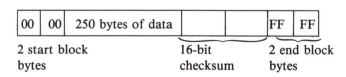

| 00 | 00 | 250 bytes of data | | | FF | FF |

2 start block bytes                   16-bit checksum            2 end block bytes

Write a subroutine which outputs a block of data in this format by repetitively calling the subroutine of Problem 8.4, and is called with the index register pointing to the start of a table of 250 data bytes stored in memory.

8.6 A commonly used interface to printers is the Centronics parallel interface which performs data transfers using seven or eight parallel data lines and two handshake lines. The handshake lines take the form of a strobe output pulse from the computer indicating when output data are valid, and an acknowledge output from the printer indicating when it is capable of receiving the next character (see margin figure). Indicate how an MC6821 PIA could be configured to provide seven data output lines and two handshake lines according to the Centronics interface convention, and write an assembly language subroutine to output ASCII characters held in accumulator A in accordance with the convention.

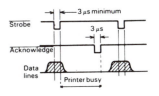

8.7 Data transfers via the Centronics interface described in Problem 8.6 are to be performed under interrupt control. Show how the PIA would be reconfigured and the subroutine modified to achieve this.

8.8 Data are transferred between a floppy disk system and an MC68HC11 microcomputer system using a test and transfer mechanism. Estimate the maximum data rate which the MC68HC11 can tolerate without missing data if it operates at 1 MHz clock rate. Explain any assumptions made in calculating this figure.

# 9 System software

**Objectives**

☐ To introduce the software tools required as part of a useful general-purpose computer system.

☐ To explain the function of an operating system program, and its relationship with other computer programs.

☐ To describe the tools required for developing applications programs in assembly and high-level languages.

☐ To explain how programs written as a number of separate modules may be combined into a single machine code program.

The previous chapter concentrated on discussing the hardware required to build up a useful and flexible general-purpose computer system, and on some of the design decisions which must be made. A vital part of any general-purpose computer is the system software, or software tools which are used in conjunction with the computer hardware. Without the system software the computer is rather like a car without petrol; although the basic mechanics of the system exist, there is no way of actually using it. This chapter concentrates on the software tools which are required to turn a general-purpose computer into a useful computer system for applications programming, for microprocessor applications development, or for use as a business or administrative system. Some insight into the types of program required can be gained by considering the various tasks which might be undertaken using a general-purpose computer.

The computer hardware defines the *potential* performance of the computer (processing power, storage capacity, etc.); the system software specifies the *achieved* performance (i.e. whether the hardware is used effectively).

In business and commercial applications, application software such as word processing, database management and accounting packages may be purchased as part of the computer system in addition to the normal system software described here.

## Loader

As suggested earlier, the first requirement when a computer is switched on is some kind of *loader* program which can be used to load any other program from the backing storage medium into memory prior to execution. A simple example of a suitable program for loading software from magnetic tape has already been described. In most modern computers the loader would be a rather larger program stored in ROM and designed to read programs from a disk, as shown in Fig. 9.1.

The concept of using one piece of software to enable another (generally more complex) piece of software to be run is called *bootstrapping*. Thus the loader program provides a method of bootstrapping other more complex programs (for example, a disk operating system as described in the next section). This approach is taken to minimise the use of the computer system memory; the loader program which resides permanently in ROM typically occupies only about 1 kbyte of memory, and therefore frees most of the remaining memory for other programs. The loader program is also often combined with a simple *monitor* or *debugger* program which may be used to debug machine code programs, and also to verify operation of the computer hardware without requiring access to a backing

The term *bootstrapping* refers to the use of an existing computer facility to enable a new, more sophisticated facility to be made operational.

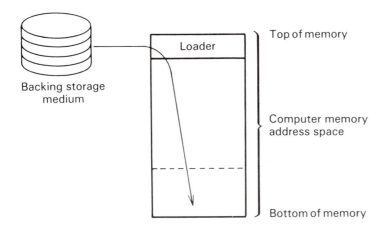

Fig. 9.1  Operation of a loader program.

storage medium. The monitor communicates via the system console, but otherwise provides very much the same facilities as described in Chapter 8.

A different type of computer may also be used for bootstrapping, by making use of *cross-software*. For example, a program may be written for a microprocessor such as the MC6809 on a minicomputer or mainframe computer, using an assembler written in a language which is available on the large computer, such as PASCAL, C, or FORTRAN. The assembler program which runs on the mini- or mainframe computer is known as a *cross-assembler* because it produces machine code for the microprocessor and not for the computer on which the assembler is run. The machine code program can then be transferred to the target computer either in PROMs or via any of the other storage media described in Chapter 8, or it can be downloaded directly via a serial or parallel communication link.

When microprocessors were first introduced, this was a common way of developing applications software for them, because microcomputer development systems based on the microprocessor were not initially available.

### Disk operating system

Software which enables programs to be loaded from (and stored on) backing storage media can be combined with facilities which handle the display terminal(s) and other computer peripherals such as printers, plotters, and so on, to provide a general-purpose control program. This *operating system* program generally makes use of floppy or hard disks as the main backing storage medium, because of the ease of randomly accessing different areas of disk containing different files. Hence the program is known as a *disk operating system* (DOS), and Fig. 9.2 illustrates its operation.

A disk operating system provides two fundamental facilities. First, it provides a mechanism for communication between the computer and the user by handling input and output to the user's console and executing the commands specified by the user. Second, it provides a mechanism for program storage and retrieval, though generally in a rather more flexible and sophisticated form than the simple loader program. Through the medium of the operating system users are able to access source files and call up text editors to make changes to them.

In this discussion, a single user of the computer system is assumed; note, however, that many computers are designed to serve multiple users simultaneously. The operating system then simply allocates short time slots to each user in turn.

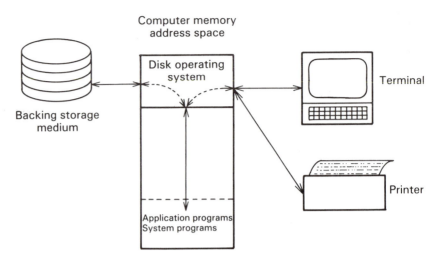

Fig. 9.2   Operation of a disk operating system.

They can then assemble or compile the source code (as appropriate) to produce machine code programs, and the machine code can be loaded into memory and executed, all under the control of the operating system.

Files, which may contain machine code, ASCII coded source text, data or any other information, are stored on the disk in a format defined by the operating system, and are accessed via *filenames*. The filenames, which are simply mnemonics chosen by the user to reflect the contents of a file, are stored in a directory which can be examined by the user. Manipulation of files — for example, assembly of an assembly language source file to produce machine code — can then be performed simply by referring to the file using its filename. In a similar way, all the other system programs described in this chapter are accessed through an operating system.

The directory also identifies where the file is stored physically on the disk, but this information is generally only required by the operating system, and so is concealed from the user.

The operating system also provides a number of housekeeping utility programs which are necessary so that the user can maintain his files on the disk in an orderly fashion. Typically, the operating system includes the following:

(a) *Directory listing* so that the user can determine what files are on the disk, their size, when they were created and other useful information.
(b) *File erasing* so that unwanted files may be removed from the disk to free space for other purposes.
(c) *File renaming* so that filenames may be changed if required.
(d) *File transfer* so that files may be copied to another disk for backup purposes or for duplication.
(e) *File listing* so that the contents of text files may be printed.
(f) *File execution* so that machine code files may be loaded into memory and executed.

Notice that this requirement implies that the computer system should include at least two backing storage devices (for example, two floppy disks).

The files to be executed may be system software programs or they may be the user's application programs.

In addition, operating systems may include many other more advanced and specialised facilities which are beyond the scope of this discussion.

Finally, the operating system provides a straightforward mechanism to enable the user to access terminals, printers and storage devices connected to the computer from within his application programs. Access is achieved by executing subroutine calls to standard subroutines within the operating system which control these devices. This saves the user from needing a detailed knowledge of the interface characteristics of the peripheral devices connected to the computer if he simply wishes to run application programs which access the standard computer peripherals under the control of the operating system.

## Text editor

Given a loader for bootstrapping the operating system when the computer is switched on, and the ability to manipulate files stored on a disk storage system, the user's next requirement is generally a facility for developing application programs in a high-level language or assembly language. In either case, the application program is initially written as a source code text file using a *text editor*. The editor program must therefore provide a mechanism for inputting the source code program and saving it on disk, and subsequently facilities must also be available for making changes, corrections and additions to the source program.

Word processors are essentially advanced text editors which include many additional features not required in editing computer source programs, such as text formatting and pagination, underlining, super- and subscripting.

Three types of activity are involved in using a text editor. First, the user must identify the text which is to be manipulated, or the place at which text is to be inserted in the file. This requires a *pointing* operation to specify where the change is to be made. Second, the user must specify the *operation* or *command* which is to be performed. Typical editing operations will include insertion of new text, deletion of text, and substitution of new text for old. In each case, the change may be made on a character, word, or line basis. More sophisticated editors also include commands to search a complete file for occurrences of a specified character string, and optionally replace this with a new string. They may also provide facilities for merging separate files or subdividing files. Finally, having specified the required editor command, the user must type in the replacement text or new text if the command requires it.

Computer text editors can be categorised into two broad types: *line-based* and *screen-based*. Screen-based editors are the simplest to use because the display terminal represents a *window* on the text file, and the pointing operation is achieved by using cursor keys on the terminal to position the cursor where a change is to be made. If the user wishes to move outside the range of the current display window, the screen is scrolled up or down to position the window at the required place in the file. Commands are generally displayed using a simple menu positioned on a fixed 'status' area of the screen, and selected by typing the first letter of the command or using special command function keys. Thus the text editor is simple and straightforward to use, and the effect of executing a command is immediately obvious on the screen.

User-friendliness is an important aspect in the design of a text editor, since most programmers spend a very large proportion of their time inputting and editing source text files.

Unfortunately, screen-based editors cannot always be used because they require facilities which may not be available on the computer. First, a relatively high serial communication rate (perhaps 9600 baud) is required between the console and the computer, so that operations such as moving the text window in the file, which requires the complete screen to be rewritten, can be achieved sufficiently rapidly (within 1–2 seconds). Second, pointing operations which make use of cursor positioning are only meaningful on a display terminal which has the facility for the computer to specify the cursor coordinates directly. Some terminals do not have this facility, and hence cannot be used in this way. Furthermore, printing terminals are sometimes also used as editing devices, and in this case the concept of a cursor is obviously meaningless.

If a screen-based editor cannot be used, the alternative is to use a line-based editor. All operations in this case are referred to a specified line in the source file. The line may be specified using a line number, or it may be identified using an *invisible cursor*. In this latter case, commands are executed to move the invisible cursor through the file, and the current cursor position within the file can be determined by causing the editor to list the current line on the terminal. Line-based editors generally require much greater memory on the part of the user and hence require significant training before competence is achieved.

Historically, line-based editors were developed before screen editors, because cursor-addressable display terminals were not widely available for early computers.

### Assemblers and compilers

Once a source file has been prepared using a text editor, the next stage is to convert the program to machine code using an assembler (if the program is written in assembly language) or a compiler (if in a high-level language). Most of the important features of assemblers and compilers have already been introduced in Chapter 6. For short programs, the facilities introduced so far prove quite adequate; as larger and more complex programs are written, however, some disadvantages begin to become apparent.

As the size of the source program increases, the time required to assemble or compile the program also increases as does the editing time (since it takes longer to locate the required part of the program within the file). Thus the efficiency of the programmer begins to fall. One way to resolve this problem is to split the program into a number of separate source modules, each of which can be edited and assembled or compiled separately. A mechanism is then required to build the various program segments together into a final machine code program. Another related problem also may become apparent; this is a need to be able to segment and separate different parts of a program physically in memory. As an example, in developing a microprocessor application, it may be required to specify one memory area for program and data constants which will be stored in ROM, and a separate non-contiguous area for data variables stored in RAM. Furthermore, at the time the program is written, the final allocation of memory may not be known. Thus a simple mechanism for *relocating* the program to different memory addresses is needed.

This is very easily achieved if a top-down structured design strategy has been adopted (see next chapter).

### *Relocatable assemblers and linking loaders*

One way to achieve this is by a simple modification to the loader and assembler or compiler programs described earlier. The assembler or compiler program is now designed to produce *relocatable object code* rather than absolute machine code. This means that wherever an absolute memory address is specified within the machine code file, this address is now specified as an address relative to zero and tagged by the assembler or compiler. Thus if the program is actually loaded starting at address 0, all the addresses specified within the program are correct. If, however, it is desired to load the program at any other base address, the base address can be specified to the loader, and is added as an offset to all tagged

NB: Unlike a machine code file, the object code file produced by a relocatable assembler is not directly executable.

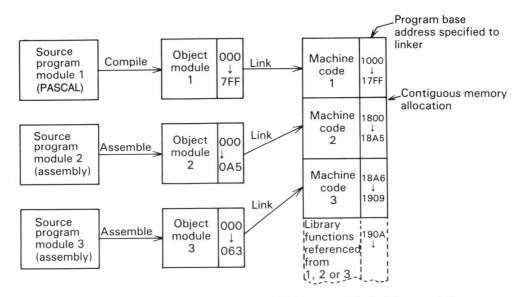

Fig. 9.3    Linkage of separately compiled or assembled object modules.

addresses in the object code file to produce a machine code program which executes correctly at any specified address in memory. An assembler or compiler program which includes this feature is generally known as a *relocatable* assembler or compiler.

One advantage of this scheme is that it can be used to help build together a number of program modules which have been written and compiled or assembled separately, as is shown in Fig. 9.3. Because the loader used to produce the final machine code program must now be capable of linking together a number of separately prepared object code files it is called a *linking loader* or *linkage editor*. The linking loader includes two important features which are not present in the simple loaders described previously. First is the ability to specify explicitly the base address of each object module so that modules may be built into a single contiguous machine code file by specifying the start address of each machine code module to follow immediately the final address of the preceding module. If required, however, modules may also be linked non-contiguously to conform with a non-contiguous allocation of physical memory.

The second requirement of the linking loader is a facility for resolving cross-references between separately compiled or assembled source modules, since modules invariably reference each other via subroutines, addresses of variables, and so on. As an example, module 2 in Fig. 9.3 might be a subprogram of the main program which is coded as module 1. This presents a problem in compiling module 1, since a label which refers to subprogram 2 is unmatched when module 1 is compiled, and hence causes a syntax error. The problem is resolved by defining additional *directives* which enable specified labels to be made *global* references, that is, labels which may be referenced from other separately compiled or assembled modules. A table of these global references is built up during linking of the various program modules, and references can then be resolved once final memory addresses have been allocated to each machine code module. Fig. 9.4 shows how a reference to module 3, a subroutine of module 2, can be resolved once the actual machine code addresses corresponding to module 2 are known.

Apart from the obvious advantage of allowing large programs to be split into more manageable modules, the use of a linking loader has a number of other benefits. First, it allows modules written in a number of different languages to be combined within the final machine code program. Thus, in the example of Fig. 9.3 the main program module, 1, might be written in a high-level language such as PASCAL, while modules 2 and 3 could be written in assembly language. This would allow program development to be predominantly in the high-level language for speed of development, but with the facility to use assembly language for small, hardware-dependent subroutines which cannot be implemented in a high-level language.

Another advantage is that a library of standard functions can be built up, and this library can be scanned by the linking loader when the machine code file is being built. Any function referenced by the program can then be built into the final machine code automatically. Typically, the sorts of function which might form part of the library would include arithmetic functions, input/output to standard devices such as terminals, printers and disks, and data format conversions (for example, between BCD, hexadecimal and binary).

Fig. 9.4 gives an example of the directives which are required to specify the cross-references between two separate modules written in MC68HC11 assembly language. the directive XREF (eXternal REFerence) indicates that the specified label(s) are references to addresses which are defined in a different program module. The directive XDEF (eXternal DEFinition) identifies a label which is to be considered global, that is, accessible from other modules. If the labels referenced by XREF directives are not matched by corresponding XDEF directives in other program modules, an error is reported when the user attempts to link his object code files together.

*Macro-assemblers*

One further common feature of assemblers should be introduced at this stage. This is the *macro*, a pseudo-instruction which, when encountered by the assembler during assembly of a program module, is substituted by a previously defined group of instructions. This facility may be used by the programmer to define new instructions in the assembly language which are made up of groups of conventional assembly language instructions. Since macros can take and pass back several parameters, quite complex functions can be generated as macros. As an example, Walker describes the use of macro facilities within the MC6809 macro-assembler to generate all the control structures of a structured high-level language such as PASCAL, and includes a much more detailed description and explanation of macros than can be given here.

**Debuggers and simulators**

Once a program has been written and assembled or compiled, the next stage is to run the program and verify its operation. Even programs written by experienced

The Motorola MC68HC11 macro-assembler reference manual also defines a number of directives which allow program and data areas for a particular application to be defined separately. These directives are placed before the appropriate program statement or data definitions. Examples are:

PSCT — Program SeCTion
BSCT — Base SeCTion
DSCT — Data SeCTion

The uses of macros and conditional assembly are explained very clearly in: Walker, G. *Towards a structured 6809 assembly language*, BYTE, pp 370–382, November 1981 and pp. 198–228, December 1981. This reference also contains an interesting example of the application of these techniques.

```
*   =================================================================
*   ILLUSTRATION OF MC68HC11 GLOBAL DIRECTIVES
*   — module 2
*   =================================================================
*   The directive XREF defines a label which occurs
*   outside module 2.
            XREF    MOD3
*   The directive XDEF defines labels which are global
*   and may be accessed from other modules.
            XDEF    PARAM1, PARAM2
*   -----------------------------------------------------------------
*   The labels PARAM1 and PARAM2 refer to the address of two
*   parameters which are to be accessible from module 3
*
PARAM1      RMB     1
PARAM2      RMB     1
*   -----------------------------------------------------------------
*   Start of program module 2.
MOD2        .
            .
            JSR   MOD3   * MOD3 is assembled separately
            .
            .
            RTS
*   -----------------------------------------------------------------
```

When module 2 is assembled, the assembler leaves a two-byte space after the JSR opcode. When modules 2 and 3 are linked, the linker correlates external references with external definitions, and can then fill in the missing subroutine address in module 2.

```
*   =================================================================
*   ILLUSTRATION OF MC68HC11 GLOBAL DIRECTIVES
*   — module 3
*   =================================================================
*   The directive XREF defines a label which occurs
*   outside module 3.
            XREF        PARAM1,PARAM2
*   The directive XDEF defines a label which is global and
*   may be accessed from other modules.
            XDEF        MOD3
*   -----------------------------------------------------------------
*   Start of program module 3
MOD3        .
            .
            LDAA   PARAM1   * get first parameter
            .
            LDAB     PARAM2   * get second parameter
            .
            .
            RTS
*   -----------------------------------------------------------------
```

The external reference to the addresses PARAM1 and PARAM2 are resolved using exactly the same process as described above. In this case the operand addresses following the LDA and LDB opcodes are left blank when module 3 is first assembled.

Fig. 9.4   Global directives in MC68HC11 assembly language.

and expert programmers very seldom work correctly to begin with. It is very difficult to foresee all the ways in which a program algorithm is executed and invariably algorithm faults are shown up when the program is first tested. To cater for this, debuggers and simulators are required to test a program.

If the program is written in the computer's native assembly language, then often it is possible to load the machine code program into the computer's memory and execute it under the control of a *monitor* program of the type already discussed. If, however, the program has been written using a cross-assembler, then it cannot be executed directly, but instead a *simulator* software package is often provided which interprets each target machine code instruction and modifies the memory locations in the host computer to simulate the action of the program on the target computer registers, memory and input/output circuits. If the configuration of the application computer is very different from that of development computer, it may not be possible fully to debug the software within the development system. In this case, in-circuit emulation facilities such as those described in Chapter 8 are used to complete the debugging process.

By their nature, programs written in high-level languages tend to be easier to debug than those written in assembly languages. Many algorithm faults cause errors which are trapped by the run-time package included in the language implementation (for example, numeric overflow of a variable). Often the error messages provide the programmer with sufficient evidence of the source of the fault to enable him to surmise exactly what has gone wrong. Furthermore, it is relatively easy to include additional diagnostic statements in a high-level language program to dump intermediate values of variables or flag when particular statements are executed and hence establish where a fault lies. Nevertheless, debugging programs for high-level languages are also available and under some circumstances can prove invaluable for tracing the execution of a program.

**Summary**

A number of software tools required as part of a general purpose computer system have been introduced in this chapter. The tools have been introduced as they would be encountered by a user who wished to use the computer to develop applications programs written in high-level or assembly languages, or in a combination of both. First of all, a loader or bootstrap program is required to load the computer's main control program, the disk operating system, into memory from disk. Via the DOS, the user can manipulate files stored on floppy or hard disk, and can execute other system programs or applications programs. Applications programs are developed using a text editor to input the program, edit it, and save it on the disk. The source program may then be compiled or assembled to produce an object code file, or directly to machine code if the program comprises only a single module. Programs made up of several separately compiled or assembled modules may be linked to form a single executable machine code file using a linking loader. Finally, faults in the program may be found using a variety of debugging and simulation tools.

# Microprocessor application design example

10

☐ To introduce the elements of microprocessor application design—system specification, hardware design and software design—through the vehicle of an example design problem.

**Objectives**

The final chapter of this book is intended to give an insight into the process of designing dedicated microprocessor applications involving both hardware and software design procedures. The design process is illustrated using a simple design example, a microprocessor-controlled central heating system. The design example is realistic in the sense that a number of commercial microprocessor-based products exist which fulfil this function; the design specification for the example has been simplified to enable the principles underlying the design process to be more readily appreciated. Some enhancements to the basic design are proposed as problems for the student.

Because the design example has been simplified to make the underlying design principles clearer, the use of a microprocessor may initially appear an unnecessary complication. Remember that a full microprocessor-controlled central heating system would include a number of additional features which would justify the use of a microprocessor, and make the product more attractive. Examples are given in Problems 10.1–10.3.

## System specification

As in most areas of engineering design, the first problem is fully and accurately to specify the requirements of the design; this is not a trivial task. The specification can be subdivided into two parts: first, the technical specification of the design, covering the task(s) which the product fulfils and criteria to be met; and second, the mechanism of project management, which includes liaison between personnel involved, project documentation, timescales, and agreed monitoring procedures for the project. This chapter is primarily concerned with the technical aspects of the design process, and thus project management is not considered in detail; nevertheless, the importance of having effective project management in the field of microprocessor application design cannot be overestimated.

In developing a specification, two particular points must be borne in mind. First, it is very difficult to draft a specification which is unambiguous, as has already been shown. This problem becomes particularly evident when the engineer is required to liaise with people working outside his own field to develop the specification. The same statement can often be interpreted in a number of different ways depending upon the background of the person reading it. In such cases the safest approach is to ensure that the eventual users of the product are involved in defining its design at a very early stage, and that mechanisms are built into the design procedure which will permit iterations of the design to be made as the product develops. Often, a simulation of the product can be produced at an early stage and with relatively little effort, and this approach is particularly recommended where naive users are involved.

One advantage of a microprocessor-based design is the flexibility which it imparts; retrospective modifications can often be made simply by software changes, and simulations can easily be performed.

Second, most specifications admit a variety of possible solutions. The engineer's objective is thus not only to produce *a* solution which achieves the specification, but to ensure that his solution is *the best* solution, whether measured in terms of cost or performance. Often, it is not clear what defines the best solution, since performance may be traded against unit cost. Furthermore, development cost must also be amortised against projected sales, and increased development effort may often result in a lower unit cost. Thus market research also plays an important part in defining the product specification.

In this design example, the specification has been chosen to duplicate the functions of a standard central heating thermostat system. In practice, such a specification would be unrealistic because there is little point in spending money on a microprocessor to duplicate a function which can be performed perfectly adequately using existing technology. Thus a practical microprocessor-based central heating controller would have to offer facilities which enhanced the performance of the system, such as greater flexibility and/or energy saving. By simplifying the specification for the purpose of the example, however, an unambiguous specification can easily be generated because the operation of a standard central heating system is well understood.

### Specification: microprocessor-controlled central heating

The microprocessor-controlled central heating system is required to duplicate the control functions of a standard electromechanical central heating system. The system has two temperature sensors, a room temperature sensor and a water temperature sensor. Both sensors consist of analogue devices connected to analogue-to-digital convertors with a sampling time of 100 µs. Each convertor produces an 8-bit digital output representing a temperature of 0–127°F for the room sensor and 0–255°F for the water temperature sensor.

These figures have been deliberately chosen to simplify the processing in the microprocessor, while representing realistic ranges of temperature control. Other figures could equally well be chosen, but would require increased arithmetic processing.

Room sensor resolution = 1/2°F
Water sensor resolution = 1°F
Again the figures have been chosen to simplify processing: in each case the resolution of the thumbwheel is 1°F.

This paragraph states the algorithm which the controller must obey.

At this stage, the designer would in practice settle for two electromechanical thermostats if given this specification!

Corresponding to the two sensors are two temperature controls. The room temperature control uses two BCD thumbwheels and is capable of specifying a room temperature in the range 0–99°F. The water temperature control is similar but employs an extra bit to enable temperatures in the range 0–199°F to be specified.

Outputs from the controller are required to control the boiler (*on* or *off*) and a water pump which pumps hot water round the radiators. If the room temperature is higher than the room temperature setting, both the pump and the boiler should be switched off. Otherwise, if the water temperature is higher than the water temperature setting, the boiler should be switched off and the pump should be switched on. Only if the water temperature and the room temperature are below their settings should the boiler and the pump be switched on.

The first stage of the design process is normally a *feasibility evaluation*. The objective here is to consider all possible alternative solutions to the specification, including non-microprocessor-based solutions. Typically, options which might be considered would include a random logic implementation or, at the other end of the scale, an implementation using a standard computer system. At this stage the choice may self-evidently be to use a microprocessor because the system complexity is too great to contemplate random logic, or because the cost of a full computer system cannot be justified. It is because so many applications lie between these two extremes that a large market for microprocessors exists.

Having decided to investigate a microprocessor-based solution, a number of further options open up. The microprocessor market can be broadly divided into two areas: single-chip microcomputers such as the MC68HC11 (containing not only the microprocessor CPU, but also memory and input/output interfaces on a single device); and general-purpose microprocessors such as the MC68000 and ARM. Single-chip devices are the cheapest in large volumes; not only can the actual chip be very cheap, but the reduction in components reduces the tooling and labour costs of assembling the printed circuit board which contains the microcomputer and any other components. Against this, however, the single-chip device generally has a restricted memory address space and a limited number of input/output lines, which may rule out its use in particular applications.

Prices as low as £1 per unit are quoted for large-scale (e.g. > $10^5$) applications of some very simple 4-bit single-chip microcomputers.

Many microprocessor applications can best be addressed using a general-purpose 8- or 16-bit microprocessor. This is particularly true of applications which involve the manipulation of alphanumeric characters (for example, the design of computer peripheral equipment) since such characters are normally represented using an 8-bit word. For more intensive applications a wide range of 32-bit microprocessors are available, at a considerable price premium. Usually, the area which a particular microprocessor application addresses within this field is self-evident.

Often any microprocessor within the appropriate broad market sector identified above is capable of fulfilling the specification; the choice of which microprocessor to use is then based upon prior experience and available development facilities. There is seldom any point in devoting time to detailed comparisons between rival manufacturers' components which address the same market sector, since if performance is sufficiently marginal that these variations are important, the extra cost of a more powerful class of device (for example, a 16-bit rather than 8-bit microprocessor) is likely to be more than outweighed by the reduced complexity of the development task.

The guidelines given here are necessarily very broad, and are not appropriate in all cases; nevertheless, they reflect the situation in the vast majority of microprocessor applications.

In the particular application considered here, two designs will be considered, one based upon the MC68000 general-purpose microprocessor and the other based upon the MC68HC11 microcontroller. These design choices are constrained by the requirement to use example processors featured in the book, rather than because these are necessarily the best choices for the implementation. In fact, a practical microprocessor-controlled central heating controller would certainly be implemented using a single-chip microcomputer since the application is relatively simple and aimed at a high-volume market. The use of the MC68000 for the first example, although introducing unnecessary complexity and cost, allows some of the issues concerned with configuring memory and input/output devices for a general-purpose microprocessor application hardware design to be explored.

Even within the single-chip microcomputer market sector, however, many alternatives exist. First, there are many different families of single-chip microcomputers, manufactured by all of the main microprocessor semiconductor manufacturers. Motorola, for example, currently manufactures the following single-chip microcomputer families:

- *MC6804 family* — very low-cost microcontrollers. Although actually implemented as 1-bit serial devices, these microcontrollers appear to the user as 8-bit parallel devices.
- *MC6805 family* — low-cost, low pin-count, mid-range microcontrollers. These devices include on-chip drivers for LED and LCD displays, serial and

Although most of these families were originally implemented using NMOS (N-channel MOS) technology, current designs are based upon Motorola's HPMOS (High Power MOS) fabrication technology. This is reflected in the designation of the devices as MC68HCxx, e.g. MC68HC11.

parallel interfaces, A/D and D/A converters and timers. Their CPU architecture is (like the MC68HC11) derived from the MC6800, but in this case is stripped down rather than enhanced by removing the B accumulator and associated instructions.

- *MC6811 family* — high-end 8-bit microcontroller family derived from the earlier MC6801 microcontroller. Enhanced performance through an expanded MC6800 instruction set, more input/output capabilities and larger and more versatile on-chip memory options. Can also be expanded using off-chip memory and input/output.
- *MC68300 family* — 32-bit microcontroller for high performance applications such as laser printer controllers, fax machines, etc.

Each basic architecture is described as a 'family' because a variety of different configurations of the architecture is available, each with its own part number. Table 10.1 shows the different components available within the MC68HC11 family. As can be seen, different variants can have up to 24 kbytes of ROM or EPROM, between 192 and 1024 bytes of RAM, up to 2 kbytes of EEPROM, multi-channel 8- or 10-bit analogue-to-digital converters, and between 32 and 66 digital input/output pins, in addition to serial interfaces and timers. As will be apparent from the review of Motorola single-chip microcomputer families above, even the MC68HC11 may be overspecified for the application considered here, and in practice the MC68HC05 or MC68HC04 families might be a better choice.

### Hardware design—MC68000-based solution

The design procedure for the microprocessor hardware and interface should, like the software design, follow a process of stepwise refinement. The outline hardware design should be developed before beginning any detailed software design because any substantial changes to the proposed hardware may have a significant impact upon the proposed software as well. In general, it is best to conduct the hardware and software design processes in parallel, since many of the design decisions to be taken involve consideration of hardware/software tradeoffs. Production requirements such as testing and field repair should be considered from the outset of the design process; it is much easier to include them at this stage than to add them later on.

Often the tradeoff to be made is between using the processor more intensively, and providing extra hardware to offload peripheral functions. The first option tends to reduce final unit cost at the expense of increased development cost.

*Input/output requirements*

The initial hardware design procedure involves identifying the component requirements of the microprocessor system in terms of ROM, RAM and input/output. Consider first of all the input/output requirements for the microprocessor-controlled central heating system:

| A/D convertors | $2 \times 8$ bits | input |
| | 2 bits | output ('start sampling') |
| Room temperature setting | 8 bits | input |
| Water temperature setting | 9 bits | input |
| Pump control | 1 bit | output |
| Boiler control | 1 bit | output |

**Table 10.1  The MC68HC11 single-chip 8-bit microcomputer family (© Motorola)**

| Device | ROM (kb) | EPROM (kb) | RAM (bytes) | EEPROM (bytes) | A/D | Serial | Timer | PWM | CE | I/O | Package | Comments |
|---|---|---|---|---|---|---|---|---|---|---|---|---|
| 68HC11A0 | – | – | 256 | – | 8-ch, 8-bit | SCI + SPI | 3 in, 6 out | – | – | 38 | 52/FN, 64/FU | PRU* 68HC24 |
| 68HC11A1 | – | – | 256 | 512 | 8-ch, 8-bit | SCI + SPI | 3 in, 5 out | – | – | 38 | 52/FN, 64/FU | PRU* 68HC24 |
| 68HC11A8 | 8 | – | 256 | 512 | 8-ch, 8-bit | SCI + SPI | 3 in, 5 out | – | – | 38 | 52/FN, 64/FU | |
| 68HC11E0 | – | – | 512 | – | 8-ch, 8-bit | SCI + SPI | 3 in, I/O, 4 out | – | – | 38 | 52/FN, 64/FU | PRU* 68HC24 |
| 68HC11E1 | – | – | 512 | 512 | 8-ch, 8-bit | SCI + SPI | 3 in, 1I/O, 4 out | – | – | 38 | 52/FN, 64/FU | PRU* 68HC24 |
| 68HC11E9 | 12 | – | 512 | 512 | 8-ch, 8-bit | SCI + SPI | 3 in, 1I/O, 4 out | – | – | 38 | 52/FN, 64/FU | |
| 68HC11L6 | 16 | – | 512 | 512 | 8-ch, 8-bit | SCI + SPI | 3 in, 1I/O, 4 out | – | – | 46 | 68/FN, 64/FU | |
| 68HC11D0 | – | – | 192 | – | – | SCI + SPI | 3 in, 1I/O, 4 out | – | – | 32 | 40/P, 44/FN | |
| 68HC11D3 | 4 | – | 192 | – | – | SCI + SPI | 3 in, 1I/O, 4 out | – | – | 32 | 40/P, 44/FN | |
| 68HC11F1 | – | – | 1024 | 512 | 8-ch, 8-bit | SCI + SPI | 3 in, 1I/O, 4 out | – | 4 | 46 | 68/FN, 64/FU | Non-multiplexed bus |
| 68HC11G5 | 16 | – | 512 | – | 8-ch, 10-bit | SCI + SPI | 3 in, 3I/O, 4 out | 4, 8-bit | – | 66 | 84/FN | Event counter |
| 68HC11G7 | 24 | – | 512 | – | 8-ch, 10-bit | SCI + SPI | 3 in, 3I/O, 4 out | 4, 8-bit | – | 66 | 84/FN | Event counter |
| 68HC11K4 | 24 | – | 768 | 640 | 8-ch, 8-bit | SCI + SPI | 3 in, 1I/O, 4 out | 4, 8-bit | 4 | 62 | 80/QFP, 84/FN | 0.5 Mbyte addressing |
| 68HC711D3 | – | 4 | 192 | – | – | SCI + SPI | 3 in, 1I/O, 4 out | – | – | 32 | 40/P, 44/FN | Available windowed |
| 68HC711E9 | – | 12 | 512 | 512 | 8-ch, 8-bit | SCI + SPI | 3 in, 1I/O, 4 out | – | – | 38 | 52/FN | Available windowed |
| 68HC711L6 | – | 16 | 512 | 512 | 8-ch, 8-bit | SCI + SPI | 3 in, 1I/O, 4 out | – | – | 38 | 68/FN, 64/FU | Available windowed |
| 68HC711G5 | – | 16 | 512 | – | 8-ch, 10-bit | SCI + SPI | 3 in, 3I/O, 4 out | 4, 8-bit | – | 66 | 84/FN | Available windowed |
| 68HC711K4 | – | 24 | 768 | 640 | 8-ch, 8-bit | SCI + SPI | 3 in, 1I/O, 4 out | 4, 8-bit | 4 | 62 | 80/QFP, 84/FN | Available windowed |
| 68HC811E2 | – | – | 256 | 2048 | 8-ch, 8-bit | SCI + SPI | 3 in, 1I/O, 4 out | – | – | 38 | 52/FN | |

\* Port Replacement Unit

Hence, the total input/output requirement is for 37 lines, comprising 33 inputs and four outputs.

One solution to this requirement would be to use three MC6821 PIAs, which would leave 11 spare bits which could be used for possible future expansion of the controller, and this is the solution which is considered here, for reasons of familiarity. In this particular application, however, the use of PIAs might not be justified because of the simplicity of the required interfaces. For example, simple transmission gates (see Chapter 5) would suffice for the inputs in this case because the data read from the inputs are continuously available. Similarly, simple latches could be used for the outputs driving the pump and boiler. A further alternative would be a mixture of these two extremes, where a single PIA would be demultiplexed to provide the required number of inputs and outputs using external logic. Thus the best hardware choice for implementing the input and output interfaces would have to be made by considering both the development costs and the production costs of the alternatives.

In addition to the input/output components, circuitry is required to ensure that upon switching on power to the system, the required pulse sequence to the RESET input of the MC68000 is provided, so that program execution begins correctly.

Problems 10.1–10.3 give examples of how the controller might be extended to increase its appeal and make better use of the processing power of the microprocessor.

See Problem 10.2.

*Program store*

In estimating the program store requirements for a microprocessor application, there is no real substitute for previous experience. In this case it is likely that considerably less than 1 kbyte of program store is required, since the required function is very simple. Although memory devices of this size have been used in the past, continuously increasing levels of integration in memory design mean that it is no longer practical to use such a small amount of memory (a larger chip is actually cheaper!) and a typical small ROM chip (the 2764 EPROM — see Fig. 10.1(a)) would now contain 8 kbytes of memory. Furthermore, a minimum of two such chips is required in an MC68000 system to match the 16-bit word memory organisation, one for the least significant byte of memory and one for the most significant byte. The use of these devices at least provides plenty of opportunity to expand the system!

Fortunately, errors in these estimations are not usually catastrophic, since additional components can be added to the system subsequently.

It is clear from the size of a minimum system based upon the MC68000 that in practice a single-chip microcomputer, with its more modest amounts of memory, is the more appropriate choice to implement the central heating controller.

*Data store*

A similar estimation process is required to decide the likely amount of RAM required. In this case, a first estimate might be that about 10 bytes of RAM would

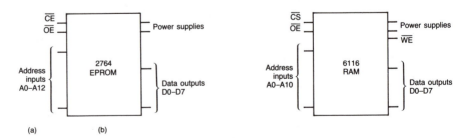

Fig. 10.1 EPROM and RAM pin connections.

be required for temporary data variables, while another 20 bytes would be needed for the stack. To simplify memory design in this small system, static rather than dynamic memory would be used. RAM is commonly available in several 'widths', 1-bit, 4-bit and 8-bit (byte-wide), but to minimise the chip count in a small system, byte-wide memory should be chosen. Again, even the smallest currently practical static memory component is vastly larger than is required for the application, and furthermore, a minimum of two chips would be needed to provide the required 16-bit word organisation. The static RAM chips chosen in this case are 6116 RAM devices, each of which provides 2 kbytes of storage (see Fig. 10.1(b)).

*Memory configuration*

The next stage in the hardware design process is to decide how the memory address space is allocated between the various components interfaced to the buses. For applications such as this one, where only a small fraction of the full address space is actually utilised, a major objective of the memory allocation process is to minimise the number of additional components required to decode ROM, RAM and PIA addresses. This process is known as *minimal address decoding*. The underlying principle of minimal address decoding is to use *don't care* address states where possible. This results in the physical component (for example, the ROM chip) being duplicated at a number of different addresses within the microprocessor address space. The duplication is acceptable as long as no attempt is made to access a device at a memory address which overlaps the memory allocation of another component. The process is best understood by considering how it would be applied to the design example.

Fig. 10.2 illustrates the general approach taken in allocating memory for an

If a single-chip implementation is used, the memory configuration is fixed by the chip design.

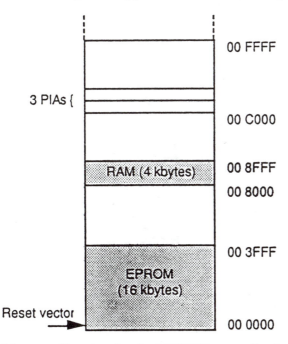

Fig. 10.2  Memory allocation for the MC68000 controller implementation.

Interrupt vectors would also be stored in the bottom 1 kbyte of memory, except that none are required in this application.

application using the MC68000. The 16 kbytes of EPROM, 4 kbytes of RAM and three PIAs obviously have to be placed within the total MC68000 address space of 16 Mbytes. The actual addresses used for each device are relatively unimportant, except that EPROM is required at the bottom of memory in order to store a non-volatile reset vector and initial system stack pointer value at addresses 0–7. Also, there may be some advantage in arranging for all the components to appear within a limited area of the memory (for example, the bottom 64 kbytes) so that efficient addressing modes with short (16-bit) operand addresses can be used. A further design objective is to minimise the number of additional logic components required to decode the addresses used in the application using minimal address decoding as outlined above.

The next stage is to develop a detailed memory allocation for the components defined in the previous sections. The allocation chosen is illustrated in Figs 10.2 and 10.3 and Table 10.2 and explained below.

The solution shown is not the only minimal solution. The student may wish to consider alternatives. (*Hint*: consider the effect on the memory map of altering the choice of 'don't care' address bits.)

Consider first of all the decoding required for the ROM chips. Address inputs A0–A12 on the EPROM chips are decoded internally by the ROM and would be connected to address bus outputs A1–A13 from the MC68000. The EPROM providing the lower byte of data would have its data outputs connected to data bus lines D0–D7 on the MC68000, and the other EPROM, providing the upper data byte, would have its data outputs connected to D8–D15 on the MC68000. This allows the MC68000 to read two bytes of data (a 16-bit word) simultaneously, made up of a byte from each of the two EPROMs. Further address decoding circuitry, which uses the $\overline{UDS}$ and $\overline{LDS}$ lines to allow bytes of data to be read individually, is described later. The two RAM chips are addressed in exactly the same way except that only MC68000 address lines A1–A11 are decoded internally by the chips.

If the aim is to use only the bottom 64 kbytes of memory, then only MC68000 address lines A14 and A15 are needed to select or deselect the physical memory components. Address lines A16–A23 are unused and are not physically connected in this application. This has the effect that the bottom 64 kbytes of the 16 Mbyte address space are actually replicated 256 times through the address space. Since the (correctly running) application program will never access these addresses, and there is no requirement to place any further physical components within the address space, this is immaterial.

**Table 10.2  Minimal address decoding for the MC68000-based microcontroller**

| Device | \<-- MC68000 address lines (A15–A1) --\> | | | | | | | | | | | | | | | | Address From | To |
|---|---|---|---|---|---|---|---|---|---|---|---|---|---|---|---|---|---|---|
| | 15 | 14 | 13 | 12 | 11 | 10 | 9 | 8 | 7 | 6 | 5 | 4 | 3 | 2 | 1 | | From | To |
| EPROM 0 | | | <------------decoded on chip------------> | | | | | | | | | | | | | | 00 0000 | 00 3FFF |
| RAM | 1 | 0 | | | <--------decoded on chip--------> | | | | | | | | | | | | 00 8000 | 00 8FFF |
| PIA1 | 1 | 1 | | | | | | | | | 1 | rs1 | rs0 | | | | 00 C030 | 00 C037 |
| PIA2 | 1 | 1 | | | | | | | | 1 | | rs1 | rs0 | | | | 00 C028 | 00 C02F |
| PIA3 | 1 | 1 | | | | | | | 1 | | | rs1 | rs0 | | | | 00 C018 | 00 C01F |

EPROM selected when A15 = 0; RAM, PIAs not selected
RAM selected when A15 = 1 and A14 = 0; EPROM, PIAs not selected
PIAs selected when A15 = 1 and A14 = 1; EPROM, RAM not selected. Individual PIAs selected using A3, A4 and A5

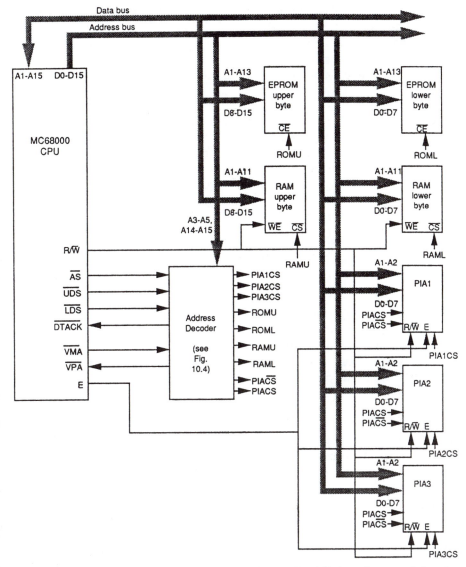

Fig. 10.3 Block diagram of hardware for MC68000-based central heating controller.

A15 is therefore used to select the EPROM and deselect the RAM and PIAs. This has the effect that the 16 kbytes of EPROM are replicated twice in the lower half of the 64-kbyte address space, at addresses 0–003FFF and 004000–007FFF, but the remaining components only appear at addresses in the range 008000–00FFFF. From the programmer's point of view a single 16-kbyte block of memory would be considered to exist at addresses 0–003FFF, and the reset vectors could thus be stored at the bottom of this memory, with the program origined anywhere convenient above the bottom 1 kbyte of exception vector address space.

In a similar way, A14 can be used to select the RAM and deselect the PIAs.

In practice, the connections are more complex than this, due to the need to include the address strobe ($\overline{AS}$) signal and the $\overline{UDS}$ and $\overline{LDS}$ lines: see the section below on the detailed address decoder design.

This results in the RAM appearing replicated four times in the address space between addresses 008000 and 00BFFF, and the PIAs appearing between 00C000 and 00FFFF.

Finally, each PIA can be addressed uniquely using address lines A3, A4, and A5 for PIA 1, 2 and 3, respectively. Thus the respective addresses at which the PIAs appear are as follows:

| *PIA1* (A3) | *PIA2* (A4) | *PIA3* (A5) |
|-------------|-------------|-------------|
| *C008–C00F* | | |
| | *C010–C017* | |
| C018–C01F | C018–C01F | |
| | | *C020–C027* |
| C028–C02F | | C028–C02F |
| | C030–C037 | C030–C037 |
| C038–C03F | C038–C03F | C038–C03F |
| . | . | . |
| . | . | . |
| . | . | . |

Notice that although the addresses of the PIAs overlap at some points in the address space, they are uniquely addressable at the first (lowest address) occurrence of each PIA. In this case, therefore, PIA1 would be addressed at addresses C008–C00F, PIA2 at addresses C010–C017 and PIA3 at addresses C020–C027 within the program.

Each PIA occupies eight bytes in an MC68000 application rather than four bytes as described in Chapter 5, because the CPU always reads a byte from the PIA as the lower byte of a 16-bit word. PIA1 registers therefore occupy addresses C008, C00A, C00C and C00E, for example.

### Address decoder and control logic

The remainder of the required address decoding and control logic is shown in Figs 10.3 and 10.4. As can be seen from Fig. 10.3, the logic is best understood by breaking it down into two components: first, two control bus signals connected directly to the memory and PIAs; and second, a set of control bus signals from the MC68000 which are combined with some of the address lines within the address decoder to generate the specific chip select and chip enable signals required by the individual memory and input/output chips.

The first of the control bus connections shown in Fig. 10.3 is the read/write line (R/$\overline{\text{W}}$), which is connected directly to the corresponding R/$\overline{\text{W}}$ inputs of the PIAs and to the $\overline{\text{WE}}$ inputs of the RAM chips. The second control bus signal is the MC68000 E output which connects to corresponding E inputs on each PIA. The MC68000 E output is provided for compatibility with MC6800-family 8-bit peripherals (such as the PIA), and simulates one of the clock signals generated by the MC6800 and MC6809 processors, to which the MC6821 was originally intended to interface.

Since the EPROMs are read-only devices, there is no need to connect the R/$\overline{\text{W}}$ line to them.

The control signals generated by the address decoder (Fig. 10.4) can be broken down into three groups. First, a group of four signals (ROMU, ROML, RAMU and RAML) are generated to enable each RAM and ROM chip individually. This allows the MC68000 to read either a byte or a word of memory at a time. Next, a group of five signals (PIACS, PIA$\overline{\text{CS}}$, PIA1CS, PIA2CS and PIA3CS) is used to enable each PIA at the appropriate address in memory. Finally, the signals $\overline{\text{DTACK}}$ and $\overline{\text{VPA}}$ are generated by the address decoder to satisfy the

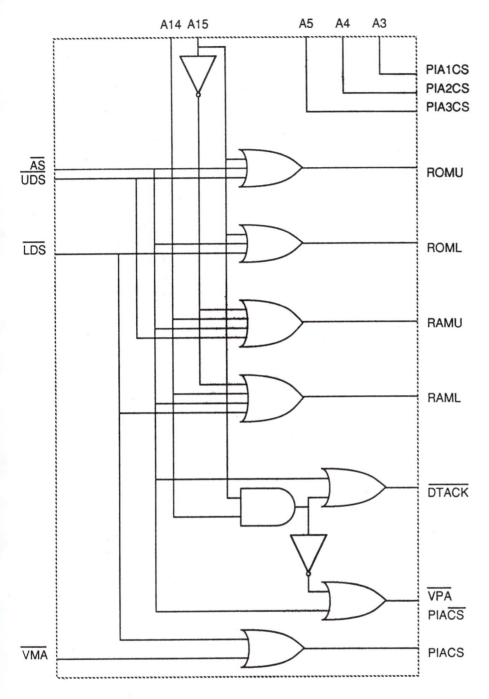

Fig. 10.4   Address decoder for MC68000-based central heating controller.

MC68000 asynchronous memory data transfer and synchronous I/O data transfer protocols.

Consider first the requirements for the chip enable (EPROM) and chip select (RAM) signals for the four memory chips. The upper-byte EPROM must be enabled only when A15 is low and $\overline{AS}$ is low and the upper data strobe ($\overline{UDS}$) control line is low. Since the EPROM is enabled for a logic 0 at its $\overline{CE}$ input, the required logic function is a logical OR of these three inputs. A similar logic function is required for the lower-byte EPROM, except that in this case, A15 and $\overline{AS}$ are logically ORed with the lower data strobe signal ($\overline{LDS}$). In the case of the two RAM chips, a similar address decoding function is required as for ROMU and ROML, respectively, except that the RAMs are enabled when A15 is high and A14 is low.

The main difference is that the address strobe and data acknowledge signals on the MC68000 are asserted low, not high.

MC68000 accesses to RAM and EPROM are made using an asynchronous protocol similar to that illustrated in Fig. 4.2, hence the address decoder not only has to decode address bus signals to select the appropriate memory chip, but also has to generate a data acknowledge signal ($\overline{DTACK}$) in response to the address strobe ($\overline{AS}$) control signal from the MC68000. This signal requires $\overline{DTACK}$ to pulse low for any memory access within the range 000000–00BFFF where the RAM and EPROM are placed. Hence the $\overline{DTACK}$ signal should go low only when $\overline{AS}$ is low and either A15 = 0 or A15 = 1 and A14 = 0. This logic function can be simplified to the following Boolean expression:

$$\overline{DTACK} = \overline{AS} + A14.A15$$

Full details of MC68000 bus timing are beyond the scope of this book: refer instead for example to Clements, A. *Microprocessor Systems Design: 68000 hardware software and interfacing* (PWS, 1987).

and thence implemented using an AND gate and an OR gate as shown in Fig. 10.4. As will be apparent, the delay between assertion of $\overline{AS}$ by the MC68000 and assertion of $\overline{DTACK}$ is defined purely by the propagation delay through the address decoder, so the access times of the EPROM and RAM chips must be fast enough to meet the requirements of the MC68000 read and write cycle protocols under these conditions.

This asynchronous memory access protocol used by the MC68000 is not suitable for interfacing to MC6800-family peripheral devices such as the PIA and ACIA, which expect a synchronous protocol of the type shown in Fig. 4.1. To interface to these devices, the MC68000 therefore generates a valid memory address ($\overline{VMA}$) signal as used for synchronous memory accesses by the MC6800 and MC6809 microprocessors. Where a synchronous memory access is required rather than an asynchronous memory access, the address decoder circuitry must generate a valid peripheral address ($\overline{VPA}$) input to the MC68000 in response to $\overline{AS}$, instead of the $\overline{DTACK}$ described above. The $\overline{VPA}$ signal should be asserted low only when A14 = 1, A15 = 1 (an address in the range allocated to the PIAs) and $\overline{AS}$ = 0. This is achieved by inverting the output of the AND gate fed by A14 and A15 and inputting the result to an OR gate along with $\overline{AS}$. The same signal is also connected to the $\overline{CS}$ input of each of the PIAs.

A further CS input on each PIA is connected to the output of a NOR gate which is fed by the $\overline{LDS}$ and $\overline{VMA}$ MC68000 outputs. This ensures that the PIAs are only enabled when $\overline{VMA}$ is asserted low and the CPU addresses the lower byte of a word. The final CS PIA input is used to select each PIA individually according to the address output on the address bus, by connecting it to A3, A4 and A5 for PIA1, PIA2 and PIA3, respectively.

Although the logic of Fig. 10.4 fulfils the function required of the address decoder, AND and OR gates have been used for clarity in this example. In practice, a further design stage of rationalising the components to minimise the number of chips used in the final implementation (for example, by implementing the complete decoder using only NAND logic) could now be undertaken. In addition, other peripheral circuitry for the MC68000, such as a power on reset circuit, and connections for DMA and interrupt inputs (neither of which is used in this application) have also been omitted for clarity. Furthermore, although the address decoder design is adequate, it is certainly not an ideal implementation of the $\overline{\text{DTACK}}$ function. In most system implementations the RAM and EPROM will not necessarily have the same access times (typically, EPROM is slower than RAM). An improved $\overline{\text{DTACK}}$ design would allow for this by including a programmable delay (achieved by a counter fed from the CPU clock), rather than responding immediately to $\overline{\text{AS}}$.

### Hardware design 2 — MC68HC11-based solution

Compared with the MC68000-based hardware design outlined above, the MC68HC11 design is very much simpler, because the complete microcontroller can be implemented on a single chip. The initial design stage again involves identifying likely input/output, program memory and data memory requirements for the application. These requirements are largely unchanged for the MC68HC11 implementation, except that memory is organised in 8-bit rather than 16-bit words, and the MC68HC11 can include an eight-channel A/D converter on chip, thus reducing the number of parallel input/output lines required as compared with the MC68000 implementation. Thus the hardware resources required for the MC68HC11 are:

2 × 8-bit A/D converters;
17 bits digital input;
2 bits digital output;
1 kbyte program store;
30 bytes data store.

Comparison of these requirements with the alternative MC68HC11 configurations listed in Table 10.1 shows that the smallest variant which includes an A/D converter on chip is the 68HC11A8, which would thus be the appropriate choice in this case. Once the specific version of the MC68HC11 has been chosen, the corresponding memory map is also defined: in this case, the memory map for the 68HC11A8 has already been shown in Fig. 2.14.

If A/D conversion was provided externally, the cheaper 68HC11D3 could be used. Comparison of overall production costs for these two alternatives would be needed to determine the best choice.

### Software design

Software is best written by a process of stepwise refinement which starts by expressing the program algorithm in very broad terms, and then breaks each block down into successively more detailed sub-blocks. The process continues until a complete detailed implementation results. One approach is to code the algorithm using the constructs of a structured high-level language such as PASCAL. Flow charts can be used for algorithm coding, but this often results in

This is known as a *top-down* strategy.

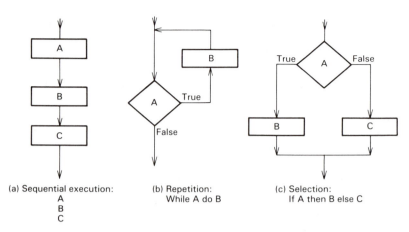

Fig. 10.5   Acceptable constructs in structured programming.

(a) Sequential execution:
A
B
C

(b) Repetition:
While A do B

(c) Selection:
If A then B else C

PASCAL has the advantage that the language was specifically designed to promote top-down design.

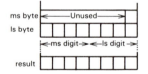

This algorithm is intended for an MC68HC11 implementation. How would it change if written for the MC68000?

At this stage, the programmer can reconsider his initial estimated physical memory requirements, and adjust these if necessary.

'spaghetti code' unless rigid rules are applied as to the constructs allowed.

The only three acceptable constructs are those shown in Fig. 10.5. The fundamental characteristic of each of these constructs is that it contains only a single entry and a single exit point, thus simplifying the process of following the execution sequence and preventing convoluted structures. At first sight, the simple nature of these three constructs would appear to limit the complexity of the algorithm which can be expressed. This is not the case, however, since each construct can contain any combination of the three constructs within it at the next greater level of detail, in accordance with the top-down strategy.

Using the top-down approach, a first-level algorithm implementing the central heating controller may be written using pseudo-PASCAL, as shown in Fig. 10.6. Procedures requiring further refinement may then be extracted from this highest-level algorithm and developed in greater detail. As the detail increases, the programmer needs to approach the architecture of the hardware more closely, and to begin to define the internal data structures which are to be used.

In this example, a procedure for converting BCD temperatures to binary is required. In one case the conversion is of an 8-bit number, while in the second a 9-bit number is required. Thus it makes sense to choose a data format for the numbers which allows the same procedure to perform the conversion on either number. The Figure in the margin illustrates a suitable format which uses two bytes to represent each BCD number, even though a single byte would be sufficient in one case, so that the two numbers are stored compatibly. For the 8-bit BCD number, the most significant (9th) bit is simply set to zero. Given this format a conversion procedure may now be written, as shown in Fig. 10.7.

As can be seen, detail included in the algorithm is now becoming sufficiently clear that the actual assembly language program can be written as an obvious extension of the algorithm expression. Before this final step is taken, however, two further points must be addressed. First, the programmer must define the variables used within the program implementation and allocate suitable storage for them in the physical memory address space where RAM resides. Second, the mechanisms to be used for communicating data between the main program and the various subtasks must be considered.

180

```
Program heatcontrol;
var (*defined later*);
BEGIN
load stackpointer;
initialise data store;
initialise PIAs;
REPEAT forever
  read roomsetting;
  convert roomsetting to binary;
  roomsetting : = roomsetting*2;
  read roomtemp;
  IF roomtemp > roomsetting
  THEN
    BEGIN
      switch off boiler;
      switch off pump
    END;
  ELSE
    BEGIN
      read watersetting;
      convert watersetting to binary;
      read watertemp;
      IF watertemp > watersetting
      THEN
        BEGIN
          switch off boiler;
          switch on pump
        END
      ELSE
        BEGIN
          switch on boiler;
          switch on pump
        END
    END;
END.
```

PASCAL is said to be a *self-documenting* language. Observe how easy it is to understand the program algorithm by reading the pseudo-PASCAL implementation.

Fig. 10.6   Outline software structure written in pseudo-Pascal.

*Data variable allocation*

By examining the algorithm developed so far, it is now possible to identify the variables to be used in implementing the central heating controller, and to allocate their storage in memory, starting from the first address in RAM:

In an MC68000 implementation, roomsetting and watersetting would be stored as 16-bit (word) variables, to simplify their manipulation.

| | | |
|---|---|---|
| roomtemp | (8-bit binary integer) | 0 |
| roomsetting | (8-bit BCD integer) | { 1 |
| | | 2 |
| roomsettingbinary | (8-bit binary integer) | 3 |
| watertemp | (8-bit binary integer) | 4 |
| watersetting | (9-bit BCD integer) | { 5 |
| | | 6 |
| watersettingbinary | (8-bit binary integer) | 7 |

Notice how the statements in this pseudo-PASCAL procedure begin to resemble assembly language statements. The student should not begin to write assembly language until it can be an almost automatic translation process from the language used to express the algorithm.

**Procedure BCD-to-binary;**
```
BEGIN
    acca := lsbyte;                          (* acca — accumulator A*)
    acca := acca AND $0F;                    (* $ — hexadecimal *)
    result := acca;
    acca := lsbyte;                          (* lsbyte — least significant *)
    acca := acca/16;                         (* byte of BCD number *)
    WHILE acca < > 0 DO
            BEGIN
                    result := result + $0A;
                    acca := acca – 1
            END:
    acca := msbyte;                          (* msbyte — most significant *)
    acca := acca AND $01;                    (* byte of BCD number *)
    IF acca < > 0
    THEN
            result := result + $64
END.
```

Fig. 10.7   BCD to binary conversion procedure.

To simplify the implementation of the subroutine specified in Fig. 10.7, the memory allocation has been chosen so that the parameters passed to the subroutine and those returned from the subroutine (roomsetting/roomsettingbinary and watersetting/watersettingbinary) are stored in exactly the same format and sequence in each case. The advantage of this is seen shortly.

*Inter-task communication*

Three methods exist for communicating information between one part of a program and another. Broadly, the choice of which method to use depends upon the amount of data to be communicated. In order of increasing quantity, the methods are:

*Arguments:* Data are passed to the subroutine and returned to the main program using specified registers. The subroutine expects that these registers will always contain the required information whenever it is called. The register may contain the data themselves, or it may contain an address pointer to the data. In the MC68HC11 microprocessor, this method is rather limited, since there are only two primary registers, accumulators A and B, and hence only two parameters can be passed backwards and forwards directly. The 16-bit index register can, however, be used as a pointer to a string of parameters stored in a data table in RAM in order to pass a larger numbers of parameters. In the MC68000, more registers are available for parameter passing, but these registers are not automatically saved in the event of an interrupt or other exception. Thus to achieve re-entrancy a stack frame mechanism of the type discussed in Worked Example 7.4 *et seq.* is required.

*Common data store:* A second alternative is to pass data between the main program and the subroutine using a common area of the data store. This area can then be accessed using direct addressing, or any other addressing mode. It is the responsibility of the main program to ensure that the contents of the specified data area are appropriately initialised before the subroutine is called, and to extract any results from this area when the subroutine has been completed. Clearly, the common data area can be as large as necessary, within the overall constraints of physically available memory. If the common data store is accessed using direct addressing, a disadvantage of the approach is that it is only re-entrant for read-only data. If this is a problem, an alternative is to use a stack frame as illustrated in Worked Example 7.4: this produces fully re-entrant code, without imposing any limitations on the number of parameters which can be passed.

*Backing store:* For very large quantities of data, there may be no alternative other than to write the data out to a backing storage device such as a disk, and for the subroutine subsequently to read the data back as it processes them. Obviously, this method of passing data has important implications for the hardware required to implement the application, and also for the execution speed of the program.

In this specific application accumulators A and B on the MC68HC11 could be used to pass the 2-byte BCD watersetting or roomsetting temperature to the conversion subroutine and a single accumulator could pass back the result. Alternatively, the index register could be set to point to the first byte of the BCD temperature, and the other bytes accessed using the indexed addressing mode as follows:

An important advantage of the argument method of communicating parameters on the MC68HC11 is that it produces a *re-entrant* subroutine, that is, a subroutine which may be executed both as part of the main program and also within an interrupt process. In this case it is essential to ensure that if the routine is suspended during an interrupt and then executed upon a different set of data within the interrupt routine, then the original data being processed are not destroyed. Data stored in registers or pointed to by registers are preserved because the registers are automatically stacked, but data written into a common data area may corrupt data previously saved there.

In the MC68000 implementation, any of the registers D0–D7 could be used to pass parameters and/or return results.

```
                 .
                 .
            LDX      roomsetting
            JSR      BCDtobinary
                 .
                 .
BCDtobinary LDAA     0,X          *accesses m.s. BCD byte
                 .
            LDAA     1,X          *accesses l.s. BCD byte
                 .
            STAA     2,X          *saves binary result
            RTS
                 .
```

Having set up the required communication mechanisms and specified the storage areas for program and data variables, the time has now come to write the detailed assembly language implementation of the algorithm. This should be almost a mechanical process, and hence the likelihood of coding errors is minimised.

**Exercise 10.1** Complete the design example by writing the detailed assembly language code to implement the algorithm for the central heating controller. The code should include assembler directives where appropriate, and should be fully documented.

### Summary

The final chapter of this book has introduced a general design methodology to be used in the development of microprocessor applications, and illustrated it with a specific design example. The importance of a structured approach to both software and hardware design has been emphasised. It is hoped that the advice given in this chapter helps the student to avoid the more obvious pitfalls associated with microprocessor and computer applications design. There is, however, no substitute for experience in this field.

### Problems

10.1 The microprocessor controlled central heating system is to be enhanced by the inclusion of a real-time clock which interrupts the processor at one second intervals. The time may be read from this clock as six BCD digits (most significant digit first) which are continuously available at the output of a 24-bit latch. Explain how the remaining spare input/output lines of the PIA could be interfaced to the clock, and write an interrupt subroutine which reads the time into three consecutive addresses in RAM labelled hours, minutes and seconds.

10.2 The microprocessor-based central heating controller is to be implemented using a single MC6821 PIA. Design hardware to implement the required 37 input/output lines by multiplexing the 16 data lines available on the PIA.

10.3 An enhanced microprocessor-based central heating controller is to be designed. The device will control the boiler and the pump as previously, but will be able to be programmed by the user with a number of timed 24-hour temperature cycles. The interface to the user will be implemented using a 4 × 4 key-switch array (see Problem 8.1), and six seven-segment LED numeric displays. The system will be implemented using a real-time clock as described in Problem 10.1, and a single multiplexed PIA. The 16 key-switches represent the digits 0–9 and a number of control functions. These will allow three different programmes each containing four time and temperature settings programmable between 0000 and 2359 to be specified. The facility to review the programmes using the display must also be provided. Develop outline software and hardware designs for the enhanced central heating controller.

10.4 A microprocessor-controlled doorbell plays one of 24 different tunes (selected by switches) when the button is pushed. Develop a specification and outline hardware and software design for the doorbell which shows how the microprocessor can generate tunes.

10.5 A feasibility study is to be conducted to examine the use of a microprocessor-based controller for traffic light control. Develop a specification and outline design for a controller which controls two sets of lights at a crossroads.

# Appendix A

**ASCII character codes and their binary representation**

| | | | | | b6 | 0 | 0 | 0 | 0 | 1 | 1 | 1 | 1 |
|---|---|---|---|---|---|---|---|---|---|---|---|---|---|
| | | | | | b5 | 0 | 0 | 1 | 1 | 0 | 0 | 1 | 1 |
| | | | | | b4 | 0 | 1 | 0 | 1 | 0 | 1 | 0 | 1 |

| b3 | b2 | b1 | b0 | Row | Column 0 | 1 | 2 | 3 | 4 | 5 | 6 | 7 |
|---|---|---|---|---|---|---|---|---|---|---|---|---|
| 0 | 0 | 0 | 0 | 0 | NUL | DLE | SP | 0 | @ | P | ` | p |
| 0 | 0 | 0 | 1 | 1 | SOH | DC1 | ! | 1 | A | Q | a | q |
| 0 | 0 | 1 | 0 | 2 | STX | DC2 | " | 2 | B | R | b | r |
| 0 | 0 | 1 | 1 | 3 | ETX | DC3 | # | 3 | C | S | c | s |
| 0 | 1 | 0 | 0 | 4 | EOT | DC4 | $ | 4 | D | T | d | t |
| 0 | 1 | 0 | 1 | 5 | ENQ | NAK | % | 5 | E | U | e | u |
| 0 | 1 | 1 | 0 | 6 | ACK | SYN | & | 6 | F | V | f | v |
| 0 | 1 | 1 | 1 | 7 | BEL | ETB | ' | 7 | G | W | g | w |
| 1 | 0 | 0 | 0 | 8 | BS | CAN | ( | 8 | H | X | h | x |
| 1 | 0 | 0 | 1 | 9 | HT | EM | ) | 9 | I | Y | i | y |
| 1 | 0 | 1 | 0 | 10 | LF | SUB | * | : | J | Z | j | z |
| 1 | 0 | 1 | 1 | 11 | VT | ESC | + | ; | K | [ | k | { |
| 1 | 1 | 0 | 0 | 12 | FF | FS | , | < | L | \ | l | \| |
| 1 | 1 | 0 | 1 | 13 | CR | GS | – | = | M | ] | m | } |
| 1 | 1 | 1 | 0 | 14 | SO | RS | . | > | N | ^ | n | ~ |
| 1 | 1 | 1 | 1 | 15 | SI | US | / | ? | O | _ | o | DEL |

*Notes:*

1 Binary codes for lower- and upper-case letters are identical except for bit 5, which is reset for upper case and set for lower case.

2 Numerals 0–9 are represented by ASCII codes 30–39 hex. Thus bits 0–3 represent the number directly in binary.

3 On most VDU keyboards, control codes can be generated by depressing the *control* key and an alphabetic character key simultaneously. The control key has the effect of resetting bit 6 of the alphabetic character, thus control codes NUL to US are represented by *control*-@ to *control*- _ respectively. (For example, *control*-I produces code HT (horizontal tab).)

| | | | | |
|---|---|---|---|---|
| NUL | Null | | DC1 | Device control 1 |
| SOH | Start of heading | | DC2 | Device control 2 |
| STX | Start of text | | DC3 | Device control 3 |
| ETX | End of text | | DC4 | Device control 4 |
| EOT | End of transmission | | NAK | Negative acknowledge |
| ENQ | Enquiry | | SYN | Synchronous idle |
| ACK | Acknowledge | | ETB | End of transmission block |
| BEL | Bell | | CAN | Cancel |
| BS | Backspace | | EM | End of medium |
| HT | Horizontal tab | | SUB | Substitute |
| LF | Line feed | | ESC | Escape |
| VT | Vertical tabulation | | FS | File separator |
| FF | Form feed | | GS | Group separator |
| CR | Carriage return | | RS | Record separator |
| SO | Shift out | | US | Unit separator |
| SI | Shift in | | SP | Space |
| DLE | Data link escape | | DEL | Delete |

# Appendix B

**Register transfer language for processor operations**

In order to describe the data transfer operations which are performed when a computer executes instructions, a *register transfer language* is used. The language provides a formalised notation which can be used to express both data transfers and arithmetic or logical processing. The following list gives symbols which are commonly used, together with their meanings:

| | |
|---|---|
| $\rightarrow$ | 'is transferred to' |
| ( ) | 'contents of' |
| + | 'plus' |
| – | 'minus' |
| * | 'multiplied by' |
| / | 'divided by' |
| AND | 'bitwise logical AND operation' |
| OR | 'bitwise logical OR operation' |
| XOR | 'bitwise logical exclusive OR operation' |
| $\ll$ n | 'shift left n bits' |
| $\gg$ m | 'shift right m bits' |

The expression to the left of the arrow must always evaluate to a data value; the expression to the right must always evaluate to an address.

*Examples*

1  $D \rightarrow L$
The data D are transferred to destination address L.

2  $(M) \rightarrow N$
The contents of address M are transferred to address N.

3  $((M)) \rightarrow N$
The contents of the address pointed to by M (the contents of the contents of M) are transferred to address N.

4  $D \rightarrow (N)$
The data D are transferred to the address pointed to by N.

5  $D*2 \rightarrow N$
The data D are multiplied by 2 (equivalent to shift left one bit) and the result is transferred to destination address N.

6  $(M) + 10 \rightarrow N$
Ten is added to the contents of address M and the result is transferred to address N.

7  $(A) - 1 \rightarrow A$
The contents of address A are decremented and the result stored back in address A.

8  $D \rightarrow L-50$
The data D are transferred to the address L minus 50.

9  $D \rightarrow (L) - 50$
The data D are transferred to the address pointed to by L, minus 50.

The letters D, L, M N and A have no particular significance, and are chosen simply for illustration. In practice, the letters used are dependent on the context (for example, A and B to represent accumulators A and B, M to represent memory, SP to represent a stack pointer, and so on.)

Double brackets to the left of the arrow, or single brackets to the right of the arrow are each used to represent indirect addressing.

A could represent an address in memory or a register depending upon the context of the statement.

# Appendix C

## MC68HC11 microprocessor instruction set © Motorola

| Source Form(s) | Operation | Boolean Expression | Addressing Mode for Operand | Opcode | Operand(s) | Bytes | Cycle | Cycle by Cycle* | S | X | H | I | N | Z | V | C |
|---|---|---|---|---|---|---|---|---|---|---|---|---|---|---|---|---|
| ABA | Add Accumulators | A+B→A | INH | 1B | | 1 | 2 | 2-1 | - | - | ↕ | - | ↕ | ↕ | ↕ | ↕ |
| ABX | Add B to X | IX+00:B→IX | INH | 3A | | 1 | 3 | 2-2 | - | - | - | - | - | - | - | - |
| ABY | Add B to Y | IY+00:B→IY | INH | 18 3A | | 2 | 4 | 2-4 | - | - | - | - | - | - | - | - |
| ADCA (opr) | Add with Carry to A | A+M+C→A | A IMM | 89 | ii | 2 | 2 | 3-1 | - | - | ↕ | - | ↕ | ↕ | ↕ | ↕ |
| | | | A DIR | 99 | dd | 2 | 3 | 4-1 | | | | | | | | |
| | | | A EXT | B9 | hh ll | 3 | 4 | 5-2 | | | | | | | | |
| | | | A IND,X | A9 | ff | 2 | 4 | 6-2 | | | | | | | | |
| | | | A IND,Y | 18 A9 | ff | 3 | 5 | 7-2 | | | | | | | | |
| ADCB (opr) | Add with Carry to B | B+M+C→B | B IMM | C9 | ii | 2 | 2 | 3-1 | - | - | ↕ | - | ↕ | ↕ | ↕ | ↕ |
| | | | B DIR | D9 | dd | 2 | 3 | 4-1 | | | | | | | | |
| | | | B EXT | F9 | hh ll | 3 | 4 | 5-2 | | | | | | | | |
| | | | B IND,X | E9 | ff | 2 | 4 | 6-2 | | | | | | | | |
| | | | B IND,Y | 18 E9 | ff | 3 | 5 | 7-2 | | | | | | | | |
| ADDA (opr) | Add Memory to A | A+M→A | A IMM | 8B | ii | 2 | 2 | 3-1 | - | - | ↕ | - | ↕ | ↕ | ↕ | ↕ |
| | | | A DIR | 9B | dd | 2 | 3 | 4-1 | | | | | | | | |
| | | | A EXT | BB | hh ll | 3 | 4 | 5-2 | | | | | | | | |
| | | | A IND,X | AB | ff | 2 | 4 | 6-2 | | | | | | | | |
| | | | A IND,Y | 18 AB | ff | 3 | 5 | 7-2 | | | | | | | | |
| ADDB (opr) | Add Memory to B | B+M→B | B IMM | CB | ii | 2 | 2 | 3-1 | - | - | ↕ | - | ↕ | ↕ | ↕ | ↕ |
| | | | B DIR | DB | dd | 2 | 3 | 4-1 | | | | | | | | |
| | | | B EXT | FB | hh ll | 3 | 4 | 5-2 | | | | | | | | |
| | | | B IND,X | EB | ff | 2 | 4 | 6-2 | | | | | | | | |
| | | | B IND,Y | 18 EB | ff | 3 | 5 | 7-2 | | | | | | | | |
| ADDD (opr) | Add 16-Bit to D | D+M:M+1→D | IMM | C3 | jj kk | 3 | 4 | 3-3 | - | - | - | - | ↕ | ↕ | ↕ | ↕ |
| | | | DIR | D3 | dd | 2 | 5 | 4-7 | | | | | | | | |
| | | | EXT | F3 | hh ll | 3 | 6 | 5-10 | | | | | | | | |
| | | | IND,X | E3 | ff | 2 | 6 | 6-10 | | | | | | | | |
| | | | IND,Y | 18 E3 | ff | 3 | 7 | 7-8 | | | | | | | | |
| ANDA (opr) | AND A with Memory | A•M→A | A IMM | 84 | ii | 2 | 2 | 3-1 | - | - | - | - | ↕ | ↕ | 0 | - |
| | | | A DIR | 94 | dd | 2 | 3 | 4-1 | | | | | | | | |
| | | | A EXT | B4 | hh ll | 3 | 4 | 5-2 | | | | | | | | |
| | | | A IND,X | A4 | ff | 2 | 4 | 6-2 | | | | | | | | |
| | | | A IND,Y | 18 A4 | ff | 3 | 5 | 7-2 | | | | | | | | |
| ANDB (opr) | AND B with Memory | B•M→B | B IMM | C4 | ii | 2 | 2 | 3-1 | - | - | - | - | ↕ | ↕ | 0 | - |
| | | | B DIR | D4 | dd | 2 | 3 | 4-1 | | | | | | | | |
| | | | B EXT | F4 | hh ll | 3 | 4 | 5-2 | | | | | | | | |
| | | | B IND,X | E4 | ff | 2 | 4 | 6-2 | | | | | | | | |
| | | | B IND,Y | 18 E4 | ff | 3 | 5 | 7-2 | | | | | | | | |
| ASL (opr) | Arithmetic Shift Left | | EXT | 78 | hh ll | 3 | 6 | 5-8 | - | - | - | - | ↕ | ↕ | ↕ | ↕ |
| | | | IND,X | 68 | ff | 2 | 6 | 6-3 | | | | | | | | |
| | | | IND,Y | 18 68 | ff | 3 | 7 | 7-3 | | | | | | | | |
| ASLA | | | A INH | 48 | | 1 | 2 | 2-1 | | | | | | | | |
| ASLB | | | B INH | 58 | | 1 | 2 | 2-1 | | | | | | | | |
| ASLD | Arithmetic Shift Left Double | | INH | 05 | | 1 | 3 | 2-2 | - | - | - | - | ↕ | ↕ | ↕ | ↕ |
| ASR (opr) | Arithmetic Shift Right | | EXT | 77 | hh ll | 3 | 6 | 5-8 | - | - | - | - | ↕ | ↕ | ↕ | ↕ |
| | | | IND,X | 67 | ff | 2 | 6 | 6-3 | | | | | | | | |
| | | | IND,Y | 18 67 | ff | 3 | 7 | 7-3 | | | | | | | | |
| ASRA | | | A INH | 47 | | 1 | 2 | 2-1 | | | | | | | | |
| ASRB | | | B INH | 57 | | 1 | 2 | 2-1 | | | | | | | | |
| BCC (rel) | Branch if Carry Clear | ?C=0 | REL | 24 | rr | 2 | 3 | 8-1 | - | - | - | - | - | - | - | - |
| BCLR (opr) (msk) | Clear Bit(s) | M•($\overline{mm}$)→M | DIR | 15 | dd mm | 3 | 6 | 4-10 | - | - | - | - | ↕ | ↕ | 0 | - |
| | | | IND,X | 1D | ff mm | 3 | 7 | 6-13 | | | | | | | | |
| | | | IND,Y | 18 1D | ff mm | 4 | 8 | 7-10 | | | | | | | | |
| BCS (rel) | Branch if Carry Set | ?C=1 | REL | 25 | rr | 2 | 3 | 8-1 | - | - | - | - | - | - | - | - |
| BEQ (rel) | Branch if = Zero | ?Z=1 | REL | 27 | rr | 2 | 3 | 8-1 | - | - | - | - | - | - | - | - |

| Source Form(s) | Operation | Boolean Expression | Addressing Mode for Operand | Opcode | Operand(s) | Bytes | Cycle | Cycle by Cycle* | S | X | H | I | N | Z | V | C |
|---|---|---|---|---|---|---|---|---|---|---|---|---|---|---|---|---|
| BGE (rel) | Branch if ≥ Zero | ? N ⊕ V = 0 | REL | 2C | rr | 2 | 3 | 8-1 | - | - | - | - | - | - | - | - |
| BGT (rel) | Branch if > Zero | ? Z + (N ⊕ V) = 0 | REL | 2E | rr | 2 | 3 | 8-1 | - | - | - | - | - | - | - | - |
| BHI (rel) | Branch if Higher | ? C + Z = 0 | REL | 22 | rr | 2 | 3 | 8-1 | - | - | - | - | - | - | - | - |
| BHS (rel) | Branch if Higher or Same | ? C = 0 | REL* | 24 | rr | 2 | 3 | 8-1 | - | - | - | - | - | - | - | - |
| BITA (opr) | Bit(s) Test A with Memory | A•M | A IMM | 85 | ii | 2 | 2 | 3-1 | - | - | - | - | ↕ | ↕ | 0 | - |
| | | | A DIR | 95 | dd | 2 | 3 | 4-1 | | | | | | | | |
| | | | A EXT | B5 | hh ll | 3 | 4 | 5-2 | | | | | | | | |
| | | | A IND,X | A5 | ff | 2 | 4 | 6-2 | | | | | | | | |
| | | | A IND,Y | 18 A5 | ff | 3 | 5 | 7-2 | | | | | | | | |
| BITB (opr) | Bit(s) Test B with Memory | B•M | B IMM | C5 | ii | 2 | 2 | 3-1 | - | - | - | - | ↕ | ↕ | 0 | - |
| | | | B DIR | D5 | dd | 2 | 3 | 4-1 | | | | | | | | |
| | | | B EXT | F5 | hh ll | 3 | 4 | 5-2 | | | | | | | | |
| | | | B IND,X | E5 | ff | 2 | 4 | 6-2 | | | | | | | | |
| | | | B IND,Y | 18 E5 | ff | 3 | 5 | 7-2 | | | | | | | | |
| BLE (rel) | Branch if ≤ Zero | ? Z + (N ⊕ V) = 1 | REL | 2F | rr | 2 | 3 | 8-1 | - | - | - | - | - | - | - | - |
| BLO (rel) | Branch if Lower | ? C = 1 | REL | 25 | rr | 2 | 3 | 8-1 | - | - | - | - | - | - | - | - |
| BLS (rel) | Branch if Lower or Same | ? C + Z = 1 | REL | 23 | rr | 2 | 3 | 8-1 | - | - | - | - | - | - | - | - |
| BLT (rel) | Branch If < Zero | ? N ⊕ V = 1 | REL | 2D | rr | 2 | 3 | 8-1 | - | - | - | - | - | - | - | - |
| BMI (rel) | Branch if Minus | ? N = 1 | REL | 2B | rr | 2 | 3 | 8-1 | - | - | - | - | - | - | - | - |
| BNE (rel) | Branch if Not = Zero | ? Z = 0 | REL | 26 | rr | 2 | 3 | 8-1 | - | - | - | - | - | - | - | - |
| BPL (rel) | Branch if Plus | ? N = 0 | REL | 2A | rr | 2 | 3 | 8-1 | - | - | - | - | - | - | - | - |
| BRA (rel) | Branch Always | ? 1 = 1 | REL | 20 | rr | 2 | 3 | 8-1 | - | - | - | - | - | - | - | - |
| BRCLR(opr) (msk) (rel) | Branch if Bit(s) Clear | ? M• mm = 0 | DIR | 13 | dd mm rr | 4 | 6 | 4-11 | - | - | - | - | - | - | - | - |
| | | | IND,X | 1F | ff mm rr | 4 | 7 | 6-14 | | | | | | | | |
| | | | IND,Y | 18 1F | ff mm rr | 5 | 8 | 7-11 | | | | | | | | |
| BRN (rel) | Branch Never | ? 1 = 0 | REL | 21 | rr | 2 | 3 | 8-1 | - | - | - | - | - | - | - | - |
| BRSET(opr) (msk) (rel) | Branch if Bit(s) Set | ? ($\overline{M}$)•mm = 0 | DIR | 12 | dd mm rr | 4 | 6 | 4-11 | - | - | - | - | - | - | - | - |
| | | | IND,X | 1E | ff mm rr | 4 | 7 | 6-14 | | | | | | | | |
| | | | IND,Y | 18 1E | ff mm rr | 5 | 8 | 7-11 | | | | | | | | |
| BSET(opr) (msk) | Set Bit(s) | M + mm → M | DIR | 14 | dd mm | 3 | 6 | 4-10 | - | - | - | - | ↕ | ↕ | 0 | - |
| | | | IND,X | 1C | ff mm | 3 | 7 | 6-13 | | | | | | | | |
| | | | IND,Y | 18 1C | ff mm | 4 | 8 | 7-10 | | | | | | | | |
| BSR (rel) | Branch to Subroutine | See Special Ops | REL | 8D | rr | 2 | 6 | 8-2 | - | - | - | - | - | - | - | - |
| BVC (rel) | Branch if Overflow Clear | ? V = 0 | REL | 28 | rr | 2 | 3 | 8-1 | - | - | - | - | - | - | - | - |
| BVS (rel) | Branch if Overflow Set | ? V = 1 | REL | 29 | rr | 2 | 3 | 8-1 | - | - | - | - | - | - | - | - |
| CBA | Compare A to B | A – B | INH | 11 | | 1 | 2 | 2-1 | - | - | - | - | ↕ | ↕ | ↕ | ↕ |
| CLC | Clear Carry Bit | 0 → C | INH | 0C | | 1 | 2 | 2-1 | - | - | - | - | - | - | - | 0 |
| CLI | Clear Interrupt Mask | 0 → I | INH | 0E | | 1 | 2 | 2-1 | - | - | - | 0 | - | - | - | - |
| CLR (opr) | Clear Memory Byte | 0 → M | EXT | 7F | hh ll | 3 | 6 | 5-8 | - | - | - | - | 0 | 1 | 0 | 0 |
| | | | IND,X | 6F | ff | 2 | 6 | 6-3 | | | | | | | | |
| | | | IND,Y | 18 6F | ff | 3 | 7 | 7-3 | | | | | | | | |
| CLRA | Clear Accumulator A | 0 → A | A INH | 4F | | 1 | 2 | 2-1 | - | - | - | - | 0 | 1 | 0 | 0 |
| CLRB | Clear Accumulator B | 0 → B | B INH | 5F | | 1 | 2 | 2-1 | - | - | - | - | 0 | 1 | 0 | 0 |
| CLV | Clear Overflow Flag | 0 → V | INH | 0A | | 1 | 2 | 2-1 | - | - | - | - | - | - | 0 | - |
| CMPA (opr) | Compare A to Memory | A – M | A IMM | 81 | ii | 2 | 2 | 3-1 | - | - | - | - | ↕ | ↕ | ↕ | ↕ |
| | | | A DIR | 91 | dd | 2 | 3 | 4-1 | | | | | | | | |
| | | | A EXT | B1 | hh ll | 3 | 4 | 5-2 | | | | | | | | |
| | | | A IND,X | A1 | ff | 2 | 4 | 6-2 | | | | | | | | |
| | | | A IND,Y | 18 A1 | ff | 3 | 5 | 7-2 | | | | | | | | |

| Source Form(s) | Operation | Boolean Expression | Addressing Mode for Operand | Opcode | Operand(s) | Bytes | Cycle | Cycle by Cycle* | S | X | H | I | N | Z | V | C |
|---|---|---|---|---|---|---|---|---|---|---|---|---|---|---|---|---|
| CMPB (opr) | Compare B to Memory | B − M | B IMM | C1 | ii | 2 | 2 | 3-1 | - | - | - | - | ↕ | ↕ | ↕ | ↕ |
| | | | B DIR | D1 | dd | 2 | 3 | 4-1 | | | | | | | | |
| | | | B EXT | F1 | hh  ll | 3 | 4 | 5-2 | | | | | | | | |
| | | | B IND,X | E1 | ff | 2 | 4 | 6-2 | | | | | | | | |
| | | | B IND,Y | 18 E1 | ff | 3 | 5 | 7-2 | | | | | | | | |
| COM (opr) | 1's Complement Memory Byte | $FF − M → M | EXT | 73 | hh  ll | 3 | 6 | 5-8 | - | - | - | - | ↕ | ↕ | 0 | 1 |
| | | | IND,X | 63 | ff | 2 | 6 | 6-3 | | | | | | | | |
| | | | IND,Y | 18 63 | ff | 3 | 7 | 7-3 | | | | | | | | |
| COMA | 1's Complement A | $FF − A → A | A INH | 43 | | 1 | 2 | 2-1 | - | - | - | - | ↕ | ↕ | 0 | 1 |
| COMB | 1's Complement B | $FF − B → B | B INH | 53 | | 1 | 2 | 2-1 | - | - | - | - | ↕ | ↕ | 0 | 1 |
| CPD (opr) | Compare D to Memory 16-Bit | D − M:M + 1 | IMM | 1A 83 | jj  kk | 4 | 5 | 3-5 | - | - | - | - | ↕ | ↕ | ↕ | ↕ |
| | | | DIR | 1A 93 | dd | 3 | 6 | 4-9 | | | | | | | | |
| | | | EXT | 1A B3 | hh  ll | 4 | 7 | 5-11 | | | | | | | | |
| | | | IND,X | 1A A3 | ff | 3 | 7 | 6-11 | | | | | | | | |
| | | | IND,Y | CD A3 | ff | 3 | 7 | 7-8 | | | | | | | | |
| CPX (opr) | Compare X to Memory 16-Bit | IX − M:M + 1 | IMM | 8C | jj  kk | 3 | 4 | 3-3 | - | - | - | - | ↕ | ↕ | ↕ | ↕ |
| | | | DIR | 9C | dd | 2 | 5 | 4-7 | | | | | | | | |
| | | | EXT | BC | hh  ll | 3 | 6 | 5-10 | | | | | | | | |
| | | | IND,X | AC | ff | 2 | 6 | 6-10 | | | | | | | | |
| | | | IND,Y | CD AC | ff | 3 | 7 | 7-8 | | | | | | | | |
| CPY (opr) | Compare Y to Memory 16-Bit | IY − M:M + 1 | IMM | 18 8C | jj  kk | 4 | 5 | 3-5 | - | - | - | - | ↕ | ↕ | ↕ | ↕ |
| | | | DIR | 18 9C | dd | 3 | 6 | 4-9 | | | | | | | | |
| | | | EXT | 18 BC | hh  ll | 4 | 7 | 5-11 | | | | | | | | |
| | | | IND,X | 1A AC | ff | 3 | 7 | 6-11 | | | | | | | | |
| | | | IND,Y | 18 AC | ff | 3 | 7 | 7-8 | | | | | | | | |
| DAA | Decimal Adjust A | Adjust Sum to BCD | INH | 19 | | 1 | 2 | 2-1 | - | - | - | - | ↕ | ↕ | ↕ | ↕ |
| DEC (opr) | Decrement Memory Byte | M − 1 → M | EXT | 7A | hh  ll | 3 | 6 | 5-8 | - | - | - | - | ↕ | ↕ | ↕ | - |
| | | | IND,X | 6A | ff | 2 | 6 | 6-3 | | | | | | | | |
| | | | IND,Y | 18 6A | ff | 3 | 7 | 7-3 | | | | | | | | |
| DECA | Decrement Accumulator A | A − 1 → A | A INH | 4A | | 1 | 2 | 2-1 | - | - | - | - | ↕ | ↕ | ↕ | - |
| DECB | Decrement Accumulator B | B − 1 → B | B INH | 5A | | 1 | 2 | 2-1 | - | - | - | - | ↕ | ↕ | ↕ | - |
| DES | Decrement Stack Pointer | SP − 1 → SP | INH | 34 | | 1 | 3 | 2-3 | - | - | - | - | - | - | - | - |
| DEX | Decrement Index Register X | IX − 1 → IX | INH | 09 | | 1 | 3 | 2-2 | - | - | - | - | - | ↕ | - | - |
| DEY | Decrement Index Register Y | IY − 1 → IY | INH | 18 09 | | 2 | 4 | 2-4 | - | - | - | - | - | ↕ | - | - |
| EORA (opr) | Exclusive OR A with Memory | A ⊕ M → A | A IMM | 88 | ii | 2 | 2 | 3-1 | - | - | - | - | ↕ | ↕ | 0 | - |
| | | | A DIR | 98 | dd | 2 | 3 | 4-1 | | | | | | | | |
| | | | A EXT | B8 | hh  ll | 3 | 4 | 5-2 | | | | | | | | |
| | | | A IND,X | A8 | ff | 2 | 4 | 6-2 | | | | | | | | |
| | | | A IND,Y | 18 A8 | ff | 3 | 5 | 7-2 | | | | | | | | |
| EORB (opr) | Exclusive OR B with Memory | B ⊕ M → B | B IMM | C8 | ii | 2 | 2 | 3-1 | - | - | - | - | ↕ | ↕ | 0 | - |
| | | | B DIR | D8 | dd | 2 | 3 | 4-1 | | | | | | | | |
| | | | B EXT | F8 | hh  ll | 3 | 4 | 5-2 | | | | | | | | |
| | | | B IND,X | E8 | ff | 2 | 4 | 6-2 | | | | | | | | |
| | | | B IND,Y | 18 E8 | ff | 3 | 5 | 7-2 | | | | | | | | |
| FDIV | Fractional Divide 16 by 16 | D/IX → IX; r → D | INH | 03 | | 1 | 41 | 2-17 | - | - | - | - | - | ↕ | ↕ | ↕ |
| IDIV | Integer Divide 16 by 16 | D/IX → IX; r → D | INH | 02 | | 1 | 41 | 2-17 | - | - | - | - | - | ↕ | 0 | ↕ |
| INC (opr) | Increment Memory Byte | M + 1 → M | EXT | 7C | hh  ll | 3 | 6 | 5-8 | - | - | - | - | ↕ | ↕ | ↕ | - |
| | | | IND,X | 6C | ff | 2 | 6 | 6-3 | | | | | | | | |
| | | | IND,Y | 18 6C | ff | 3 | 7 | 7-3 | | | | | | | | |
| INCA | Increment Accumulator A | A + 1 → A | A INH | 4C | | 1 | 2 | 2-1 | - | - | - | - | ↕ | ↕ | ↕ | - |
| INCB | Increment Accumulator B | B + 1 → B | B INH | 5C | | 1 | 2 | 2-1 | - | - | - | - | ↕ | ↕ | ↕ | - |
| INS | Increment Stack Pointer | SP + 1 → SP | INH | 31 | | 1 | 3 | 2-3 | - | - | - | - | - | - | - | - |

| Source Form(s) | Operation | Boolean Expression | Addressing Mode for Operand | Machine Coding (Hexadecimal) Opcode | Operand(s) | Bytes | Cycle | Cycle by Cycle# | S | X | H | I | N | Z | V | C |
|---|---|---|---|---|---|---|---|---|---|---|---|---|---|---|---|---|
| INX | Increment Index Register X | IX + 1 → IX | INH | 08 | | 1 | 3 | 2-2 | - | - | - | - | - | ↕ | - | - |
| INY | Increment Index Register Y | IY + 1 → IY | INH | 18 08 | | 2 | 4 | 2-4 | - | - | - | - | - | ↕ | - | - |
| JMP (opr) | Jump | See Special Ops | EXT | 7E | hh ll | 3 | 3 | 5-1 | | | | | | | | |
| | | | IND,X | 6E | ff | 2 | 3 | 6-1 | | | | | | | | |
| | | | IND,Y | 18 6E | ff | 3 | 4 | 7-1 | | | | | | | | |
| JSR (opr) | Jump to Subroutine | See Special Ops | DIR | 9D | dd | 2 | 5 | 4-8 | - | | | | | | | |
| | | | EXT | BD | hh ll | 3 | 6 | 5-12 | | | | | | | | |
| | | | IND,X | AD | ff | 2 | 6 | 6-12 | | | | | | | | |
| | | | IND,Y | 18 AD | ff | 3 | 7 | 7-9 | | | | | | | | |
| LDAA (opr) | Load Accumulator A | M → A | A IMM | 86 | ii | 2 | 2 | 3-1 | - | - | - | - | ↕ | ↕ | 0 | - |
| | | | A DIR | 96 | dd | 2 | 3 | 4-1 | | | | | | | | |
| | | | A EXT | B6 | hh ll | 3 | 4 | 5-2 | | | | | | | | |
| | | | A IND,X | A6 | ff | 2 | 4 | 6-2 | | | | | | | | |
| | | | A IND,Y | 18 A6 | ff | 3 | 5 | 7-2 | | | | | | | | |
| LDAB (opr) | Load Accumulator B | M → B | B IMM | C6 | ii | 2 | 2 | 3-1 | - | - | - | - | ↕ | ↕ | 0 | - |
| | | | B DIR | D6 | dd | 2 | 3 | 4-1 | | | | | | | | |
| | | | B EXT | F6 | hh ll | 3 | 4 | 5-2 | | | | | | | | |
| | | | B IND,X | E6 | ff | 2 | 4 | 6-2 | | | | | | | | |
| | | | B IND,Y | 18 E6 | ff | 3 | 5 | 7-2 | | | | | | | | |
| LDD (opr) | Load Double Accumulator D | M → A, M + 1 → B | IMM | CC | jj kk | 3 | 3 | 3-2 | - | - | - | - | ↕ | ↕ | 0 | - |
| | | | DIR | DC | dd | 2 | 4 | 4-3 | | | | | | | | |
| | | | EXT | FC | hh ll | 3 | 5 | 5-4 | | | | | | | | |
| | | | IND,X | EC | ff | 2 | 5 | 6-6 | | | | | | | | |
| | | | IND,Y | 18 EC | ff | 3 | 6 | 7-6 | | | | | | | | |
| LDS (opr) | Load Stack Pointer | M:M + 1 → SP | IMM | 8E | jj kk | 3 | 3 | 3-2 | - | - | - | - | ↕ | ↕ | 0 | - |
| | | | DIR | 9E | dd | 2 | 4 | 4-3 | | | | | | | | |
| | | | EXT | BE | hh ll | 3 | 5 | 5-4 | | | | | | | | |
| | | | IND,X | AE | ff | 2 | 5 | 6-6 | | | | | | | | |
| | | | IND,Y | 18 AE | ff | 3 | 6 | 7-6 | | | | | | | | |
| LDX (opr) | Load Index Register X | M:M + 1 → IX | IMM | CE | jj kk | 3 | 3 | 3-2 | - | - | - | - | ↕ | ↕ | 0 | - |
| | | | DIR | DE | dd | 2 | 4 | 4-3 | | | | | | | | |
| | | | EXT | FE | hh ll | 3 | 5 | 5-4 | | | | | | | | |
| | | | IND,X | EE | ff | 2 | 5 | 6-6 | | | | | | | | |
| | | | IND,Y | CD EE | ff | 3 | 6 | 7-6 | | | | | | | | |
| LDY (opr) | Load Index Register Y | M:M + 1 → IY | IMM | 18 CE | jj kk | 4 | 4 | 3-4 | - | - | - | - | ↕ | ↕ | 0 | - |
| | | | DIR | 18 DE | dd | 3 | 5 | 4-5 | | | | | | | | |
| | | | EXT | 18 FE | hh ll | 4 | 6 | 5-6 | | | | | | | | |
| | | | IND,X | 1A EE | ff | 3 | 6 | 6-7 | | | | | | | | |
| | | | IND,Y | 18 EE | ff | 3 | 6 | 7-6 | | | | | | | | |
| LSL (opr) | Logical Shift Left | (diagram: ← C b7 b0 0) | EXT | 78 | hh ll | 3 | 6 | 5-8 | - | - | - | - | ↕ | ↕ | ↕ | ↕ |
| | | | IND,X | 68 | ff | 2 | 6 | 6-3 | | | | | | | | |
| | | | IND,Y | 18 68 | ff | 3 | 7 | 7-3 | | | | | | | | |
| LSLA | | | A INH | 48 | | 1 | 2 | 2-1 | | | | | | | | |
| LSLB | | | B INH | 58 | | 1 | 2 | 2-1 | | | | | | | | |
| LSLD | Logical Shift Left Double | (diagram: ← C b15 b0 0) | INH | 05 | | 1 | 3 | 2-2 | - | - | - | - | ↕ | ↕ | ↕ | ↕ |
| LSR (opr) | Logical Shift Right | (diagram: 0 → b7 b0 C) | EXT | 74 | hh ll | 3 | 6 | 5-8 | - | - | - | - | 0 | ↕ | ↕ | ↕ |
| | | | IND,X | 64 | ff | 2 | 6 | 6-3 | | | | | | | | |
| | | | IND,Y | 18 64 | ff | 3 | 7 | 7-3 | | | | | | | | |
| LSRA | | | A INH | 44 | | 1 | 2 | 2-1 | | | | | | | | |
| LSRB | | | B INH | 54 | | 1 | 2 | 2-1 | | | | | | | | |
| LSRD | Logical Shift Right Double | (diagram: 0 → b15 b0 C) | INH | 04 | | 1 | 3 | 2-2 | - | - | - | - | 0 | ↕ | ↕ | ↕ |
| MUL | Multiply 8 by 8 | A x B → D | INH | 3D | | 1 | 10 | 2-13 | - | - | - | - | - | - | - | ↕ |

| Source Form(s) | Operation | Boolean Expression | Addressing Mode for Operand | Opcode | Operand(s) | Bytes | Cycle | Cycle by Cycle* | S | X | H | I | N | Z | V | C |
|---|---|---|---|---|---|---|---|---|---|---|---|---|---|---|---|---|
| NEG (opr) | 2's Complement Memory Byte | 0 – M → M | EXT | 70 | hh ll | 3 | 6 | 5-8 | - | - | - | - | ↕ | ↕ | ↕ | ↕ |
|  |  |  | IND,X | 60 | ff | 2 | 6 | 6-3 |  |  |  |  |  |  |  |  |
|  |  |  | IND,Y | 18 60 | ff | 3 | 7 | 7-3 |  |  |  |  |  |  |  |  |
| NEGA | 2's Complement A | 0 – A → A | A INH | 40 |  | 1 | 2 | 2-1 | - | - | - | - | ↕ | ↕ | ↕ | ↕ |
| NEGB | 2's Complement B | 0 – B → B | B INH | 50 |  | 1 | 2 | 2-1 | - | - | - | - | ↕ | ↕ | ↕ | ↕ |
| NOP | No Operation | No Operation | INH | 01 |  | 1 | 2 | 2-1 | - | - | - | - | - | - | - | - |
| ORAA (opr) | OR Accumulator A (Inclusive) | A + M → A | A IMM | 8A | ii | 2 | 2 | 3-1 | - | - | - | - | ↕ | ↕ | 0 | - |
|  |  |  | A DIR | 9A | dd | 2 | 3 | 4-1 |  |  |  |  |  |  |  |  |
|  |  |  | A EXT | BA | hh ll | 3 | 4 | 5-2 |  |  |  |  |  |  |  |  |
|  |  |  | A IND,X | AA | ff | 2 | 4 | 6-2 |  |  |  |  |  |  |  |  |
|  |  |  | A IND,Y | 18 AA | ff | 3 | 5 | 7-2 |  |  |  |  |  |  |  |  |
| ORAB (opr) | OR Accumulator B (Inclusive) | B + M → B | B IMM | CA | ii | 2 | 2 | 3-1 | - | - | - | - | ↕ | ↕ | 0 | - |
|  |  |  | B DIR | DA | dd | 2 | 3 | 4-1 |  |  |  |  |  |  |  |  |
|  |  |  | B EXT | FA | hh ll | 3 | 4 | 5-2 |  |  |  |  |  |  |  |  |
|  |  |  | B IND,X | EA | ff | 2 | 4 | 6-2 |  |  |  |  |  |  |  |  |
|  |  |  | B IND,Y | 18 EA | ff | 3 | 5 | 7-2 |  |  |  |  |  |  |  |  |
| PSHA | Push A onto Stack | A → Stk, SP=SP–1 | A INH | 36 |  | 1 | 3 | 2-6 | - | - | - | - | - | - | - | - |
| PSHB | Push B onto Stack | B → Stk, SP=SP–1 | B INH | 37 |  | 1 | 3 | 2-6 | - | - | - | - | - | - | - | - |
| PSHX | Push X onto Stack (Lo First) | IX → Stk, SP=SP–2 | INH | 3C |  | 1 | 4 | 2-7 | - | - | - | - | - | - | - | - |
| PSHY | Push Y onto Stack (Lo First) | IY → Stk, SP=SP–2 | INH | 18 3C |  | 2 | 5 | 2-8 | - | - | - | - | - | - | - | - |
| PULA | Pull A from Stack | SP=SP+1, A ← Stk | A INH | 32 |  | 1 | 4 | 2-9 | - | - | - | - | - | - | - | - |
| PULB | Pull B from Stack | SP=SP+1, B ← Stk | B INH | 33 |  | 1 | 4 | 2-9 | - | - | - | - | - | - | - | - |
| PULX | Pull X from Stack (Hi First) | SP=SP+2, IX ← Stk | INH | 38 |  | 1 | 5 | 2-10 | - | - | - | - | - | - | - | - |
| PULY | Pull Y from Stack (Hi First) | SP=SP+2, IY ← Stk | INH | 18 38 |  | 2 | 6 | 2-11 | - | - | - | - | - | - | - | - |
| ROL (opr) | Rotate Left | C b7 ← b0 C | EXT | 79 | hh ll | 3 | 6 | 5-8 | - | - | - | - | ↕ | ↕ | ↕ | ↕ |
|  |  |  | IND,X | 69 | ff | 2 | 6 | 6-3 |  |  |  |  |  |  |  |  |
|  |  |  | IND,Y | 18 69 | ff | 3 | 7 | 7-3 |  |  |  |  |  |  |  |  |
| ROLA |  |  | A INH | 49 |  | 1 | 2 | 2-1 |  |  |  |  |  |  |  |  |
| ROLB |  |  | B INH | 59 |  | 1 | 2 | 2-1 |  |  |  |  |  |  |  |  |
| ROR (opr) | Rotate Right | C b7 → b0 C | EXT | 76 | hh ll | 3 | 6 | 5-8 | - | - | - | - | ↕ | ↕ | ↕ | ↕ |
|  |  |  | IND,X | 66 | ff | 2 | 6 | 6-3 |  |  |  |  |  |  |  |  |
|  |  |  | IND,Y | 18 66 | ff | 3 | 7 | 7-3 |  |  |  |  |  |  |  |  |
| RORA |  |  | A INH | 46 |  | 1 | 2 | 2-1 |  |  |  |  |  |  |  |  |
| RORB |  |  | B INH | 56 |  | 1 | 2 | 2-1 |  |  |  |  |  |  |  |  |
| RTI | Return from Interrupt | See Special Ops | INH | 3B |  | 1 | 12 | 2-14 | ↕ | ↕ | ↕ | ↕ | ↕ | ↕ | ↕ | ↕ |
| RTS | Return from Subroutine | See Special Ops | INH | 39 |  | 1 | 5 | 2-12 | - | - | - | - | - | - | - | - |
| SBA | Subtract B from A | A – B → A | INH | 10 |  | 1 | 2 | 2-1 | - | - | - | - | ↕ | ↕ | ↕ | ↕ |
| SBCA (opr) | Subtract with Carry from A | A – M – C → A | A IMM | 82 | ii | 2 | 2 | 3-1 | - | - | - | - | ↕ | ↕ | ↕ | ↕ |
|  |  |  | A DIR | 92 | dd | 2 | 3 | 4-1 |  |  |  |  |  |  |  |  |
|  |  |  | A EXT | B2 | hh ll | 3 | 4 | 5-2 |  |  |  |  |  |  |  |  |
|  |  |  | A IND,X | A2 | ff | 2 | 4 | 6-2 |  |  |  |  |  |  |  |  |
|  |  |  | A IND,Y | 18 A2 | ff | 3 | 5 | 7-2 |  |  |  |  |  |  |  |  |
| SBCB (opr) | Subtract with Carry from B | B – M – C → B | B IMM | C2 | ii | 2 | 2 | 3-1 | - | - | - | - | ↕ | ↕ | ↕ | ↕ |
|  |  |  | B DIR | D2 | dd | 2 | 3 | 4-1 |  |  |  |  |  |  |  |  |
|  |  |  | B EXT | F2 | hh ll | 3 | 4 | 5-2 |  |  |  |  |  |  |  |  |
|  |  |  | B IND,X | E2 | ff | 2 | 4 | 6-2 |  |  |  |  |  |  |  |  |
|  |  |  | B IND,Y | 18 E2 | ff | 3 | 5 | 7-2 |  |  |  |  |  |  |  |  |
| SEC | Set Carry | 1 → C | INH | 0D |  | 1 | 2 | 2-1 | - | - | - | - | - | - | - | 1 |
| SEI | Set Interrupt Mask | 1 → I | INH | 0F |  | 1 | 2 | 2-1 | - | - | - | 1 | - | - | - | - |
| SEV | Set Overflow Flag | 1 → V | INH | 0B |  | 1 | 2 | 2-1 | - | - | - | - | - | - | 1 | - |

| Source Form(s) | Operation | Boolean Expression | Addressing Mode for Operand | Opcode | Operand(s) | Bytes | Cycle | Cycle by Cycle# | S | X | H | I | N | Z | V | C |
|---|---|---|---|---|---|---|---|---|---|---|---|---|---|---|---|---|
| STAA (opr) | Store Accumulator A | A → M | A DIR | 97 | dd | 2 | 3 | 4-2 | - | - | - | - | ↕ | ↕ | 0 | - |
| | | | A EXT | B7 | hh ll | 3 | 4 | 5-3 | | | | | | | | |
| | | | A IND,X | A7 | ff | 2 | 4 | 6-5 | | | | | | | | |
| | | | A IND,Y | 18 A7 | ff | 3 | 5 | 7-5 | | | | | | | | |
| STAB (opr) | Store Accumulator B | B → M | B DIR | D7 | dd | 2 | 3 | 4-2 | - | - | - | - | ↕ | ↕ | 0 | - |
| | | | B EXT | F7 | hh ll | 3 | 4 | 5-3 | | | | | | | | |
| | | | B IND,X | E7 | ff | 2 | 4 | 6-5 | | | | | | | | |
| | | | B IND,Y | 18 E7 | ff | 3 | 5 | 7-5 | | | | | | | | |
| STD (opr) | Store Accumulator D | A → M, B → M + 1 | DIR | DD | dd | 2 | 4 | 4-4 | - | - | - | - | ↕ | ↕ | 0 | - |
| | | | EXT | FD | hh ll | 3 | 5 | 5-5 | | | | | | | | |
| | | | IND,X | ED | ff | 2 | 5 | 6-8 | | | | | | | | |
| | | | IND,Y | 18 ED | ff | 3 | 6 | 7-7 | | | | | | | | |
| STOP | Stop Internal Clocks | | INH | CF | | 1 | 2 | 2-1 | - | - | - | - | - | - | - | - |
| STS (opr) | Store Stack Pointer | SP → M:M + 1 | DIR | 9F | dd | 2 | 4 | 4-4 | - | - | - | - | ↕ | ↕ | 0 | - |
| | | | EXT | BF | hh ll | 3 | 5 | 5-5 | | | | | | | | |
| | | | IND,X | AF | ff | 2 | 5 | 6-8 | | | | | | | | |
| | | | IND,Y | 18 AF | ff | 3 | 6 | 7-7 | | | | | | | | |
| STX (opr) | Store Index Register X | IX → M:M + 1 | DIR | DF | dd | 2 | 4 | 4-4 | - | - | - | - | ↕ | ↕ | 0 | - |
| | | | EXT | FF | hh ll | 3 | 5 | 5-5 | | | | | | | | |
| | | | IND,X | EF | ff | 2 | 5 | 6-8 | | | | | | | | |
| | | | IND,Y | CD EF | ff | 3 | 6 | 7-7 | | | | | | | | |
| STY (opr) | Store Index Register Y | IY → M:M + 1 | DIR | 18 DF | dd | 3 | 5 | 4-6 | - | - | - | - | ↕ | ↕ | 0 | - |
| | | | EXT | 18 FF | hh ll | 4 | 6 | 5-7 | | | | | | | | |
| | | | IND,X | 1A EF | ff | 3 | 6 | 6-9 | | | | | | | | |
| | | | IND,Y | 18 EF | ff | 3 | 6 | 7-7 | | | | | | | | |
| SUBA (opr) | Subtract Memory from A | A − M → A | A IMM | 80 | ii | 2 | 2 | 3-1 | - | - | - | - | ↕ | ↕ | ↕ | ↕ |
| | | | A DIR | 90 | dd | 2 | 3 | 4-1 | | | | | | | | |
| | | | A EXT | B0 | hh ll | 3 | 4 | 5-2 | | | | | | | | |
| | | | A IND,X | A0 | ff | 2 | 4 | 6-2 | | | | | | | | |
| | | | A IND,Y | 18 A0 | ff | 3 | 5 | 7-2 | | | | | | | | |
| SUBB (opr) | Subtract Memory from B | B − M → B | B IMM | C0 | ii | 2 | 2 | 3-1 | - | - | - | - | ↕ | ↕ | ↕ | ↕ |
| | | | B DIR | D0 | dd | 2 | 3 | 4-1 | | | | | | | | |
| | | | B EXT | F0 | hh ll | 3 | 4 | 5-2 | | | | | | | | |
| | | | B IND,X | E0 | ff | 2 | 4 | 6-2 | | | | | | | | |
| | | | B IND,Y | 18 E0 | ff | 3 | 5 | 7-2 | | | | | | | | |
| SUBD (opr) | Subtract Memory from D | D − M:M + 1 → D | IMM | 83 | jj kk | 3 | 4 | 3-3 | - | - | - | - | ↕ | ↕ | ↕ | ↕ |
| | | | DIR | 93 | dd | 2 | 5 | 4-7 | | | | | | | | |
| | | | EXT | B3 | hh ll | 3 | 6 | 5-10 | | | | | | | | |
| | | | IND,X | A3 | ff | 2 | 6 | 6-10 | | | | | | | | |
| | | | IND,Y | 18 A3 | ff | 3 | 7 | 7-8 | | | | | | | | |
| SWI | Software Interrupt | See Special Ops | INH | 3F | | 1 | 14 | 2-15 | - | - | | 1 | - | - | - | - |
| TAB | Transfer A to B | A → B | INH | 16 | | 1 | 2 | 2-1 | - | - | - | - | ↕ | ↕ | 0 | - |
| TAP | Transfer A to CC Register | A → CCR | INH | 06 | | 1 | 2 | 2-1 | ↕ | ↕ | ↕ | ↕ | ↕ | ↕ | ↕ | ↕ |
| TBA | Transfer B to A | B → A | INH | 17 | | 1 | 2 | 2-1 | - | - | - | - | ↕ | ↕ | 0 | - |
| TEST | TEST (Only in Test Modes) | Address Bus Counts | INH | 00 | | 1 | ** | 2-20 | - | - | - | - | - | - | - | - |
| TPA | Transfer CC Register to A | CCR → A | INH | 07 | | 1 | 2 | 2-1 | - | - | - | - | - | - | - | - |
| TST (opr) | Test for Zero or Minus | M − 0 | EXT | 7D | hh ll | 3 | 6 | 5-9 | - | - | - | - | ↕ | ↕ | 0 | 0 |
| | | | IND,X | 6D | ff | 2 | 6 | 6-4 | | | | | | | | |
| | | | IND,Y | 18 6D | ff | 3 | 7 | 7-4 | | | | | | | | |
| TSTA | | A − 0 | A INH | 4D | | 1 | 2 | 2-1 | - | - | - | - | ↕ | ↕ | 0 | 0 |
| TSTB | | B − 0 | B INH | 5D | | 1 | 2 | 2-1 | - | - | - | - | ↕ | ↕ | 0 | 0 |
| TSX | Transfer Stack Pointer to X | SP + 1 → IX | INH | 30 | | 1 | 3 | 2-3 | - | - | - | - | - | - | - | - |
| TSY | Transfer Stack Pointer to Y | SP + 1 → IY | INH | 18 30 | | 2 | 4 | 2-5 | - | - | - | - | - | - | - | - |

| Source Form(s) | Operation | Boolean Expression | Addressing Mode for Operand | Machine Coding (Hexadecimal) | | Bytes | Cycle | Cycle by Cycle* | Condition Codes | | | | | | | |
|---|---|---|---|---|---|---|---|---|---|---|---|---|---|---|---|---|
| | | | | Opcode | Operand(s) | | | | S | X | H | I | N | Z | V | C |
| TXS | Transfer X to Stack Pointer | IX − 1 → SP | INH | 35 | | 1 | 3 | 2-2 | - | - | - | - | - | - | - | - |
| TYS | Transfer Y to Stack Pointer | IY − 1 → SP | INH | 18 35 | | 2 | 4 | 2-4 | - | - | - | - | - | - | - | - |
| WAI | Wait for Interrupt | Stack Regs & WAIT | INH | 3E | | 1 | *** | 2-16 | - | - | - | - | - | - | - | - |
| XGDX | Exchange D with X | IX → D, D → IX | INH | 8F | | 1 | 3 | 2-2 | - | - | - | - | - | - | - | - |
| XGDY | Exchange D with Y | IY → D, D → IY | INH | 18 8F | | 2 | 4 | 2-4 | - | - | - | - | - | - | - | - |

*Cycle-by-cycle number provides a reference to Tables 10-2 through 10-8 which detail cycle-by-cycle operation.
    Example: Table 10-1 Cycle-by-Cycle column reference number 2-4 equals Table 10-2 line item 2-4.

**Infinity or Until Reset Occurs

***12 Cycles are used beginning with the opcode fetch. A wait state is entered which remains in effect for an integer number of MPU E-clock cycles (n) until an interrupt is recognized. Finally, two additional cycles are used to fetch the appropriate interrupt vector (14 + n total).

dd  = 8-Bit Direct Address ($0000 – $00FF) (High Byte Assumed to be $00)
ff   = 8-Bit Positive Offset $00 (0) to $FF (255) (Is Added to Index)
hh  = High Order Byte of 16-Bit Extended Address
ii   = One Byte of Immediate Data
jj   = High Order Byte of 16-Bit Immediate Data
kk  = Low Order Byte of 16-Bit Immediate Data
ll   = Low Order Byte of 16-Bit Extended Address
mm = 8-Bit Bit Mask (Set Bits to be Affected)
rr   = Signed Relative Offset $80 ( – 128) to $7F ( + 127)
       (Offset Relative to the Address Following the Machine Code Offset Byte)

# Appendix D

## D.1 ARM microprocessor instruction set

**ARM Instruction set**

*Data processing instructions*

*ADC: Add with carry*

Syntax:      ADC <destination>, <operand1>, <operand2>

Operation:    Destination = operand1 + operand2 + carry

Description:   The ADC instruction is identical to the ADD instruction (below), but also adds the carry flag to the result. If the carry flag is set, i.e. the last instruction resulted in a number which was too large to hold in a single 32-bit register, then 1 is added to the result. This is useful if it is required to perform 64-bit addition using two instructions. The least significant words are first added using the ADD instruction; if the result of the addition overflows, the carry flag is set. The ADC instruction is then used to add the most significant words, taking into account any overflow from the previous addition.

Example:     ADC    R0,R3,R4   ; Set R0 = R3 + R4 if carry flag clear
                                   ; Set R0 = R3 + R4 + 1 if carry flag set

*ADD: Addition*

Syntax:      ADD <destination>, <operand1>, <operand2>

Operation:    Destination = operand1 + operand2

Description:   ADD performs the arithmetic addition of its two operands, and stores the result in the destination register. The result is valid both for unsigned numbers and signed 2s complement numbers.

Example:     ADD    R0,R3,R4   ; Set R0 = R3 + R4
              ADD    R0,R0,R1   ; Set R0 = R0 + R1

*AND: Logical AND*

Syntax:      AND <destination>, <operand1>, <operand2>

Operation:    destination = operand1 and operand2

Description:   This instruction performs a logical bitwise AND operation between operand1 and operand2. The result of the operation is placed in the destination register. AND is particularly useful for clearing certain bits in a word. For example:

|             |                                              |
| ----------- | -------------------------------------------- |
| operand1    | %10110101110101001100001110101101            |
| operand2    | %01010111010111010011111010001101            |
| destination | %00010101010101000000001010001101            |

Example:   AND    R2,R6,R3                    ; Set R2 = R6 AND R3

*BIC: Bit clear*

Syntax:       BIC <destination>, <operand1>, <operand2>

Operation:    destination = operand 1 AND (NOT (operand2))

Description:  The BIC instruction provides a useful way of clearing (forcing to zero) certain bits within a data word, whilst leaving the others unchanged. Operand1 in the instruction is the data word to be modified. Operand2 is called the *bit mask*. A set bit (one) in the bit mask will force the corresponding bit in the data word to be reset when the instruction is executed. A zero bit in the bit mask will leave the corresponding bit in the data word unchanged. The modified data word is placed in the destination register. For example:

|             |                                              |
| ----------- | -------------------------------------------- |
| operand1    | %10110101110101001100001110101101            |
| operand2    | %00000000000000001111111100000000            |
| destination | %10110101110101000000000010101101            |

Example:   BIC    R0,R0,R1    ; Consider R1 = %1111
                             ; Clear low 4 bits in R0

*CMN: Compare negative*

Syntax:       CMN <operand1>, <operand2>

Operation:    Compare the sizes of operand1 and − operand2

Description:  CMN performs an exactly equivalent operation to CMP (below), except that it compares operand1 with the negative of operand2. Note that, unlike the MVN instruction (below), the 2s complement negative of operand2 is formed before the comparison, not the 1s complement value. Hence the operation performed for the comparison is:

operand1 + operand2

Example:                          ; Consider R0 = 7, R1 = − 8, R2 = 9
           CMN    R0,R1          ; C set, Z clear, N set, V clear
           CMN    R0,R2          ; C clear, Z clear, N clear, V clear

*CMP: Compare*

Syntax:       CMP <operand1>, <operand2>

Operation:    Compare the sizes of operand1 and operand2

Description:  The instruction is used to compare two operands, and to reflect the result of the comparison in the status flags. The operation which is performed is identical to the SUB instruction:

operand1 − operand2

The result of the subtraction is discarded (hence there is no destination register); only the status flags are affected:

| | | |
|---|---|---|
| Carry | C | Set if operand1 < operand2 (unsigned) |
| Zero | Z | Set if operand1 = operand2 (signed or unsigned) |
| Negatve | N | Set if operand1 − operand2 < 0 (signed) |
| Overflow | V | Set if operand1 < 0 and operand2 > 0 (signed) and operand1 − operand2 > 0 (signed) i.e. the result has overflowed from what should be a negative value to a positive value |

Example:

```
                              ; Consider R0 = 7, R1 = − 8, R2 = 9
CMP    R0,R1                  ; C clear, Z clear, N clear, V clear
CMP    R1,R9                  ; C clear, Z clear, N set, V clear
CMP    R0,R2                  ; C set, Z clear, N set, V clear
```

## EOR: Logical exclusive OR

Syntax:      EOR <destination>, <operand1>, <operand2>

Operation:   destination = operand1 EOR operand2

Description: This instruction performs a logical bitwise EOR operation between its two operands. The result of the operation is placed in the destination register. The EOR operation results in a binary 1 only if one of the two inputs is 1 and the other is 0. EOR is especially useful for toggling the values of the bits in one of the operands. If one of the inputs to EOR is 1, then the result will be the complement of the other input. If one of the inputs is 0, then the result will be equal to the other input. For example:

```
operand1      %10110101110101001100001110101101
operand2      %01010111010111010011111010001101
destination   %11100010100010011111110100100000
```

Example:   EOR    R7,R2,R3          ; Set R7 = R2 EOR R3

## MLA: Multiplication with accumulate

Syntax:      MLA <destination>, <operand1>, <operand2>, <sum>

Operation:   destination = (operand1 * operand2) + sum

Description: This instruction performs a similar operation to the MUL instruction (below). The difference is that the contents of the register given in the sum field are added into the result of the multiplication before storing it in the destination register. Like MUL, operand1 and operand2 must be simple registers, and must observe the same restrictions.

MLA is used to keep a running total of a series of multiplications. If the sum register is specified as being the same as the destination, then the result of each multiplication will be accumulated in the destination register.

Example:      MLA    R0,R1,R2,R0           ; Set R0 = (R1 * R2) + R0

## MOV: Move data

Syntax:      MOV <destination>, <operand2>

Operation:    destination = operand2

Description:    The MOV operation is used to move data into the destination register. The source of the data to be moved is given in operand2. Note that the MOV instruction is an example of a *unary* operator, as it operates on only one operand (cf. the majority of the instructions in this section, which are *binary* operators).

Example:      MOV    R12, R0       ; Set R12 = R0
                MOV    R15, R14     ; Return from subroutine

## MVN: Move inverted data

Syntax:      MVN <destination>, <operand2>

Operation:    destination = NOT (operand2)

Description:    MVN performs an identical operation to MOV, except that operand2 is inverted by the ARM before being moved to the destination register. This can be useful for moving 2s complement negative values into the destination register. The 2s complement is formed by complementing the binary value (the *1s complement or not* operation) and adding 1 to the result. If operand2 contains 9, then the result stored in destination will in fact be $-10$.

Example:      MVN    R0,R1        ; Set R0 = $-$ (R1 + 1)
                                        ; If R1 = 9 then R0 = $-10$

## MUL: Multiplication

Syntax:      MUL <destination>, <operand1>, <operand2>

Operation:    destination = operand1 * operand2

Description:    This instruction performs a 32-bit multiplication between operand1 and operand2. If the two operands are interpreted as being signed 2s complement numbers, then the result may also be treated as being signed. Certain restrictions exist about how the operands may be specified. Operand2 must be a simple register, the destination and operand1 must be different registers, and R15 may not be used as the destination register.

Example:      MUL    R0,R1,R2      ; See R0 = R1 * R2

## ORR: Logical OR

Syntax:      ORR <destination>, <operand1>, <operand2>

| Operation: | destination = operand1 OR operand2 |

| Description: | This instruction performs a logical bitwise OR operation between operand1 and operand2. The result of the operation is placed in the destination register. ORR is particularly useful for setting certain bits within a word. For example: |

operand1    %1011010111010100110000111010 1101
operand2    %0101011101011101001111101000 1101
result      %1111011111011101111111111101 01101

| Example: | ORR    R2,R6,R3          ; Set R2 = R6 OR R3 |

*RSB: Reverse subtract*

| Syntax: | RSB <destination>, <operand1>, <operand2> |

| Operation: | destination = operand2 – operand1 |

| Description: | Like the SUB instruction (below), RSB performs the arithmetic subtraction of its operands. However, in this case the subtraction is reversed, and operand1 is subtracted from operand2. At first sight, this seems like a waste of an instruction. However, operand2 can be specified in several ways, and can include shift and rotation operations. The RSB instruction ensures that either of the operands can be specified in the more flexible format. |

| Example: | RSB    R0,R7,R14          ; Set R0 = R14 – R7 |

*RSC: Reverse subtract with carry*

| Syntax: | RSC <destination>, <operand1>, <operand2> |

| Operation: | destination = operand2 – operand1 – not (carry) |

| Description: | The RSC instruction performs a reverse subtract operation while taking account of a previous borrow in the carry flag. It is identical to the SBC instruction, except that operands 1 and 2 are reversed, to allow the different operand formats to be used with operand2. |

| Example: | RSC    R3,R0,R8          ; Set R3 = R8 – R0 if carry 1 (no borrow) |
| | ; Set R3 = R8 – R0 – 1 if carry 0 (borrow) |

*SUB: Subtract*

| Syntax: | SUB <destination>, <operand1>, <operand2> |

| Operation: | Destination = operand1 – operand2 |

| Description: | SUB performs the arithmetic subtraction of its second operand from its first operand. The result is stored in the destination register. The result is valid both for unsigned numbers and for signed 2s complement numbers. |

| Example: | SUB    R10, R2, R4          ; Set R10 = R2 – R4 |

*SBC: Subtract with carry*

Syntax:          SBC <destination>, <operand1>, <operand2>

Operation:     destination = operand1 – operand2 – not (carry)

Description:    SBC allows multi-word subtraction to be performed in the same way as ADC allows multi-word addition. In this case the carry flag is used to indicate that a 'borrow' occurred when subtracting two words, and that this borrow should be taken into account when subtracting the next two words. The subtract operations, SUB and SBC affect the carry flag in one of two ways:

If a borrow is generated, then the carry is cleared (0)

if a borrow is not generated, then the carry is set (1)

When multi-word subtraction is performed, a borrow from the least significant word means that an extra one must be subtracted from the next word. However, a borrow results in the carry flag being 0, not 1 as would be expected. To compensate for this, the ARM inverts the carry flag before using it in the SBC instruction, resulting in the operation:

destination = operand1 – operand2 – not (carry)

Example:       SBC     R3,R0,R8    ; Set R3 = R0 – R8 if carry 1 (no borrow)
                                    ; Set R3 = R0 – R8 – 1 if carry 0 (borrow)


*TEQ: Test equivalence*

Syntax:          TEQ <operand1>, <operand2>

Operation:     Bitwise comparison between operand1 and operand2

Description:    TEQ compares the two operands by performing a bitwise EOR operation between them. If they are identical, the zero flag Z is set, otherwise Z is cleared. TEQ does not modify the carry flag C, and so it can be used in place of CMP if the value of C must be preserved. The results of the EOR are discarded, hence no destination field is required.

operand1       %10110101110101001100001110101101
operand2       %00000000000000001111111100000000

Example:       TEQ     R10,R11     ; Compare R10 and R11
                                      ; Z set if R10 and R11 equal


*TST: Test bits*

Syntax:          TST <operand1>, <operand2>

Operation:     Test whether particular bits in a word are 1s or 0s

Description:    TST is used to test whether bits are set in a word. One operand is the data word to be tested and the other operand is a bit mask, selecting which bits in the data word are to be tested. If any bits in the mask which are set have a corresponding bit in the data word which is also set, then the result of the bit test is positive, and the zero flag Z is set (to 1). If none of the bits set in the mask have corresponding bits which are set in the data word, then the result of the bit test is negative, and the Z flag is cleared (to 0).

TST performs a logical AND between operand1 and operand2. The results of the AND are discarded hence no destination field is required. Only the status flags are affected. For example:

operand1      %10110101110101001100001110101101
operand2      %00000000000000000000000000000011

Zero flag set, as bit 0 of operand1 was set. If bit 0 of operand1 was clear, the zero flag would be cleared.

Example:      TST      R0,R1              ; Check whether R0 and R1 have
                                         ; any common set bits

## Shift and rotate operations

Shift and rotate operations are performed by the barrel shifter, and can be appended to any of the data processing operations in the previous section. They are applied to operand2 of the data processing instruction before execution of its function.

### LSL: Logical shift left
### ASL: Arithmetic shift left

Syntax:       LSL #n
              LSL Rx
              ASL #n
              ASL Rx

Operation:    Logical and arithmetic shift left operations are identical. A shift left operation of n places moves all the bits n positions to the left. For each 1-bit left shift, an extra zero bit is shifted into bit 0 of the register on the right hand side. Bit 31 of the data, shifted out of the left hand side of the register, is shifted into the carry flag.

Example:      LSL #4       ; shift left four places ( = multiply by 16)
              ASL R2       ; if R2 has 4 stored in it, has same effect as above.

### LSR: Logical shift right

Syntax:       LSR #n
              LSR Rx

Operation:    A shift right operation of n places moves all the bits n positions to the right. Extra zero bits are shifted into bit 31 of the register on the right-hand side. Bit 0 of the data, shifted out of the right hand side of the register, is shifted into the carry flag.

Example:      LSR #6       ; shift right 6 places ( = divide by 64)
              LSR R2       ; if R2 has 10 stored in it, divides by 1024

*ASR: Arithmetic shift right*

Syntax:      ASR #n
               ASR Rx

Operation:  An arithmetic shift right operation of n places moves all the bits n positions to the right. The original contents of bit 31 are also retained in bit 31 (this preserves the sign bit for a signed 2s complement number, hence the mnemonic). Bit 0 of the data, shifted out of the right-hand side of the register, is shifted into the carry flag.

Example:    ASR #2      ; shift right 2 places ( = divide by 4)
               ASR R2      ; if R2 has 8 stored in it, divides by 256

*ROR: Rotate right*

Syntax:      ROR #n
               ROR Rx

Operation:  A rotate right operation of n places moves all the bits n positions to the right. Unlike the shift operations, bits shifted out of the right-hand side of the register are shifted into the left-hand side of the register in a cyclic manner. A copy of the original contents of bit 0 is also shifted into the carry flag.

Example:    ROR #3      ; rotates specified register contents 3 bits right

*RRX: Rotate right with extend*

Syntax:      RRX

Operation:  The RRX operation always rotates data right by one bit only. Operation is similar to the 'ROR' function, except that the carry flag acts as an additional bit in the rotation. Thus bit 0 of the register is rotated right into the carry flag, and the carry flag contents are rotated right into bit 31 of the register.

Example:    RRX     ; rotate right 1 bit, including carry flag

*Processor/memory transfers*

*LDR: Load register from memory*

Syntax:      LDR  Rx, < address >
               LDRB Rx, < address >

Operation:  The LDR instruction loads a single 32-bit word (or 8-bit byte if the LDRB mnemonic is used) into the specified register from the specified address in memory. The memory address can be specified using any of the addressing modes described in Chapter 7.

Example:    LDR    R0, [R1]    ; Load R0 from address specified in R1
                                        ; (Register Indirect addressing)
               LDR    R3, Buffer   ; Load R3 from address specified by label Buffer
                                        ; (Program Counter relative addressing)

*STR: Store register in memory*

Syntax:       STR   Rx, <address>
              STRB Rx, <address>

Operation:    The STR instruction stores a single 32-bit word (or 8-bit byte if the STRB mnemonic is used) into memory from the specified register. The memory address can be specified using any of the addressing modes described in Chapter 7.

Example:      STR      R0,[R1]        ; Store R0 to address specified in R1
                                      ; (Register Indirect addressing)
              STR      R3,Buffer      ; Store R3 to address specified by label Buffer
                                      ; (Program Counter relative addressing)

*LDM: Load multiple registers from memory*

Syntax:       LDM <stack type> <base register>(!), {register list}

Operation:    The LDM instruction is used to load the contents of the registers specified in the register list sequentially from memory, starting at the address specified by the contents of the base register. Registers are loaded in a processor-defined order. The base register can be any register, but it is convention that R13 (also known as SP) is used as the stack pointer. When used to implement a memory stack, the write-back option (!) is required.

Example:      LDMFD  SP!, {R0–R7,PC}      ; unstack R0–R7 and exit from
                                             subroutine

*STM: Store multiple registers in memory*

Syntax:       STM <stack type> <base register>(!),{register list}

Operation:    The STM instruction is used to store the contents of the registers specified in the register list sequentially in memory, starting at the address specified by the contents of the base register. Registers are stored in a processor-defined order. The base register can be any register, but it is convention that R13 (also known as SP) is used as the stack pointer. When used to implement a memory stack, the write-back option (!) is required.

Example:      STMFD  SP!, {R0–R7,LR}      ; stack R0–R7 and the link register

*Branches*

**B: Branch**

Syntax:       B <address>

Operation:    The branch instruction causes program execution to branch to the specified address. The address is specified as a 24-bit 2s complement offset, allowing branches to anywhere in the ARM address space. In assembly language, it is normally specified using a label.

Example:    B Loop        ; branch to the address identified by the label Loop

*BL: Branch with link*

Syntax:     BL <address>

Operation:  The branch with link instruction causes program execution to branch to the specified address. The address is specified as a 24-bit 2s complement offset, allowing branches to anywhere in the ARM address space. In assembly language, it is normally specified using a label. In addition, the address of the instruction after the BL instruction is stored in the link register (R14). This implements a primitive subroutine call mechanism.

Example:    BL PrintString       ; branch to the subroutine at address PrintString

*Software interrupt*

*SWI: Software interrupt*

Syntax:     SWI <number>

Operation:  The software interrupt instruction provides the only method by which a user mode program can access resources controlled by the supervisor mode. For example, in an Archimedes microcomputer this includes all I/O devices and systems available under the operating system. The number included after SWI is ignored by the instruction itself but is used as a parameter to specify the system resource required.

Example:    SWI &02       ; Software Interrupt to print a text string

## D.2 ARM summary instruction set

*Data processing instructions*

All data processing instructions except MUL and MLA have the following format:

| 31  28 | 27 26 | 25 | 24  21 | 20 | 19  16 | 15 12 | 11  0 |
|--------|-------|----|--------|----|--------|-------|-------|
| Cond   | 00    | I  | Opcode | S  | Rn     | Rd    | Operand2 |

**Assembly language format:** <Opcode mnemonic> (Cond. mnemonic) (S)  Rd, Rn, Operand2

| Mnemonic | Meaning | Opcode | | Condition mnemonic | Cond |
|---|---|---|---|---|---|
| AND | Logical AND | 0000 | | EQ (EQual) | 0000 |
| EOR | Logical Exclusive OR | 0001 | | NE (Not Equal) | 0001 |
| SUB | Subtract | 0010 | | CS (Carry Set) | 0010 |
| RSB | Reverse Subtract | 0011 | | CC (Carry Clear) | 0011 |
| ADD | Add | 0100 | | MI (MInus) | 0100 |
| ADC | Add with Carry | 0101 | | PL (PLus) | 0101 |
| SBC | Subtract with Carry | 0110 | | VS (oVerflow Set) | 0110 |
| RSC | Reverse Subtract with Carry | 0111 | | VC (oVerflow Clear) | 0111 |
| TST | Test and mask | 1000 | | HI (Higher) | 1000 |
| TEQ | Test Equivalence | 1001 | | LS (Lower or Same) | 1001 |
| CMP | Compare | 1010 | | GE (Greater or Equal) | 1010 |
| CMN | Compare Negative | 1011 | | LT (Less Than) | 1011 |
| ORR | Logical OR | 1100 | | GT (Greater Than) | 1100 |
| MOV | Move | 1101 | | LE (Less than or Equal) | 1101 |
| BIC | Bit Clear | 1110 | | AL (ALways) | 1110 |
| MVN | Move Negative | 1111 | | NV (NeVer) | 1111 |

**I: Immediate operand bit.** This defines exactly what operand2 is. If the I bit is 0, operand2 is a register, with the register number held in bits 0–3 and the shift applied to that register in bits 4–11. If the I bit is 1, operand2 is an immediate value, with bits 0–7 holding the 8-bit value, and bits 8–11 holding the shift applied to that value.

**S: Set condition codes.** If this bit is set to 0, the condition codes are not altered after the instruction has been executed. If it is set to 1, they are altered.

**Rn: First operand register**

**Rd: Destination register**

**Multiply and Multiply-Accumulated** have the following format:

| 31    28 | 27          22 | 21 | 20 | 19      16 | 15      12 | 11       8 | 7      4 | 3      0 |
|---|---|---|---|---|---|---|---|---|
| Cond | 000000 | A | S | Rn | Rd | Rs | 1001 | Rm |

**Assembly language format:** <MUL> (Cond. mnemonic) (S)   Rd, Rm, Rs
  ;Rd = Rm*Rs
  <MLA> (Cond. mnemonic) (S)   Rd, Rm, Rs, Rn
  ;Rd = Rm*Rs + Rn

**A: Accumulate bit.** 0 = multiply, 1 = multiply with accumulate

*Memory access instructions*

Memory access instructions comprise two groups: simple data transfer (LDR and STR) and block data transfer (LDM and STM).

### Simple data transfer: LDR (Load Register) and STR (Store Register)

| 31 | 28 | 27 26 25 | 24 | 23 | 22 | 21 | 20 | 19  16 | 15  21 11 | 0 |
|---|---|---|---|---|---|---|---|---|---|---|
| Cond | | 01 | I | P | U | B | W | L | Rn | Rd | Offset |

**Assembly language formats:**

| | |
|---|---|
| Pre-indexed instruction: | <Opcode mnemonic> (Cond. mnemonic) (B) Rd,[Rn(,offset)](!) |
| Post-indexed instruction: | <Opcode mnemonic> (Cond. mnemonic) (B) Rd,[Rn(,offset)] |
| Program-relative format: | <Opcode mnemonic> (Cond. mnemonic) (B) Rd,<address> |

**I: Immediate offset bit.** Defines content of bits 0–11 using same coding scheme as for the data processing instructions.

**P: Pre/Post-indexing bit.** 0 = post-indexing (offset added after transfer); 1 = pre-indexing (offset added before transfer).

**U: Up/Down bit.** 0 = down (offset subtracted from base); 1 = up (offset added to base).

**B: Byte/Word bit.** 0 = transfer word; 1 = transfer byte.

**W: Write-back bit.** 0 = no write back; 1 = write final address into Rn (indicated by ! in assembly language).

**L: Load/store bit.** 0 = store to memory; 1 = load from memory

**Rd: Destination/Source register**

**Rn: Base register** points to the base (start) of a block of data; the effective address in memory is given by adding the offset to the base address.

### Multiple data transfer: LDM (load multiple register) and STM (store multiple register)

| 31 | 28 | 27  25 | 24 | 23 | 22 | 21 | 20 | 19  16 | 15 | 0 |
|---|---|---|---|---|---|---|---|---|---|---|
| Cond | | 100 | P | U | S | W | L | Rn | Register list | |

**Assembly language format:** <Opcode mnemonic> (Cond. mnemonic)<type> Rn(!), {list}

**P, U, W, L bits:** As for the single data transfer instructions above. The P and U bits define the stack type as follows:

| PU | Stack type |
|----|-----------|
| 00 | ED (Empty, Descending) |
| 01 | EA (Empty, Ascending) |
| 10 | FD (Full, Descending) |
| 11 | FA (Full, Ascending) |

(An alternative equivalent method of defining the stack in terms of increment/decrement before/after operations is also possible.)

**S: PSR and Force user mode.** 0 = Do not load PSR or force user mode; 1 = Load PSR or force user mode.

**Rn: Base register** points to the base (start) of the stack; the address is incremented or decremented by four bytes as each register is stored or loaded.

*Branch instructions*

| 31      28 | 27      25 | 24 | 23                                    0 |
|------------|------------|----|-----------------------------------------|
| Cond       | 101        | L  | Address offset                          |

**Assembly language format:** <B> (L) (Cond. mnemonic) <address>

**L: Link bit.** 0 = Branch; 1 = Branch with link

**Address.** This is specified as a 24-bit address encoded as a program counter offset.

*Software interrupt instruction*

| 31      28 | 27      24 | 23                                 0 |
|------------|------------|--------------------------------------|
| Cond       | 1111       | Expression field (ignored by ARM)    |

**Assembly language format:** SWI <expression>

**Expression.** This field is ignored by the ARM, but it is normally decoded by subsequent software and used to determine in detail what supervisor action should be taken.

*Key to assembly language format statements:*

| | |
|--|--|
| <angle brackets> | contain essential components of the statement |
| (round brackets) | contain optional components of the statement |
| [square brackets] | indicate indirection in assembly language and are part of the assembler syntax |
| {curly brackets} | indicate a list of registers and are part of the assembler syntax |

# Appendix E

**MC68000 microprocessor instruction set**

**Table E.1 MC68000 basic instruction types**

| Mnemonic | Description | Mnemonic | Description |
|---|---|---|---|
| ABCD | Add decimal with extend | MOVE | Move |
| ADD | Add | MOVEM | Move multiple registers |
| AND | Logical AND | MOVEP | Move peripheral data |
| ASL | Arithmetic shift left | MULS | Signed multiply |
| ASR | Arithmetic shift right | MULU | Unsigned multiply |
| Bcc | Branch conditionally | NBCD | Negate decimal with extend |
| BCHG | Bit test and change | | |
| BCLR | Bit test and clear | NEG | Negate (2s complement) |
| BRA | Branch always | | |
| BSET | Bit test and set | NOP | No operation |
| BSR | Branch to subroutine | NOT | Ones complement |
| BTST | Bit test | OR | Logical OR |
| CHK | Check register against bounds | PEA | Push effective address |
| CLR | Clear operand | RESET | Reset external device |
| CMP | Compare | ROL | Rotate left without extend |
| DBcc | Test condition, decrement, branch | ROR | Rotate right without extend |
| DIVS | Signed divide | ROXL | Rotate left with extend |
| DIVU | Unsigned divide | ROXR | Rotate right with extend |
| EOR | Exclusive OR | RTE | Return from exception |
| EXG | Exchange | RTR | Return and restore |
| EXT | Sign extend | RTS | Return from subroutine |
| JMP | Jump | SBCD | Subtract decimal with extend |
| JSR | Jump to subroutine | | |
| LEA | Load effective address | Scc | Set conditional |
| LINK | Link stack | STOP | Stop |
| LSL | Logical shift left | SUB | Subtract |
| LSR | Logical shift right | SWAP | Swap data register halves |
| | | TAS | Test and set operand |
| | | TRAP | Trap |
| | | TRAPV | Trap on overflow |
| | | TST | Test |
| | | UNLK | Unlink stack |

**Table E.2  Variations of MC68000 basic instruction types**

| Type | Variation | Description | Type | Variation | Description |
|------|-----------|-------------|------|-----------|-------------|
| ADD | ADD | Add | MOVE | MOVE | Move |
| | ADDA | Add address | | MOVEA | Move address |
| | ADDQ | Add quick | | MOVEQ | Move quick |
| | ADDI | Add immediate | | MOVE from SR | Move from status register |
| | ADDX | Add with extend | | MOVE to SR | Move to status register |
| | | | | MOVE from CCR | Move from condition codes |
| AND | AND | Logical AND | | MOVE to CCR | Move to condition codes |
| | ANDI | And immediate | | MOVE USP | Move user stack pointer |
| CMP | CMP | Compare | NEG | NEG | Negate |
| | CMPA | Compare address | | NEGX | Negate with extend |
| | CMPM | Compare memory | | | |
| | CMPI | Compare immediate | OR | OR | Logical OR |
| | | | | ORI | OR immediate |
| EOR | EOR | Exclusive OR | | | |
| EORI | Ex-OR imme-diate | | SUB | SUB | Subtract |
| | | | | SUBA | Subtract address |
| | | | | SUBI | Subtract immediate |
| | | | | SUBQ | Subtract quick |
| | | | | SUBX | Subtract with extend |

**Table E.3 MC68000 memory addressing modes**

| Motorola mode name | Motorola notation | Addressing mode in this book |
|---|---|---|
| Data-register direct | Dn | implied |
| Address-register direct | An | implied |
| Immediate | #data | immediate |
| Absolute long | Abs.L | direct |
| Absolute short | Abs.W | direct |
| Address register indirect | (An) | register indirect |
| — with postincrement (see note) | (An)+ | register indirect with auto-post-increment |
| — with predecrement (see note) | –(An) | register indirect with auto-pre-decrement |
| Address register indirect with displacement | d.16(An) | based |
| Address register indirect with index | d.8(An,Xn) | based indexed (short) |
| Address register indirect with index | d.8(An,Xn.L) | based indexed (long) |
| Program counter with displacement | d.16(PC) | relative |
| Program counter with index | d.8(PC,Xn) | relative indexed (short) |
| Program counter with index | d.8(PC,Xn.L) | relative indexed (long) |

*Note.* If An is A7 (a stack pointer), and the operand size is 'byte', the increment or decrement is 2, to keep the stack pointer on a word boundary (i.e. even).

Notation:

| | |
|---|---|
| Dn | Data register n (D0 to D7) |
| An | Address register n (A0 to A7) |
| Xn | Data register n or Address register n |
| PC | Program counter |
| data | expression yielding a 3-, 8-, 16- or 32-bit value |
| Abs.L | a 24-bit memory address |
| Abs.W | a 16-bit memory address, sign extended to 24 bits |
| d.8 | expression yielding an 8-bit value, sign extended before use |
| d.16 | expression yielding a 16-bit value, sign extended before use |

In the tables which follow, each instruction mnemonic may be able to specify any or all of three possible data sizes: byte (B), word (W) or long word (L). The *size* column defines which sizes are allowed for each mnemonic. Where no entry appears in the size column, the operation is unsized. The intended data size for the instruction is identified by adding the suffix .B, .W or .L at the end of the mnemonic. Where only one data size is allowed for a particular instruction, no extension is required, unless stated otherwise in the notes. If the mnemonic extension .B, .W or .L is omitted a .W extension is assumed.

Condition code operations are defined as follows:
- – Not affected
- • Set or reset according to the result of the operation
- ? Undefined
- 0 Set to zero
- 1 Set to one

**Table E.4 Data movement instructions**

| Mnemonic | Operands | Size | XNZVC | Notes | Operation |
|----------|----------|------|-------|-------|-----------|
| MOVE  | src,dst  | B,W,L | – • • 0 0 | 11  | (src)→dst |
| MOVEA | src,An   | W,L   | – – – – – | 1   | (src)→An |
| MOVEQ | #data,Dn | L     | – • • 0 0 | 2   | data→Dn |
| MOVEP | Dn,dst   | W,L   | – – – – – | 3   | (Dn)→dst |
| MOVEP | src,Dn   | W,L   | – – – – – | 3   | (src)→Dn |
| MOVEM | src,regs | W,L   | – – – – – | 4,5 | (src)→regs |
| MOVEM | regs,dst | W,L   | – – – – – | 5,6 | (regs)→dst |
| MOVE  | src,CCR  | W     | – – – – – | 7,8 | (src)→CCR |
| MOVE  | CCR,dst  | W     | – – – – – | 7,8 | (CCR)→dst |
| MOVE  | src,SR   | W     | • • • • • | 7,9 | (src)→SR |
| MOVE  | SR,dst   | W     | – – – – – | 7,9 | (SR)→dst |
| MOVE  | An,USP   | L     | – – – – – | 9   | (An)→USP |
| MOVE  | USP,An   | L     | – – – – – | 9   | (USP)→An |
| | | | | | |
| LEA   | src,An   | L     | – – – – – | 10  | src→An |
| PEA   | src      | L     | – – – – – | 10  | src→–(SP) |
| SWAP  | Dn       | L     | – • • 0 0 |     | (Dn[0..15])↔(Dn[16..31]) |
| EXG   | Dn,Dm    | L     | – – – – – |     | (Dn)↔(Dm) |

*Notes.* Unless otherwise stated in the notes below, src may be any of the 14 addressing modes in Table E.3 and dst may be any mode except immediate, relative or relative indexed.

Neither src nor dst may be address registers if the instruction size is byte (B).

1  MOVE does not allow the destination to be an address register: use MOVEA instead.

2  The entire instruction is encoded as a single word (hence the mnemonic MOVE Quick) if the destination is a data register, the size is long and the source is an immediate operand in the range $-128$ to $+127$.

3  src or dst may only use based mode. These instructions are designed to transfer data to/from peripheral devices which are byte-orientated. Such devices occupy only one byte of the 16-bit data bus and appear as consecutive odd or consecutive even addresses. The word or long word in the data register is split into bytes which are transferred to/from alternate bytes of memory beginning at an address identified by based addressing.

4  src may not be a register, or use register indirect with pre-decrement, or immediate addressing.

5  regs is a list of general registers; when using the Motorola assembler, ranges are denoted by dashes (D2–D5), and multiple names and ranges are separated by slashes (A2/D2–D5/SP/D0). The order of the registers in the assembly language instruction is irrelevant; registers are moved in an order predetermined by the CPU hardware.

6  dst may only use direct, register indirect, register indirect with pre-decrement, based and based indexed modes.

7  src or dst may also not use address register direct (implied) addressing.

8  The source operand is a word, but only the low-order byte is copied to CCR.

9 Privileged instruction, executed only in supervisor state. A TRAP occurs if execution in user state is attempted.

10 src may only be direct, register indirect, based, based indexed, relative or relative indexed.

11 Both src and dst can be memory addresses: this is the only instruction for which this is possible.

**Table E.5 Arithmetic operations**

| Mnemonic | Operands | Size | XNZVC | Notes | Operation |
|----------|----------|------|-------|-------|-----------|
| ADD  | src,dst   | B,W,L | $\bullet\bullet\bullet\bullet\bullet$ | 1 | (dst) + (src) → dst |
| ADDA | src,An    | W,L   | $-----$ | 2 | (dst) + (src) → dst |
| ADDI | #data,dst | B,W,L | $\bullet\bullet\bullet\bullet\bullet$ | 3 | (dst) + data → dst |
| SUB  | src,dst   | B,W,L | $\bullet\bullet\bullet\bullet\bullet$ | 1 | (dst) − (src) → dst |
| SUBA | src,An    | W,L   | $-----$ | 2 | (dst) − (src) → dst |
| SUBI | #data,dst | B,W,L | $\bullet\bullet\bullet\bullet\bullet$ | 3 | (dst) − (src) → dst |
| NEG  | dst       | B,W,L | $\bullet\bullet\bullet\bullet\bullet$ | 4 | 0 − (dst) → dst |
| ADDX | src,dst   | B,W,L | $\bullet\bullet\bullet\bullet\bullet$ | 5 | (dst) + (src) + X→dst |
| SUBX | src,dst   | B,W,L | $\bullet\bullet\bullet\bullet\bullet$ | 5 | (dst) − (src) − X→dst |
| NEGX | dst       | B,W,L | $\bullet\bullet\bullet\bullet\bullet$ | 4 | 0 − (dst) − X → dst |
| ABCD | src,dst   | B     | $\bullet ? \bullet ? \bullet$ | 5 | $(dst)_{10} + (src)_{10} + X$→dst |
| SBCD | src,dst   | B     | $\bullet ? \bullet ? \bullet$ | 5 | $(dst)_{10} - (src)_{10} - X$→dst |
| NBCD | dst       | B     | $\bullet ? \bullet ? \bullet$ | 4 | $0 - (dst)_{10} - X$→dst |
| MULS | src,Dn    | W     | $-\bullet\bullet00$ | 4 | (Dn)*(src)→Dn |
| MULU | src,Dn    | W     | $-\bullet\bullet00$ | 4 | (Dn)*(src)→Dn |
| DIVS | src,Dn    | W     | $-\bullet\bullet\bullet0$ | 4 | (Dn)/(src)→Dn |
| DIVU | src,Dn    | W     | $-\bullet\bullet\bullet0$ | 4 | (Dn)/(src)→Dn |
| CLR  | dst       | B,W,L | $-0100$ | 4 | 0→dst |
| EXT  | Dn        | W,L   | $-\bullet\bullet00$ |   | (Dn) sign extended → Dn |

*Note.* Unless otherwise stated in the notes below, src may be any of the 14 addressing modes in Table E.3, and dst may be any mode except immediate, relative or relative indexed.

1 Either src or dst must be a data register.
2 dst must be an address register.
3 This mnemonic forces immediate addressing. If data is in the range $+1$ to $+8$, the entire instruction is encoded as a single word: this can be forced using ADDQ, SUBQ.
4 src or dst may also not be address register direct (implied).
5 src and dst must either both be data registers, or both use auto-decrement mode.

**Table E.6 Compare, test, and bit manipulation instructions**

| Mnemonic | Operands | Size | XNZVC | Notes | Operation |
|---|---|---|---|---|---|
| CMP | src,Dn | B,W,L | – • • • • | | (Dn) – (src) |
| CMPA | src,An | W,L | – • • • • | | (An) – (src) |
| CMPI | #data,dst | B,W,L | – • • • • | 1 | (dst) – data |
| CMPM | src,dst | B,W,L | – • • • • | 2 | (dst) – (src) |
| TST | dst | B,W,L | – • • 0 0 | 1 | (dst) – 0 |
| BSET | bnum,dst | B,L | – – • – – | 1,3 | Test and set bit bnum of dst |
| BCLR | bnum,dst | B,L | – – • – – | 1,3 | Test and clear bit bnum of dst |
| BCHG | bnum,dst | B,L | – – • – – | 1,3 | Test and change bit bnum of dst |
| BTST | bnum,dst | B,L | – – • – – | 1,3 | Test bit bnum of dst |
| TAS | dst | B | – • • 0 0 | 1,4 | Test and set msb of dst |
| Scc | dst | B | – – – – – | 1,5 | if cc is true then 1s→dst else 0s→dst |

*Note.* Unless otherwise stated in the notes below, src may be any of the 14 addressing modes in Table E.3, and dst may be any mode except immediate, relative or relative indexed.

1  src and/or dst may also not be address register direct (implied).
2  dst and src can only be register indirect with post-increment.
3  bnum may specify a data register or an immediate operand only. If dst is a data register, then the size must be long and the range of bnum is 0 to 31. Otherwise, the size is byte and bnum must be in the range 0 to 7.
4  This operation has an indivisible read-modify-write operation for use as a semaphore primitive in multiprocessor systems.
5  In the mnemonic, cc denotes one of

| | | |
|---|---|---|
| CC | carry clear (0) | not C |
| CS | carry set (1) | C |
| EQ | equal | Z |
| GE | greater or equal | (N and V) or (not N and not V) |
| GT | greater than | (N and V and not Z) or (not N and not V and not Z) |
| HI | high | not C and not Z |
| LE | less than or equal | Z or (N and not V) or (not N and V) |
| LS | low or same | C or Z |
| LT | less than | (N and not V) or (not N and V) |
| MI | minus | N |
| NE | not equal | not Z |
| PL | plus | not N |
| VC | no overflow | not V |
| VS | overflow | V |
| T | true | |
| F | false | |

**Table E.7 Logical instructions**

| Mnemonic | Operands | Size | XNZVC | Notes | Operation |
|---|---|---|---|---|---|
| AND | src,dst | B,W,L | $- \bullet \bullet 0\,0$ | 1,2 | (dst) AND (src)→dst |
| ANDI | #data,dst | B,W,L | $- \bullet \bullet 0\,0$ | 2 | (dst) AND data→dst |
| OR | src,dst | B,W,L | $- \bullet \bullet 0\,0$ | 1,2 | (dst) OR (src)→dst |
| ORI | #data,dst | B,W,L | $- \bullet \bullet 0\,0$ | 2 | (dst) OR data→dst |
| EOR | Dn,dst | B,W,L | $- \bullet \bullet 0\,0$ | 2 | (dst) EOR (Dn)→dst |
| EORI | #data,dst | B,W,L | $- \bullet \bullet 0\,0$ | 2 | (dst) EOR data→dst |
| NOT | dst | B,W,L | $- \bullet \bullet 0\,0$ | 2 | ~ (dst)→dst |
| ORI | #data,CCR | B | $\bullet \bullet \bullet \bullet \bullet$ | | data OR (CCR)→CCR |
| ANDI | #data,CCR | B | $\bullet \bullet \bullet \bullet \bullet$ | | data AND (CCR)→CCR |
| EORI | #data,CCR | B | $\bullet \bullet \bullet \bullet \bullet$ | | data EOR (CCR)→CCR |
| ORI | #data,SR | W | $\bullet \bullet \bullet \bullet \bullet$ | 3 | data OR (SR)→SR |
| ANDI | #data,SR | W | $\bullet \bullet \bullet \bullet \bullet$ | 3 | data AND (SR)→SR |
| EORI | #data,SR | W | $\bullet \bullet \bullet \bullet \bullet$ | 3 | data EOR (SR)→SR |

*Note.* Unless otherwise stated in the notes below, src may be any of the 14 addressing modes in Table E.3, and dst may be any mode except immediate, relative or relative indexed.

1 Either src or dst must be a data register.
2 src and/or dst may also not be address register direct (implied).
3 Privileged instruction, executed only in supervisor state. A TRAP occurs if execution in user state is attempted.

**Table E.8 Shift and rotate instructions**

| Mnemonic | Operands | Size | XNZVC | Operation |
|---|---|---|---|---|
| ASL | cntdst | B,W,L | $\bullet \bullet \bullet \bullet \bullet$ | (dst) ≪ cnt→dst; 0→lsb; msb→C,X |
| ASR | cntdst | B,W,L | $\bullet \bullet \bullet \bullet \bullet$ | (dst) ≫ cnt→dst; (msb)→msb; lsb→C,X |
| LSL | cntdst | B,W,L | $\bullet \bullet \bullet 0 \bullet$ | (dst) ≪ cnt→dst; 0→lsb; msb→C,X |
| LSR | cntdst | B,W,L | $\bullet \bullet \bullet 0 \bullet$ | (dst) ≫ cnt→dst; 0→msb; lsb→C,X |
| ROL | cntdst | B,W,L | $- \bullet \bullet 0 \bullet$ | (dst) ≪ cnt→dst; (msb)→C,lsb |
| ROR | cntdst | B,W,L | $- \bullet \bullet 0 \bullet$ | (dst) ≫ cnt→dst; (lsb)→C,msb |
| ROXL | cntdst | B,W,L | $\bullet \bullet \bullet 0 \bullet$ | (dst) ≪ cnt→dst; (msb)→C,X; (X)→lsb |
| ROXR | cntdst | B,W,L | $\bullet \bullet \bullet 0 \bullet$ | (dst) ≫ cnt→dst; (lsb)→C,X; (X)→msb |

*Note.* There are three different formats for 'cntdst':

Dm, Dn — Data register Dn is shifted by the amount specified in the six low-order bits of data register Dm.

#cnt, Dn — Data register Dn is shifted by cnt (shift range 1 to 8).

dst — The memory word at location dst is shifted by one bit. The only operand size is 'word' and the following modes may *not* be used: immediate, relative and relative indexed.

**Table E.9 Program control instructions**

| Mnemonic | Operands | Size | XNZVC | Notes | Operation |
|---|---|---|---|---|---|
| JMP | addr | | - - - - - | 1 | Addr→PC |
| JSR | addr | | - - - - - | 1 | (PC)→ – (SP); Addr→PC |
| BRA | addr16 | | - - - - - | 2,3 | (PC) + addr16→PC |
| BSR | addr16 | | - - - - - | 2,3 | (PC)→ – (SP);<br>(PC) + addr16→PC |
| Bcc | addr16 | | - - - - - | 2,3,4 | if cc is true, (PC) +<br>addr16→PC |
| DBcc | Dn, addr16 | W | - - - - - | 2,4 | if cc is false then (Dn) – 1→Dn;<br>if (Dn) ≠ –1<br>then (PC) + addr16→PC |
| RTS | | | - - - - - | | ((SP)) + →PC |
| RTR | | | ● ● ● ● ● | | ((SP)) + →CCR; ((SP)) + →PC |
| RTD | | | - - - - - | 5 | ((SP)) + →PC: (SP) + disp→SP |
| LINK | An,#disp | | - - - - - | 5 | (An)→ – (SP); (SP)→An;<br>(SP) + disp→SP |
| UNLK | An | | - - - - - | | (An)→SP; ((SP)) + →An |

*Notes*

1  addr specifies the effective address of the jump target using any addressing mode except immediate, auto-increment or auto-decrement.

2  addr16 defines a target address within 32 kbytes of the instruction.

3  If the target address is within 128 bytes of the program counter, a short form of the instruction can be generated.

4  In the mnemonic, cc denotes one of

| | | |
|---|---|---|
| CC | carry clear (0) | not C |
| CS | carry set (1) | C |
| EQ | equal | Z |
| GE | greater or equal | (N and V) or (not N and not V) |
| GT | greater than | (N and V and not Z) or<br>(not N and not V and not Z) |
| HI | high | not C and not Z |
| LE | less than or equal | Z or (N and not V) or (not N and V) |
| LS | low or same | C or Z |
| LT | less than | (N and not V) or (not N and V) |
| MI | minus | N |
| NE | not equal | not Z |
| PL | plus | not N |
| VC | no overflow | not V |
| VS | overflow | V |
| T | true | |
| F | false | |

5  disp is a 16-bit 2s complement integer in the range – 32 768 to 32 767.

**Table E.10 System control instructions**

| Mnemonic | Operands | Size | XNZVC | Notes | Operation |
|----------|----------|------|-------|-------|-----------|
| NOP | | | − − − − − | | No operation |
| RTE | | | • • • • • | 1 | Return from exception |
| STOP | #data | W | • • • • • | 1 | data→SR, halt CPU |
| RESET | | | − − − − − | 1 | Reset external devices |
| TRAP | #vector | | − − − − − | 2 | (PC)→ − (SSP); SR→ − (SSP); (vector)→PC |
| TRAPV | | | − − − − − | | if V is true then TRAP |
| CHK | src,Dn | W | − • ? ? ? | 3 | if (Dn)<0 or (Dn)>(src) then TRAP |

*Notes*

1 Privileged instruction, executed only in supervisor state. A TRAP occurs if execution in user state is attempted.
2 Vector is in the range 0 to 15.
3 src may use any addressing mode except address register direct.

**Acknowledgement**

Because the MC68000 has so many different combinations of instructions, addressing modes and data types, it is very difficult to produce a concise yet comprehensive description of its instruction set. Motorola literature offers a two-page instruction summary (insufficiently detailed for practical use) or a 200+ page programmer's reference manual (comprehensive, but hardly practical as an Appendix). Though differing in the detailed information given, organisation, and grouping of instructions, the layout of the tables above is based upon a structure developed by John F. Wakerly in *Microcomputer Architecture and Programming* (Wiley, 1981). As the best compromise between detail and conciseness which I could find, the basic design of this Appendix follows Wakerly's model. Any errors resulting from reorganisation and augmentation of the material contained within are purely my responsibility, however.

# Appendix F

## Example ARM and MC68000 programs for Chapter 6

### Example ARM machine code program

As the ARM has no direct addressing mode, in this example the PC relative mode is used (see Chapter 7). It is assumed that the switches and LEDs are stored at the two bytes immediately following the code.

| Coding | Register transfers | Hex. machine code |
|---|---|---|
| Load switches to register 0 | (switches)→R0 | E5DF 0004 |
| Store register 0 to LEDs | (R0)→leds | E5CF 0001 |
| Branch back to start | | EAFF FFFC |

In the first two instructions, the last three hex. digits specify a 12-bit 2s complement byte offset from the program counter. In the last instruction, a 24-bit word offset is encoded as the last six hex. digits. Each offset also makes allowance for the ARM instruction pipeline.

### Example MC68000 machine code program

| Coding | Register transfers | Hex. machine code |
|---|---|---|
| Move switches to D0 | ($7004)→D0 | 1038 7004 |
| Move D0 to lights | (D0)→$7000 | 11C0 7000 |
| Branch back to start | | 60F6 |

### Example ARM assembly language code program (see Fig. F.1)

This assembler listing was produced using an Acorn ARM macro-assembler running on an Acorn Archimedes microcomputer. The assembler can only produce *relocatable* object code, which is subsequently linked by a linking loader (see Chapter 9), hence it is not possible to produce absolute code directly, and no ORG directive is thus available.

The loop execution times are calculated on the assumption of a 10 MHz clock rate. All data processing instructions execute in one clock cycle, the load instruction in three cycles, the store instruction in two cycles and branches in five cycles. Hence the inner delay loop takes six cycles or 0.6 $\mu$s. The delay count should actually be 166 667, but due to the limited encoding capabilities of the ARM immediate addressing mode (see Chapter 7), the nearest value which can be encoded with a single instruction is 165 888 (think about it!).

As in the machine code example, because the ARM has no direct addressing mode, program counter relative addressing has been used, with the switches and LEDs assumed to be placed immediately after the program code (see the listing). In practice, a non-contiguous area of memory would normally be used for input/output, and would be addressed using register indirect addressing.

As is illustrated by this example, the ARM instruction execution speed is typically five to ten times faster than the MC68000.

```
 2 00000000          ;Program to display switch settings on LEDS
 3 00000000          ;after a delay of five (5) seconds.
 4 00000000          ;============================================
 5 00000000          ;
 6 00000000          ; A. C. Downton    May 1991
 7 00000000          ;
 8 00000000          ;--------------------------------------------
 9 00000000          ;
10 00000000          ;Define registers used:
11 00000000          ;
12 00000000        0 R0        RN      0
13 00000000        1 R1        RN      1
14 00000000        2 R2        RN      2
15 00000000        3 R3        RN      3
16 00000000          ;
17 00000000 00028800 delay     EQU     165888       ;nearest encodable!
18 00000000          ;
19 00000000          ;************************************************
20 00000000          ;
21 00000000          ;Main program:
22 00000000          ;Reads switches and compares with previous
23 00000000          ;stored value. if different inserts a 5
24 00000000          ;second delay and then outputs new value to
25 00000000          ;LEDs. Also updates previous stored value.
26 00000000          ;
27 00000000                    AREA    DELAY,CODE
28 00000000                    ENTRY
29 00000000          ;
30 00000000 E5DF002D start     LDRB    R0,switch    ;read switches
31 00000004 E5DF3028           LDRB    R3,swstrd    ;read variable
32 00000008 E1500003           CMP     R0,R3        ;values different?
33 0000000C 0AFFFFFB           BEQ     start        ;branch if no change
34 00000010          ;
35 00000010          ;5 second time delay
36 00000010          ;
37 00000010 E3A01032           MOV     R1,£50       ;50*0.1 sec loop
38 00000014 E3A02BA2 loop1     MOV     R2,£delay    ;inner loop, 0.1 sec
39 00000018 E2522001 loop2     SUBS    R2,R2,£1     ;dec inner loop
40 0000001C 1AFFFFFD           BNE     loop2        ;branch if <0.1 secs
41 00000020 E2511001           SUBS    R1,R1,£1     ;dec outer loop
42 00000024 1AFFFFFA           BNE     loop1        ;branch if < 5 secs
43 00000028          ;
44 00000028          ;output to LEDs and modify stored value
45 00000028          ;
46 00000028 E5CF0004           STRB    R0,swstrd    ;modify stored value
47 0000002C E5CF0002           STRB    R0,leds      ;output switches
48 00000030          ;
49 00000030          ;repeat complete loop
50 00000030          ;
51 00000030 EAFFFFF2           B       start
52 00000034          ;
53 00000034          ;************************************************
54 00000034          ;
55 00000034          ;Temporary storage for switch settings,
56 00000034          ;and addresses for switches and leds input/output
57 00000034          ;
58 00000034          RWstorage
59 00000034                    ^       RWstorage
60 00000034 00000034 swstrd    £       1
61 00000034 00000035 switch    £       1
62 00000034 00000036 leds      £       1
63 00000034          ;
64 00000034                    END
```

Fig. F.1   Example ARM assembly language code program.

**Example MC68000 assembly language code program** (see Fig. F.2)

This assembler listing was produced by a native MC68000 assembler running on a MC68000-based microcomputer under the Unix operating system. The assembler can only produce *relocatable* object code, which is subsequently linked by a linking loader (see Chapter 9), hence it is not possible to produce absolute code directly, and no ORG directive is thus available. The loop execution times are calculated on the assumption of an 8 MHz clock rate.

```
 1                          |==================================================
 2                          | Program to display switch settings on LEDS
 3                          | after a delay of five (5) seconds.
 4                          |==================================================
 5                          |
 6                          | A.C.Downton June 1987
 7                          |
 8                          |--------------------------------------------------
 9                          |
10                          |Define constants:
11                          |       Time delay = 0.1 sec. @ 8MHz
12                          |       Switch address = $7004
13                          |       Leds address = $7000
14                          |
15          0000 7831       delay   = 30769           |(30769*3.25uS=0.1s)
16          0000 7004       switch  = $7004           |switch port address
17          0000 7000       leds    = $7000           |LEDs port address
18                          |
19                          |--------------------------------------------------
20                          |
21                          |Temporary storage for switch settings
22                          |
23   00 0000                swstrd: .space  1
24   00 0002                        .even             |force to even address
25                          |
26                          |**************************************************
27                          |
28                          |Main program:
29                          |Reads switches and compares with previous
30                          |stored value. If different inserts a 5
31                          |second delay and then outputs new value to
32                          |LEDs. Also updates previous stored value.
33                          |
34   00 0002 1039 0000 7004 start:  move.b  switch,d0
35   00 0008 B039 0000 0000'        cmp.b   swstrd,d0 |has setting changed
36   00 000E 6700 FFF2              beq     start     |branch if no change
37                          |
38                          |5 second time delay
39                          |
40   00 0012 7232                   moveq   #50,d1    |outer loop, 50*0.1 sec
41   00 0014 343C 7831      loop1:  move.w  #delay,d2 |inner loop, 0.1 sec
42   00 0018 5342           loop2:  subq.w  #1,d2     |dec. inner loop (1uS)
43   00 001A 6600 FFFC              bne     loop2     |bra <1/2 sec? (2.25uS)
44   00 001E 5301                   subq.b  #1,d1     |decrement outer loop
45   00 0020 6600 FFF2              bne     loop1     |branch if <5 secs.
46                          |
47                          |Output to LEDs and modify stored value
48                          |
49   00 0024 13C0 0000 0000'        move.b  d0,swstrd |modify stored value
50   00 002A 13C0 0000 7000         move.b  d0,leds   |output switches
51                          |
52                          |Repeat complete loop
53                          |
54   00 0030 6000 FFD0              bra     start
55                          |
56   00 0034                        .end
```

Fig. F.2   Example MC68000 assembly language code program.

**Table F.1 Equivalent directives in standard ARM, MC68HC11 and MC68000 assembly languages.**

| ARM | MC68HC11 | MC68000 | Description |
| --- | --- | --- | --- |
| ORG | ORG | ORG | Program origin address |
| END | END | END | Program end point |
| # | RMB | DS.B, DS.W DS.L or DS | Reservation of storage |
| DCB, DCW or DCD | FCB, FCC | DC.B, DC.W DC.L or DC | Specification of program data |
| EQU | EQU | EQU | Equate symbol to value |

(All the assemblers also define many other directives, but these are the most commonly encountered.)

# References

1 Attikiouzel, J. *Pascal for Electronic Engineers* (Van Nostrand Reinhold, 1984).

2 Bacon, J. *The Motorola MC68000. An Introduction to Processor, Memory and Interfacing* (Prentice Hall, 1986).

3 Bardeen, J., Brattain, W.H. *Physical Principles Involved in Transistor Action*, Bell Systems Technical Journal, v. 28, pp. 239–277, April 1949.

4 Bartee, T.C. *Digital Computer Fundamentals* (5th edition) (McGraw-Hill, 1981).

5 Clements, A. *Microprocessor Systems Design: 68000 hardware, software and interfacing* (PWS, 1987).

6 Forester, T. (ed.) *The Microelectronics Revolution* (Blackwell, 1980).

7 Ginns, M. *Archimedes Assembly Language: the complete programming course* (2nd edition) (Dabs Press, 1989).

8 Metropolis, N., Howlett, J., Rota, G.-C. *A History of Computing in the Twentieth Century* (Academic Press, 1980).

9 *Motorola 8 bit Microprocessor and Peripheral Data Handbook* (Motorola, 1983).

10 *The MC68HC11 Microcontroller Family*, BR411/D Rev 1 (Motorola, 1990).

11 *MC68HC11 HCMOS Single-chip Microcontroller* (Motorola, 1988).

12 *Motorola MC68000 16/32 bit Microprocessor Programmer's Reference Manual* (4th edition) (Prentice Hall, 1984).

13 *Motorola MC68000 Data Sheet*.

14 Nichols, K.G., Zaluska, E.J. *Theory and Practice of Microprocessors* (Edward Arnold, 1982).

15 Osborne, A. *An Introduction to Computers, Volume 1: Some Basic Concepts* (2nd edition) (Osborne/McGraw-Hill, 1980).

16 Peatman, J.B. *Microcomputer Based Design* (McGraw-Hill, 1977).

17 Randell, B. (ed.) *The Origins of Digital Computers* (Springer-Verlag, 1973).

18 Stonham, T.J. *Digital Logic Techniques: principles and practice* (2nd edition) (Van Nostrand Reinhold, 1987).

19 Turing, A. *On Computable Numbers with an Application to the Entscheidungsproblem*, Proceedings of the London Mathematical Society, v. 42, pp. 230–265, 1937.

20 *VL86C010 RISC CPU Data Sheet* (VLSI Technology, 1989).

21 Walker, G. *Towards a Structured 6809 Assembly Language*, BYTE, pp. 370–382, November 1981 and pp. 198–228, December 1981.

The Acorn RISC machine (ARM) is fabricated for ACORN by VLSI Technology Ltd, and as well as being used within the Acorn Archimedes range of microcomputers, is also sold as a separate 32-bit microprocessor family for use in embedded applications.

# Answers to exercises and problems

☐ Some of the problems and exercises, particularly in the later chapters of the book, are design problems. By their nature, design problems have many solutions, and it is not possible to specify definitive answers here. In some cases, a few guidelines have been given as to how the problem should be approached; further guidance and assessment of the student's proposed solution are best obtained from his supervisor or lecturer.

**Chapter 2**

E2.1

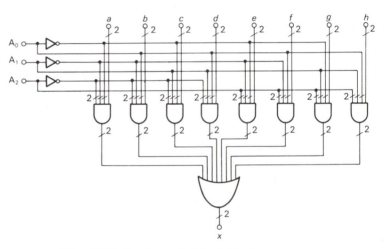

Fig. ANS. 1   One-of-eight 2-bit data selector.

E2.2   The transfer must be effected by temporarily storing one of the register's contents in a third register; the contents of the second register may then be transferred to the first register, and the contents of the temporary register transferred to the second register. Thus a minimum of three clock pulses will be required. Example transfers:

(A) → D
(B) → A
(D) → B

Notice that the contents of the temporary register are overwritten during execution of the instruction. Most computer architectures include a number of 'unnamed' temporary registers so that this type of operation can be supported without corrupting any of the normal CPU registers.

P2.1   $1.26 \times 10^7$ bits (12 Mbits).

P2.2   17 bits.

P2.3    4096 AND gates; each contains 13 inputs.

P2.4    Each AND gate would contain only 12 inputs; the read/write line would not be required.

P2.5    128 AND gates; each contains 7 inputs. (In addition, 4096 2-input AND gates would be needed to detect the coincidence of a row and a column address; these would normally be combined as part of the flip-flop.

Observe how much less logic is needed for a two-dimensional memory array; this is one reason why memory chips use this structure.

## Chapter 3

E3.1    Truth table of a 1-bit subtractor:

| Borrow in | A | B | Difference A − B | Borrow out |
|:---:|:---:|:---:|:---:|:---:|
| 0 | 0 | 0 | 0 | 0 |
| 0 | 0 | 1 | 1 | 1 |
| 0 | 1 | 0 | 1 | 0 |
| 0 | 1 | 1 | 0 | 0 |
| 1 | 0 | 0 | 1 | 1 |
| 1 | 0 | 1 | 0 | 1 |
| 1 | 1 | 0 | 0 | 0 |
| 1 | 1 | 1 | 1 | 1 |

E3.6    Binary:
(a) 1011   (b) 11110011   (c) 1110101101000   (d) 1000100111011001
(e) 0.1   (f) 101.001   (g) 11011.11   (h) 10110010.101
Octal:
(a) 13   (b) 363   (c) 16550   (d) 104731
(e) 0.4   (f) 5.1   (g) 33.6   (h) 262.5
Hexadecimal:
(a) B   (b) F3   (c) 1D68   (d) 89D9
(e) 0.8   (f) 5.2   (g) 1B.C   (h) B2.A
BCD:
(a) 0001 0001           (b) 0010 0100 0011
(c) 0111 0101 0010 1000     (d) 0011 0101 0010 1000 1001
(e) 0.0101              (f) 0101.0001 0010 0101
(g) 0010 0111.0111 0101     (h) 0001 0111 1000.0110 0010 0101

E3.7    (a) 0100 0000 0001         (b) 1100 1111 0010
(c) 0111 1111 1000         (d) 1001 1000 1100
(e) 1011 1111 1111         (f) 0011 0000 1110
(g) 1000 0000 1000         (h) 0110 0111 0100

E3.8    (In each case, the most significant bit of the number is assumed to be the sign bit.)
(a) 94   (b) −97   (c) −1939   (d) −497   (e) −17333   (f) 32496

E3.9    A 32-bit 2s complement integer has a range of $\pm 2^{31}$ ($= \pm 2.15 \times 10^9$) and a resolution of 1. The range and resolution of a 32-bit floating point number depend upon the division of bits between the mantissa and exponent, but with a suitable choice (see the example given) both increased resolution and a higher range can be achieved, though not simultaneously.

Floating point format is the equivalent of scientific notation on a calculator.

E3.10    There is built-in redundancy in the floating point format; using the format described the number 8 could equally well be represented as $0.5 \times 2^4$, $1 \times 2^3$, $2 \times 2^2$, etc. By representing the exponent as a power of 16 rather than 2, the range of numbers which can be expressed is increased at the expense of reduced redundancy. In the example given, the range will be $16^{\pm 128}$ or approximately $10^{\pm 154}$.

E3.11    As might be expected, the required operations are straightforward on the MC68000, and can be performed on bytes, words (16 bits) or long words (32 bits) of data. For example, the instruction sequence for performing the operation on *bytes* would be as follows:

```
MOVE.B   $0100,D0   *Load register D0 from address 100 hex.
ADD.B    $0180,D0   *Add contents of address 180 hex. to D0
MOVE.B   D0,$0200   *Store contents of D0 at address 200 hex.
```

The code resulting from this is as follows:

| | | |
|---|---|---|
| 1000 | 1038 | *load* opcode |
| 1002 | 0100 | operand address |
| 1004 | D038 | *add* opcode |
| 1006 | 0180 | operand address |
| 1008 | 11C0 | *store* opcode |
| 100A | 0200 | operand address |

The exact opcode value needed is defined by the value of various *fields* within the instruction word which define the addressing mode, data type, etc. Refer to Chapter 7 for details.

P3.1    Hexadecimal:
(a) 400   (b) 1000   (c) 4000   (d) 10000   (e) 40000   (f) 100000
(g) 400000   (h) 1000000
Decimal:
(a) 1024   (b) 4096   (c) 16384   (d) 65536   (e) 262144   (f) 1048576
(g) 4194304   (h) 16777216
Octal:
(a) 2000   (b) 10000   (c) 40000   (d) 200000   (e) 1000000
(f) 4000000   (g) 20000000   (h) 100000000

P3.2    (a) 10 bits   (b) 12 bits   (c) 14 bits   (d) 16 bits
(e) 18 bits   (f) 20 bits   (g) 22 bits   (h) 24 bits

P3.3    (a)      0011 1000 (38)
            + 0100 0111 (47)
            = 0111 1111 (7F) Binary
            = 1000 0101 (85) BCD
        (b)      0001 1001 (19)
            + 0110 1000 (68)
            = 1000 0001 (81) Binary
            = 1000 0111 (87) BCD

The result of this binary addition of two BCD numbers is a number where the least significant digit is outside the allowable range. A decimal adjust accumulator (MC6800) instruction must, therefore, be provided to adjust the result to the correct BCD value. In this case the BCD overflow is corrected by adding 6 to the result.
In the second example, BCD overflow again occurs, but the half-carry bit (carry between bits 3 and 4) is set. The decimal adjust accumulator instruction must detect this and again add 6 to the result.

The algorithm required to correct a two-digit BCD number after binary addition is:

```
BEGIN (* Decimal Adjust Accumulator *)
      IF leastsignificantdigit > 9 OR halfcarry = TRUE
      THEN result:- result + 6
END (* Decimal Adjust Accumulator *)
```

For BCD numbers of greater than two digits, the same algorithm is applied to each digit in turn starting from the least significant digit.

P3.4  32-bit floating point format:  range       $\pm 10^{\pm 77}$
                                     resolution   1 in $10^7$
       64-bit floating point format:  range       $\pm 10^{\pm 77}$
                                     resolution   1 in $10^{17}$

P3.5  (a)  (i)   79, 183, 16, 0
           (ii)  182, 112, 4, 183, 112, 0
           (iii) 200, 69, 76, 79, 161
      (b)  (i)   20407, 4096
           (ii)  –24576, 1207, 28672
           (iii) –14267, 19532, 20385
      (c)  (i)   4*, *7, 10, 0
           (ii)  *6, 70, 04, *7, 70, 00
           (iii) *8, 45, 4*, 4*, 4*, *1
                 (The asterisks indicate a binary number which is not a valid
                 BCD digit.)
      (d)  (i)   0.6227741
                 (Floating point numbers are usually normalised so that the
                 mantissa is represented as a fraction between 0.5 and 1.)
           (ii)  Not floating point numbers since 48 bits is not an integer
                 number of 32-bit words.
           (iii) As (ii).
      (e)  (i)   0, 7, DLE, NUL (The m.s.b. is ignored if not used as a parity
                 check.)
           (ii)  6, p, EOT, 7, p
           (iii) H, E, L, L, O, ! (In this case the m.s.b. is compatible with an
                 odd parity scheme.)
      (f)  (i)   CLRA
                 STAA     $1000
           (ii)  LDAA     $7004
                 STAA     $7000
           (iii) EORB     #45
                 INCA
                 INCA
                 CLRA
                 CMPA     *,X
                 (The asterisk indicates that the base address is not specified
                 since the opcode is the last byte in the sequence.)

In general it is not possible to determine the intended format of the data in the examples. Some possibilities can be excluded, however, where codes which are not compatible with the assumed data format occur. Thus many of the examples cannot represent BCD numbers since values larger than 9 are specified. Similarly, example (iii) cannot represent MC68HC11 machine code because the final instruction does not include an operand. It may be noted that (i) and (ii) are reasonably meaningful if interpreted as MC68HC11 machine code, while (iii) is meaningful if interpreted as ASCII characters. Other interpretations are also possible, however, and cannot be excluded.

# Chapter 4

E4.1  Refer to Appendix C. Notice that some instructions require more cycles
      to execute than might be surmised theoretically from the data transfers
      which are required. Sometimes additional clock cycles are required for
      internal CPU operations.

E4.2  The MC68HC11 ALU may be deduced to contain the following inputs
      and outputs:

Four bits are allocated for function select because the ALU is required to perform 15 distinct functions: Add, Add with carry, AND, Bit test, Compare, Complement, Decimal Adjust, Decrement, Exclusive OR, Increment, Multiply Negate, OR, Subtract, and Subtract with carry.

| *Inputs* | | *Outputs* | |
|---|---|---|---|
| Data input byte 1 | 8 bits | Data outputs byte | 8 bits |
| Data input byte 2 | 8 bits | Status output bits | 5 bits |
| Carry input | 1 bit | | |
| Function select | 4 bits | | |
| TOTAL | 21 bits | TOTAL | 13 bits |

Thus a ROM with 21 address input bits and 13 data output bits would be required to implement the MC6800 ALU ( $= 2.1 \times 10^6$ 13-bit words).

E4.3  The ARM ALU may be deduced to contain the following inputs and outputs:

| *Inputs* | | *Outputs* | |
|---|---|---|---|
| Data input word 1 | 32 bits | Data output word | 32 bits |
| Data input word 2 | 32 bits | Status output bits | 4 bits |
| Carry input | 1 bit | | |
| Function select | 4 bits | | |
| TOTAL | 69 bits | TOTAL | 36 bits |

Thus a ROM with 69 address input bits and 36 data output bits would be required to implement the ARM ALU — clearly impracticable!

E4.4  (a) $Z = 1$   (b) $N = 0$   (c) $Z + (N \oplus V) = 1$
(d) $Z + (N \oplus V) = 0$   (e) None

E4.5  Refer to Appendix C.

E4.6  Stack corruption can also occur if insufficient memory is allocated to the stack. In this case, during program execution the stack pointer may be decremented below the bottom of the allocated memory area to an area containing program, data variables or no physical memory at all, with consequently unpredictable results.

P4.1  Refer to Appendix C.

'Shift and Add' executes faster than repetitive addition (particularly for large numbers), but requires more code. Repetitive addition can be coded very compactly, but will require the loop to be executed a very large number of times for large binary numbers. The student is encouraged to code both methods and compare code length and execution time for each.

Note that the result must be expressed as a 16-bit 2s complement number if the multiplier and multiplicand are 8-bit 2s complement numbers.

P4.2–
P4.6  A number of possible algorithms exist for performing binary multiplication; some are computationally more efficiently than others. The method suggested on page 28 (shift and add) is one alternative; another is repetitively to add the multiplicand to itself while decrementing the multiplier once for each addition until the multiplier is reduced to zero (repetitive addition).

If the numbers to be multiplied are represented in the 2s complement format, they cannot be multiplied directly. Any negative number must first be 2s complemented before being multiplied. After multiplication, the sign of the result is a logical exclusive OR function of the signs of the original two numbers. If the result should be negative the (positive) result must be 2s complemented again to produce the final 2s complement representation.

**Chapter 5**

E5.1  2-kbyte ROMs have internal address decoding for address bits A0–A10. A15 is used for distinguishing between the program and input/output port addresses. Thus any of the address lines A11–A14 are available for decoding and distinguishing between the two ROMs. A single address line, connected directly to one device, and through an inverter to the other, will have the effect of selecting one device when the appropriate address bit is 1 and the other when the address bit is 0. It is best to use the lowest unconnected address line for this function, because this will cause the ROMs to be contiguously addressed in the MC68HC11 address space. The required address decoding logic is shown in the margin Figure. (If the ROMs have more than one chip select input (CS), the NAND gates shown may not be required.)

E5.2

```
                *
                * Subroutine to perform a test and transfer input
                * from a data port at address 80 hex., controlled
                * by a status signal, the m.s.b. of a port at 81 hex.
                *
B6 00 81 INPUT  LDAA  $81      * Read the status port
84 80           ANDA  #$80     * Mask off all except bit 7
27 F9           BEQ   INPUT    * repeat loop if bit 7 not set
B6 00 80        LDAA  $80      * data available, read data port
39              RTS            * return from subroutine
   ↑
```

(Machine code corresponding to the specified assembly language code.)

E5.3    The time to respond to an interrupt request comprises:
(a) the time to complete the current instruction;
(b) the time to save the current program status;
(c) the time to load the program counter with the interrupt service routine address.

The first of these (a) is variable depending upon the point in instruction execution at which the interrupt request is received, and has a minimum value of 0. Program status is saved by saving all CPU registers (except the stack pointer) on the stack one byte at a time. This requires 9 $\mu$s (see Fig. 5.6) plus a further 1 $\mu$s for the final post-decrement of the stack pointer to the next free stack address. Finally, the interrupt address must be loaded one byte at a time from addresses FFF8 and FFF9 hex. This requires an additional 2 $\mu$s. Thus the minimum time to respond to an interrupt request will be 12 $\mu$s. In practice, the MC68HC11 control logic does not code these operations in the most efficient possible sequence, and additional unused clock cycles occur at various points.

Notice that the time to respond to an interrupt request is very processor-dependent, and is particularly influenced by the number of processor registers saved when an interrupt request occurs.

P5.1

```
        *
        * Program to copy 8 latching push-buttons at 7004 hex.
        * to 8 LEDS at 7000 hex.
        *
LOOP    LDAA    $7004    * read the switches
        STAA    $7000    * copy to the LEDS
        BRA     LOOP     * repeat the program
```

P5.2    The maximum time to respond to a change in input occurs when the input is sampled immediately before an external change in its value occurs, and is equal to the loop execution time, in this case 11 $\mu$s.

The program reads address 7004 hex. and writes to address 7000 hex. Thus it assumes that these addresses correspond physically with the push-buttons and LEDs respectively. Furthermore, it is assumed that the output from the push-buttons is continuously available, and that data can be written to the LEDs at any time, since in each case direct transfer is used to perform the input/output operation.

P5.3

```
                *
                * Program to initialise a PIA for parallel data
                * transfer to a printer.
                * PIA base address is 8000 hex.
                *    Peripheral interface register A is connected to
                *    the 8 data lines.
                *    The printer status signal is connected to CA1
                * Test and transfer data output is performed by reading
                * printer status on bit 7 of control register A (CRA).
                *
INIT    CLRA                    * output 0 to CRA
        STAA    $8001           * (selects direction register)
        STAA    $8000           * output 0 to direction register
                                * (set data register to all inputs)
        LDAA    #$04            * bit 2 = 1 selects data register
                                * bit 1 = 0 sets CRA7 on -ve
                                *  transition
                                * bit 0 = 0 disables interrupts
                                *  from PIA
                                * bits 5, 4, 3 not used.
        STAA    $8001           * (Select data register and
                                *  CA1 status input)
        RTS                     * return from subroutine
```

P5.4

```
                *
                * Program to output a byte of data to the printer
                * using test and transfer method.
                * address and bit assignments as shown above.
                *    Data byte is in accumulator A on entry.
                *
PRINT   LDAB    $8001           * read control register  A
        ANDB    #$80            * mask off all except bit 7
        BEQ     PRINT           * repeat until printer ready
        STAA    $8000           * output data
        RTS                     * return from subroutine
```

P5.5    For data output initiated by an interrupt request from the printer, an
interrupt request must be generated by the 1-to-0 transition of the
printer ready line. Thus the line 'LDAA #$04' in P5.4 would be
replaced by:

```
        LDAA    #$05            * bit 2 = 1 selects data register
                                * bit 1 = 0 sets CRA7 on -ve transition
                                * bit 0 = 1 enables interrupts from PIA
                                * bits 5, 4, 3 not used.
```

In addition, the IRQA output of the PIA must be connected to the
MC68HC11 IRQ input.

If two similar printers are configured using the two data ports on the
PIA, each control register in the PIA (CRA and CRB) would be con-
figured as described above. The two interrupt outputs from the PIA,
IRQA and IRQB, would be logically ORed together and connected to

the IRQ input of the MC68HC11. When either printer interrupts the processor, the processor must determine which printer has requested service. It does this by examining the status bits CRA7 and CRB7 in turn and determining which is set. The processor can then branch to a specific service routine for the printer which has interrupted and set its status flag.

P5.6    Five cascaded decade counters will be required to divide the MC68HC11 1 MHz clock down to 0.1 s pulses. Either edge of the counter output pulse can be fed into the CA1 (or CB1) input to a PIA. The PIA is then configured to generate an interrrrupt pulse on the required clock edge by suitably programming the appropriate control register.

P5.7    Additional cascaded decade and modulo-6 counters can be used to generate seconds, tens of seconds, minutes, tens of minutes, hours and tens of hours outputs from the real-time clock. Each decade or modulo-6 counter will provide one BCD digit of the real-time clock output. Since each PIA comprises 16 data lines, four digits can be connected to the PIA in parallel. A further PIA could be used for the final two digits, but a cheaper solution is to multiplex the digits using, for example, one data port to read two digits at a time, and a second port to provide the control outputs to the multiplexer. The software required to read the time will depend on the exact configuration of hardware chosen.

This process is known as *polling interrupts* because each interrupting device is interrogated (polled) in turn to determine whether it was the source of the interrupt request.

In this case, the output from the counter could be fed directly to the MC68HC11 IRQ input, but in many cases a PIA will be required to read data (the time) each time the real-time clock interrupts (see P5.7)).

Single-chip implementations of the function specified in this problem are commonly available for use in real-time microprocessor systems.

An alternative approach to this problem would be to implement the six-digit clock using software, by writing an interrupt routine which updates six BCD variables in memory each time an interrupt is received.

## Chapter 6

E6.1
```
*
* MC68HC11 shift left program
*
SHL     LDAA    #01         * initialise shifting register
        CLC                 * clear carry flag
LOOP    BSR     DELAY       * delay 0.1 seconds
        STAA    $7000       * output to lights address
        ASLA                * shift one bit left
        BCC     LOOP        * repeat loop if carry not set
        BRA     SHL         * start again if carry set
*
* 0.1 second delay subroutine
*
DELAY   LDX     #16667      * loop counter set to 16667
DLAY1   DEX                 * decrement counter (3 $\mu$S)
        BNE     DLAY1       * loop if not zero (3 $\mu$S)
        RTS                 * return after 16667 × 6 $\mu$s = 0.1 s
```

This subroutine generates a fixed delay of 0.1 s; more generally useful would be a subroutine which could generate variable delays according to a parameter passed into the routine. How would the subroutine be modified to do this?

E6.2    (a) Program algorithm specified in pseudo-Pascal:

program reactiontimer(switches, lamps);
var countertimer:integer, switches:boolean;
begin

The required delay is passed to
the delay procedure as a
parameter.
true = no switches pressed.

By executing instructions in this
sequence, the measured
reaction time is rounded up to
the nearest 0.01 s.

```
repeat forever
    set countertimer to zero;
    delay(5 seconds);
    while switches = true do
    begin
        read(switches);
        delay(10ms);
        increment countertimer;
        write(countertimer)
    end;
    while switches = false do
    begin
        read(switches)
    end;
end.
```

(c) A number of algorithms for generating pseudo-random numbers
have been published. A simpler alternative in this case is to initiate
a counter (for example, a suitable processor register) which will
increment and overflow until the user of the reaction timer releases
the switch after reading his reaction time from the LED. Since the
time elapsing before this occurs is fairly random and asynchronous
with respect to counting, the number in the counter when the switch
is released can be used to generate a random time delay.

**Chapter 7**

E7.1    Total distinct items to remember for the three processors are:

    ARM:       25 instructions + 9 addressing modes = 34 items
    MC68HC11:145 instructions + 4 addressing modes = 149 items
    MC68000:   56 instructions + 14 addressing modes
                    + 3 data types = 73 items.

As might be guessed, in spite of the fact that the MC68000, and
particularly the ARM, have far greater processing capabilities than the
MC68HC11, their instructions sets are in fact significantly easier to use
than the MC68HC11, because of their regularity and orthogonality.

E7.3

In this case, the output from
the counter could be fed
directly to the MC68HC11 IRQ
input, but in many cases a PIA
will be required to read data
(the time) each time the
real-time clock interrupts (see
P5.7)).

```
*
* Indexed addressing example program
*
START   LDX     #0      * initialise index register
        CLRA            * accumulator stores partial sum
LOOP    ADDA    $20,X   * add array element to partial sum
        STAA    $40,X   * store result in new array
        INX             * increment to next element
        CPX     #10     * past last element?
        BNE     LOOP    * repeat loop if not
```

E7.4
```
*
* Register indirect assessing example program
*
```

```
        START   LDAB   #10      * set up loop counter
                CLRA            * accumulator stores partial sum
                LDX    #$20     * initialise pointer to first array
                LDY    #$40     * initialise pointer to second array
        LOOP    ADDA   0,X      * add array element to partial sum
                INX             * increment pointer
                STAA   0,Y      * store result in second array
                INY             * increment pointer
                DECB            * decrement loop counter
                BNE    LOOP     * repeat if loop counter not zero
```

Notice how it is necessary to use two registers in this example, whereas a single register was sufficient for the equivalent indexed addressing example.

E7.5   The advantage of the stack frame mechanism is its *generality*: it can be used to pass any arbitrary number of parameters to a subroutine. By contrast, registers can be used for passing parameters, but in the case of the MC68HC11, only two parameters could be passed this way. The use of a generally applicable method is important in a high-level language compiler, to ensure that the same mechanism can be used, regardless of the number of parameters specified for a particular procedure or function by the programmer.

E7.6   The code given in Worked Example 7.4 would fail if SUB1 in turn called another subroutine using the same stack frame mechanism, because the contents of the X register (stack frame pointer) would be overwritten by setting up the stack frame pointer in the second subroutine. To avoid this problem, the previous stack frame pointer should itself be saved on the stack as the first instruction of the subroutine, and restored as the last instruction. The code for SUB1 would now be:

```
        SUB1    PSHX           save previous frame pointer
                TSX            (S)→X address register
                .
                (some intervening instructions)
                .
                LDAA   4,X     restore 2nd parameter to A
                LDAB   5,X     restore 1st parameter to B
                .
                (the rest of the subroutine code)
                .
                TXS            reset stack pointer to frame pointer
                PULX           restore previous frame pointer
                RTS
```

These two instructions are implemented by a single instruction in the MC68000: LINK.

Note that the offset from the frame pointer is increased by two to allow for the bytes allocated on the stack to store the previous frame pointer.

These two instructions are implemented using the UNLK (unlink) instruction on the MC68000.

P7.1   Implied (or inherent) address instruction are listed in Appendices C, D and E.

P7.2   See Appendix D.

P7.3   See Appendix E.

P7.4   A common use for an indirect jump instruction is to implement the equivalent of the CASE statement in PASCAL: the jump instruction points to a data variable which is set up according to the result of a test condition, and thereby selects which of a number of addresses the instruction jumps to.

P7.5  (See E7.6)

The solution to E7.6 supports requirement (ii) of this problem. In addition, the use of a stack to pass parameters inherently meets requirement (iii) because re-entrant or recursive subroutines will not overwrite the parameters of the routine which calls them. For full support, local variables used within the subroutine should also be stored on the stack; this is achieved by allocating a suitable area immediately below the stack frame pointer for these variables. Local variables are then accessed with a *negative* offset from the frame pointer, while parameters are accessed with a *positive* offset.

Requirement (i) is generally met in one of two ways. The simplest method is to specify a particular register (e.g. the A accumulator) as containing the returned functional value: this is acceptable because functions are always defined to return only a *single* parameter. Alternatively, and more generally, the stack mechanism can again be used, by allocating additional space on the stack before calling the subroutine. At the end of the subroutine, the functional result is then placed on the stack in the allocated space.

Example code for the MC68HC11:

```
        PSHB
        PSHA            Push B then A onto system stack
        DES             Make space for functional result
        JSR   SUB1      Jump to subroutine
        PUL   A         Transfer functional result to A
        INS             Restore the stack pointer to its original position
        INS
```

The subroutine would have the following format:

```
SUB1    PSH   X         Save previous frame pointer
        TSX             Set up new frame pointer
        DES             Allocate a byte for local variables
                        (repeat for each local variable)
        LDAA 5,X        Restore 2nd parameter to A
        LDAB 6,X        Restore 1st parameter to B
        STAA  −1,       Save 1st local variable
        STAB  −2,       Save 2nd local variable
                .
        STAA 4,X        Store functional result
        TXS             Reset stack pointer to frame pointer
        PUL   X         Restore previous frame pointer
        RTS             Return from subroutine
```

Any MC68HC11 16-bit register can be used as a frame pointer.

Additional adjustment to offset (cf. E7.6) is to allow for byte allocated for functional result.

Readability is improved by defining local variable offsets with suitable labels using EQU directives. Local variable storage is deallocated at the end of the subroutine.

Note that the instruction TXS automatically ensures that the stack pointer is repositioned correctly at the end of the subroutine.

# Chapter 8

E8.1     *
        * E8.1 ACIA initialisation routine

```
          *
          *
          ACIAINIT   MOVE.B   #%00001101,$8000   Set 7 data bits, 1 stop
                                                 bit, odd parity
                                                 Store in control register
                     RTS                         Return from subroutine
E8.2      *
          * E8.2 ACIA data read with error checking
          *
          READCH     BTST.B   #0,$8000           Read status port
                                                 Mask off all except RDRF bit
                     BEQ      READCH             Loop if no byte received
                     MOVE.B   $8000,D1           Read status port again
                     MOVE.B   $8001,D0           Read data port
                     AND      #$70,D1            Mask all except bits 4, 5, and
                                                 6
                     BEQ      END                Branch if none of 4, 5 or 6 set
                     OR       #$80,D1            Else set bit 7
          END        RTS                         Return from subroutine
E8.3      *
          * E8.3 Test and transfer magnetic tape reader
          *
          READ       LDAA     $6002              Read PB data port
                     ANDA     #$80               Mask off all except bit 7
                     BNE      READ               Loop until data not valid
          READ1      LDAA     $6002              Read PB data port
                     ANDA     #$80               Mask off all except bit 7
                     BEQ      READ1              Loop until data valid
                     LDAA     $6000              Data valid; read it
                     RTS                         Return from subroutine
E8.4      **************************************************************
          *
          * Routine to load magnetic tape in Motorola S record format
          *
          *    If an error occurs in any record, the routine returns
          *    FF hex. in A after reading the erroneous record, else
          *    0 is returned in A when the whole file has been read.
          **************************************************************
          *
          * Start tape motor
          *
          SLOAD      LDAA     #$01               Motor start signal = 1
                     STAA     $6002              Output to control bit
          *
          * Wait for tape valid signal
          *
          LOOP1      LDAA     $6002              Read motor status port
                     ANDA     #$02               Mask off all except bit 1
                     BEQ      LOOP1              Loop if tape not valid
```

The % symbol indicates a binary number in Motorola assembly language.

The first three instructions are executed until the end of the data valid pulse is detected.

The next three instructions are executed until the beginning of the next data valid pulse is detected.

This example implementation includes only minimal error checking, using the checksum on each record as a whole: in practice, much more extensive byte-by-byte error checking could (and should) be carried out.

```
*
* Look for record header character 'S'
*
SLOAD1    BSR     READ       Read a character
          CMPA    #'S'       is it 'S'?
          BNE     SLOAD1     loop if not record start
                             character
*
* Check whether data or end of file
*
          BSR     READ       Read next character
          CMPA    #'9'       end of file?
          BEQ     SLOAD9     terminate reading blocks if so
          CMPA    #'0'       data block?
          BNE     SLOAD1     error if not 0; start again
*
* Read two hex. digits (record length)
* Store block in buffer at 1000 hex.
*
          LDX     #$1000     initialise buffer pointer
          BSR     RDBYTE     get a byte from two hex. digits
          STAA    0,X        store record length in buffer
          INX                increment pointer
          TFR     A,B        copy record length to counter
                             register
*
* Read remainder of block
*
LOOP2     BSR     RDBYTE     read next two hex. digits
          STAA    0,X        store in buffer, increment
                             pointer
          INX
          DECB               decrement counter
          BNE     LOOP2      loop if record not complete
*
* Stop tape motor
*
          LDAA    #$00       Reset motor start bit
          STAA    $6002      Output to control bit
*
* Process S record
*
* First byte is record length; put in B accumulator
* Next two bytes are the load address; put in Y register
* Copy all data bytes to specified load address
* Accumulate checksum.
*
          LDX     #$1000     Pointer to first byte
          LDB     ,X         get record length in B
```

The header character 'S' is used to synchronise to the start of the record.

The tape motor is stopped before processing each record; thus processing of each block can take as long as is required.

In practice, the amount of processing required here could

| | SUBB | #3 | adjustment for data bytes alone |
| | LDAA | #0 | initialise checksum |
| | ADDA | 0,X | record length is first byte of checksum |
| | INX | | |
| | LDY | 0,X | Load address →Y |
| | ADDA | 0,X | load address bytes are part of checksum |
| | INX | | |
| | ADDA | 0,X | |
| | STA | CHKSUM | Save checksum as variable in memory |
| LOOP3 | LDAA | 0,X | Get data byte from buffer |
| | INX | | |
| | STAA | 0,Y | Store data byte at load address |
| | INX | | |
| | ADDA | CHKSUM | add to running checksum total |
| | STAA | CHKSUM | save running checksum back in memory |
| | DECB | | decrement loop counter |
| | BNE | LOOP3 | loop if data bytes not complete |

*

* Last byte is 1s complement checksum; add to running checksum,
* increment, if result is zero, record was read correctly
*

| | LDAA | 0,X | Get checksum from buffer |
| | ADDA | CHKSUM | add to running checksum total |
| | INCA | | increment 1s complement |
| | BEQ | SLOAD | if result zero, record read OK |
| | LDA | #$FF | else error in checksum |
| SLOAD9 | RTS | | return from subroutine |

*
* _____
*

* Read one data byte (two hex. digits) from the magnetic tape
* Byte is returned in A accumulator
*

| RDBYTE | BSR | READ | Read 1st hex. digit |
| | BSR | MAKHEX | convert to least sig. nibble |
| | ASLA | | move to most sig. nibble |
| | ASLA | | |
| | ASLA | | |
| | ASLA | | |
| | PSHA | | save on stack |
| | BSR | READ | read 2nd hex. digit |
| | BSR | MAKHEX | convert to least sig. nibble |
| | ANDA | #$0F | clear bits 4–7 |

Side notes:

be carried out as the data are read; this may not always be the case, however.

It might be sensible to check that the specified load address corresponds to physically available memory: this can be done by reading back the value stored at the load address and comparing it with the value initially stored.

The checksum stored with the S record is the 1s complement of the sum of the other bytes in the record; adding 1 gives the 2s complement, and adding this to the running checksum should give zero.

```
                    ORA       0,S            OR most sig. nibble into A
                    INS                      adjust stack pointer
                    RTS                      return from subroutine
      *
      * _____
      *
      * Convert hex. digit character '0'–'9', 'A'–'F', to 4-bit nibble
      * Hex. digit is passed in A, nibble is returned as bits 0–3 of A
      *
      MAKHEX        SUBA      #$30           subtract ASCII numeric offset
                    CMPA      #$09           is result less than or equal to
                                             9?
                    BLE       MAKH1          branch if so, result obtained
                    SUBA      #$07           subtract additional ASCII
                                             character offset
      MAKH1         RTS                      return from subroutine
      *
      * _____
      *
      * Read one byte of data from magnetic tape
      * Data is returned in the A accumulator
      *
      READ          LDAA      $6001          read the control port
                    ANDA      #$80           mask off all except bit 7
                    BEQ       READ           loop if bit 7 not set
                    LDAA      $6000          data is valid: read data port
                    RTS                      return from subroutine
      *
      ************************************************************
```

Some additional checks that each data character was within the range '0'–'9', 'A'–'F' would be appropriate here.

# Index